STICKY DOGS AND STARDUST

THE SECOND INNINGS

SCOTT OLIVER

First published by Fairfield Books in 2025

fairfield books

Fairfield Books
Bedser Stand
Kia Oval
London
SE11 5SS

Typeset in Garamond and Proxima Nova
Typesetting by Rob Whitehouse

This book is printed on paper certified
by the Forest Stewardship Council

Every effort has been made to trace copyright and any oversight
will be rectified in future editions at the earliest opportunity

All rights reserved. No part of this book may be reproduced, sold, utilised
or transmitted in any form or by any electronic or mechanical means,
including photocopying, recording or by any information storage and
retrieval system, without prior permission in writing from the publishers

The views and opinions expressed in this book are those of the author
and do not necessarily reflect the views of the publishers

© 2025 Scott Oliver
ISBN 978-1-915237-43-9

A CIP catalogue record for is available from the British Library

Printed by CPI Group (UK) Ltd

STICKY DOGS AND STARDUST

THE SECOND INNINGS

SCOTT OLIVER

To Mum and Dad

Contents

Foreword   09

Introduction   11

01 Jesse Ryder   14
at New Brighton

02 Rohan Kanhai / Lance Gibbs   37
at Ashington / Whitburn (and Aberdeenshire, Blackpool, Crompton, St Annes / Burnley)

03 Kim Hughes & Terry Alderman   80
at Watsonians

04 Richie Richardson   103
at Thames Ditton, Blackpool, Gateshead Fell, Swansea and Burnmoor

05 Marnus Labuschagne – Steve Smith – Travis Head   141
at Plymouth, Sandwich – Sevenoaks Vine – Ventnor

06 Mohammad Yousuf   162
at Bowling Old Lane, Pudsey Congs and Smethwick

07 Chris Cairns / Ryan Harris   **182**
at Bacup / Lowerhouse

08 Muthiah Muralidaran   **212**
at Leicester Ivanhoe

09 Abdul Qadir (and Imran Khan)   **231**
at Hanging Heaton and Stenhousemuir (and Wakefield)

10 Dennis Lillee   **257**
at Haslingden

11 Joel Garner   **271**
at Littleborough, Moorside and Glastonbury

12 Morne Morkel / Mohammad Asif   **301**
at Endon / Ashcombe Park

13 Michael Holding / Andy Roberts   **330**
at Rishton / Haslingden

Foreword

"Pro". That's how you were known when you signed as professional in northern league cricket. Not just the whole club but the whole town looked up to you. You were expected to deliver.

I played Lancashire League cricket, arguably the most famous of all the leagues. Wesley Hall, Bob Simpson and Eddie Barlow were all "Pro" at my club, Accrington. They left an indelible impression on me as a star-struck young cricketer dreaming of playing for England.

Before then, as a very young lad, I was even more star-struck. I remember buying the league handbook every year and trying to get the autographs of all the pros. I'd pay threepence to go into 'the enclosure' – the ringed-off area in front of the pavilion – and fill the handbook with the autographs of these great players, these wonderful characters of the game. Phadkar, Mankad, Umrigar, Hazare, Gupte: magical names of players from a far-off land. There was Everton Weekes, Fazal Mahmood, Hugh Tayfield, Lance Gibbs, Collie Smith, Conrad Hunte. The list is world-class in every way, iconic cricketers rubbing shoulders with amateurs. That was the real starting point of my love for the game. It got me hooked.

Growing up quickly from being that star-struck young boy to quite an outstanding young player in the area, it was a big step to be put into the first XI at 15, opening the batting against top-class professionals. I could stay in but I couldn't hit it off the square! You grew up very quickly. Every ground would have a barracker, who was a notable personality and known to everyone in the area. There was Big Roland at Enfield, Jackie Barnes at Haslingden. If you played a maiden out, they were on your case. At Accrington, we had a contingent who went on the bus to away matches. They were called 'the Heavenly Choir'. They'd give it heaps. They got stuck into everyone. Fantastic.

I got my first fifty when I was 17, batting with Eddie Barlow against the fearsome Roy Gilchrist at Lowerhouse. There was a battery of quick bowlers in the league – Charlie Griffith, Chester Watson, Lester King, Des Hoare – and, as a regular occurrence, a number of players who'd study the fixtures before booking their holidays. It was the vintage era for league professionals. The game was very popular and the grounds were full. The social side was vibrant – if you've got Wesley Hall and Bobby Simpson, you'd want to rub shoulders with these guys. There was tremendous local interest and rivalry. Everyone would clamour to buy the *Evening Telegraph Pink* to see what Alf Thornton had to say.

Testing yourself against the overseas pros was a fabulous grounding and remains a special part of the recreational game, even if the names are no longer quite the top-notchers – at least, not when they're in their prime. Times change, of course, but there's still something unique in the way cricket pits the amateur against the professional. It's a magic that no other sport can match.

Wherever I went in the game, I always had a connection to my club, and it was always my intention to go back into league cricket after I'd finished playing at Lancashire. I had two years as pro at Accrington, then three as amateur. We had 2,500 on when Viv came with Rishton – which definitely helped with my collection on the day! – but even he didn't always find it easy. The pro is there to be knocked down by the amateurs, who want to get into him, which raises their game. And it raises the pro's game. It's all eyes on you. Responsibility. Being the main man at Accrington helped a young Shane Warne no end. It made him get his act together when he was doing all sorts of daft things.

The glory days of the overseas pro may have gone but the memories remain. They were the most marvellous of times. Scott's book captures the colour and sense of occasion of it all, the drama, the characters among the amateurs, even the supporters and committeemen, getting into the heart of the club game as I knew it at both ends of my playing days – and not only the game in Lancashire but in many other corners of the country where a tussle with the superstar pro would often bring the amateurs nightmares, sometimes dreams come true, occasionally both.

So sit back and read all about them in Scott's excellent account. There are some great names here. You will know them all.

David Lloyd, spring 2025

Introduction

For a book that (apparently) wasn't really a book – it looked and felt and smelt like a book, yet was (arguably) perhaps an anthology, a quorum of standalone freelance articles gathered together in a lightbulb moment and beefed up with six or seven more stories to make it into not-quite-a-book – for that to have picked up one of the cricket lit 'majors' was a lovely surprise, to say the least.

In one sense, however, it wasn't a complete surprise. After all, the vast majority of cricketers are recreational players and the vast majority of cricket literature isn't concerned with the recreational game. And understandably so. Nevertheless, I knew from both my own cricket induction – listening rapt to gifted storytellers in the bar – and subsequently scratching about in the club game as a journalist that there was an ocean of salty yarns to be explored. I hoped, as the accidental Sticky Dogs project gathered steam, there would be an appetite to read some of them.

An ocean is a big thing, of course, but the superstar pro angle was a good way in, a good way to bring some of the stories to life. To quote the introduction for the first book, since I can't say it any better: "No other sport offers up stories quite like the ones collected in these pages. Only cricket – and especially the club cricket of England and the British Isles – allows recreational players to rub shoulders with international stars and even superstars in a fully competitive context, providing them with some of the most cherished memories of their lives."

This volume was both conceived and commissioned as a book. The research was deeper. Where the original versions of the stories in the first volume often involved me haggling with editors over the wordage, this one had no such constraints. I was allowed to find my natural length (perhaps I needed to be a tad shorter?). Initially, there were again 22 chapters, but nine of these have had to be set aside for the Third Innings, both to de-risk the publisher's potential bankruptcy and to allow holiday readers not to breach their luggage allowance. To revisit the metaphor from the previous Introduction: if the last book ranged from "two-minute ditties" through "hefty mid-sized workouts" up to "17-minute Sun

Ra Arkestra space-jazz experimentalism", this one is heavy on the space-jazz, figuratively speaking.

The length of some of the chapters here is in part because some of the stories, unlike most of those in the first book, involved multiple clubs and multiple leagues, much of it worth more than a cursory gloss. It is also because the research threw up more material. But mainly it's because I wanted to explore more of those ocean waters, so to speak. The superstar cricketer remains the hook, the great whale at the centre of things, but at times I have opened things out onto the wider ecosystem: the characters, the folklore, the anecdotes, history and splashes of colour, whatever came into view in those vast, uncharted depths, localities largely unknown to the cricket literature. (On which note, and magnificently, when I was using Android's voice recognition software to turn scrawled notes into text, my pronunciation of "Garner" was habitually rendered as "Ghana" – that is, until I started rolling out that first 'r', taking the enunciation down into a valley and up again over a hill: *Garrr-nurr*. At which point it started to produce the correct spelling. Even the AI felt the Big Bird's Lancashire connection!)

Another difference is that the superstar's voice is almost entirely absent, save for a few citations from autobiographies. There were no direct interviews, whereas five or six of the subjects in the first book very kindly shared their memories. For one reviewer, "rather than detract from the stories, this helps fuel the air of mystique of when some of these gods of cricket took to the field alongside, or against, mere mortals". I'm more than happy to make a virtue of a necessity.

Despite there being only 13 chapters here, these nevertheless cover 20 cricketers (with a few more tangents about other legendary if not quite so famous club pros), or 21 with the slightly tenuous inclusion of Imran Khan (on the basis that I got sent some amazing photos of him playing club cricket, and he gets four or five paragraphs in that chapter!). Only three fewer than the first book, then.

Given its journalistic origins, the first volume had more than its fair share of glamorous cricketers (these being what an editor was more likely to commission). There was Viv, Sobers, Warne, Wasim, ABdV, Gilchrist, Donald, Marshall, Curtly, KP, Shane Bond and so forth. While the present volume might not be quite so full of super-sexy A-listers, the assembled line-up is not short of its VIPs and Pantheon members. Of the 21 named players on the contents page, 16 feature in the all-time top 100 Test ratings, either with bat or ball. There are 11 who have been to No.1 in the world at some point in their career, five who reached No.2, two who made it to No.3 and another who topped out at No.4. Sexy enough.

As ever, the stories were greatly enhanced by the contributions of the various interviewees who shared their memories and stories (there are, of course, always more people to be spoken to, ways in which these work-in-progress stories could be expanded, but only so much oxygen in a diver's tank…). Sincere thanks to everyone who indulged me. Special mentions, however, must go to the following people who went above and beyond to supply me with materials: Mick Moore (St Annes); Stewart Oliver, David Bell and Duncan Scott (Watsonians); Martin Pickles and Mike Young (Blackpool); John MacNeil and Duncan Walker (Stenhousemuir); Martin Ball and Bob Gregory (Ashcombe Park). Thanks also to Brian Heywood for his submission, to Ali Saad for the Imran Khan photos, to Samir Aga and Benj Moorehead for their collection of useful materials, to Ben and Dinah for all the lifts, to Paul Johnston for reading some early versions of the chapters, and to Matt Thacker and the team at Fairfield for their patience and support.

Scott Oliver, spring 2025

1

Jesse Ryder
at New Brighton

With his porn-star name and rock-star game, Jesse Ryder ought to have been one of New Zealand cricket's Hall of Famers – a lavishly gifted batting all-rounder who in the end made two cult albums then disappeared. Alas, the final body of work is not sufficient to squeeze Ryder in past the Pantheon's bouncers (which is unfortunate for one so fond of a messy night out), but there were enough sightings of his coruscating talent, enough solid bullets on the CV, for a 60-minute special of *What Might Have Been*.

In the space of six Test innings against India in 2009, he made 102 at Hamilton, 201 at Napier and 103 at Ahmedabad. There were three ODI hundreds, the last of them from 46 balls in what turned out to be the final month of his international career. He won six Player of the Match awards for New Zealand, the first for a savage 79* against England alongside 'Baz' McCullum, a game in which Anderson, Broad and Swann were pumped for a combined 0/102 from nine overs. As for the bustling seamers that proved so productive during three post-ostracism seasons with Essex, there may only have been five Test wickets but these did include Rahul Dravid, Gautam Gambhir, Michael Clarke and Brad Haddin. With violent pick-ups and short-arm pulls, elegant lofted extra-cover drives and velvety hands, the chubby boy from Napier certainly had game.

The reasons for Ryder's unfulfilled potential can be triple-distilled into a single word: alcohol. Which, as the philosopher Homer (J. Simpson) famously defined it, was "the cause of, and solution to, all of life's problems". As for why Jesse so frequently sought solace in the bottle, even with the mounting evidence of the damage it was doing to his career, this might require a skilled psychiatrist, although it would doubtless have a fair bit to do with his mother, Heather, walking out on his father when he was a small boy, leaving him in the care of a cricket-loving though somewhat dissolute man who was rarely at home and who, when Jesse was 14, dropped him off at a mate's house, telling him he'd see him in a week, only to move to Australia. Spitballing here, but maybe he had abandonment issues affecting his self-esteem, which was then 'managed' through boozy intoxication, a place where it's easy to feel king for an hour – or comfortable, at least. The only real boundaries Jesse knew were those he smote at cricket.

Some years before Ryder started to accumulate the formidable list of misdemeanours that eventually led to New Zealand Cricket deciding enough was enough, he spent a happy summer on the Wirral with New Brighton CC in the Liverpool & District Cricket Competition, a strong league that had seen its share of handy pros if not quite the *bona fide* superstars found elsewhere in the county palatine of Lancashire. It also had a tradition for home teams supplying visitors with free jugs of ale to lubricate the early stages of post-match conviviality, which in retrospect may not have been what Jesse's doctor would have ordered, particularly when half his teammates were his age or younger. Which is to say, enthusiastic sesh companions.

New Brighton were original members of 'The Comp', and had never been relegated. They had won a maiden title in the 1970s, two in the '80s and three under the captaincy of Tim Watkins in the '90s, going toe-to-toe with a formidable Bootle side in the process. Having called time in 2000, Watkins was "cajoled out of injury-based retirement" by a friend at Huyton CC in 2003. In early 2007, with New Brighton having finally escaped the months-long threat of a substantial points deduction (and thus demotion) over the alleged use of an ineligible player, Watkins and his 43-year-old dicky shoulder were talked into rolling back the years at Rake Lane – a now non-bowling No.11 essentially there to shepherd the talented crop of youngsters blooded over the previous five years: opener Matt Thompson; keeper-batter Paul Hale; all-rounder Martyn Evans, who later played for Cumberland; and twins James and David While, North of England under-15s teammates of Johnny Bairstow a few years earlier. Watkins was "the grown-up in the room, a steady hand on the tiller" and brought with him from Huyton the dependable middle-order batting of Lawrence 'Loggsy' Wilson and the quality left-arm spin of Ashraf Nawab, who would end his career with over

1,000 top-flight LDCC scalps. They just needed a pro capable of pushing them back into the top half of the table. The clock was ticking. Feelers were put out.

The New Brighton faithful had grown accustomed to seeing Test cricketers leading the charge. In 2002, 'The Rakers' signed 30-year-old Sri Lankan seamer Eric Upashantha two weeks after he'd sent down 8-0-65-1 in a ten-wicket trouncing at Old Trafford; he put together solid numbers but New Brighton finished joint-eighth out of 12. The next two years saw his compatriot Chandika Hathurusingha in the hotseat, the 35-year-old with 26 Test caps averaging mid-40s with the bat, almost 30 with the ball, ultimately leading to finishes of joint-fourth and an underwhelming joint-eighth. The following season, the 34-year-old Zimbabwean Test leggie Paul Strang inspired a third-place finish, but they slipped back to joint-ninth in 2006, with Shabbir Ahmed – the fastest Pakistani to 50 Test wickets before his action was blackballed – taking over from Strang for the final six weeks.

Eventually, New Brighton's 11th-hour feelers threw up a name for 2007: JD Ryder – younger, less well credentialed, more of a risk. "The Jesse signing came while cobbling things together, late in the day," recalls Watkins. "It was through Steven Hirst, the agent, a Kiwi. He said, 'I think this guy might be very good, but I'm not 100 per cent sure.' We had no other irons in the fire, so we took him."

Ryder may not have been an international cricketer, but he was no greenhorn. He had five seasons under his belt as a full-time pro, including a New Zealand 'A' tour. His 36 first-class appearances had yielded an average of 45 and two State Championship finals for Wellington, with a 71 and match figures of 5/54 in the most recent. He was percolating through, although no one on the Wirral knew much about him. Martyn Evans had spent the winter in New Zealand a couple of years earlier, so asked around for references as the decision was being mulled over. "My mate in Napier said, 'Oh my god, he's amazing. He's the next big thing over here. Just be wary, he likes his piss.' Those exact words."

* * *

Jesse Ryder was hungover for his New Brighton debut, away at Fleetwood Hesketh, although he did have the courtesy to inform

Watkins about this in advance, as he would on each occasion he turned up a little crispy from his nocturnal shenanigans. Part of the problem on that front, his captain believes, is that Ryder was billeted "a ten-minute walk from the club and a ten-second stroll from a pub", the Magazine Hotel, overlooking the Mersey. This had been an early port-of-call on the eve-of-debut debauch, from which his new teammates had slunk away with the pro still very much in the throes of things. "There were rumours of a mother-daughter combo and that all three had gone home together," says Evans, "although Jesse has never let on."

Ryder was also a week late arriving, with no one able to recall why, although in his absence New Brighton engaged his compatriot Iain O'Brien as sub pro, a game that went so badly for him that he returned his fee. Evans had nipped out Northern's 19-year-old South African pro Francois Haasbroek with the score on 21, after which they waited 233 runs for a second breakthrough, future Nottinghamshire skipper Steven Mullaney making 116 – the first of six hundreds that year as the 20-year-old racked up 1,308 runs at a strike rate of 118 – while Carl Hey stroked 150* en route to what remains the LDCC's all-time record run aggregate of 1,467. Tough day. O'Brien had two of his 22 Test caps at the time, and finished with 0/74 from 13 overs, which in his view was not worthy of remuneration. Northern had been champions for the first time in 2005 and were emerging as one of the league's powerhouses – indeed, in subsequent years, besides a glut of local prizes, they've won a pair of Lancashire knockouts and reached three national finals – yet they would finish only fourth in 2007, despite these mammoth run-piles, a sign of how competitive things were at the sharp end of the Comp. If you can't turn up daisy-fresh, you'd better be good when you're frazzled.

Arriving in Southport for the Fleetwood Hesketh game, Jesse splashed his face with cold water, jogged off the previous night's toxins, strapped on his pads and walked out at 12/1. It was a tough batting day – only one of his teammates would make it past 15 – and the pro would have to get stuck in against Jamaican left-arm spinner Nikita Miller, who went on to collect 50 ODI appearances for West Indies, as well as seamer Mohammad Azam, who'd played a smattering of first-class cricket in Pakistan. Counter-punching judiciously, Ryder was still there at 119/8 as Andrew Evans joined him and hung around long enough for the pro to dab a pair of twos to third man to bring up three figures. Jesse departed at 167/9, stumped, with 105 from 130 balls, including eight fours and five sixes on this wide, rectangular ground. "He slog-swept Nikita Miller onto the social club roof," recalls Martyn Evans, "one of the biggest hits I've ever seen. Massive, massive hit."

Defending 184, Evans was then pulled for six from the first ball of the innings, losing the new ball and thereby denying his brother a crack at the other end after a spud-standard spare was produced. Instead, Nawab would open up and bowl unchanged, collecting 3/77 from 25 overs, although Hesketh had inched up to 159/7, needing 26 more, when the ball was tossed back to Ryder, who had earlier knocked over the first three. Bang, bang, bang he went, finishing with 6/18 from 9.5 overs, as well as a pair of insouciant snaffles to see off both first-class players, completing what was, by any measure, a reasonably steady first impression. "That was our first look under the bonnet," says Watkins, "and we all thought: oh my god, this fella can play!" He then got stuck into the complimentary jugs, where he was equally talented. Later in the summer, he would neck a four-pint pitcher in 21 seconds.

Ryder's debut had given the team an instantaneous shot of belief. Twenty-four hours earlier, says Evans, "We didn't have any thought of pushing for the league. We knew we'd be quite competitive and were hoping the pro would add to that." Now, the dreamier members at New Brighton were thinking about a tilt at the title, although they knew that any challenge would have to go through the reigning champions, a formidable Bootle team set up to push for the national knockout by their captain of 21 years, the 49-year-old Ian Cockbain.

Released by Lancashire in 1983 after six years on the staff, 'Coey' promptly became the first Comp batter for 20 years to make 1,000 runs in a season, repeating the trick three times more. Those blond curls would finish with 29,979 runs for the club, as well as 8,575 Minor Counties Championship runs at 41.4 for Cheshire, who he skippered for 11 years, leading them to a NatWest giant-killing of Northamptonshire in 1988. As captain of the Minor Counties XI for five seasons, he took 70 off the '93 Australians – Warne included – and in 1995 oversaw a shock win over the West Indians at Reading as well as a giant-killing of Leicestershire in the B&H Cup, in which he top-scored with 65*. But his finest hour came at Marlow in 1992, a two-dayer against the World Cup-winning Pakistanis – Waqar Younis and Mushtaq Ahmed in the attack – when he followed 45* in the first innings by reaching the final over of a 250 chase on 73* with nine wickets down and 12 required. "First ball, I skipped down the wicket and hit Aamer Sohail over extra-cover for a one-bounce four," he later recalled. "Then I had a big whoosh and could have been stumped. I remember thinking: 'Come on, don't be stupid. Don't overhit.'" A swept six "put the willies up them", but two dots left two needed from one, at which point Cockbain "ran down again and hit him over the top for four, and I don't think I stopped running for 20 minutes!" There were few flies on Coey, and thus of the teams he led.

Bootle had won nine LDCC titles in Coey's 21 years at the helm. They were also the most successful Comp side in the prestigious Lancashire knockout, contested by the top four teams from a dozen of the county's leagues, culminating in an Old Trafford final (New Brighton, from pre-1974 Cheshire, did not compete). They won it in 1988, lost back-to-back finals in '97 and '98, before landing it again in 2004, '05 and '06. They would win it in 2007, too, a four-year streak that has never been matched.

Bootle also had an affinity for the *Liverpool Echo*'s knockout competition, which began in 1974 and was played as midweek T20 games before the bells and whistles of an end-of-season, two-innings Sunday final. After failing to score three runs off CEL Ambrose of Chester Boughton Hall's last over in 1986, they won it the next two years, regained it in 1995 and '99, then reeled off four in a row between 2002 and 2005. All of which was child's play compared to their taste for the LDCC's knockout competition, the Ray Digman Trophy, launched in 1980. Bootle won their first in 1987 (adding it to the league title and Echo to make it a treble), their next in 1990 (a double with that year's title) and another in 1993. The pattern suggested they would win it again three years later, in 1996, which they did, from where the list of winners reads: Bootle, Bootle, Bootle, Bootle, Bootle, Bootle, Wigan, Wallasey, Bootle, Bootle and Bootle. In 2007, Jesse's season, it was also Bootle. For the next four years after that, it was Bootle, Bootle, Bootle and Bootle – 14 triumphs in 16 seasons. An absurd trophy machine.

To recap, then: Bootle were coming off a 2006 season that had brought them a treble (Comp, Digman, Lancs Cup). The year before that had brought them a different treble (Digman, Echo, Lancs Cup). The 2004 season was the full house: Comp, Digman, Echo, Lancs Cup. Ten out of 12 majors won over three years. Coey's boys lay in wait at the end of May for Jesse and his superhero cape. In the interim, New Brighton would chuck another five wins on their streak.

* * *

When Ryder arrived on Merseyside, his teammates weren't even aware that he bowled. Once disabused of the notion that he was a one-trick pony, at times thereafter he would take the new ball, at others come on third change. Whatever, mate. "He wasn't a reluctant bowler," recalls Watkin, "but it's fair to say there was an amicable negotiation at times. He was a very shy, modest bloke, a shrug-your-shoulders sort of character. He was very chilled about how we played our cricket, and wasn't bothered if I didn't put the ball in his hands. But if he felt the mojo was with him, we'd ride the wave."

The 151-run win over St Helens Recs on his next outing brought Ryder 2/13 from a five-over new ball burst – both men bowled for ducks – having earlier chipped one into the ring for 15 in a total of 262/9, Martyn Evans scoring 99 from No.7 before being run out from the last ball of the innings after a Monty Panesar dive had left him floundering short of his ground.

A week later, on home debut, Jesse plundered 85 against Hightown as New Brighton racked up 277/5 in 43 overs, allowing a very early declaration (these were timed games, with a last 20 overs called, in which the team batting first could do so all day if the mood took them). The visitors had reached 58/0 when the ball was tossed to the pro, who promptly took a hat-trick: caught behind, lbw, lbw. Hightown came up 148 runs short, giving New Brighton a second straight 25-point haul (it was 20 for a bat-second win). "Jesse used to amble in off five paces and either bash people on the pad or go through them," says Evans. "He was deceptively quick at times."

On May's first bank holiday Monday, New Brighton grafted out 212/9, Ryder chipping in a breezy 57, then sending down 10-3-20-4 as Leigh – a team that would win just once all season – fell 92 short. For a bloke they didn't know could bowl, Ryder's 15/70 from four games represented a pleasant surprise. Nawab had 13/89 in his last three, and Ryder was staggered the spinner had never played first-class cricket. "We suddenly thought we could win any type of game, from anywhere," says Evans, "because with Jesse we had a second gun bowler."

Nevertheless, Ryder was only given two overs in his next outing, which came the following Thursday – albeit this was in the pool stage of the Friends Provident Trophy for Ireland, for whom he was sharing overseas pro duties with Nantie Hayward. Ireland skipper Trent Johnston took a hat-trick, yet they were rolled for 63 by Gloucestershire to lose by 185, less than two months after beating Pakistan in the World Cup. Jesse made a single, and took 0/13 off two.

Two days later, back on the Wirral, Ryder bagged 4/43 as Lytham were hustled out for 183. After tea, he was pinned lbw for 15 – the start of a 13-game run in the league yielding only one 50-plus score – but his teammates dug deep for a three-wicket win, the only one in the division on a showery afternoon, to keep the good times rolling. And rolling. On into the witching hour. Indeed, unless otherwise stated, we should assume every win was celebrated heartily. Certainly by Mr Ryder.

Thus it was that a few early birds at John Lennon Airport the following morning saw a somewhat worse for wear professional cricketer waiting to catch his Dublin flight for the 11am start against Essex (think Foreign Secretary Boris Johnson in the departure lounge at Perugia after an off-book soirée at the Tuscan villa of an 'ex'-KGB agent). Ravi Bopara knocked Jesse over for two, following up with a hundred in a seven-wicket stroll, with Ryder not being asked to bowl. Six days later, back across the Irish Sea, Ryder pummelled 48 at Maghull in New Brighton's 248/7 then played a support role with 2/33 from 17 overs as the hosts came up 115 short, with four wickets taken by the 37-year-old former Transvaal seamer Louis Botes – the Rakers' pro in the early-90s, who then married the scorer, stayed and became English qualified – to secure the sixth straight win. New Brighton were 34 points clear at the summit.

Aside from the disappointment, for a team of Reds, of Liverpool's 2-1 midweek defeat to AC Milan in Athens in the Champions League final, everything in the garden was rosy as the acid test of those title credentials loomed into view. 'The Bootle game'. Say that phrase today at Rake Lane, 18 summers and several stoushes down the track, and they will know exactly what you're talking about.

* * *

Belief was bouyant ahead of the top-of-the-table clash. But then, this was Bootle, over whom New Brighton had prevailed just once in 14 LDCC encounters in the 2000s, and that required 105* from Paul Strang to turn 56/4 into a successful chase of 240. If six Jesse-inspired wins on the bounce were the early scenes in *The Wolf of Wall Street*, Jordan Belfort and cohorts snorting and wheeler-dealing their way to feelings of invincibility, Bootle was the IRS turning up and asking to look at the accounts. Any doubts that had started shuffling from the shadows and into the centre of the psychic dancefloor were not, strictly speaking, *irrational* fears, for if idle moments had brought rumination on reputations, on the institutional heft embodied in that Bootle crest, then pessimism – or, at least, trepidation at a bubble about to burst – was the entirely rational response. The brain had run its simulations, scenarios had been war-gamed out, and the ones in which you win necessarily appeared slightly fanciful. But then, it is only from the madness of unshakeable optimism that great underdog deeds are forged. *If we can be just ten per cent better… If our big players deliver… If we can find a way to flip the pressure… If we can make that crest weigh heavy with expectation as the reality around it starts to shift course…*

Cockbain, an infectiously garrulous personality with a will to win made from steel, was of course the principal agent of Bootle's long hegemony, not least their ability to attract top players from across the North West. Crossing the Mersey alongside him was his 20-year-old son, Ian Cockbain Jr, a batter who would go on to play 250 games of professional cricket for Gloucestershire, Adelaide Strikers and others. There was the 21-year-old left-arm spinner Stephen Parry, who would play 249 games as a full-time pro, mainly at Lancashire, as well as making seven white-ball appearances for England, one more than Bootle's No.4, the 38-year-old Graham Lloyd, middle-order fulcrum of Lancashire's 1990s one-day trophy machine. The other seven weren't too shabby, either, even with the unavailability of David Snellgrove, the Comp's leading run-scorer in two of the previous five seasons and, 16 years later, England over-50s' World Cup-winning captain. Their opening bowlers were Adam Warren, Tasmanian born but with one List 'A' appearance for Yorkshire, and Will Purser, a future stalwart of the leagues around Manchester and a Minor Counties player for Staffordshire. First change was veteran Australian seamer Ronnie Davis, famous for dismissing Dean, Mark and Steve Waugh in a Sydney Grade game, and pro in the 1990s for Chorley in the Northern League, when the club reached three straight national knockout finals.

New Brighton won the toss and opted to bat. A cold, blustery wind blew off the Irish Sea, making driving difficult down the road on the Royal Liverpool links at Hoylake, never mind on a slow, nibbly pitch at Rake Lane. Matt Thompson fell in the first over, bringing Ryder to the crease. The score edged up to 38/1 when John While gave Warren a second wicket and Lloyd a second slip catch, but Jesse found a resolute partner in keeper Paul Hale and at 79/2 a solid foundation looked to have been laid. Whereupon Ryder slapped Davis to Parry at cover and the last eight wickets tumbled for 27 runs, Davis collecting 5/37, Parry sending down 8.5-6-7-3. The imperial Bootle machine, laying waste to another tribe.

Sandwiches were consumed, tea supped, hope sought. New Brighton needed Jesse to come to the party (which, to be fair, was a decent bet). He went steady on the cake. He knew the pitch was capricious and that, with 106 to defend and no Botes in the ranks, he might have to bowl unchanged throughout – death or glory.

Bootle survived the opening cut and thrust, reaching 41 without loss, before Evans trapped 'Mini Coey' lbw then snuck one through Lloyd, either side of Ryder nicking off Craig Prince for 24. At 48/3, New Brighton had a faint sniff, yet Parry and Gavin Reynolds, a good enough player to make unbeaten half-centuries for Lancashire second XI, slowly ground away and by 92/3, with just 15 required, the caretaker set off on final rounds before lights out. Nine, ten, jack considered jumping in the shower.

At which point, a Jesse jaffa burst through Parry. Next over, eyeing up the short-cut home, Reynolds slog-swept Nawab clean, hard and flat, only to find Evans in the flightpath, who safely took a reverse-cup, head-high catch a foot inside the rope: 92/5. WinViz bumped the New Brighton chances, but they were still barely out of single digits, not with Cockbain Snr and his nous held back in case things got ticklish. "It was a pretty bleak day," recalls Purser. "We were crammed in the dressing-room with the lights on and wrapped up in sweaters, because it was pretty dark and very chilly outside. Wickets started to tumble and Coey Senior was going berserk."

Wicket-keeper Neil Williams was joined by Warren. Eight runs were eked out, bringing up three figures, then Ryder crashed one into Williams's castle, bringing Purser to the crease at 100/6, seven required. "Jesse's bowling had looked fairly innocuous," adds Purser. "A gentle run-up and some bustling medium pace. All of sudden, though, he started to get the ball going both ways. He was the type of bowler who hit the bat harder than expected and he began to extract movement off the pitch."

Warren took two runs off Nawab, bringing the target to within one hit – one sweet connection for a would-be hero – an attempt at which cost him his wicket as the spinner snuck one through the glory-mow: 102/7. Purser followed next over, smashed on the front pad by Ryder: 102/8. Still five needed. Finally, the Cockbain Insurance Policy entered. Hale was up to the stumps, a high-wire act with so few runs up the sleeve. A fifth-ball single for Cockbain left Davis facing the Ryder radar, which locked in the target and once more crashed ball into stumps: 103/9. Razor-blade tension.

Another Cockbain single off Nawab brought him back down to face Jesse: three needed, keeper up, only deep cover out sweeping in front of the bat. Jesse hit the wicket hard, the ball nipped back, flicked the pad and – is that a bit of glove? – was gathered by Hale. A huge appeal followed – eleven players, a few dozen spectators, the dead ancestors of New Brighton players past and present – and all eyes fell on the man in the white coat, not least those of the Comp's most legendary local player, now imploring – no, *daring* the umpire. Time had stopped for a fag break.

And then the finger went up. After which, bedlam. Pandemonium. #limbs. Bodies in Brownian motion, in delirious shock, in ecstasy – although not the Bootle skipper, obviously. "Coey was bulletproof," observes Evans. "He'd had 20-plus years as skipper. It was *huge* for the umps to give it. He was effing and jeffing all the way off, but he battered it."

"It was one of the great games," adds Watkins, "where Jesse and Ashraf – mainly Jesse – brought us back from the absolute dead. Jesse was carried off, and rightly so. It took a few of us to lift him, mind, 'cos he's a big lad. But it was an unbelievable game. Roy of the Rovers stuff."

"We won by two runs after taking seven for 12 against the best team we'd ever seen in our area, who'd been dominant for ten years," continues Evans. "That half-hour will forever be legendary in this club's history. It's the best game I've ever been involved in, my absolute favourite – including winning the league as captain in 2015. They were just so, so good and the way we won it was totally crazy. Just mad."

"The beer was flowing in the bar afterwards," Watkins confirms. "Bootle were always the same: fantastic winners, fantastic losers. Coey said to me: 'We've got the best team, you've got the best player.' It was true. Jesse was head-and-shoulders the best player in the Comp. This was the day we thought the team has got a bit of a chance. We turned a corner – changed the psyche of the team."

New Brighton were 35 points ahead of Lytham in second and had opened up a 49-point buffer over Bootle, who sat in fourth. Jesse had sent down a folkloric spell of 19.3-6-44-6 but he had a game for Ireland the following morning, down at The Oval, so the sensible course of action would have been a couple of scoops then home for a mug of Ovaltine and a piece of cheese on toast before bed. The celebrations were giddy that night, however, the sort that might have had Bootle-born Jamie Carragher saying "you've won nothing, get down the tunnel". But this was a major step forward, a puncturing of several days' slow-release pressure and several hours' suffocating tension. Cavort away, boys, but keep the caveats in mind; realise the job can only be completed with the utmost sobriety.

* * *

At 4:45am the alarm began its noisy assault on Sleeping Beauty. He stretched out a meaty right mitt and shut down the din. By 5am there was a taxi outside, tooting and blaring. Sleeping Beauty paid no heed. Instead, he turned off his phone and rolled over, a throbbing head flopping back down to the sanctuary of his pillow. Surfacing at 10:30, around the time of the scheduled toss in London, he sent a text message to the Ireland coach, Phil Simmons, informing him that he had missed his flight, which had been due in around two-and-a-half hours earlier. As it happened, Ireland's game against Surrey was a wash-out, which Jesse may briefly have reasoned provided him with rain-card vindication. But Simmons was not at all amused, and despite another game at Hove the next day, Ryder's contract was immediately annulled.

"Jesse must have just decided he didn't fancy going," says Watkins. "He'd gone out with the lads, who were all buzzing, and got bladdered. The taxi's turned up, and he's just turned over: can't be arsed. I got a phone call from him, late morning: 'I've missed my flight. Can I play tomorrow?' We'd got Wallasey on the bank holiday Monday. 'Yes you can, Jesse.' He told me later he regretted agreeing to play for Ireland."

Nine months later, in Christchurch, Ryder would hurl abuse at hospital staff treating a hand he had gashed badly when punching the window of a toilet door in a city-centre bar. In January 2009, after a drunken night in Wellington, he slept through a Black Caps team meeting and was too hungover to train. In July 2010, he was censured for rowdy behaviour while intoxicated in a hotel during an indoor tournament. In March 2012, he was dropped for an ODI against South Africa after he and Doug Bracewell had hit the pop in the hotel bar. In March 2013, after a year of sorting out his life – counselling, kickboxing, cricket training, taking a dietary supplement that incurred a six-month doping ban – he was brutally assaulted outside a bar in Christchurch, leaving him in a coma with a fractured skull and punctured lung. In February 2014, a late-night pub visit on the eve of a Test against India – he was next batting cab off the rank, Ross Taylor was injured, so Tom Latham came in for his debut instead – led to his omission from the following month's World T20 in Bangladesh, when he was the incumbent New Zealand opener in a format that ought to have made him a superstar. And that was that for his international career. You can lead a horse to water.

It is a long rap sheet – the sort of career in which 'maverick' doubles as a euphemism for 'pisshead' – although Watkins says he only ever had one "domestic" with Jesse. "I took a call from the owner of the property he was staying in, a relative of a club member. 'I need you to come down. There's been some damage caused.' They'd had a bit of a party and somebody had honked up on the rug. They'd then rolled it up and stuck it behind the couch. We had to placate him and pay for the cleaning."

With Ryder having "missed his flight", New Brighton were delighted to have him for the game at Wallasey, a leisurely ten-minute stroll up the road – "Thankfully," says Evans, "Jesse was not provided with a car". Like their neighbours, Wallasey were one of the Comp's founding group of 11 clubs and they had a more recent league title than their derby rivals, having won their first in 2000 – Brad Haddin clubbing 697 runs in 13 games at 63.36 – then backed it up in 2002, the first of Paul Strang's three years there before switching to the Rakers. Indeed, the club had been something of a Zimbabwean exclave through the 1990s, with several cast members from the "we flippin' murdered 'em" series turning out at the Wallasey Oval. Skipper Alastair Campbell had a middling year in 1995 but had made 1,123 runs at 66 in 1993, with Heath Streak also appearing in five games that summer. Grant Flower compiled 1,049 runs at 95.36 in 1996, a warm-up for the December rumble with Bumble's England. Strang's brother Bryan, the left-arm swing bowler, spent 1997 and '98 at the club, while in 1991 an 18-year-old Guy Whittall – who once famously woke up with a crocodile under his bed (in Africa, not the Wirral) – had been New Brighton's overseas.

New Brighton scrapped their way up to 189/9, 'Loggsy' Wilson with a third fifty of the campaign, Ryder chipping in 36, before the visitors laid siege to Wallasey's batting as they attempted to extend their winning streak to eight. Three wickets had already been lopped off before Ryder was introduced to the attack. He took the next six, 56/3 becoming 83/9, New Brighton's momentum now that of river rapids after torrential rain. Enter No.11 Barrie Beaver, determined to build some sort of obstacle. The heavy charcoal skies started to drip water. As the light grew iffier and the drizzle harder, Beaver blocked that river, defending his castle for 27 balls while No.6 Richie Conlan stood firm at the other end. Eventually, the rain grew too persistent and the players left the field, still almost an hour left in the game and 17 precious points on the line for New Brighton.

"We came off and locked ourselves in the changing rooms using a leg pole from the bowling machine," recalls Wallasey's David Miles. "I remember a few pitch inspections and outfield trudges by the umpires but I wouldn't know if it actually stopped raining as we remained locked inside. I think Richie Conlan even went for a shower. The umpires called a halt when there was less than the mandatory ten minutes left. We still had the usual social drinks after, but Jesse disappeared shortly after drinking a four-pint jug in one go!" The first two pints were to celebrate figures of 11.5-5-17-6, the second two to drown sorrows as the unbeaten run was ended, the lead over Lytham trimmed back to 23 points.

If Jesse's bowling was a revelation – overall, he had 33/207 at 6.3 apiece by the end of May – his batting had entered a mid-season slump that saw ten league fixtures pass by without a half-century, although there was a bludgeoned 147* against Irby in the Liverpool Echo T20 knockout, with sixes smote into nearby bus stops on Rake Lane and others clearing 40-foot nets by the scoreboard and the school behind that, finally landing in a neighbouring garden hitherto considered beyond cricket-ball range.

New Brighton picked up a win in their next outing, 17-year-old John While making 129 in an imposing total of 279/4 declared, while Ryder followed a disappointing 13 with 4/96 from 20.2 overs, taking the final wicket – opposite number Patrick Jackson, clean bowled for 140 – as Southport & Birkdale's gallant chase got within 23 of victory. It would be six games before they won again, however, a run that saw them slide back to fifth in the table.

* * *

The trip to Ormskirk was always a challenge. The club had won five LDCC titles between 1971 and 1980, then entered a long period of retrenchment from which they emerged in 1999 with victory at Old Trafford in the Lancashire knockout. They lost the final in the next two years, the bitter pill of the second sweetened by a first Comp title in 21 years and a second straight Liverpool Echo win. They were an emerging powerhouse. Indeed, in 2008, with bouncer addict Neil Wagner spearheading the attack, they would land another Comp title, since when there have been four more, a run of six LDCC T20 wins in seven years, and a major splash at national level. In 2013, they lost a washed-out T20 final to Wimbledon in a bowl-off; four years later, with future England spinner Tom Hartley and England Lions batter Josh Bohannon in the side, they went down by 12 runs to Wanstead & Snaresbrook in the 45-over version. It was a tricky assignment, although Paul Hale's 21st birthday promised a good evening for Jesse and the boys however things panned out at Brook Lane.

Ormskirk's 34-year-old Sri Lankan pro, Suwanji Madanayeke, a tidy left-arm spinner who finished with 369 first-class scalps at 22 apiece, knocked over the first three wickets after New Brighton had elected to bat, including Ryder for four. Wilson and the birthday boy made 70s but the going was tough and almost 59 overs were needed to post 243/9 declared. Alas, there would be no Ryder heroics this time as Ormskirk romped home for the loss of only three wickets. Comp legend John Armstrong added 75 to the pile that would eventually put him in the 10,000 club; his opening partner Matthew Glayzer made 46; there was 49 from No.3 Jack Kelliher, a former England under-15s captain and fiery redhead later to collect a three-year ban from the Saddleworth League for striking an opponent with his bat *on his way to the crease*; and the job was finished with unbeaten 20-odds from Ian Glayzer and an 18-year-old John Simpson, future wicket-keeping stalwart of Middlesex and Sussex. Ryder managed 1/79 from 13.1 sprayed overs. "It was a very flat pitch against a very good line-up," muses Evans. Disappointing. Still, win or lose…

"Jesse didn't get home till 3am," adds Evans. "On Monday! He had to be escorted out of a nightclub by a good mate of ours on Sunday night. At one stage, he drank a bottle of Jim Beam straight down. I'd also seen him down a bottle of wine in seven seconds. He could certainly drink, but he didn't do it around the club's old guard at the bar in the club. It was usually done at house parties."

New Brighton were still 27 points clear at this juncture, heading into a home game against a Huyton team that would win only one of 26 league games. Jesse failed to dip bread, however, registering his only duck of the season, while a muscle niggle restricted him to nine overs. Huyton had evidently been irked by Tim Watkins nabbing Nawab and Wilson as he returned to Rake Lane, and hung on determinedly for the draw, seven down. More disappointment. Air was coming out of tyres, and with an injured Jesse unable to make the trip along the Welsh coast to Colwyn Bay, New Brighton were rucked for 126 and went down by four wickets, 6/57 taken by the 34-year-old former Indian Test seamer Debasis Mohanty.

Bootle had gone top, but Northern, in sixth, were only 22 points back at the halfway mark. Meanwhile, Colwyn Bay were on an eight-game winning streak that would make them, by the end of June, the fourth team to hold the lead in the title race. At the end of a week that saw Tony Blair replaced as Prime Minister by Gordon Brown, New Brighton's game at Northern was abandoned without a ball bowled. A week later, having picked up 5/66 to keep Fleetwood Hesketh to 220, Jesse sounded the bugle on 17 and was stumped, New Brighton hanging on, eight down and 80 short. It was one win in seven since the Bootle heist, while Ryder was averaging a tick over 21 since his last fifty, two months earlier. The next three games, against bottom-half teams, provided an opportunity to get the juices sluiced.

He started by crashing 132 against St Helens Recs – dismissed by C Lyon (arf) after adding 211 with John While – before Louis Botes, with 7/39, including a hat-trick, eased them to a 165-run win. The game against Hightown, who had Yusuf Pathan sub-proing, was then lost to the weather, before Jesse took 6/28 against a dismal Leigh side that would finish bottom of the pile. Watkins, who missed the game, thinks it was a grave error to win the toss and bowl, restricting themselves to a 20-point win. "They were crap that year," he says. "For some unknown reason, we stuck them in. We bowled them out for 50-odd and knocked them off in ten seconds. It was my fault for not leaving instructions. I was laissez-faire and didn't want to micromanage from a distance." Still, they were back up to second, nine points behind Bootle and leading Colwyn Bay, Northern and next opponents Lytham by seven, 11 and 17 respectively. Nip and tuck.

The game up at Lytham would typify the sort of quandary that a cavalier overseas pro provides. The home team battled their way to 226 all out in 55 overs, a good effort from the Rakers with no Botes or Nawab in the attack and Jesse going at fours. New Brighton's reply seemed to be progressing sweetly at 160/3, the game three-quarters won, when Ryder miscued one of Jimmy Wisniewski's leggies to the long-on boundary for a brutal but not match-securing 86. Still, Evans made his way to 60 with no further alarms and at

189/4, with 38 more required, the game was five-sixths won. At which point the last six wickets were swept away for 19 runs. Time was not a factor, either: there were 67 balls left when Lytham's 6' 7" pro, Marcus Sharp – who 12 years earlier had knocked over Brian Lara, Carl Hooper and Jimmy Adams when the Minor Counties beat the West Indians at Reading – cleaned up the last man to finish with 5/67 from 22.2 unchanged overs.

The good news was that not much had changed: New Brighton still trailed the leaders by nine points, only now those leaders were Colwyn Bay on 301 points, followed by Bootle (300), New Brighton (292), Lytham (290), Northern (280) and Ormskirk (278) in an incredibly tight title race. Seven days later, half-centuries for John While and Matt Thompson offset a single-figure score from the pro and, with 253 to defend and Maghull up to 141/3, Jesse roared in to knock over top-scorer Dave Roots, trap Andrew Symes lbw (breaking his toe in the process), and clean-bowl the last five to finish with 7/66. New Brighton were back on top; Bootle away was next.

* * *

How do you evaluate an overseas pro? By what metrics, which intangibles? For some, it boils down to cold, hard stats. For others, it is a question of the matches and trophies they win. For others still, it is more about the *dreams* of winning trophies that their performances and presence allow to feel within reach. We all run on hope. For many, however, it comes down to what the pro 'puts back in' to the club.

New Brighton were delighted with Ryder, and after the trip to Bootle they would offer him terms to return in 2008. Jesse accepted without hesitation, although requested they give him less money because he wished to skip the mandatory Friday night coaching duties with the kids – not necessarily because Fridays were prime bender terrain, but because he just couldn't find it in him to be a combination of bottomless enthusiasm and buttoned-up responsibility. That was not a costume he felt comfortable wearing. However, if putting back into the club means spending money there, then Ryder was supremely dedicated. "He put 60 per cent of his wages behind the bar," says

Evans. Watkins reckons 95 per cent. "If you held his hand and he was comfortable with what was around him, he was awesome," the skipper adds. "If you were asking him to be a grown-up, it was a struggle."

Jesse's body language in New Zealand colours didn't always exude steely determination, but his New Brighton teammates knew he was all-in, despite the blasé air and slumped shoulders. "Any more laid back he'd have been lying down," says Evans, "but he fought tooth-and-nail for us, and at times bowled himself into the ground. He loved it, and was massively up for it."

The trip to Wadham Road was the only Comp game that started that afternoon, albeit over two hours late. Bootle won the toss and decided to field, giving themselves the easier route to victory in a truncated game, as well as the option of shutting up shop if things headed south. Ronnie Davis snuck one through John While, then trapped Jesse lbw for nine. Adam Warren chipped in with a couple of middle-order wickets and Will Purser mopped up the rest, finishing with 5/20, Thompson top-scoring with 19 on a treacherous pitch as New Brighton mustered 74 all out. Could lightning strike twice?

A run out got things going for the Rakers, then Botes took out Cockbain Jr and Jesse dismissed Reynolds: 11/3. The 45-year-old John Hitchmough, a veteran of 66 games for Cheshire and called out of retirement the previous week, was cleaned up by Botes: 20/4. Stephen Parry and Graham Lloyd steadied the ship, but with the score on 47 Botes trapped Lloyd in front and five runs later picked up Parry for a resolute 27, courtesy of a fine catch by Ryder. The favour was then returned as Ryder scalped Purser: 59/7. With Cockbain Snr unavailable, the Bootle bottle was once more under the microscope. Another five runs were hewn from the rock face. Eleven more needed, the gloaming descending fast, bowling side very much still fancying their chances. At just after 6:30, however, the umpires conferred and decided it was simply too dark to continue. "We were gutted," says Evans, "because we thought we had them. Even though they only needed 11 to win, they had scars from the first game." In the end, both teams picked up five points, the same as their rivals, meaning the top six were separated by 20 points with five to play.

The August bank holiday weekend brought New Brighton 49 points from a pair of wins. On the Saturday, at Trafalgar Road,

Southport & Birkdale's much-loved Lancashire out-ground, Nawab took 6/28 to turn 213/2 into 238 all out. Patrick Jackson followed his 121 by trapping Jesse for 35 when the visitors were cruising along at 122/2. Half an hour later it was 152/7 and the goose looked cooked, only for Nawab to smear 48* from No.9, supported by Tom Jones's 31, to keep the New Brighton noses in front as Bootle trounced Leigh by 140 runs. On the Monday, Bootle beat Hightown by 138, with Purser picking up 9/25, making it imperative New Brighton saw off Wallasey in the derby.

Batting first, the Rakers had reached 42 when the first wicket fell. Jesse then smoked 57 of the 74 scored while he was at the crease but succumbed when set to cut loose, with Hale's 61 steering the home team to 217 all out. Wallasey never threatened to get them, subsiding to 73/9 before a late flurry added 48 more and saved a little face, Ryder picking up 4/25 from 15.2 overs of quality medium-fast bowling. With three to play, New Brighton were 11 points clear of Bootle, with Ormskirk at home the last major hurdle to navigate. Bootle were at fourth-placed Lytham.

This time, New Brighton opted to bowl first, partly through apprehension of Ormskirk's batting power though mainly a strategic decision to accept a 20-point win, thereby remaining – assuming both they and Bootle won – at least six points clear, with relegated Huyton and a Mohanty-less Colwyn Bay left to play. It looked a good call at 17/2, Jesse striking twice, but clinical batting from Matt Glayzer (63), John Simpson (47) and Ian Glayzer (43), along with some irritating lower-order biffing from skipper Adam Waterhouse (26*), left New Brighton a chase of 250 on a wicket taking spin. Big pressure. Over to you, Jesse?

The scoreboard read 29/1 when Jesse slunk out to the middle, Matt Thompson feathering a catch to Simpson off the lively seamers of 18-year-old Nicky Caunce, who would join the Lancashire staff a couple of years later and take nine wickets on debut for the second XI. Two runs later, James While skipped past one from Madanayeke to be stumped. Hale stuck around with Jesse to add 41 before falling to another nick behind, just when the scoreboard had again started to glimmer optimistically. Madanayeke then won an lbw decision against Evans to make it 93/4. But Jesse was blazing away, scoring at a run a ball, handling the Sri Lankan, bullying the others, Loggsy providing calm support as 66 were added. At 159/4, with Jesse on 90 from 85 balls, including seven fours and six sizeable sixes, the game – perhaps the season as a whole – had entered 'another half-hour of this' territory. At which point came a stiletto knife through the heart: Waterhouse's nagging in-swingers snuck one through a big Jesse mow and crashed into timber. Shit.

Out came David While, Rake Lane numb with shock. The score nudged up to 180/5: 70 more. But there was time pressure in play, a need to keep things ticking, and Waterhouse was going at under threes while Madanayeke whirled away menacingly at the other end. Eventually, While succumbed, caught in the outfield off the spinner. Almost immediately, Wilson ran at the pro and gave Simpson a second stumping. Madanayeke then found the edge of Jones's bat and Simpson did the rest. Second-teamer Richard Williams, in at No.10, was stumped second ball, and New Brighton were nine down, 55 short.

In came the rarely-called-upon Watkins, the only New Brightonian with a title-winner's medal on his mantelpiece. Nawab struck a couple of fours, smote a couple of sixes. Watkins got one away to the boundary. They were up to 224/9. Fifteen minutes remained. Everybody had everything crossed, hoping for a Houdini. "I walked down and told Ashraf not to charge the spinner. I said we could get them at the other end, but sure enough that's what happened: he was almost run out, he was that far down." Simpson had four stumpings and seven victims overall, a Comp record. Madanayeke had 7/64. New Brighton had only emptiness, which not even booze could fill.

"Jesse couldn't have done any more," reflects Evans, with a touching acceptance of amateur responsibility, a hearty conviction that it's no good being a one-man band, before adding: "Well, he could have hit a big hundred and won us the game. But he was 22 years old. I think at 25 he'd have done that. Fact is, we let Jesse down. We kept running past their left-arm spinner."

Bootle, meanwhile, had never really looked in trouble, although Lytham had rallied from 65/6 to 145/6 in pursuit of 220, before eventually folding for 157. The Bootle machine had gone five points clear of New Brighton, six ahead of Northern, and had two of the bottom four to play.

* * *

There were regrets, but no recriminations. A miracle still might be possible, although the geography – Bootle being over the water, but barely a couple of miles for your average crow – was not congenial for the fates to engineer a lucky break with the weather, a benign *force majeure*. The penultimate Saturday saw Ryder thrash 85 before being run out, mid-carnage, New Brighton declaring as soon as the fifth batting point was pocketed. Huyton, already down and devoid of the spoiler's doggedness of earlier in the season, were then flattened for 29 in 17 overs, Jesse taking 6/11. The game finished at 4:40pm. Bootle would need another 80 minutes to secure their win. These 80 minutes represented the final chance, but there was to be no hurricane, no blizzard, no earthquake.

On the final afternoon, Bootle had signed and sealed their win before New Brighton shook off a stout Colwyn Bay challenge, Jesse taking the final four wickets in a 32-run win having earlier clubbed 113 out of a 286/6 rage-compiled in 41.5 overs. The dream was not to be. The engraver pulled out his trusty Bootle stencil and scratched away. Still, to return to the Ten Commandments (and Jesse was nothing if not an Old Testament guy): *win or lose, always booze*. His teammates took their disappointment and their hangovers to the Cheshire Cup final the following day, where they were trounced by Oulton Park.

Bootle, meanwhile, had already added that fourth straight Lancashire knockout and fourth straight Ray Digman to a fourth Comp title in five years, although Ormskirk retained the Echo to deny them the quadruple. Fifteen major trophies out of 20 in five years, 13 out of 16 in the last four. There's no shame in being bested by such a team, and New Brighton had come within a fag paper – within a clutch of *what-ifs* – of slaying Goliath. What if they'd batted first against Leigh and picked up the 25 points? What if they'd taken that last Wallasey wicket – that damn Beaver – before the rains? What if Jesse had converted the 86 at Lytham or the 90 against Ormskirk into mummy hundreds? Time heals, but it is difficult to entirely purge the sting from these what-might-have-beens.

"The Ormskirk game is what cost us," asserts Evans. "There was never a thought that he could have done more, though. It never crossed our minds. We knew we wouldn't have been anywhere near where we were without him. Yes, 15 years later, maybe you start thinking about the Ormskirk game, the Lytham game, when he was set and got out. But we didn't step up and back him up. That's how I see it. That's how everyone sees it."

Ryder's final tally was 1,047 runs (fourth most) at 49.85, along with 79 wickets (second behind Mohanty's 83) at 11.30, third in the averages among bowlers with 20 wickets or more. It promised much for 2008, but by February he was making a T20 and ODI debut against England. A central contract followed, then an apologetic phone call to Merseyside, slightly more sincere than the SMS he'd sent to PV Simmons. New Brighton finished third that summer, Wagner's Ormskirk pipping Bootle on the final afternoon.

Ryder's next UK jaunt was not until 2014, the first of his three seasons at Essex. Evans and a friend paid him a visit, watching a T20 game in Chelmsford. "Jesse didn't have a drink the whole two nights we were there," he recalls. "He'd had the world at his feet. He just sometimes chose the wrong path. He couldn't go in a pub and not have a drink."

The following year, 2015, Evans led New Brighton to a first title in 17 years and ahead of the 2019 season agreed terms with Ryder for a romantic return to Rake Lane, 12 years on. The visa and contracts were sorted, but a family illness prevented him from coming. Nevertheless, the mark he left on the place endures. "Everybody at New Brighton will say he was the best cricketer we've ever seen at our club," Evans asserts. "We've had local legends and very good overseas pros, but he was just different. At times, he was playing a different game."

A very good season it had been, but not quite good enough. Still, they will always have The Bootle Game.

2

Rohan Kanhai and Lance Gibbs
at Ashington / Whitburn (and Aberdeenshire, Blackpool, Crompton, St Annes / Burnley)

With the obvious exception of 1992, when Durham graduated from Minor Counties heavyweights to first-class lightweights – it would not take them long to bulk up – perhaps no season was greeted with quite so much giddy anticipation in the North East as the summer of 1964, when for the first time in its history this club cricket hotbed would count two active internationals among its professional ranks. They weren't any old players, either: Lance Gibbs, returning for a second season at Whitburn in the Durham Senior League, was the No.1 bowler in the world, while Rohan Kanhai, about to embark on a maiden campaign with Ashington of the Northumberland County League, was the No.2 batter, behind only his Test skipper, Garry Sobers. The cricket-loving folk of Tynemouth and Wearmouth, South Shields and Sunderland, North Shields and Newcastle had seen plenty of them on the television the previous summer, too, as West Indies ran out 3-1 winners in the inaugural Wisden Trophy. Now came the chance for an intimate viewing.

The stories of Lancelot Richard Gibbs and Rohan Bholalall Kanhai would of course be indelibly intertwined. Born within 15 months of each other on the northern shores of Guyana, they each played 79 Tests for West Indies, 58 of them alongside one another. In 1968, when county cricket opened up fully to overseas players, they embarked upon six years together at Warwickshire, where they became legends. During the first two years of bedding in with the Bears, the phlegmatic Gibbs averaged mid-to-low 20s, the feisty Kanhai low-to-mid-40s. In 1970, Kanhai's 68.18 average trailed only Sobers at Notts. In 1971, Gibbs's 123 wickets (at 18.84) were 21 clear of anyone else as Warwickshire finished runners-up, earning him his *Wisden* Cricketer of the Year laurels the following April. That summer of '72, the 36-year-old Kanhai and 37-year-old Gibbs, averaging 59.87

and 26.48 respectively, helped Warwickshire go unbeaten through the season, bringing the pennant to Edgbaston for just the third time, the first for 21 years. Gibbs called it quits at the end of 1973, playing on in Test cricket, while his mate stayed four more years, until he was 41, by which time his nickname was 'Silver Fox'.

The diminutive Kanhai's dancing feet and savagely pugnacious back-foot game beguiled all that saw them, prompting Sunil Gavaskar, Alvin Kallicharran and even Bob Marley to name sons of theirs after him. He was intense, occasionally moody, a pocket battleship with a streak of wizardry. The unflappable Gibbs was tall and pencil slim, memorably described by David Frith as having "bulbous but dreamy eyes, close cropped hair and the loosest of gaits" that gave him "the appearance of a New Orleans trombonist". Spells were woven with exceedingly long fingers, a high-jumper's rhythmical high-stepping approach into a chest-on delivery, and an astute tactical brain, and in February 1976 he would become Test cricket's all-time leading wicket-taker, finishing with 309 at 29.09, a record held until DK Lillee went past him almost six years later.

Through Birmingham, British Guiana and the West Indies these gilded cricketing pathways were beaten out alongside each other – but also in the North East, when they were already in their late-20s and well-seasoned Test cricketers who had shone on that '63 Test tour, Kanhai picking up his *Wisden* Cricketer of the Year the following spring, just before his arrival in Ashington. Between March 1962 and early 1968, he never left the top four of the Test batting rankings. Gibbs was world No.1 for four unbroken years.

These were *bona fide* superstars – the equivalent, perhaps, of Virat Kohli and Ravichandran Ashwin rocking up for a season somewhere today – and the *Sunday Sun*, the region's go-to broadsheet for sports results, paid them £1,000 apiece for a weekly column (over £17,200 in today's money) in which they would hold forth on the local game, throw out a few thoughts on that summer's Ashes and offer some fairly rudimentary coaching tips, supposedly 'eternal verities' that perhaps come over to the modern reader as platitudes. For instance, Kanhai's batting *do's* included: "get to the pitch of the ball when playing forward"; "play every ball on its merits"; "concentrate all the time". And the *don'ts*: "hit across the ball"; "back away"; "try to cut a good length ball"; "take your eyes off the ball".

His compatriot's were only moderately less no-shit-Sherlockian: "you must read the wicket to be a spinner", he proffers, while advising his fellow tradesmen to "spin the ball as much as you can", "use the crease", "watch the footwork" and "try different things in nets". At times, it seems, their editor nudged them into choppier waters, deeper into the currents of the local scene, something to get tongues wagging and give the proto-clickbait headlines some heft – a risk with benefit matches on the horizon and bumper gates desired.

The paper also had their superstar columnists pick a team from the best amateurs they encountered in their league endeavours, an XI they would skipper in a challenge match – a sort of quasi-*Britain's Got Talent* in which this chosen cream would play for the honour of their respective league, their respective minor county, and, whatever the result, would go away with a spring in their step knowing one of the world's top players had thought them half-decent. Time's arrow has since flown another 60 years, but for those who survive, octogenarians now, these are the sort of newspaper cuttings still cherished.

* * *

Gibbs's first club cricket gig was at Burnley. He had picked up 11 Test caps in three years by the time he arrived at Turf Moor in 1961, the three most recent on the momentous 1960-61 tour of Australia in which West Indies were led for the first time by a black (and professional) captain, Frank Worrell. Gibbs sat out the first two – a tie in Brisbane, defeat at the MCG – but in the third, at Sydney, his 3/46 and 5/66 were pivotal to West Indies levelling the series. The fourth Test, in Adelaide, was drawn thanks only to the Aussies' last pair stonewalling for 109 excruciatingly tense minutes, Gibbs having earlier picked up a hat-trick (and Kanhai twin hundreds). Back in Melbourne for the decider, West Indies lost by two wickets, although Gibbs's match analysis of 79.4-37-142-6 (and these are eight-ball overs) further burnished his reputation, unequivocally marking him out as a world-class operator. Yet status counted for very little in the Lancashire League – maybe a couple of weeks' grace if the esteemed finger was slow in being pulled out – where demanding crowds accustomed to international stars were interested only in results. Especially at

Burnley, who had more league titles than all but Nelson and more trophies than everyone bar Nelson and East Lancs.

A whole cohort of Lancashire-bound West Indians had arrived alongside Gibbs at Tilbury Docks in April. Chester Watson at Church and Seymour Nurse at Ramsbottom were, like Gibbs, making their Lancashire League bow. Conrad Hunte was back for a fifth season at Enfield (the previous two having brought 1,437 and 1,125 runs) and Wes Hall for a second at Accrington, for whom he had taken 100 wickets in 1960 – not enough to stop Bacup taking the crown, spurred on by Roy Gilchrist's 126 scalps. Of the 14-strong professional cadre, 11 had Test experience, with the likes of Frank 'Typhoon' Tyson at Todmorden, Johnny Wardle at Nelson and Rawtenstall's Chandu Borde among Gibbs's direct adversaries, those he had to best in order to buy him his breathing space. Reputations forged on international fields would provide scant protection from the carpers and grousers if he didn't adapt to pitches and expectations. Indeed, given Gibbs's haplessness with the bat, even at this level – the season would bring him just 65 runs – his bowling would have to sizzle.

Burnley were Worsley Cup holders, their fourth in ten years since the inimitable Cec Pepper – leggies, larrups, effin', jeffin' – had inspired them to a double in 1950. They won another championship in 1956, but the next season slipped to 12th, whereupon they signed 24-year-old West Indian off-spinning all-rounder Collie Smith, one of *Wisden*'s Cricketers of the Year, who shot them back up to second in 1958 and helped them win the Worsley Cup, played as timeless single-innings games over however many consecutive weeknights it took to achieve a result.

In the opening round of the following year's competition, Burnley were drawn away at cross-town rivals Lowerhouse. OG Smith would pile up a record 306*, including 56 fours – several of them out of the ground, although sixes were only counted as such at half-a-dozen venues (the Lowerhouse Lane and Liverpool Road sides, but not the others, were added to the list in 1963, before universal standardisation of six-hits in 1968). At the peak of the carnage, the game was almost abandoned due to a lack of balls, only for four to be thrown back over the wall in one go. Burnley eventually declared at 523/9 – each night the stand-in skipper dropped by the regular captain's house and was told to bat on – and went on to win by 376, another record that still stands. Ninety-five days later, however, Smith would be dead, failing to regain consciousness after a 4:30am car crash as Garry Sobers drove him and fellow Jamaican Tom Dewdney to an exhibition match in London.

Three days after Smith's demise, with the Lancashire League committee refusing to countenance calling the game off, Burnley fulfilled their final fixture of the season, at home to Rawtenstall – sub pro Roy Gilchrist took 8/59 to win the game, seven of them bowled – which was preceded by a memorial service led by Smith's landlord, Reverend Walter Ridyard. Neighbours Burnley FC were represented by chairman Bob Lord, manager Harry Potts and winger Jimmy McIlroy, who, an hour later, ran out to face West Bromwich Albion, sustaining a shoulder injury that kept him off the field for 13 minutes while he was strapped up (Burnley already having used their one permitted substitute). McIlroy returned to the fray to help secure a 2-1 win, and by the time Indian swing-bowling all-rounder Dattu Padkhar had arrived in April 1960, the Clarets were en route to what remains their most recent top-flight title. When Gibbs turned up a year later, Burnley were in the European Cup quarter-final, ultimately eliminated by a 75th-minute Uwe Seeler strike in Hamburg, while finishing a creditable fourth in the league. The town was abuzz and, as the summer sport took over the back pages, Gibbs needed to avoid being a buzzkill.

It started well, with a win over Hall's Accrington. A week later, Gibbs took 5/33 against Rishton, although rain had the final say. He bowled steadily in a nerve-shredding one-wicket win over Haslingden, took 5/39 in a rout of Rishton, then a pair of seven-fors in home-and-away derby wins against Lowerhouse. Burnley were top. Everything was groovy. The jazz trombonist was satisfying the natives' need for cawing one-upmanship.

At which point came a 13-match run yielding only two wins. Gibbs managed just one wicket at Todmorden and Church, none at Enfield, three at Colne, only four times picking up more than that. He dismissed Seymour Nurse against Rammy, but figures of 9-4-51-3 were not flattered by comparison with fellow offie Jack Schofield, a wily veteran who sent down 15-7-18-3. As the grumbles grew more frequent, Burnley slowly lost touch with leaders Accrington. There was an uptick in August, with four wins out of five ultimately pushing them up to a creditable joint-second finish. They had five batters in the top 18 of the averages, yet bungled run chases with the pressure on proved costly.

Meanwhile, Wes Hall's heroics secured Accrington a first title for 45 years. The skipper, Lindon Dewhurst, was presented with the trophy during the tea interval at Ramsbottom on the season's final afternoon, with the game followed by the traditional champagne celebration. The team then hopped on an open-top bus and headed back up the Rossendale Valley to be greeted in Accrington by a huge crowd outside the town hall. There they attended a civic reception hosted by the mayor and local MP, after which everyone repaired to the Commercial Hotel for drinks and buffet, where Hall was presented with a club tie and cap. Different times.

Gibbs had finished with a respectable 90 wickets – only Hall, with 106, had more – which cost him 11.72 apiece, within a run of Tyson (10.93) and also trailing the Reverend Wesley and Rishton offie Jimmy Smith. It was a solid enough campaign, but not one that brought him much joy in the face of crowds as proprietorial (for their two shillings' worth) as they were parochial. "Everything is taken so seriously – the result is the thing, not good cricket," he would write later in the *Sunday Sun*, following up with the arm-ball. "When we won, everything was great: people would have a drink and take you home by car. But when we lost, quite another matter!" Gibbs was after a change of scenery, and soon got news of an offer from the North East.

***

While Gibbs was in Burnley, Kanhai was in his fourth year on the club pro circuit, having been first tapped up as a 21-year-old pup on West Indies' 1957 tour by Aberdeenshire CC. That un-Guyanese, north-easterly corner of Caledonia was not as difficult a sell as might be imagined, for Mannofield Park was the best appointed ground in Scotland, with a true pitch and serried banks of wooden benches for its often lively crowds. Bradman had played his last game on British soil there, scoring 123* at the end of the 1948 Invincibles' tour, and Kanhai's three years in the Granite City would see him reach Bradmanly heights as the best of Forfarshire,

Fifeshire, Clackmannanshire, Stirlingshire and others in the Scottish Counties Championship failed, unsurprisingly, to solve the puzzle he presented. He topped both run charts and averages in all three seasons in Aberdeen, each year a little more awesomely: 533 at 76.14 in 1958, then 623 at 89 in 1959, and 766 at 109.42 in 1960. Bish, bash, bosh. West Lothian were certainly sick of the sight of him; his scores against them were 89, 103*, 84*, 138*, 151* and 102* for an average of 667. Alas, there were no championships: Perthshire won it in the first two seasons – indeed, they would win 17 in a 20-year stretch from 1953 – and Clackmannan the third.

In 1961, Kanhai switched to moneybags Blackpool of the Northern League, which had been formed by a dozen aspirational clubs splitting from the Ribblesdale League nine years earlier. He was following in illustrious footsteps. In 1939, the 34-year-old Harold Larwood, drummed out of county cricket in the acrimonious aftermath of Bodyline, took 68 league wickets at 10.5 while running a sweet shop in town, while the club engaged Jim Parks Snr for their debut Northern League campaign.

In 1953, a month before Stanley Matthews was inspiring the Tangerines to FA Cup final glory, Bill Alley was enticed over from Colne, where he had been the first – and still only – player to score 1,000 league runs in five successive seasons. A boxing champion, bouncer and blacksmith in his native Australia, later a Test umpire after an Autumn-blooming career at Somerset, Alley was even more prolific at Stanley Park than he had been in the Lancashire League, again topping four figures in each of his four seasons – including what remains a club record 1,345 in 1949, at an eye-watering 149.44 – while averaging 115.36 overall, all in front of crowds regularly in excess of 5,000. A tough act to follow. As, indeed, was Kanhai's immediate predecessor, Hanif Mohammad, who likewise topped both league averages and run charts in his two seasons at Blackpool – 1,134 at over 103 taking them to the title the year before Kanhai stepped into his slippers. The 1,000-run mark had been breached five times in nine Northern League seasons, all of them by Blackpool pros. Over to you, Rohan.

This was the dawn of the swingin' sixties, with 150,000 holidaymakers descending on Blackpool each summer for the golden sands, donkey rides and fish and chips; for the Pleasure

Beach, amusement arcades and bingo halls; for the ballrooms and piers, with their heaving rock 'n' roll nights and packed houses for Morecambe and Wise, Tommy Cooper, Ken Dodd and Bruce Forsyth at the Winter Gardens, the ABC, the Grand. They tumbled in through the turnstiles at Stanley Park, too, making life very lucrative for these batting greats the club had engaged, and with his hair swept up in the 'candy floss', Teddy Boy style, Kanhai brought his own slice of fast-footed glamour to town. Score a few runs, count the collection and then head out onto the promenade, into the heart of things. In September 1963, he would marry Phyllis Brenda Hague, a former Miss Blackpool.

With a pair of Test double-hundreds in his first two years for the West Indies, Kanhai's appetite for runs was evidently voracious, and there were those twin centuries in Adelaide a couple of months before first rolling down the Golden Mile. Predictably enough, he too topped runs and averages in both his seasons in Blackpool, making it five out of five as a club pro.

In 1961, with the pro chipping in 919 runs at 65.64, Blackpool finished joint-second behind Leyland, while Kanhai shot them to victory in the Slater Cup (which, in a 12-team league, meant only three rounds, or four for four sides). He scored 58* in the first round, a ten-wicket win over Leyland Motors. In the semis, a five-wicket win over Darwen, the contribution was 74* as 112 were knocked off. In the final, it was 86* as Kendal's 122 were overhauled. There was a hint of genius to it all, and a hefty streak of professional ruthlessness.

The following year's Slater Cup brought 60 in the first-round win over Leyland, 81* in the semis against Fleetwood, and 52 out of 98 all out in the final, which Blackpool lost to Darwen (to save you the maths, that's a Slater Cup average of 205.5). Still, Blackpool went one better and won the league, and Kanhai was even more dominant, amassing 1,165 runs – 450 more than the next best – at 83.21, with six tons, five more than anyone else. Having taken Lancaster for 153* in his first year, he upped it to 156 in 1962. Special K.

The Seasiders were keen to have him back after West Indies' tour of England in '63, but at the end of that trip, sitting out a tour game at Scarborough, Ashington, backed by Charlie Chisholm, a local bookie, swooped in with a bigger offer. It was too good to refuse and Rohan rolled the dice. In one of his early *Sunday Sun* columns, first impressions formed, he would suggest that the standard was better in the Northern League, although added that he "could never get used to the sheer intensity and surliness" of the cricket over there, something of a diplomatic salvage operation. He can't have disliked Lancashire too much – he eventually settled on the Fylde coast, calling his old pal Sonny Ramadhin in Saddleworth every fortnight until the latter passed away in 2022, and he is still there today as he approaches a 90th birthday.

* * *

Between the cumulonimbus of his Burnley exit and the fanfare of his arrival at Whitburn in April 1962, Lance Gibbs had turned in one of Test cricket's all-time great bowling performances against India in Barbados, one that was sure to have had the Wearsiders salivating in anticipation. The Guyanese was of course a byword for pressure-building parsimony, finishing with a career economy-rate of 1.98 in Tests, and here, as the Indians battled for over 185 overs to save the game, he returned figures of 53.3-37-38-8, this after being 0/31 off 35. It was both a coming-of-age and a Test career-best, as it would remain. If anything encapsulated the challenge facing the local amateurs as they tackled the Durham Senior League's first ever £1,000 pro – Gibbs picked up £40 a week, just a year after professional football's maximum wage of £20 a week had been abolished – then his post-lunch spell on the fifth day in Bridgetown was it: an astonishing 15.3-14-6-8. There weren't going to be too many freebies.

Whitburn's glory days were its long-gone trio of consecutive Durham Senior League titles in the 1920s, with another championship in 1950 the only one in the 30 years before Gibbs's arrival. Sunderland (with 13 titles) and Durham City (eight) were the perennial heavyweights, yet Whitburn, despite finishing rock-bottom of the table in 1961, had grounds for optimism ahead of the new season – and not only due to the scarcely plausible capture of Gibbs by a club from a small mining village sitting a handful of into-the-wind, step-and-fetch hits from the Wearside clifftops, a club that hadn't engaged a pro of any description for four years, not since local lad Nev Lorraine. Other things were changing, too.

The club's gently sloping ground on East Street had originally been developed in 1862 at Whitburn Hall on land donated by Sir Hedworth Williamson, the eighth baronet. By the time Gibbs arrived a century later, the hall had been converted into apartments, although vestiges of the estate's Grecian-columned terrace still flanked the northern boundary when in 1961 the 11th baronet, Sir Nicholas Hedworth Williamson, sold both ground and hall to Laurie Evans, a local builder and vice-chairman of Sunderland Football Club. That winter, Evans pushed through bold plans to build a new, two-storey pavilion with a large upstairs balcony, on which the ribbon was cut just in time for the unveiling of the West Indian superstar as he set about making some happier memories – both for himself and a club taking its leap into the unknown.

"As the wind whipped in off the North Sea, the club chairman Percy Bell and Penelope Evans, daughter of the new owner Laurie Evans, opened the new pavilion," writes Jonathan Wilson, a native of Whitburn (and keen purveyor of sub-Gibbsian offies) who didn't even realise Gibbs had played for his village team, a story he investigates in a masterful and poignant essay detailing trips 'home' from London to look after his mother as she slides into dementia, exploring the themes of roots, memory and identity as he documents the unravelling of his mam's coherent, memory-bound self (it was her casual remark that first alerted Wilson about Gibbs's stint in Whitburn) and his own fading memories and deracination. "This, said Bell," continues Wilson, "would be 'the greatest season in the history of the club'. Could one player, even a *bona fide* great like Lance Gibbs, really make that much difference? Gibbs himself seemed uncertain: the photo in the *Sunderland Echo* shows him swaddled in at least two jumpers, looking distinctly uncomfortable."

Gibbs was billeted three miles south in Sunderland, living with Mrs Hutchinson and her two daughters overlooking Roker Park – the municipal amenity, not the football stadium – built on land donated by Hedworth Williamson in 1880. "It was very near the football ground," Gibbs would recollect to Wilson almost 60 years later, "and they warned me to get home early when there was football on." When football wasn't on, he would frequent Wetherall's nightclub, with teammates Alan Alder, freshly returned from dog-training duty with the RAF in Cyprus, and Cliff Bell his minders. Prior to the

1962 season, the club itself had no bar for post-match libations. Team selection was held at The Jolly Sailor, just up the road. It was, indeed, a Brave New World.

His Whitburn colleagues had had a look at him in the nets, Gibbs bowling in a long overcoat to combat the Nordic winds, but the job of facing his first ball in the Senior League fell to Ken Longstaff – the name, if ever there were one, of some fabled smiter, descendent of the Merry Men. Longstaff opened the batting for Boldon, the pit village three miles west, and as a 14-year-old boy had cycled all the way to London to watch the Olympics, while there dropping in at The Oval to see Bradman's final Test (as in: b Hollies 0 and that mythic .94). An ardent Methodist who inherited his father's grocer's shop near East Boldon station, Longstaff was good enough to play for his county – he bagged a pair in 1959 when Durham played the Indians in Sunderland, where a 17-year-old Colin Milburn gave notice with a rollicking ton – and certainly would not have been unduly daunted as he saw Gibbs mark out that long run of his. "When spin bowlers opened the bowling," Longstaff told Wilson, "they often wouldn't waste the new ball bowling spin: they'd try and swing it. I was facing the first ball. I saw him take a long run and I thought he would bowl swing."

Watching on from the boundary was a teenage Barry Emmerson, Whitburn's future chairman but back then more interested in news coming through the wireless about Sunderland's attempt to pick up the win they needed at Swansea City in the final match of the season to gain promotion back to English football's top flight after a four-year absence. "Lance Gibbs was the Shane Warne of his day," he says, "so for him to come to a small village just up the road from Sunderland was incredible."

Meanwhile, on that cool, bright late-April day, Gibbs was coming in at Longstaff. It wasn't swing. "He'd taken such a long run," Longstaff added, "and the whip of his arm – I thought nobody could be bowling spin at that pace, but then it turned back…" Indeed it did: straight into the stumps. "He had terrifically long fingers," the defeated batter would later muse. "He could wrap his index finger round the ball."

"Ken came off shaking his head," says Emmerson, "and throughout the years I've always said to him 'I remember you getting out first ball of the season to Lance Gibbs'. It got to the stage where he'd say, 'Bugger off, will you'."

Gibbs finished with 4/32, and despite the county skipper of 16 summers, Don Hardy, making a fighting 48, Boldon fell for 61, which Whitburn knocked off – albeit six down, hinting at struggles later in the season. On his home debut the following Saturday, Gibbs took 7/53 as Seaham Harbour were bowled out for 164, following up with 53 – which would turn out to be his highest score for the club and the falsest of dawns – yet Whitburn came up 32 short. A week later, it was 4/30 off 19 in a return to winning ways, then 5/48 off 28 in an abandonment with Burnmoor, before Whitburn reeled off six straight victories, at five points apiece, that saw them surge eight points clear at the top, Gibbs contributing 7/52 in a first win over North Durham for six years, then 7/73, 6/56 (in front of 1,500 spectators at Sunderland), 7/33, 4/33 and 4/66. The juggernaut looked unstoppable, the bottom-to-top fairytale half-penned.

By that stage, Gibbs had 55 wickets in ten games at 8.71 a pop. But three weeks later – after three straight defeats in which batting frailties could not be PR-ed by any amount of spin – he broke a finger diving forward to take a low catch at cover against Chester-le-Street and was forced to sit out six rounds of matches. Whitburn lost that match, too, along with every other one for the remainder of the season, barring a shaky run chase against Seaham Harbour. As the nights shortened, Gibbs took 7/40 as Eppleton were rolled for 91, only for Whitburn to crash to 74 all out. He then bagged 6/33 as Gateshead Fell were rucked for 53, only for Whitburn to collapse to 32 in reply. After two months of daydreaming up in the thin air at the summit, they slid back to a ninth-place finish. Gibbs topped the league bowling averages with 84 wickets at 8.4. Sort out the batting by the time he returned in 1964, and they would be competitive.

* * *

When Gibbs and Kanhai arrived in the North East for the 1964 season, they did so not only as the world's No.1 bowler and No.2 batter but as key components in the West Indies' landmark 3-1 series win over the England of Trueman, Statham, Barrington, Cowdrey and Dexter the previous summer. Kanhai was the leading run-scorer in the series, with 497 at 55.52, while Gibbs – whose pro's seat at Whitburn had been kept warm by Nasim-ul-Ghani, at one time the youngest cricketer to have taken a Test five-for – pocketed 11/157 and 7/127 in the wins at Old Trafford and Headingley. His series haul of 26 wickets at 21.3 apiece was behind only Trueman's 34 and the 32 taken by Charlie Griffith, who was heading to Burnley for the summer, pitting his wits against Ramsbottom's Seymour Nurse and Bacup's Basil Butcher. Griffith's new-ball partner, Wes Hall, took up a new post at Great Chell of the North Staffordshire & South Cheshire League, where he would be going toe-to-toe with Norton's Garry Sobers. The black-and-white BBC highlights had given the future opponents of these stars a (grainy) picture of what lay in store.

Like Whitburn, Ashington was a coastal pit settlement, and its supporters were notoriously fervent and invariably raucous as the game started to pinch tight, particularly when the visitors had come from the big city – as was the case when Percy Main visited Langwell Crescent for Kanhai's debut – or from farming country up the Tyne valley. "The atmosphere was electric when Kanhai came out with McGrady," reported the *Sunday Sun* after Ashington had been set 135 in an hour and a half. Tyne-Tees TV was there to film Kanhai survive a huge lbw shout second ball – insert your own variant of the 'crowd has come to see…' line – and "the gasp of relief around the field was plainly audible". He was soon cooking, picking up Atkinson's opening offering for a big six over midwicket and reaching 50 in half an hour, whereupon the 18-year-old Alan Hardy had him caught at deep square leg with his own first ball.

Ashington got home with three balls to spare thanks to George Walton, a Northumberland stalwart of the 1950s who suffered badly from ulcers and would regularly have the county side's 12th man administer him milk and biscuits at long leg between overs. Once completing two centuries on a single day for the Northumbrians, his 51-minute second-innings effort helping knock off 146 in 17 overs against Cheshire, Walton also responded to his defeated teammates' timorous tales of Staffordshire's young quick-bowling tyro Ken Higgs by lashing him for 26 in the first over of the return game. Here, after his first up-close look at Kanhai, Walton told *The Journal*: "I am quite sure most Northumberland League ground records will be broken this season when this finest aggressive batsman-entertainer in the world makes his appearances."

Bob Dunning, at the time a starry-eyed 14-year-old and later both Ashington's first-team captain and chairman, is in no doubt that Kanhai was the biggest name ever drawn to the County League, an honour previously held by Indian Test leggie Chandu Borde, who had picked up 100 wickets in a season for South Northumberland in the mid-1950s. "When Ashington played at South North," says Dunning, "Tommy Simpson got a ton. Tommy was a little left-hander, Ashington through and through, with no gloves, a block, a square cut and a mow over midwicket. Eye like a shithouse rat, though. After the game, Borde singled out Tommy and asked 'Mr Simpson', as he called him, how he picked his leggy and his googly. 'Easy', Tommy said, pointing to the far side of the ground. 'Your leg-spinner went in that tennis court and the googly went into the one next door.'"

The day after the Percy Main game brought Kanhai's opening *Sunday Sun* column, a first pebble dropped in the water. Here he speculated about how his presence might shape his team's games – "some clubs, for example, may well now leave Ashington only two hours to score, say, 200-odd runs, and consider it a generous target!" – which proved uncannily (or *cannily*) prophetic. He also predicted a second template: Ashington romping adventurously up to a 200-plus total, leaving the opposition plenty of time to chase, only for them to see the dangled carrot and refuse it like a vegetable-averse child – a standard and perfectly acceptable cricketing strategy for under-gunned sides, of course.

This second template played out almost to the letter in Ashington's next game, as they declared on a sprightly 202/4. Kanhai made 55 before being run out, Walton chipped in 42* and the former Leicestershire batter Ken Smith, father of Warwickshire's David and Paul, compiled a steady 60, although he would leave the club in mid-season, his accumulator's style seemingly at odds with Rohanball's demand for all teams to "score at 80 runs an hour" and penalties for persistent slow play, because "public interest must be constantly created, held and then stimulated". Kanhai would eventually find a willing, cudgelling sidekick in Colin Cairns, a miner and later groundsman at Ashington who represented the county at cricket, bowls and snooker.

After tea, Morpeth stodged their way to 126/7, Geoff Woodman taking an hour and a half over his 17* as the resolve not to be cast as belly-tickled suckers kicked in, whatever Rohan might say about it in the *Sun*. "I cannot see crowds ever improving" with this approach, he would grouse, preaching about attacking cricket to the benighted denizens of these recalcitrant rivalries with an evangelical air shared by Gibbs south of the Tyne. "We sent down nearly two dozen long-hops and full tosses to tempt them into the game," he added, seemingly failing to grasp that the spoiling, over-my-dead-body, fuck-'em mentality was (and is) as much a northern staple as brown ale and mushy peas. Maybe the crowds liked it that way, too. Not everyone is full of the song of joy.

Nevertheless, Ashington's enterprising, Kanhai-fuelled cricket would slowly reap its rewards. The third game saw them win with well over an hour to spare, the pro unbeaten on 92 as Blythe's 167 was blitzed off. Next up, at Benwell, in the shadow of St James' Park, with Ashington left just over two hours to chase 202, Kanhai made 80 out of the first 111 before falling to Bill Golightly, an entomologist lecturing at Durham University and working with the Ministry of Agriculture, whereupon Walton called off the chase. Benwell took £50 on the gate (around £860, adjusted for inflation), more than in the whole of the previous season.

A week later came a first Kanhai ton in a nine-wicket win at Alnwick. The Ashington committee no doubt felt that scores of 50, 55, 92*, 80 and 106* represented a tidy enough start from the hired help as they looked forward to the home clash with heavyweights South Northumberland. Indeed, they had already agreed to re-sign him for 1965, which wasn't yet cut and dried with the West Indies' Test series against Australia running into May, but Kanhai nonetheless remarked that "they have been generous with me. I believe no league club in the country could match their terms." (Or, in subsequent speculations conducted in the local parlance: "Must've been a canny wage packet..." "Colliery hoose an' aaal 'ees coal.")

Having won all three home games and drawn all three away – the rewards were a flat five points for a win, one for a draw – Ashington sat second behind South North, who proceeded to compile a mammoth 238/8, effectively batting their hosts out of the game, with 140 of them scored by legendary local boy Robert Willis Smithson, a

Cambridge-educated classics teacher at Durham School – there was no Cantab Blue for cricket, with seven future Test players in the side, but he did win one for rugby – who later had Northumberland's county cup named in his honour, in part because *wor Bobby* had taken 73 off the 1956 Aussies, 76 off the 1961 Aussies, and in 1960 had won the Wilfred Rhodes Trophy as the leading batter in Minor Counties cricket. Gauntlet thrown down, Kanhai fell for nine in a limp reply of 118/7, exactly the type of game that peeved him.

He was forced to sit out the following week's league match due to a persistent knee injury, aggravated in the second leg of the Robson Cup final against the Durham Senior League's Chester-le-Street, having forgotten to insert the three extra inches of protective padding into his knee roll. Newcastle United invited him down for heat treatment – an offer they probably didn't extend to any old crocked cricketer – but he failed to recover in time and had to watch on from the sidelines as the rains came with Ashington well poised for victory, the draw pushing them back to fourth, behind South North, Benwell and Percy Main.

* * *

The 1964 season was only two weeks old when the *Sunday Sun* announced that their two £1,000 columnists would each select an amateur XI to face off in a festival game in early August, the winners to receive the princely sum of £20 (around £33 each when adjusted for inflation and divvied up) and the losers £5. More importantly, it was a chance for the Durham Senior and Northumberland County leagues to stake a claim for local pre-eminence, while the weekly columns were awaited with a keen sense of anticipation by plucky, talented amateurs hoping for the frisson of satisfaction from receiving these cricketing royals' seal of approval. Often, however, particularly with Kanhai, it was a case of where the largeprint giveth, the smallprint taketh away.

Joe Thewlis of Percy Main was "a very good cover point fieldsman" but "I suggest he concentrates just a little bit harder". Of Morpeth's Mike Crawhall, Kanhai remarked: "I like this player a lot. He's a refreshing cricketer who likes to hit the ball hard and as often as possible [whose] only real fault is that he doesn't get his left foot to the pitch when driving through the covers." He called Blyth's Graham Heatley "a great bowler" but plumps for his teammate Peter Robertson, despite him needing (a) better concentration, (b) more confidence, and (c) more care in his field placings. Alan Thompson of Benwell was "a beautiful batsman, probably the best I've seen this season", but there was also "a flaw", this being "a slight impatience and lack of concentration". The 23-year-old Durham University dental student Mike Dickinson "hits a lovely ball through the covers" but was "a bit vulnerable around his pads", while the 22-year-old apprentice auctioneer Jimmy Hunter from Alnwick was warned against "trying to bowl too fast". Still, even qualified praise from RB Kanhai was enough to put a spring in the step.

As with Kanhai, Gibbs sprinkled a little constructively-critical salt on the hard-earned plaudits, and like his compatriot restricted his selection to the amateurs, thereby precluding several strong local cricketers from among his counterparts in the DSL professional ranks. There was Ken Earl, a handsome bank clerk in Newcastle reputed to be the swiftest bowler in the land when he was in the conversation for the 1950-51 Ashes tour; Tom Angus, a lively seamer who had spent time with Middlesex and was commuting to Horden from London each weekend, partly to see his fiancée; Russell Inglis, a gnarly all-rounder who would make a top-scoring 47 as opener when, in 1973, Durham slayed Yorkshire to become the first minor county side to beat a first-class team in the Gillette Cup; Frankie Forster, a genial swing bowler at North Durham who once took the first nine Whitburn wickets only then for a colleague to drop a skier at mid off, a calamity met with a stoical "hard luck, son" before Forster went ahead and took the tenth anyway; and the South Shields pro Alec Coxon, an expat Yorkshireman who played a single Test for England in 1948, reputedly falling out with Denis Compton, before settling in the North East.

"The former Whitburn player Alan Alder remembers Coxon as 'a horrible bloke', while Barry Emerson recalls him standing in the corner, farting and swearing," writes Jonathan Wilson. "On one occasion he was banned from the bar at Whitburn for several weeks after urinating in a sink. Nonetheless, he returned to Whitburn as a coach in 1979 (when the club pro was Lance Cairns – 'bloody awful; the league had balls we called conkers,' was the New

Zealander's summation of his season there)." As a counterpoint, Coxon's Sunderland teammate, Dave McLaren, recalls "a great bloke and coach" and "coming back from games hanging on to Alec's milk-float with the club kitbag after he had had numerous pints. He said to me, 'I can do nothing with you, son!'"

Gibbs was back with Mrs Hutchinson in Roker, albeit this time with his wife, Joy, whom he had married the previous October, with Clyde Walcott as best man. After a disappointing opening day 2/56 in defeat to Eppleton that saw Gibbs laud his first festival XI pick Derek Soakell's "great exhibition of aggressive batting ... an approach that can do nothing but good for the game", Whitburn's star man was soon slotting into the groove he had shown in 1962 before that broken digit, the Villagers winning six of the next seven and romping to the top of the table by early June.

He started that run with 5/29 from 20 overs against Seaham Harbour, whose No.3 batter Freddie Allen was duly selected for the Lance Gibbs XI, but not the 14-year-old No.6, Peter Willey, whose Test career would begin the year Gibbs's ended. Against Chester-le-Street, Gibbs sent down a tidy 14-7-11-7 as the Cestrians managed just 43, although earlier Bill Routledge's seamers impressed in defeat and got him a spot at No.8 in Lance's team. Wearmouth were then bundled out for 68, Gibbs with 6/35 (and disinclined to pick anyone), after which Whitburn came unstuck against Burnmoor, Gibbs managing a single wicket but inking in the name of 21-year-old industrial painter George Bull, "a likeable lad with tremendous pace off the wicket". The team then got back to winning ways against South Shields, Gibbs taking 5/29 yet liking what he saw in the 25-year-old batter Jawad 'Joe' Hussain, a business administration student whose wife would give birth to their eldest son Mel prior to returning to Madras, where they had younger son Nasser and daughter Benazir before moving back to the UK and settling in Ilford.

The procession continued with North Durham soundly beaten, Gibbs bagging 8/25 from 20.2 overs, seven of them bowled, and the following week brought the first of four two-night midweek games, although Whitburn only needed one of them to trounce Gateshead Fell, who capitulated to 34 all out, Gibbs with 7/19 as he denied the club coffers a second night's take. By this stage, he had 41 wickets at 5.63, along with a few opinions about the state of the local game.

As with his friend's musings on the Northumbrian scene, most of it was concerned with injecting a little zing into things. "Forget this attitude ... of concentrating simply on not being beaten," Gibbs parped. "Let's say: to hang with the result for the moment. To blazes with averages and parochial pride!"

How this quasi-hippy developmentalism went down in Whitburn, who'd stumped up a grand of their hard-earned to rub everyone's noses in their superiority, is not known, yet Gibbs had other progressive ideas, too, some of which had to tread a diplomatic high wire. For instance, while he acknowledged the contribution of enthusiastic fortysomethings to club cricket, there was a sting in the tail, a perennial picture of youngsters waiting impatiently for their turn in the first team and potentially walking away from the game – which could well have been a roundabout attempt to influence selection and get some livelier fielders in the side by a spinner who was, ahem, 41 years young when he stepped away from the West Indies team. On the subject of spinners, Gibbs felt they were "becoming a rare luxury in most set-ups"; get the spinners in, he says, and he'll wager "some of Jamaica's best keg rum that we'll see the game pep up quickly enough".

Both Kanhai and Gibbs were asked early in the season what they felt was the standout feature of league cricket in the North East, and both answered, unpussyfootingly: "the pathetic standard of fielding". (Oof.) Gibbs points out that "those deadening things", the averages, don't record fielding sharpness and offers some basic tips, while Kanhai riffs on the "butter-fingers affliction" and commends Percy Main for their four run outs.

"We must make club cricket a worthwhile pastime – and a place in the first team an enviable achievement," continues Kanhai, asserting that "cricket interest in the North East is not dead", citing the 1,500-strong crowd for that Chester-le-Street cup tie. "If you make the cricket attractive enough, you'll get the spectators," he adds – to which the obvious response is: *No, mate, they're there to see you, a world-class batter.* Or rather: the way to make it attractive is to spend money on a sprinkling of stardust, a position he will explicitly advance in a later column.

* * *

Kanhai's accommodation was a pleasant flat on Alexandra Road in Ashington. He spent some of his spare time coaching at the grammar school and plenty more playing cards and dominoes at the cricket club or the Universal Social Club, a short hop from home. "He was – is – a very articulate man with a deep knowledge of cricket," says Bob Dunning. "He could be a bit moody at times, but everyone who batted with him testifies to his willingness to advise and support his batting partners."

After a week of recuperation for the knee, Rohan was ready for the club's push through the heart of the season, aware that few red carpets were going to be rolled out. The game he had missed through injury was at the famous ground at Jesmond, sometime venue for the Minor Counties XI's fixtures against international tourists and regular home of the County Club (these days, Newcastle CC), where Northumberland's pro was mandated to play: in 1975 and '76 it was Pakistan seamer Asif Masood, in '79 Dilip Doshi, the year after that Mushtaq Mohammad, in 1983 Wasim Raja, and Chris Old in '86 and '87. Ashington had them 40/6 chasing 140 when the weather intervened, but went on to win five in a row to surge clear at the top.

Against Blyth, who were knocked over for 52, Kanhai managed to get himself out for an average-wounding 11 in a futile bid to provide a few crowd-pleasing fireworks. Otherwise, the template was that Ashington would rack up over 200 before declaring, then go on to win by 50-plus margins. Against Morpeth, the pro made 107 out of 200/9 in a 55-run win. Against Tynedale, it was 74 – run out for a second time in nine knocks – as 204/5 were posted, before Fraser Suffield's 6/41 secured a 61-run victory. At Benwell Hill, he was bowled for 44 by Stewart Allen, but Ashington's 201/7 proved 56 too many. And in the 97-run win against Backworth, skipper Stan Levison pushed the boat out even further, Ashington declaring on 247/3 – Kanhai with just the 196* of them – before Levison called the boat back in as it sailed into the Atherton-Hick Strait. After a second abandonment with County Club, unbeaten Ashington finished July with another straightforward win, over Tynedale, Kanhai falling to the former Somerset seamer Mike Latham for 14 before picking up 3/7 with his jazz-hat leggies.

In amongst all this the player described in *The Journal* as "the most dynamic personality to hit Northumberland League cricket since the palmy days of Larry Liddel" had a high-summer benefit match, with 3,000 in attendance. While Sobers, Hall and Nurse were late arriving from Manchester "due to traffic jams on the road", Kanhai treated the crowd to a sparkling 69, earning him a £37 collection (getting on for £650). After tea, WW Hall bowled RW Smithson first ball with a flat-out delivery, Sobers making 54.

In his next column, Kanhai pushed for more clubs to sign Test pros, to ramp up the glamour and the clamour, repudiating the idea that they hog the game and hamper development: "I don't think that anyone can dispute that top professionals can act as a stimulant to the game and an inspiration to individuals" (indeed, Mr Kanhai, here I am trawling through 1960s newspaper clippings). It was, in Kanhai's depiction, a virtuous circle, with Ashington's membership having doubled since his arrival and the extra money slated for extending the clubhouse, thereby potentially bumping revenues. "What with the increased social activity and the development of the ground as the scene of some of the season's most attractive festival fixtures, the present big room and bar are hardly sufficient to satisfy the demand for space."

Benefit done, there was also the opportunity for a little more candour in his weekly musings (and an opportunity missed for a 'Kanhai tell you something?' strapline by the sub-editors). Levelling some mild criticism at the standard of umpiring – from which, anecdotally, he had apparently profited, although he merely pointed out that "opposing batters have been victims of some of the most grotesque umpiring decisions" – he received a significant amount of blowback, the chunter waves and umbrage ripples extending south of the Tyne. Legends they may have been, but the locals weren't necessarily going to sit back and have house guests point out everything that was wrong with the upholstery, the lighting, the feng shui. "We in Durham, especially the Sunderland branch, take our job very seriously," started J Blakelock, himself running the risk of offending umpires from beyond his home city. Meanwhile, 'Poor Old Umpire, Co. Durham' – anonymity undermined by listing some of his cricketing achievements: a spell of 6/0 in which he broke two stumps; smiting 34 from an over; a 23-minute hundred – simply trumpeted: "I would like to see these Test cricketers with the white coat on". Shove that in your pipe, Rohan!

Kanhai also floated the idea of forming a North East "superleague", combining the best of the NCL, DSL and Tyneside Senior leagues, perhaps even the North Yorkshire & South Durham League. "Unquestionably, there are advantages to such a scheme," he begins, "but most of them, I believe, would favour the top teams. The smaller clubs should be encouraged to keep going by mixing with their betters and not cast aside by the richer concerns." Instead, he suggests a compromise: playoffs to decide the region's club champions. He also called for a rule change allowing teams to claim an extra six overs in the push for a definitive result, "instead of the meagre and unsatisfactory one for a draw".

Two weeks after pocketing his testimonial lolly, Kanhai commented on the quality gap between the bottom and top of the league (his three-year average against struggling Backworth, for instance, was 173.33, and it would finish north of 100 against five of the 11 rivals). Again, the correspondence bag was plumper than usual that week. "If one omits Kanhai then the present league leaders, Ashington, have one good opening bowler and two batsmen, one of whom will be shortly retiring," writes PK Fairclough of Ryhope, which is not so much an argument for the strength at the bottom of the table as an assertion that everybody was crap.

Kanhai's face would be acquainted with egg the following week when Ashington drew with bottom side Benwell Hill, who grafted their way to 182 in three and a half hours, batting on after the interval in contravention of the unwritten convention. "We were nine down at tea," recalls No.11 Hugh Dyson, "and our captain, Tom Hounsome, got up and said, 'I hope you don't think we've declared'. Tom Bell and I had to walk out through very irate Ashington supporters – the ground was absolutely packed – and it was the one and only time I was ever booed onto a cricket field."

Ashington would have an hour and 50 minutes for the chase, at the start of which, *The Journal* reported, Kanhai was clearly run out for nought but "the crowd gave it not out", an event captured by the paper's inimitable cartoonist Dudley Hallwood under the strapline: *Nivvor in the world*. On he went, briefly, reaching 27 in 15 minutes of velvety mayhem – "an exhilarating crash programme" – before Hugh

Dyson had him caught on the fence, thereby justifying his spot in the Kanhai XI (completed by Dicky Race of County Club, Tynedale's Terry Darling and Backworth keeper Brian Thain). "I had had him dropped at slip from my first ball at the game at Benwell Hill, a perfect outswinger," Dyson recalls, "so it was quite gratifying to finally get him."

Ashington called off the chase with 17 needed from the final over, nine down, the reason for which, given Kanhai's regular protestations, can only have been the pursuit of an unbeaten campaign. Another bristling member of the public dipped his pen in schadenfreude and wrote in: "I recall that when Ashington failed to bowl out Morpeth we were given a lecture on the merits of brighter cricket and told that 80 runs an hour was a must at all times." The upshot was that Kanhai now had five sub-50 scores in his last eight innings, which represented the biggest slump of his three years in the North East (a slump, true enough, containing scores of 107, 74 and 196*).

* * *

Just as things were looking good for Whitburn, with six wins from eight to start the season, they picked up one win in five through June. A drizzly two-nighter against Boldon was drawn, Gibbs having taken 5/32. He pouched 5/44 and 5/50 in a pair of abandoned Saturday games – Whitburn wobbling at 53/4 in reply to Philadelphia's 156 and well placed at 82/4 in pursuit of reigning champions Durham City's 114 when the rains came in. Before then, he had passed 50 wickets in a 124-run win over Horden, only two of which had been lbw, with the maestro revealing in his column that he had declined to appeal for all but the most palpable shouts because "leg-before is an unsatisfactory way of claiming wickets in this class of cricket".

He also rode again on his favourite hobby-horse: entertainment! Too many players were worried about their "petty dignity and pride", he suggested, adding: "you probably know the sort I mean". Then, for clarity, it was batters "crawling their way to a pathetic score": "if you can't get on, get out". Thankfully, said Lance, cup matches defeated "the stranglers" because "defensive play – the bane of the game and the poison of the box office – is inevitably ruled out".

Again, these were striking cultural differences, for there is a deep streak in the English club-cricketing psyche in which, even now, passions are mobilised by the dogged draw, the post-match bathing in a pool of give-'em-nowt satisfaction. If we can't win, don't lose. The problem, arguably, was less to do with this attitude per se than the incentives for those that pursue it – in 1960s Durham Senior League cricket, a draw meant a point apiece, no matter which team had made most of the running. As long as a points system is calibrated to reflect the balance of power in the game, Dear Lancelot, then there is *more* nuance and intrigue in the win-lose-draw format than a straight win-lose game, which can often be decided by half-time – a gargantuan score having been posted, a couple of early poles taken, and no inherent incentive to pursue the rest of the wickets – the game lumbering dully to its inevitable conclusion rather than retaining graded targets for refusing to capitulate. Gibbs saw the symptoms but not the true cause: equal reward for a wholly spoiling approach and a team trying to take the initiative.

At the end of the month, however, Gibbs got his nerve-jangling entertainment against title rivals Sunderland. Whitburn scrapped their way up to 176/8, leaving the visitors two-and-a-quarter hours to chase. A solid third-wicket partnership between Gordon Fairley, who made 54, and optician Peter Birtwistle, who chipped in with 36, meant the score had ticked past three figures before Gibbs took his first wicket. The game accelerated in the final hour, Whitburn picking up wickets and Ian Hind countering with a brisk 31. When Mel Allen started the final over, ten more were needed with two wickets in hand. Ken Biddulph cracked the first two balls for four, à la Klusener, then missed the next two, and was run out coming back for the second off the penultimate delivery: scores level, nine down. "Jack Washington swung at the vital last ball," reported the *Sunday Sun*, "and although the ball merely travelled a few yards on the leg side, the batsmen scampered home with Ken Cooper missing the stumps from close range while Washington was still out of his ground."

The mid-season mini-wobble was an opportune moment for Cooper, the new captain, to rally the troops. He had taken over in unfortunate circumstances, after a contentious game at Whitburn the previous summer against Boldon when Don Hardy had apparently edged a ball to slip with the visitors nine down and three runs shy of victory. Believing they had won, Whitburn trooped off, yet Hardy realised the umpire had given him not out and stood his ground. Whitburn refused to return, and after a lengthy disciplinary process were fined five guineas. The captain, Barry Connor, was distraught and never played cricket again. Gibbs's return was thus a long gust of cleansing air, be there a title or not.

The 3/56 Gibbs took in that last-ball loss gave him 63 wickets at the halfway mark, well on the way to the all-time Senior League record, which was the 115 that Sunderland's Alf Morris had piled up in 1912, this after 102 in 1911, 114 in 1910, 107 in 1909, 107 in 1908 and 108 in 1907 – six of the 15 occasions on which the 100-wicket barrier had been breached in 61 DSL seasons by a bowler who was second only to SF Barnes in the Minor Counties game at the time. Sunderland's Alec Coxon and South Shields' CS Nayudu had both achieved it three seasons running in the mid-1950s.

The win bumped Sunderland into a three-way tie for second place with Durham City and Whitburn, the trio sitting four points behind leaders Eppleton, who Whitburn faced the following Saturday after once more beating Gateshead Fell in a midweek two-nighter, albeit with Charlton Lamb, a 27-year-old wine merchant, making an enterprising 77 for 'The Fell', the highest score Whitburn conceded all year, Gibbs travelling to the tune of 4/93. Lamb would break the league's 51-year-old aggregate record, too, finishing with 1,031 runs, back then an extraordinary achievement for an amateur. By this juncture, Gibbs had finalised his team for the festival showpiece, adding in Lamb and the Sunderland wicket-keeper Bobby Johnson, a 26-year-old electrician, as well as Philly's Alan Glass, a 26-year-old engineer, the 31-year-old industrial joiner George March of Durham City and Ken Longstaff. These were the chosen few.

Before the staging of what was a *de facto* league rep match – a year before the League Cricket Conference launched their inter-league competition, the Rothman's Cup (later the President's Trophy), which ran until 2014 – the North East cricketing public did get to see Gibbs and Kanhai go head-to-head in a fully competitive context. It was the two-legged 'final' of the Hedworth Williamson Cup, 40 overs per side on consecutive Sundays, qualification for which entailed (a) being Whitburn, and (b) being invited to compete against Whitburn, the invitation always being sent north of the Tyne but usually to County Club. However, with Kanhai at Ashington, the enterprising

Don Kings and Frank Warrens at East Street felt it impossible not to get this fight on, so someone was deputed to put the contrite call in to their counterparts in Jesmond, explaining that they were very sorry but the glamour had to be serviced (again, the disinvited habitués' response is not recorded).

The first leg was a corker. Gibbs "came in for some punishment" in his 4/56 "but had the last laugh when he had Kanhai caught by Johnson" for an impish 57 out of Ashington's 169, a score that Whitburn exactly matched to leave things perfectly poised for the return game in Durham. Alas, rain would push it back into August. Meanwhile, the top-of-the-table clash with Eppleton saw Gibbs snare 6/64 as the visitors posted 178, a total the often shaky Whitburn batting passed for the loss of only four wickets, Gibbs chipping in an unbeaten 23. The following week they tumbled to 52/7 in pursuit of Seaham Harbour's 117, only for Doug Bell and Bill Smith to see them home without further alarm. Gibbs's 9/56 then winkled out Boldon in the final midweek game – although Whitburn had to recover from 75/5 to chase down the 179 target, Smith clubbing 86* – before a Chester-le-Street washout was followed by a 49-run win over Wearmouth, Gibbs contributing a third straight duck along with 6/25 as Whitburn sat top at the end of July, four points clear of Sunderland with seven to play, the pro with 92 wickets and counting.

* * *

Local interest in the Gibbs XI vs Kanhai XI festival game was high – 1,650 turned up at Ashington and it would doubtless have been more had the forecast not been poor – with both skippers having done their best to imbue the fixture with a sprinkling of spice, engaging in some polite, pantomime trash-talk in their columns. It was a big deal for the participants, too, although with Northumberland playing away in Cheshire, Kanhai's team had a few cry-offs and he had to spend Sunday morning on the phone – metaphorically speaking, of course – ringing round to see who was available. In the end, Gibbs's Senior League team strolled up to 80/1 – Longstaff with 44* of them – before the drizzle became a little too persistent and the players took shelter, never to return. Stoicism it had to be. The event raised £143 (almost £2,500), although there was no chance for the raffle winners to be announced, two airbeds and an autographed bat going unclaimed until further notice. Gibbs's own benefit had been and gone the previous week – Sobers, Kanhai, Hall, Griffith, Gilchrist, Nurse, Butcher – a crowd of 5,000 turning up for a game that, likewise, was truncated by rain. Available Sundays were running out for the second leg of the Hedworth Wiliamson. It was ever thus.

Ashington headed into August unbeaten in the league and, in the lead-up to the festival game, had beaten Percy Main to lift the county-wide Wilson Cup, the day after which Kanhai took 53* from Backworth in a comfortable seven-wicket win. Having won the league in 1959, '60 and '62, they were keen rather than desperate. A week later, against second-placed Benwell, the star man fell to Larry Teasdale's left-arm swingers for six, his lowest score of the season, although faced with a chase of 176 the visitors opted to stonewall for a draw and keep the gap at 7½ points, hoping someone else would do them a favour. It wasn't going to be Alnwick, who Ashington rolled for 75 to win by eight wickets while Benwell were drawing, meaning a win against third-place Percy Main would wrap up the title with two games to spare, bringing the trophy back to Langwell Crescent after its year at Tynemouth.

Whatever that game threw at them, they could count on the utmost professionalism from Kanhai, recalls Bob Dunning. "He was a real team man and, despite his big-hitting reputation, always tried to bat responsibly to bring the team home. One game in particular springs to mind at South North in an evening 20-over game, where Ashington were chasing a very good total and lost three quick wickets. The rate had crept up, so South North had four men on the leg-side boundary, tempting Rohan to hit over them. Instead, he never lifted a ball off the bottom for the rest of the game and repeatedly hit fours, perfectly in the gaps between the fielders, until Ashington won."

If Ashington's title looked a formality, Whitburn were in a much tighter struggle with a strong Sunderland team. August had begun with a league double-header, the Villagers sneaking home by two wickets after Gibbs's 6/62 had bowled South Shields out for 117, of which 'Joe' Hussain made 50. Twenty-four hours later, Gibbs swept through the 100-wicket barrier with 7/25 in an eight-wicket romp at Burnmoor, his 14th five-for in 21 games. Sunderland themselves picked up ten points from two wins to remain just four back. The eve of the Big Festival Wet Blanket brought a 50-run win over North Durham, while Sunderland, hovering over everything like a giant storm cloud, were beating Horden. And then, finally, Whitburn cracked against a Philadelphia team that had brought five coachloads of supporters to East Street. In the previous Sunday's column, angling for pro's jobs for fellow West Indians, Gibbs had said "there are some clubs, such as Philadelphia, who could, with just a bit more experience and class in the side, become a real power in the Durham Senior League." Oh, Lance.

The pitch was dry, and the visitors opted to bat first. Gibbs was handled well, a relatively costly 4/83 taking him within three of the DSL record. Faced with a stiff but hardly insurmountable chase of 177, Whitburn choked. Not a single player made double figures as 6/28 for Alan Glass shattered the hosts' batting. *How do you like them apples?* The only good news was that Sunderland came up a dozen short of Durham City's 176 when time was called, although they picked up a bonus point for scoring rate to sit two points back with three to play. After the lavish investment in both pro and pavilion, Whitburn were fretting.

The following Saturday, Gibbs claimed the DSL record with 6/52 as Horden were rolled for 124. Amid such yearning tension, however, every chase was a ticklish one and Whitburn lost nine wickets hauling in the runs, Alan Alder's 35 and a captain's 51* from Kenny Cooper doing the heavy lifting. At which point, pints of relief became pints of celebration when news came through that Sunderland had been held by Boldon. Later that evening, the first ever *Match of the Day* was broadcast – highlights of a single game only, Liverpool's 3-2 win over Arsenal – and the next day Whitburn faced Sunderland in the Saunders Cup final, back then the most prestigious knockout competition in Durham. Sunderland prevailed by 16 runs – a psychological blow, potentially, with the two teams meeting on the season's final Saturday.

Before then, Whitburn would visit reigning champions Durham City, the temptation to pop into the cathedral beforehand to offer prayers almighty. Whitburn proceeded to post a season's highest 203/9 declared before Saint Lancelot of Demerara tore through the batting with 5/17 as the hosts were routed for 68. Meanwhile, Sunderland smashed Burnmoor by ten wickets. It would go to the wire, with Whitburn, having won ten of their last 11 completed games, knowing a draw would suffice.

Twenty or so miles north, Ashington were bowling out Percy Main for 138, Kanhai then romping to a glorious unbeaten 104. "My very best cricket memories as a boy were watching Kanhai bat," recalls Vince Howe. "My dad kept wicket for the Main, and stumped Rohan in the first over for nought down the leg side. The umpire gave it not out in front of a packed ground and Rohan went on to make a brilliant century!" Ever the showman, Kanhai reached three figures with a six that both won the match and sealed the league title.

The following Saturday, presented with the manna of a final-day title showdown, the Durham Senior League's mandarins were piqued by Sunderland AFC's home game with Leeds United drawing people off the gate (further north, Kanhai would lament the primacy of football in the North East, remarking on the "acceptable entertainment" provided by Ashington – a sign of the times, no doubt, that he thought local cricket could compete as a spectacle with the Toon, although maybe in the Bruce years he'd have had a point). With Sunderland CC needing victory at Ashbrooke to force a playoff, Whitburn won the toss and inserted. Gibbs, with 3/42, played a solid second fiddle to Doug Bell's 6/60 and the hosts were knocked over for 107 – good start, though far from a done deal.

Whitburn's now-or-never reply began steadily enough, yet clouds started to close in and, as light rain fell, they ground on for half an hour to 62/3 before bad light took everyone from the field, not long after which the drizzle intensified. "As rain pelted down on Ashbrooke at 5:45 on Saturday," reported the *Echo*, "Vic Reed of Sunderland, and Ken Cooper of Whitburn, stood at the top of the pavilion steps and agreed that no more play was possible in the vital struggle between the sides." Gibbs's 126 wickets at 8.53 – a haul that remained a record until the DSL folded in 2013, and will be so forevermore – had delivered Whitburn its first title for 14 years. The boil, finally, had been Lanced.

Ashington's game was also abandoned, but they had to navigate one more match – a trip to runners-up South Northumberland – to complete their unbeaten league season. At the end of a week in which he'd scored 170 for FM Worrell's XI against an England XI at Edgbaston, Kanhai signed off with 160 in an emphatic 79-run win, his fifth ton of a campaign that had finished: P22, W13, D9, L0.

As with Whitburn's investment in Gibbs, Ashington's punt on Kanhai had paid off handsomely. While allowing his teammates to experience the thrill of playing in front of packed houses every week, Kanhai had amassed an NCL record 1,217 runs at 93.62, top on both counts for the sixth time in six English league seasons as pro. None of which was good enough to win him Ashington's Sports Personality of the Year prize, a gala affair at the Universal Club, where kitchen staff had "carved fifty loaves of bread to make beef and pease pudding sandwiches". The showpiece attraction was the Mitchell Hedges Silver Bowl – an award for miners' first-aid teams, reputedly used to bathe the infant George IV and said to be worth £2,000 (around £34,500) – which was kept overnight in Ashington police station, while the SPOTY award (and a set of golf clubs) was presented by Newcastle United manager Joe Harvey to Leeds United's Ashington-born centre-half Jackie Charlton, whose boss Don Revie watched on with Kanhai.

Where there is Revie, so there is Brian Clough, and on the day Ol' Big 'Ead's first son was born, 22 October 1964, Sunderland's injured young striker was busy drinking champagne with Gibbs in Wetherall's nightclub, his Guyanese friend not yet having departed for his winter assignments. "I have thoroughly enjoyed my stay with Whitburn, and I can honestly say I'm looking forward to 1965," Gibbs had written in his final column, before reiterating his belief that more clubs should engage big-name pros. With Kanhai carrying the day in Northumberland despite barely bowling, and the barely-batting Gibbs doing likewise in Durham, it seemed a no-brainer. Then again, with other clubs in other leagues on the lookout, there were not many of this calibre in the shop window.

When the two of them met up again in the new year for the Australia series, Lance was able to remind Rohan that he had dismissed him for 23 as Whitburn edged out the Northumbrians by nine runs in the second leg of the Hedworth Williamson Cup, although Kanhai had his readymade retort. "In one of the games, a young Ashington batsman, Bob Taylor, cover-drove Gibbs for four, a very rare event even in Tests," recalls Dunning. "Kanhai was convulsed with laughter about that and reminded Gibbs about it for the rest of the day, and probably for a while after."

* * *

Nine years on down the cricketing track, having buffed his reputation across those six summers in Birmingham, Gibbs bade farewell to the Bears in late 1973 and took up a post with the Sports Council in Guyana, continuing in the West Indies Test team until February 1976. Kanhai retired from Test cricket as captain in April '74, made 55 in the 1975 World Cup final, his valedictory West Indies appearance, but stayed on at Warwickshire until the end of a moderately disappointing benefit season in 1977, his tenth at the county, which netted him £10,500 (just shy of £60,000 in today's money). That winter, his third with the North Melbourne club – for whom he scored 1,135 runs at 47.29, not once finishing top of the Victoria Premier Cricket averages – he called Edgbaston to tell them his wife was ill and he would not be back for the summer, as planned. It was an amicable parting of the ways for a batter who, by one metric at least, was statistically the county's greatest ever: of the 34 players to have made 10,000 first-class runs for Warwickshire, Kanhai's average of 51.62 remains the highest (Nick Knight at bang-on 50 is the only other to reach that benchmark). By early 1979, however, he was back in the UK and looking for a gig, 12 years after finishing at Ashington. Enter Mel Whittle, skipper at Crompton of the Central Lancashire League, who drove over to Blackpool and persuaded him to sign.

Among the opposition pros the 43-year-old maestro would encounter were a trio of West Indian quicks: Franklyn Stephenson, Hartley Alleyne and Colin Croft, the latter released by Lancashire the previous autumn and as angry as ever. He didn't need a second invitation to offer the grand old man of West Indian batting a sniff test. "Croft was a bit of a nutcase," says Whittle, a seamer for whom the removal of the beamer from his tradesman's armoury was part of a wider anti-bowler conspiracy, "and he struck me a serious blow in a game at the Paddock [Royton], breaking a couple of fingers. Earlier, Kanhai had hit him for a couple of massive sixes, straight over the flats. The very next ball, he virtually sat on his backside and hooked Croft straight onto the bowling green." Kanhai made 58 that day and 43 in the return.

Another fiery pro Kanhai tangled with that year was Heywood's still uncapped 21-year-old, Geoff Lawson, full not only of spunk but also respect for a man who, at that juncture, he considered "the greatest player with whom I had shared a cricket field". Obviously, he bumped him. Several times. Kanhai scudded a few away over square leg, where the fielder, David Fare, started to inch back, a unilateral hunch not conveyed to the bowler. "I ended up retreating all the way to the edge," Fare recalls, "and sure enough the sixth ball of the over was top-edged and landed next to the umpire. Suffice to say 'Henry' was not best pleased, and questioned my parentage quite loudly."

In the Wood Cup semi-final against Heywood, Kanhai compiled a diligent half-century that saw Crompton edge into the final for the very first time – an astonishing record in a 14-team competition launched back in 1921. There they would meet Oldham, whose pro was another future Australian luminary of the tracksuitocracy, John Buchanan, who, despite irritating SK Warne by denying him his smokes on a three-day pre-Ashes bootcamp, spent eight years as Australia coach, encompassing back-to-back ODI World Cup wins.

Famously, Warne believed a coach should be "something you get to the ground on" and the fact that 'Buck' only had seven first-class appearances to call on did not help his credibility among the swinging dicks, although he did not lack self-assurance and at the end of that 1979 season sent an open letter to the other CLL clubs, touting his achievements at the Pollards. One such was a top-scoring 60 in the cup final as Oldham posted 174/7, before then sending down five straight maidens to put the Crompton innings behind the 8-ball. At one stage, he had 2/9 from 14 overs. Kanhai made a "scratchy" 17, full of uncharacteristic hacks, and Oldham won by 45 runs. They also won the league, although Kanhai, with 826 runs at 45.88, was top of both lists, picking up from where he had left off before his Warwickshire sojourn.

The following year, Crompton were top at the end of July and on for a first outright title since 1954 before falling away badly. Croft was touring with the West Indies, so Royton replaced him with Stephenson and, with John Holder sharing the new ball, stormed through to win the league. Crompton won the early-season home game with Royton, however, Kanhai anchoring things with 43*, but on a wet pitch at Royton he took a blow to the hand from a Stephenson delivery that flew off a length and nipped back, retiring hurt and not returning. Still, it may not be earth-shattering news to learn that he topped the CLL averages, with 1,123 runs at 74.87 – Crompton's all-time record aggregate, indeed, albeit three runs fewer than Werneth's Montserratian former World Series Cricket support actor Jim Allen, whose final tally was boosted by a folkloric 80-ball 176* against Crompton – the hundred up in an even 50 balls – with one over of Kanhai's leggies going for 664261 (area code unavailable).

Nevertheless, having waited 58 years for that maiden cup final date, Crompton made it back again, this time facing Stockport, with Kanhai's top-scoring 60 turning out to be the margin of victory. It was the only Wood Cup success in the club's history, yet terms could not be reached for 1981 and Kanhai found himself back in the Northern League for what became a three-year stint at St Annes, just down the coast from his home in Poulton-le-Fylde, his son Russell turning out in the twos. Chuck in an ostentatiously liveried Morris Ital – Dutton-Forshaw of Kings Rd stretching to the very margins of the front doors – and it was an attractive package.

While a young David Boon was struggling his way to 485 runs at a tick under 27 for Netherfield, the venerable Kanhai – bald from brow to crown, white hair banked up alongside and behind it, an Adelaide Oval of a coiffure – was reeling off six straight early-season half-centuries and once more finished top of the league averages, almost 18 runs clear of the next best. His top score was 125* against Fleetwood, whose pro, Mike Whitney, would be plucked from his £65 a week Northern League gig to make a Test debut in the Old Trafford Ashes Test when Lawson and Rodney Hogg pulled up lame. 'Fleetwood Mike' claimed DI Gower as a first Test scalp and, at the end of the series, drove back into the fishing port to find townsfolk lining the streets and holding banners proclaiming 'Welcome home, Mike!'

Kanhai's other ton that year came at his old haunt Blackpool, whose pro, Collis King, had bludgeoned 119 from 97 balls at St Annes earlier in the season. "Feast of Special K" tooted the *Blackpool*

Gazette, anticipating "more demolition jobs than Wimpey" at Stanley Park. In the end, Collis failed and Kanhai batted through for 105* out of 179/9 in a scores-level draw. Alas, he pulled a leg muscle going for the second off the last ball and was forced to sit out the following day's Slater Cup final, Mudassar Nazar deputising in a 14-run defeat to Lancaster. St Annes finished fourth in the league, sneaking into the qualification spots for the prestigious Lancashire Cup, the 'Champions League' of the Red Rose county's rich club cricket scene.

They didn't make it very far, unfortunately. The powers of the now 46-year-old Kanhai – occasionally batting in a neckerchief, giving him the air of an archaeology professor returning from a dig, or a suave conman from an Agatha Christie mystery – were inevitably on the wane, even if only imperceptibly, very much as a man loses his hair. Scandalously, for the first time in a dozen years as a club pro, Kanhai failed to win the league averages. Nor did he head the run charts, his paltry 1,085 at 60.27 leaving him second, 18 behind Lancaster's future New Zealand Test opener Trevor Franklin. There were six half-centuries and three tons. Opening the batting with Eddie Feather, who ducked out for a week to play in the Maccabiah Games for the England Jewish cricket team, he took Chorley's Keith Eccleshare – a seamer at the time, later a leggie who snared Greenidge, Kallis and Richie Richardson, and arguably the league's finest local bowler – for six fours from the opening over of the match. Meanwhile, led by Indian left-arm swing bowler Karsan Ghavri, Geoffrey Boycott's one-time nemesis, Blackpool topped the table, with St Annes finishing fourth and again qualifying for the Lancashire Cup, in which, in his final year of club cricket, the little maestro would launch the push for glory.

The 1983 league campaign produced not a single win in the first half of the season as St Annes sunk to the bottom. Then they beat the first-place team two weeks running – Kanhai with 81 against Leyland and 87 against eventual champions Preston – but come season's end only Darwen sat below them. Kanhai's relatively meagre haul of 769 runs was still the second most in the league, 18 fewer than young Victorian batter Warren Whiteside, but his average had dipped below 60 for the only time in his 13-year club career, tumbling all the way to 40.47. Booooo.

Overall, cup games included, the tally was 1,224 at 51.00 as Kanhai dug deep to script one final story, dragging St Annes along a fairytale run to the Lancashire Cup final as he squeezed out the last of the summer wine. Dismissed cheaply in the first round against Hesketh Bank of the Palace Shield, he purred his way to 140 against Orrell Red Triangle of the South West Lancashire League in the second, which happened to be the exact margin of victory. Round Three brought a daunting game against Lancaster, county champions in three of the previous four years, but Kanhai's 81* steered them to a six-wicket win. In the quarter-final, they faced Atherton of the Bolton Association and marched to a ten-wicket triumph with Kanhai (51*) happy to play second fiddle to Aussie amateur Rhys Banwell (93*). The semi-final brought a disciplined bowling performance that restricted visitors Heaton of the Bolton League to 147/8, knocked off two down with Kanhai unbeaten on 71.

Regardless of what happened in the final, making it there was described by skipper Mick Moore as "the greatest achievement since the club's championship of 1952". Three coaches were booked for the trip to Old Trafford, a familiar venue for Kanhai but a once-in-a-lifetime experience for most of his teammates. The whole club was abuzz. "However," adds Moore, "when the teams got there the groundsman said it was unfit to play that day and, as an alternative date could not be agreed, it was decided to share the trophy. Most unfortunate."

And that was that for Kanhai, bringing to an end the five-year coda of one of club cricket's greatest overseas players, some 11,981 runs at 72.60 in the can. Long before this final curtain, though, he and Gibbs would seal their legacy in the North East, back when Kanhai was less Morris Ital and more Aston Martin, in mint condition and at full throttle.

* * *

Both Gibbs and Kanhai had used the final columns of their glorious, championship-winning 1964 seasons to throw a little demotic spotlight on the aspects of a club lying beyond its shop-window first XI and the glitz of its expensively hired superstars. Gibbs advocated allowing youngsters into the main club room "to play billiards and table tennis. In this way their interest would be maintained during the close season when they would otherwise be attracted by all these new dance crazes."

For his part, Kanhai expressed gratitude to those who keep the show on the road for a small-town club: "To sustain it in times when the public have access to many counter-attractions, a steady flow of money must be sustained." He added that he loved the dog that recovered the week's haul of lost balls from practice night, and that he enjoyed the hugger-mugger of the bar, where "after the match, whatever the result, there is the inevitable inquest, and the vigorous cut and thrust of argument and dispute". This was a man who had bought into his new home from home, and how these unbeaten league champions loved him for his regular pyrotechnics. The halcyon days of the halcyon days.

The pair of them landed four weeks late for the 1965 season – this despite the Whitburn committee writing to the WICBC requesting them to change the dates of the Australia series. Instead, their salaries were deducted pro rata, while in the Lancashire League Charlie Griffith and Basil Butcher had their contracts annulled. In the meantime, West Indies lost the fifth Test on May 17, although prevailed 2-1 in the series. Gibbs took 9/80 in the Guyana victory and finished as his side's leading wicket-taker, while Kanhai averaged 46 and scored half his team's hundreds. It wasn't going to get any easier for the North East's amateurs, even though the pair of them endured an arduous journey back, flying from Trinidad to Jamaica, then on to New York, and from there to Glasgow Prestwick before sharing a taxi to Alnwick, where Kanhai disembarked just in time, Gibbs heading on south to Boldon, arriving half an hour after the start.

Having stretched out his legs and taken on caffeine, Kanhai caressed 75 of Ashington's 161/6 before falling again to Jimmy Hunter, who had heeded the previous year's advice about trying to bowl too fast. "I was the only one at Alnwick who ever got him out," says Hunter with a hum of satisfaction still palpable some six decades later. In reply, the hosts fell to 67/9 before No.11 Hunter walloped 66 in a partnership of 72 that had "Kanhai jumping up and down a fair bit at first slip".

"It was always a good head-to-head," Hunter adds. "He was a class act, maybe the best in the world at his peak, but I think he respected me as a bowler." Indeed, the pair of them got to know each other well on the long coach trip down to Stoke-on-Trent for the opening round of the Rothman's Cup against the North Staffordshire & South Cheshire League. Garry Sobers missed the game through injury, but Wes Hall decimated the County League batting with a spell of 7/13 from seven overs, eight of those runs from two Kanhai boundaries, one a hook shot that hit the concrete terracing of the covered stand at square leg and bounced all the way back to the short-leg fielder. The NCL's 78 were knocked off without too much fuss, recalls Hunter, "and on the bus on the way back we had a crate of Newcastle Export, but no bottle-opener. Kanhai says, 'My mammy gave me good teeth' and starts opening everyone's bottles in his mouth."

Kanhai's second league innings of the summer brought him 87 in a straightforward win over Tynedale, after which came a trip to Gosforth to face South Northumberland, where he had signed off with 160 the previous September. This time he upped it to 175 out of 235/3, although the game finished in a tame draw, Bobby Smithson with 88. Next he made 22* in a ten-wicket stroll against Benwell Hill, then 124 in another home win, Kanhai himself taking the final Backworth wicket to leave Ashington ten points clear of South North at the top and his own batting average at 118.25.

Another title began to look like a formality for an Ashington side still to be defeated in a league match with Kanhai in the side, the run now stretching out to 27 (or 31 if you include the four undefeated games the pro had missed while engaged against the Australians). At which point they lost four of the next seven, along with two abandonments and a draw, all of which saw them slip to third place heading into August. Kanhai's scores weren't terrible – a run of 43, 61, 127, 8, 11 – but if he failed to reach 50, the team lost. There were bowling issues, too: the 61 against County Club had underpinned a total of 227 all out, which were knocked off, eight down.

An edge-of-the-seat two-run win at Benwell in which Kanhai top-scored with 57 stopped the rot. Newly re-booted, Ashington routed Alnwick for 61 the following week, Kanhai with a showman's 30* in the chase. A week later, despite some brave umpire raising the digit when Blyth's Graham Heatley hit Kanhai on the pads when he had 22, Ashington safely negotiated a chase of 143 and returned to the top of the table. Their final game in front of the boisterous, partisan support at Langwell Crescent saw Kanhai (138*) and Colin Cairns (104*) add an unbroken 242 for the first wicket, which proved 74 too many for Tynemouth, and when the penultimate round of fixtures were washed out, Ashington headed into the final Saturday with a three-point lead over County Club, who sat one ahead of South Northumberland. All to play for.

Alas, Ashington's return game with Tynemouth fell afoul of the weather, with the covers at Preston Road unable to protect the square, and the single point picked up for the washout meant that if County Club could knock off Benwell's 138, the title was theirs for the first time in 11 years, when they had completed a run of six championships out of eight. In the end, with teatime cake not making it all the way down the gullet, they fell 11 short. Thus, if South North – for whom Smithson had made 100* as they posted 181/5 – could take ten Backworth wickets, a share of the title with Ashington was theirs. Amid the newtons of tension and the ohms of resistance, this they managed to do, winning by 69 runs.

The elements not only scuppered a fifth outright championship in seven years for Ashington, but also prevented Kanhai reaching 1,000 runs, and he had to settle for 980 at 89.10 in 14 innings – top of both lists for the seventh straight year as a club pro.

* * *

The Whitburn team Gibbs re-joined after his taxi ride from Glasgow had won four out of four before the pro's arrival, dismissing the opposition for 81, 71, 41 and 114 in the process, while Boldon were already five down when he pulled his kit and suitcase from the boot, signed a couple of autographs and headed into the fray, chipping in a solitary wicket to a fifth straight win. He took 6/23 at home to Gateshead in the next outing as Whitburn made it six out of six, then 6/79, 5/46, 6/22 and 5/37 in the next four games: business as usual. Astonishingly, however, 13 games then went by without an LR Gibbs five-for. Nevertheless, Whitburn still sat top in mid-August (and with a game in hand on Sunderland), this despite a run of one win in six, culminating in back-to-back defeats – the first, agonisingly, by one run at Durham City, the other after crashing to

83 all out against Philadelphia. Undoubtedly, they were doing their best to hand over the crown.

Gibbs then took 7/65 in victory over Horden, leaving Whitburn a point clear at the top with two to play. Forty-eight hours later, on August bank holiday, Sunderland would visit East Street to complete their programme, needing a win to keep the title race alive ahead of Whitburn's last-day trip to South Shields. A win for Whitburn and the championship was theirs, a draw and they would just need to avoid defeat in their final game to claim back-to-back titles. A large and expectant crowd turned up, gathering on the new balcony where the trophy had been held aloft 12 months earlier. Invited to bat, the home team could only muster 114, which Sunderland duly knocked off for the loss of one wicket, meaning Whitburn would have to win their last match to retain the title – or would have done had it not hosed down. The teams didn't even make it out of the pavilion. Effectively, Sunderland had won the league because they had squeezed in a game on a fine day earlier in the year. They won the next three championships, too. Whitburn had to settle for the Sunderland Echo Bowl as runners-up.

It was a disappointing end for Gibbs. He had finished the campaign with 61 wickets at over 11 apiece – bringing his overall DSL tally to 271 wickets at 9.3 – and that was that for his career in club cricket. Whitburn had undoubtedly bungled the championship race in 1965 and were looking good for it in 1962 before the pro snapped his digit, but the Durham Senior League title Gibbs's record 126 wickets delivered for Whitburn in 1964 remains the last time the club finished top of the pile. The stuff of legend.

However, Gibbs's legacy for cricket in Durham was even wider than silver baubles and golden memories. Setting out a blueprint in his *Sunday Sun* columns for sustaining the interest sparked by his and Kanhai's presence, he suggests providing incentives for progressive cricket, with prizes awarded to the players recording the fastest fifty and hundred, the best figures and the most catches. He even offered to donate one of the tankards. Two weeks later, three people running a bingo and social club in Sunderland had bequeathed four tankards, with most wicket-keeper dismissals replacing fastest fifty. Meanwhile, Norman Howe from Boldon donated a trophy for the most team runs scored in two hours, which lived on as the Savoy Trophy until the Durham Senior League was finally folded into an amalgamated Durham League in 2013, a feeder to the North East Premier League. Before then, in 1981, the *Sunday Sun* inaugurated its prestigious Player of the Year award, covering the whole region, with monthly prizes and much song and dance before the overall winner received a cash bounty, a large stash of kit and a barrelful of kudos. Little did they realise that long-fingered Lance's prints were all over it all.

* * *

The original plan with Gibbs when he signed a one-year extension with Whitburn after the championship season had been that he would rest a year and come back in 1966, but with the box-office success of the 1963 tour, the Cricket Council – forerunner of the TCCB and ECB – had invited the West Indies back early. Once again they dominated, winning 3-1, two of them by an innings. A week after Guyana had won its independence, Gibbs had match figures of 10/106 in the first Test at Old Trafford and was again West Indies' top wicket-taker in the series. Kanhai was more subdued, dragging his series average over 40 with a hundred in the dead-rubber defeat at The Oval and slipping back to the depths of No.3 in the ICC Test batting rankings. Five days after two sons of Ashington had helped England to World Cup glory over West Germany at Wembley, Kanhai had made an insouciant 45 in the innings victory at Headingley, the game wrapped up by Gibbs's 6/39.

If the North East was sad to see the back of LR Gibbs – he had signed for Warwickshire, but would have to serve a qualifying season in the second XI, only for the county game to liberalise access to overseas players once he had served it – the Charltons' success and Kanhai's return had things crackling ahead of the 1967 summer. Once again, his first game was at Alnwick, and once again Jimmy Hunter claimed his wicket – this time in the first over, albeit from the tenth delivery after a flurry of no-balls.

Scores of 8, 55 and 39* and a trio of abandonments represented a slow-ish start, but Kanhai followed up with 132 in a draw against County Club, adding 232 with Colin Cairns for the first wicket, then 66* in a win at Blyth and a scintillating 130 in 100 minutes in a draw with Tynemouth. Ashington were struggling to win games, however, harvesting just two in their first dozen outings after a pair of Kanhai 30-odds at Tynedale and Benwell Hill had sandwiched a duck at home against Percy Main. "He was run out in the first over, sent back by Colin Cairns," recalls Les Jowsey. "The ground was full at 2:30, empty by 2:40."

Languishing at that point in the bottom half of the table, Ashington promptly reeled off five straight wins, Kanhai taking 85 off Backworth, then 111* at County Club as 151 were chased down in quick time, in the process taking a liking to his opposite number, Jack van Geloven, a lugubrious Yorkshireman who had been Kanhai's deputy the previous summer, when Ashington finished seventh. "I don't know what was said, or what went on between him and Rohan," recalls Dunning, "but Rohan kept smashing the ball back at Jack at head height on his follow-through. So much so that Jack actually complained to the umpire that Kanhai was trying to kill him."

He followed up with 81* at Percy Main (for some reason batting at No.6) then 55* against Benwell Hill (the only side he didn't make at least an 80 against in three Northumberland League seasons), helping Ashington to a first home win of the season – in mid-August. After that came 62 in a heart-stopping one-run win in the return match with Backworth, which left them within striking distance of leaders South Northumberland, their next opponents, whose formidable pro, Steve Greensword, an opera-singing milkman from south of the Tyne, had just finished a seven-year stint at Leicestershire, where he had roomed initially with Dicky Bird. 'Greeny' would go on to become a legend of the Durham team and, in his late-40s, a skipper of the Minor Counties XI, his guileful military-mediums bringing a career economy rate of 3.62 in the Benson & Hedges Cup and 2.71 for Durham in the Gillette Cup. "He were a good bowler, that Greensword," opined Geoffrey Boycott.

And so it proved, as Greensword knocked over the great man for a single. Ashington's 166 proved scant challenge, Greensword's 98* in an eight-wicket cruise effectively sealing the title, and with Kanhai missing the final two matches, released to play for the Cavaliers XI, the following Saturday's trip to Morpeth was to be his final innings in the Northumberland County League. He signed off in style, carving 142* out of 205/6 in a 37-run win, to finish with 1,030 runs for the season at a tidy 103, top and top for the eighth straight year. "I thought I'd bowled him a good ball," recalls John Douglas ruefully, "and it ended up in the Old Black Swan car park." Overall, his three seasons with Ashington had brought 3,227 league runs at 94.99. Of his 48 NCL innings, 13 of them were hundreds (eight of those over 130) and 16 were fifties. Truly, the greatest player ever to grace the league.

Undoubtedly, Kanhai relished his time there, too, the affection shining through his final *Sunday Sun* column, which focussed on the famously fervent support of this most working-class of clubs, the Langwell Crescent ultras who, with a few faces changed, were still there when Steve Harmison and Mark Wood came through the ranks. "They are a partisan bunch, but this vocal encouragement is a great incentive to players striving to win a championship," Kanhai purred. "And don't they love to dispute a decision – especially if it looks like going against their own team? The conventional cricket supporters tend to look down their superior noses at noisy spectators who bring to the cricket ground the freedom of expression enjoyed in the football ground, but they are worth their weight in gold to the keyed-up batsman, bowler or fielder…" He signed up again for 1968, but Warwickshire beckoned.

As with Gibbs, Kanhai's legacy was deeper and longer-lasting even than all those extraordinary batting feats, than the trophies he helped haul in. Not only did the "superleague" that he foresaw come to pass 36 years later, with the establishment of the North East Premier League in 2000 (won 15 out of 24 times by South Northumberland, never by Ashington, who nonetheless did surf the Kanhai wave to land the next two NCL championships, the club's most recent league titles), but a visitor to the town today – arriving perhaps at the railway station, newly opened in December 2024 after being closed to passenger services since Kanhai's first summer there 60 years earlier – might decide to mooch eastward along Station Road into town, working up a thirst, where, at 1-4 Woodhorn Road, next to the Poundstretcher, he or she will see a one-storey new-build JD Wetherspoon with handsome wrought-iron signage bearing the silhouette of a diminutive batter, rocking back to slap one through the covers, a wicket-keeper up to the stumps. This is the place to slake that thirst, to chow down on a vacuum-packed kipper, a curvaceous banana, a packet of Bombay mix. Its name is The Rohan Kanhai, and in *'Spoons Carpets: An Appreciation* (no, really) Kit Caless conjectures that the underfoot textile there is inspired by that of the Overlook Hotel in *The Shining*. Be that as it may, The Kanhai, as well as an eponymous monument to the town's adopted run-machine, is, as far as is known, the only pub in the UK to be named after a long-ago professional at the local amateur cricket club – a pub, presumably, serving only the finest cuts.

3

Kim Hughes & Terry Alderman
at Watsonians

Saturday, 18 July 1981 was both a remarkable and a humdrum sort of day for the Watsonian Cricket Club in Edinburgh. Having made a respectable 177/7 against bottom side Grange, the first XI were frustrated in their attempt to pick up a first Ryden East League win of the season. Their overseas pro/coach, 34-year-old leg-spinner Bob Holland, three years on from a surprise first-class debut, four years out from his even more surprising Test bow, was steady as ever in sending down 20-8-30-3, yet he had been unable to prise out the lower order amid much pad play, Grange closing on 112/8.

Meanwhile, 'Dutchy' and his teammates were keeping close tabs on events 160 miles south in Leeds, where a bedraggled England, having sacked Ian Botham as captain after the drawn second Test at Lord's, had been asked to follow on – although they did not have to bat in perfect light on Saturday evening because the playing regulations stated that the extra hour could only be utilised if the resumption came before 6pm, and they weren't good to go until 6:05. Oh, cricket. 'Another Test match, another fiasco' snorted a headline in the *Scotsman* on Monday, by which time both teams had enjoyed a traditional rest-day piss-up chez Botham ahead of t's being crossed and i's dotted.

Holland wasn't the only one with skin in the game at Headingley. His immediate predecessor as overseas player at Watsonians had been Terry Alderman, who had trapped Graham Gooch lbw in the first innings en route to 42 wickets at 21.26 in his debut series, one scalp fewer than he had managed in his East League campaign. Four years before that, the Australia captain Kim Hughes had lit up Scottish cricket with several innings for Watsonians that are still rhapsodised over today. Whether Kim and Terry's former colleagues would have been unreservedly supporting the tourists is moot – far from the Saltire-emblazoned William Wallace stereotype, Anglophobia was rare among the cricket-playing private school system, who had a complicated relationship with the Sassenach cricketers if less so when it came to rugby union – but they were certainly hoping their two old boys shone.

Hughes had made a measured 89 in the first innings at Leeds. His team were one up in the series and almost certain to make it 2-0. Everything was going *beaut*. Then a 500/1 bet was taken, the Legend of Beef and his Monday roasting was born (no Yorkshire pudding, this), with a little help from 'Picca' Dilley's circus act and Big Bad Bob's blitz on a chilly Tuesday. That same evening, skedaddling from the Headingley wreckage, Hughes and Alderman were in the Watsonians pavilion at Myreside, sharing a consolatory catch-up beer with old colleagues ahead of the Australians' game against Scotland in Glasgow two days later.

It was as trying a defeat as can be imagined, although Kim – with a personality seemingly as impervious to self-doubt as it was to the senior-pro sniping that swirled about him – was unlikely to have brought any melancholy to Edinburgh with him. At least, such is the portrait that emerges from Christian Ryan's magisterial biography, *Golden Boy*, which lays bare the toxicity of that early-'80s Australian dressing-room, the absolute lack of faith that its two lodestars, Dennis Lillee and Rod Marsh, had in Hughes's tactical acumen, and the vituperations and bullying to which he was subjected. "So colossal was his natural confidence," asserts Ryan of his subject, "that disappointments big and small loomed like mosquitoes on a crocodile's snout."

The question Ryan explores – or, perhaps, the psychological dynamic he maps – never circles too far from this confidence, and the degree to which it was help or hindrance. At times, this trait comes across as a sort of Huck' Finn, country-boy bumptiousness – for instance, with his habit of commentating on his own shots in the nets: "Shot, Claggy!" At others, it seemed to propel an almost quixotic approach to batting, a commitment to the wow! moment – the cap-wearing cavalier who charged the quicks and hooked no matter the state of the game – and a sort of obliviousness bordering on delusion about how all this went down with colleagues. Hughes's "cocktail of good cheer, naivety and overstatement", continues Ryan, "would become a trademark of his public pronouncements, one that bugged some teammates." Whether this particular cocktail helped ease him into the sort of psychological safe space necessary for a guileless soul who found himself monstered by the macho Aussie machine – defence mechanisms to help him deal with the backbiting, assisted by a plentiful supply of grog – perhaps even Hughes himself doesn't really know. In the midst of it all, however, he certainly had game.

A few months before the 1981 Ashes, having scored a scintillating 213 against India, Hughes had risen to third in the ICC's Test batting rankings. He was Ricky Ponting's favourite player when growing up, beguiled as 'Punter' was by the audacious shot-making ability. His self-inflicted failures were legion, his peaks extraordinary. There was 113* and 84* in the 1980 Centenary Test at Lord's, Chris Old despatched to the top tier of the Lord's pavilion. Most famously, there was an even 100 on a spiteful MCG pitch against the West Indies of Holding-Roberts-Garner-Marshall, an innings rated by *Wisden* as the eighth greatest in Test history. He played "shots that others couldn't draw pictures of", observes Ryan, and no season in history of the Watsonian Cricket Club was quite so golden as the one with the Golden Boy. Hughes would himself describe it as "possibly the best six months of my life".

* * *

The man responsible for bringing Hughes to Edinburgh was Brian Adair, Watsonians' 41-year-old first team captain, opening bowler and middle-order safety valve, not to mention future president of the Scottish Cricket Union. The 38-year-old Western Australian state batter Peter Wishart had been the club's first overseas player the previous year, and ahead of the 1976 season Adair dipped into the same playing pool, studying *Australian Cricket* magazine and receiving "handwritten notes in biro on Basildon Bond paper about various cricketers" from an agent based in Wiltshire. The 22-year-old Hughes had averaged a steady 30 in his maiden Sheffield Shield campaign, and that winter followed a first-dig golden duck against the West Indian tourists with a dashing second innings hundred for WA. Adair made an offer – £1,000 for the season, with some of the fee covered by George Watson's College, where Kim would be engaged as cricket master – which was both the only offer the club made and the only one Hughes received. With his girlfriend Jenny off to study in London, Hughes accepted.

Terms had been agreed, but there came no letter of confirmation from Hughes (this was long before email, of course). Thus, the next thing Adair heard about it all was when he was called by club secretary Stewart Oliver and told that Kim was waiting at Edinburgh's Turnhouse Airport. "I was slightly annoyed that he hadn't given us any warning of his travel times," Adair would write to Christian Ryan many years later, "and did not hurry too much to pick him up. (I later found his letter of acceptance had been posted to come sea-mail!) I found him sprawled on the roundabout at our then small airport, clad in a denim suit and open-neck shirt." Adair wound down his window: "Are you Kim?" Kim it was. "Okay then, get in".

Adair ferried Hughes over to his digs at the school, where he would be living in an apartment in the boarding house run by PE teacher Duncan Scott, winner of ten rugby union caps for Scotland in the 1950s. Scott recalls fondly how "the seven- and eight-year-old boys at the school loved him. The cricketers loved him. He was a great guy. A great advert for Australian cricket."

Despite a touch of jetlag, Hughes was keen to attend that night's practice on the pristine grass nets at Myreside – an eye-opening first glimpse for the Watsonian players of that outlandish shot-making repertoire: the time, timing and touch – and as the season wore on he would habitually finish the sessions with a challenge. "He would go in without pads on, and bat with a stump or the edge of his bat," recalls teammate Stephen Lockhart. "The first person to bowl him out, he bought them a beer. My guess would be that he bought no more than three beers through the whole season. He seemed to middle almost everything. It was extraordinary."

The club Hughes had joined had celebrated their centenary the previous summer by making the final of the regional midweek knockout, the Masterton Trophy, a game they ultimately had to concede – partly due to a clash of dates with the start of a commemorative cricket week and partly to the inability of the other clubs to accommodate this. It was a competition they had never won, just as they had never before won the East League, which had been inaugurated in 1953 and won seven times by Stenhousemuir, six by Grange and four by Heriot's Former Pupils, the other six sprinkled about.

If cautious Watsonian optimism had been stoked by Kim's long-haul warm-down at nets, it was set aflame by his first hit in the middle, a pre-season friendly amid the bucolic charm of Scottish border country at Selkirk, where cow corner was not confined to wide long on but stretched around into the bovine-specked, sightscreenless expanses behind the bowler's arm and beyond. A novelty. Still, after almost being cleaned up in the first over by fellow Western Australian Ken Frankish, Hughes compiled a sprightly springtime hundred then promptly asked whether he should retire. With the whole ground lapping up the spectacle, he was told to carry on and duly stretched it out to 151, at the time the third highest score in the club's history. He followed up with 58, 75* and 70* – thereby heading into the league programme with an average of 177 and several awe-struck, jaw-slack colleagues.

Alas, the first half of the league campaign would not be quite such a carnival, with wily dogs and soft pitches forcing the man Ryan memorably describes as "the millionaire strokeplayer with a scatterbrain streak" into more graft than he was wired for. Not that it was entirely a drought. He began with 50 at Stenhousemuir in an abandoned game, the rains wiping out the next two fixtures as well. Once the sun of this famously sultry summer decided to show its face, Hughes mainly chipped in with cameos as Watsonians hit the halfway mark of the short 14-game campaign with four straight draws. "If Kim had a fault when batting," mused Adair, "it was to decide what he was going to do to the next ball before it had been bowled." There was 24 against reigning champions Royal High, 31 against Edinburgh Academicals, 63 against Carlton when they stumbled from 75/0 to 116/9 in pursuit of 179, and finally 18 at Grange, who went into the final over needing 12 to overhaul Watsonians' 213/6 and were kept to nine by Mario Maciocia, an Italian surname with a hint of Scots.

With the championship decided on percentage of possible points won – a protection against being hamstrung by bad weather – and plenty of draws elsewhere, Watsonians may have been winless at halfway yet they still sat third and very much in touch with the leaders, Heriot's. A much-needed victory was then picked up in the first game after the turnaround, at home to Stenhousemuir.

The day before, Hughes had played in an International XI against 'Stenny' for the host's own centenary celebration, and 24 hours later Tommy Dickson would wind-up his teammate John Goodall by saying Kim thought "he was basically crap and couldn't bowl. John then bowled him a perfect over, and the last ball would have been wasted on a good batsman, but Hughes was better than good and managed to nick it to the keeper. No other batsman would have got close to it. John then bowled like a wet sponge after that."

Despite Hughes falling for what would be a sole single-figure score in the league campaign, a measured 50* from the former Oxford University batter David Bell, an international at both rugby union and cricket, ensured Watsonians knocked off the 117 for the loss of six wickets, whereupon they hastened to the airport for the club's 15th annual jaunt to Ireland. Upon arrival, Hughes and Bell had a wager over which of them would be the first to kiss a stranger on leaving the hotel. The first women they encountered – the point at which the wager was settled – were nuns. The universal law of tour *omertà* has kept the bet's winner a closely guarded secret, but it is rumoured to rhyme with 'gym shoes'.

A lavish carouser – *me, in Dublin, with my reputation?* – Hughes threw himself whole-heartedly into both the *craic* and the cricket. "He always seemed able to perform after a few the night before," confirms Lockhart. There were shot-filled knocks of 43, 46 and 77 against the three Dublin clubs, Pembroke, Clontarf and Leinster, each followed by lavish banquets or barbecues to sweep them full of stomach into the night's imbibing. And so it was that by Thursday's closer, at Malahide, the tourists' casualty list was lengthy. "Even the team doctor and the by now expert scorer Jimmy Sutherland were consulted about playing," stated the tour report. Kim had to step in as skipper. The opposition had three pros and were keen. Hughes duly rattled off 111 to set up a 13-run victory and a merry morning flight back to Scotland, those already firm bonds growing tighter.

The Irish connection would not end there, for Brian Adair was involved with a touring side from the Emerald Isle called Leprechauns who somehow parlayed their way to a fixture against Essex at Chelmsford in which Hughes made 76 and launched one into the

River Can. He was playing any game he could, however jazz-hat. In one midweek friendly against Oxford University Authentics he was clean bowled by a leg-spinner and decided he would stand his ground. Somehow, the umpire failed to give it. Hughes later explained that he "didn't know what had happened". The Australian way, Broadly speaking.

For Kim, each innings – indeed, all of life – was approached as a merry adventure. Everything was lapped up, his easy bonhomie charming the pants off most who crossed his path. "He was definitely a man for the ladies," recalls Mark Everett, "and his regular Saturday night attire was an open-necked shirt, white suit and white shoes. He was never one to shy away from a pint or three, either. He was with Jenny, but let's just say that that didn't hold him back."

Hughes would have his wardrobe expanded at the club's traditional 'Crock's Supper' – a dinner held each July as a prelude to a match between the current team and the Old Boys, with the guest speaker that summer being Colin Cowdrey – during which he was presented with a bonnie Watsonians blazer, along with a kilt. The latter was the *de rigueur* attire for the annual pub-crawl up the Royal Mile, taking in around 20 hostelries, in one of which, the port of sobriety receding ever further into the distance, it was discovered that Kim was also sporting jockey shorts. "This is not what a true Scotsman does," explains Lockhart, "so he was made to disrobe in the middle of the pub in front of everyone – to great hilarity." More bonding.

The first league game after the Ireland trip was a visit to arch-rivals Heriot's at Goldenacre, which Watsonians knew as 'The Trampoline' for the spongey bite it offered the slow bowlers. Hughes fell for 24 and would describe seamer Eric Thompson, a native of the Orkneys, as the toughest bowler he faced in Scotland, but it was the spinners George Goddard and Richard Rodger, with nine wickets between them, who restricted Watsonians to 134, with Scotland opener Hamish More's unbeaten 77 taking care of the rest. Not a decisive blow, but a blow all the same.

Two days later, the team had the opportunity to erase the memory of the previous season's Masterton Trophy forfeiture and land a first ever piece of major silverware for the club. It was the 13th iteration of a competition that the clubs in and around the Scottish capital were extremely keen to win, and Stenhousemuir were to be Watsonians' opponents in the final. Hughes had contributed 35 against Edinburgh Academicals, 84* against Royal High and 50 against Stewart's-Melville to get them there. It would be a game marked by injuries, with Kim at the centre of things.

Opening the bowling with Adair, who laid down a scarcely believable spell of 7-5-2-1 in the 25-over contest, Hughes's ultra-military medium-pace contrived to hit wicket-keeper Jeff Burton on the forehead in his opening over, forcing him to leave the field with a large gash. "We all used to have a good laugh about the pace Kim bowled at, because he was very much a net bowler," says Lockhart. "The keeper was standing back as well! There was a lot of ribbing about that."

Still, Hughes finished with a floaty wee 3/24 as Stenhousemuir recovered from 29/4 to post a not-quite-middling 107/7, then it was over to the day job for the golden-locked cavalier. In the second over of the reply, he leathered a cut shot out toward the cover boundary where Stuart Rycroft, three days married, swooped to do the fielding. "The ball struck a divot and hit Stuart's cheek," recalls Tom Dickson, "fracturing it and knocking him out. Morison Zuill, the captain, was yelling 'get the ball in, get the ball in'. Stuart's wife had to be stopped from running across the field to care for him. They ran two but Kim refused to take any more as Stuart was obviously out for the count. I had never seen the ball hit so hard with such minimal effort."

Hughes skipped his way to 41 off 42 balls and the target was passed with three overs to spare, the gloaming already beginning to wrap itself around the July day despite the northerly latitude. It may have been a school night, but it was also a big night, a historic milestone reached – perhaps with more to come – and thus demanding an appropriate celebration, with Kim more than happy to oblige.

*   *   *

With one trophy in the bag, Watsonians began the five-game East League dash for home with a pair of seven-wicket wins. Hughes chipped in with 3/23 and 60 as Kirkcaldy's 105 was unfussily overhauled, before blazing 91 in Sunday's friendly at Gatehouse.

The following weekend, again failing to red-ink things, he danced his way to 47 as Royal High's paltry 78 was knocked off, ushering everyone into the bar perilously early. Next game, he was bowled by Edinburgh Academicals' left-arm spinner Jim Allen for 19, although Watsonians recovered from 34/4 to a useful 162/6 courtesy of 61 from Maciocia. Andy Lamb's geometrically linear offies then bagged 4/14 – making it 11/62 in this three-game run – but Accies, having twice appealed unsuccessfully against the light, hung on at 105/9, to much frustration. Even so, with the bonus point pocketed and chief challengers Heriot's finishing on the wrong end of a draw with Royal High, Watsonians went top with two to play: 62.5 per cent of possible points per game to 60. They couldn't, could they? The ever-bullish Kim had few doubts.

The penultimate round of matches brought third-placed Carlton to Myreside. Meanwhile, with lynchpins Hamish More and George Goddard required for Scotland's annual first-class fixture with Ireland in Glasgow, Heriot's successfully petitioned for their game with Grange to be deferred to the first free Saturday after the regular season, which appeared to be a significant advantage. Taking the bull very much by the horns, Hughes slammed 106 imperious runs, adding 193 with Bell, who made a season's best 84. Carlton declined to chase the 215 target, and four more wickets for Lamb had them in trouble, but once more they were foiled by the flinty doggedness of the last pair and a clutch of dropped catches. They may not have played, but Heriot's had returned to the top.

The sharp sting of this near-miss was treated after the match with the traditional balm of hoppy, malted medicaments, and the following morning a scratch team travelled to Greenock for a friendly, Golden Boy launching a chase of 300 by nicking off first ball to Trevor Laughlin – in two years' time, his colleague on a WSC-ravaged Test tour to West Indies – which was less than ideal prep for the league finale, although it was unlikely to have vexed Kim and his bulletproof confidence too greatly. In any case, whatever happened when Grange visited Myreside, the fate of the championship could not be decided.

Adair lost the toss and Watsonians were asked to bat. They declared at tea on 173/4 from 47 overs, KJ Hughes making 103 of them, leaving 53 overs for Grange to chase. But the sea fret was already rolling in and at 32/1 mid off could no longer see first slip so the umpires had little choice but to take everyone from the field. Hughes had finished with 556 league runs at 46.33, the latter a figure that would certainly have been improved had he cared for it in the slightest.

"He would try to hit the ball out of the ground when within reach of a hundred," Christian Ryan would write, "because this put smiles on people's faces, even if it meant getting out in the nineties, as it often did. […] 'To create some memories for myself and for other people' – that was always the boy's first aim. Only after accomplishing that would he set his mind to scoring as many runs as he possibly could. This is the reverse of nearly every other cricketer's thinking. Runs and wickets are the thing, smiles and memories happy accidents."

With conditions at the other Edinburgh games also fit only for filming scenes from *Macbeth*, Heriot's would go into their rearranged game with Grange needing an outright win to deny Watsonians their maiden league title. Meanwhile, Hughes and Co. headed out to the Scottish borders for a friendly. Communications infrastructure being what it was in 1976, the team were limited to intermittent landline calls to keep abreast of things: ignorance is bliss or ignorance is stress? Nevertheless, as the club's yearbook notes, "there were quite a few stout-hearted Watsonians at Goldenacre" to ensure there was no funny business.

While a distracted Hughes fell for 31 at St Boswells, Heriot's were busy amassing 218/6, declaring after 40 overs to leave themselves 60 to collect the ten wickets needed for the title. Seamer Peter Rhind then led the charge with a mid-innings burst of 4/0 to take out the middle order after Grange had moved steadily up to 60/2. "The more accurate Heriot's bowling had put Grange behind the clock," reported the *Scotsman*, "and Kevin Loney, first with Frank Ingham and then, after Rhind's breakthrough had left Grange at 98/7, with Guy Turner, Brian Partridge and finally, in the last four palpitating overs, John Little, saw the visitors foil Heriot's by that vital wicket […] Irishman Loney's defiant 38 took a little over two hours and will remain an unwelcome memory for Heriot's." True, although Watsonians considered commissioning a statue.

Adair and his boys were in the bar at St Boswells when the news came through. They had waited agonisingly as they heard of the seventh and eighth Grange wickets falling – still 12 overs to go! – then the ninth, leaving those dreams of historic glory to ride 24 balls on the knife-edge. The jubilation that followed had not a trace of anti-climax – no sense, when the deed was finally done, of wanting to have walked off a field to heroes' acclaim. They were champions, and there is no space for nuance or qualification in that all-encompassing rush of euphoria. True, the margin was a slim one: 0.2 per cent of their possible points per game. But a previously trophyless club had bagged a league and cup double, and Hughes was there to pop the champagne. "How timely has been the decision to have a trophy case in the pavilion!" noted the annual report.

"It was great for the elder statesman of the team who played for many years and never won it," recalls Lockhart. "Being young, I just assumed it was going to be the norm. But then Heriot's won the next seven on the trot: our arch enemies, both in rugby and cricket!"

Hughes still had a little over two weeks to bask in the glory, to cement ties, to sketch himself deeper in the institutional memory. Friday next he turned up to David Bell's wedding in Lenzie in his wide-lapelled white suit and matching flairs, a year before John Travolta strutted them out in *Saturday Night Fever*. The following day he rattled off 86 against Strathmore and the next weekend headed to Dundee to play Forfarshire in what looked like being his final innings for the club, a chance to sketch a few final flourishes of that quicksilver talent.

It was Brian Adair's final game as captain, too, and he pulled rank to open the batting alongside a man who was 19 years his junior but with whom he had grown very close – notwithstanding having knocked Hughes out of the club's single-wicket tournament in the first round. The pair added 232 together, a club record. "My job was to count up to five then run like hell on the sixth ball," Adair later recalled. He made 41; Hughes, a club record 218* in which there were 25 fours and five sixes, the one that sailed over the Forthill clubhouse believed to be the first ever to make that journey. Heads are still shaken at the majesty, the absurdity of the shot-making.

"Older Scottish observers would say Kim was the most fluent player they had seen since Rohan Kanhai at Aberdeenshire," reflects Donald Scott. "He was a tremendously exciting player. The crowds were much higher with Kim around. Just knowing he was playing, people would turn up to watch. He was that sort of person. There was never a dull moment. Other people got terribly worried about things – about their performance, or whether the coin came down heads or tails. I got the impression that Kim played for the joy of it. There aren't many cricketers who play that way."

The double-hundred took Hughes's final tally to 2,017 runs in all cricket. His five centuries were a club record, as were both the 218* and the official aggregate – excluding midweek knockabout games – of 1,711 runs at 74.39, putting him top of the averages across the whole country. "How well he has fitted in, popular with Watsonians and schoolboys alike," proclaimed the club report. Brian Adair was moved to write a letter of commendation to the Australian Cricket Board, eulogising both Hughes's cricket and his comportment. "The Scots as a race are not given to extravagant praise but the attraction of his style brought a lot of spectators to our games. You are extremely lucky in Australia to have such fine, uninhibited and technically correct stroke-players […] Kim behaved both on and off the field with exemplary sportsmanship, and his conduct at all times was a credit to Australia and the Australian cricket authorities. In these days when the manners of cricket players leave a lot to be desired, it is encouraging to see a fiercely competitive player acting properly."

With such friends in Edinburgh, the Golden Boy would not be a stranger.

* * *

If ever there were an Australian bowler suited to conditions in the British Isles, it was Terry Alderman and his devilish late swing, delivered at a lively enough clip – Hoggardian on the 1981 Ashes tour, when that shuffling run-up was *allegro moderato*, Ollie-Robinsonian by 1989, when the approach was more *andantino* – and from tight enough to the stumps to punish any slight failings in footwork, any errors in alignment. His 83 wickets at 19.34 in two Ashes series in England – in the process so tormenting Graham Gooch that his voicemail used to say, "I'm not here right now. I'm probably out… lbw to Terry Alderman" – suggest that the Western Australian could have had a mighty career were in not for dislocating his shoulder in November 1982 while attempting to rugby tackle a drunken English pitch invader at a broiling WACA, and had he not gone on the Australian rebel tour to South Africa in 1985-86. Still, 170 Test wickets at 27.15 was not to be sniffed at, and the uncapped 23-year-old who arrived in Edinburgh with his English wife Jane in April 1980 with 38 first-class appearances and 139 wickets to his name was likely to provide a stiff enough task for the East League's finest, notwithstanding the pitches' general lack of zip.

Watsonians had followed up their Hughes-inspired championship season with a runners-up finish to Heriot's in 1977, the unheralded former Western Australia Colts' Kevan Penter engaged as the overseas player-coach. In 1978, with Steve Shipley as pro, another from WA, they finished third – Heriot's again topping the table – while losing two cup finals: to Grange in the Masterton and those *bêtes noires* Heriot's in the Shish Mahal Trophy, as Scotland's national competition was then known. (At the time of writing, Watsonians are still to win the Scottish Cup, losing finals in 1983, 2012, 2017 and 2021, two of them to Heriot's.) In 1979, with yet another Western Australian Colt as pro, Earl Scarff, they finished third once more. The champions? That would be Heriot's again.

Watsonians did manage to win an unofficial Masterton final against Edinburgh Academicals that year, after three of the semi-finalists refused to play the official winners Stenhousemuir on account of their behaviour in a first-round win over Holy Cross, the Stenny skipper unilaterally signalling for his batters to leave the field with 19 runs needed from the final over as the rain – steady, not torrential – started to fall. Holy Cross assumed the game had been conceded, which was confirmed by the umpires, then subsequently denied by the visitors' captain once everyone had left the field. The rain relented and back out they went. At 9:40pm. After one ball, Stenhousemuir complained about the light. After another ball, the umpires conferred and took everyone off again. Two Holy Cross players refused to take part in the replay. The East of Scotland Cricket Association wrote to Stenhousemuir and asked them to concede, an idea given short shrift. The replay was won by Stenny, as was the quarter-final against West Lothian, at which point Watsonians, Heriot's and Edinburgh Academicals announced their boycott and the trophy was awarded to Stenhousemuir.

The Watsonian players' first look at Alderman, *four weeks before the start of the league campaign*, was a reasonably promising spell of 12-5-13-5 against Glasgow Academicals. There followed a tidy 14-3-33-2 against Clydesdale, Scottish Cup winners in three of the previous eight seasons, and 11-2-24-6 at West Lothian, who were blitzed out for 56 in a ten-wicket pre-season friendly win that was evidently not being taken as an opportunity to share the game around – which probably suited the Alderman temperament just fine, for where Kim the merry prankster had danced and romanced his way through things, Terry was a little spikier. "He was more intense and combative than Kim," asserts Stephen Lockhart. "He wasn't averse to a few verbals either, which would be expected of an opening bowler for WA and subsequently Australia."

Charismatic versus cranky might be overstating things – difficult as it is to imagine Golden Boy dropping a shoulder into an inebriated interloping spectator – yet where Hughes was relentlessly chipper, Alderman could be occasionally chippy. "Terry was also a very personable guy and a very good coach to the boys at school," reflects Donald Scott, "but he was a bit different on the field. If the slips dropped a catch, you could see him fizzing away."

The opening East League fixture brought Heriot's to Myreside. Alderman worked his way through two probing spells to finish with 6/53 from 19.1 overs as the visitors scrabbled up to 144 all out, the equally feisty Hamish More top-scoring with 36. Watsonians fell 21 short in reply, Alderman chipping in with 19 before falling to Scotland captain George Goddard, who ensured the visitors left with 20 points to their hosts' six as an early marker was laid down. Twenty-four hours later, however, revenge was exacted in the opening round of the Shish Mahal, Maciocia's 4/20 and 3/20 from Lockhart tumbling Heriot's out for 106, knocked off six down with David Bell's 36 gluing it all together.

Watsonians had no intention of being pushovers, and recorded a comprehensive 110-run win against Holy Cross the following Saturday to get their league campaign rolling, Alderman's 14.4-4-29-6 routing the visitors for 81. Nevertheless, having started with back-to-back six-fors, there would be only one more five-bag in the league, partly because of the erratic slip fielding and partly because the standard was a lot higher than the Australian visitors generally expected. Indeed, in the next round of the Shish Mahal, the pro bowled nine wicketless overs for 49 as Aberdeenshire sent them on their way. The Alderman equanimity had been tickled, the importance of sticking to tried-and-trusted strengths tested.

"Terry wasn't loath to use the bouncer," Lockhart recalls, "but he didn't overdo it. He realised that he was most effective pitching the ball up and moving it around, and the amount of play-and-missing that year was extraordinary. Besides, although he was a very fit man, he would tie his pace back to allow him to bowl the long spells we asked of him."

Alderman still found a way to chip in as the first half of the league campaign unfolded – although surprisingly for a certified No.12 in the pro game, this was just as often with the bat. After a marathon spell of 27.2-10-48-3 had not proven enough to beat Royal High, Watsonians hanging on at 128/8 in pursuit of 151, Alderman, a crease-crabbing jabber who would muster one first-class fifty from 265 attempts, ground out a crucial 46* in an occasionally shaky four-wicket win over Carlton, having earlier picked up 1/45 from 21 overs of toil. That week he celebrated a 24th birthday on the lash with club colleagues, then watched the lashing rains claim the weekend fixture against Grange. Next time out, at Edinburgh Academicals' evocative Raeburn Place ground, overlooked by Inverleith's handsome Georgian houses and the granite-hued Auld Reekie skyline, he followed a typically probing spell of 18-4-39-3 with 29* in a more straightforward win.

Such batting heights were never to be touched again, however, with the final eight East League games yielding just 38 runs at 4.75. This reversion to type began with a duck as Watsonians hung on at 98/9 in response to Stenhousemuir's 125/9, Alderman having earlier bowled 25 overs on the spin to pick up 5/45. All of which meant the trip to high-flying Heriot's to start the homeward leg of the campaign became a must-win, were any chance of hauling in the unbeaten leaders to be kept alive. It turned out to be a game spicier than the Shish Mahal menu.

Heriot's won the toss and, with the nous of six past, current or future Scotland internationals in their side, opted for first use. It was tough going, cut and thrust, Alderman proving close to unplayable in a spell of 23.3-11-28-3 as the home team were bundled out for

95. The game's principal flashpoint came when Heriot's hardboiled opener Hamish More – "a charming gentleman off the pitch," says Lockhart, "but a very different animal on it" – pulled Alderman to square leg, where Keith Flannigan held on to the chance while tumbling backward, the ball subsequently coming free. How subsequently was the nub of things.

Watsonians were happy that the catch had been completed, as were the umpires. More, it would be fair to say, was not. More, it would also be fair to say, was distinctly unchuffed about both the decision and the appeal. Volubly unchuffed. So unchuffed that he was not prepared to leave the field of play. Alderman then suggested – and this would be something of pre-watershed version of how the conversation went, the Watsonians pro drawing liberally on the stock idioms of your Aussie spearhead, your *effs* and your *cees* – that More should probably head for the pavilion, all things considered. More fired back with some choice Scots phrases of his own – two superpower nations of profanity, locked in mighty battle! – calling the umpiring disgraceful and everyone "fuckin' cheats", particularly Alderman, before two teammates appeared, one of them his brother George, and he was escorted off, raving away. He was 40 years old. And he wasn't finished there. There was more, and More wasn't any merrier when it came.

"We knew this wasn't going to be the end of it," recalls Lockhart, "because we still had to bat and we knew we were going to get it in the neck. Hamish was their wicket-keeper – a very good batsman, a pretty good keeper, although not the best you've ever seen – and he liked a chat from behind the stumps. He never stopped. But even before then, having been off the field for maybe 20 minutes, he came back over the rope with his bat in hand, waving it about and suggesting he was going to knock the head off a few of us, Terry Alderman first and foremost. And again, he had to be escorted off the pitch."

Monday's *Scotsman* referred only to the game being "marred by certain incidents that could be ascribed to over-enthusiasm", which is not how Mario Maciocia remembers it: "All hell broke loose. Such was the ensuing dreadful atmosphere that it almost reached fisticuffs. Hamish More's father was pacing around the boundary screaming abuse at Terry, and after the match George

More attempted to elbow me down the stairs as we approached the bar to have after-match drinks."

By then, Watsonians had been obliterated for 35. Off-spinner Goddard, two years away from receiving an MBE for services to cricket, did the bulk of the damage, pouching 6/21 on the Goldenacre 'trampoline'. The last realistic chance in the league had been snuffed out, Heriot's thereafter romping to a fourth straight title with 94 per cent of the possible points won. It had been a day to forget for Watsonians – albeit an unforgettable one – who now had to ensure a top-four finish for qualification for the Scottish Cup.

They started by failing to beat bottom side Holy Cross, with Alderman picking up an unwanted century: 4/100 from 21 overs, 77 off 13 in his second spell as Phil Arrowsmith had a day for the scrapbook, carving his way to 85* having been forced to slide in at No.4 after arriving late. Locum opener Javed Khan chipped in a half-century, exactly as he had predicted he would after the game at Myreside, and Holy Cross closed on 244/7, having used the maximum 58 overs, leaving 42 for the chase. Although proceedings ended in a tame draw – David Bell responded with an unbeaten 100 – it remains a mythical game at Arboretum Road, the scorecard still adorning the clubhouse wall.

"Every professional, Kim and Terry included, were surprised at the quality of club cricket in Scotland," says Lockhart. "I think it spurred Terry on to do a bit better, thinking: 'Hang on, I've just gone for 100 in 21 overs'. He would have been first down at nets on Tuesday, trying to rectify things. He worked much harder than Kim did, principally because Kim had so much natural ability."

Besides that pursuit of Scottish Cup qualification, the team did have a trophy to play for, having reached the Masterton final once again. Alderman's seven-over spells in the first three rounds had brought him 1/13, 1/25 and 2/15: two-and-a-half per over. Two days after the mild ignominy at Holy Cross, he was held back to bowl the last seven overs from one end in the final and turned in a cup-winning spell of 6-2-7-5 as Stenhousemuir were bowled out for 84, a target reached with three overs to spare, Bell unbeaten on 40, to land just the club's third major piece of silverware.

Equilibrium restored, Alderman then sent down a combined 42.1-17-65-9 over the next three East League games – wins against Royal

High and Grange sandwiching an abandonment against Carlton, who were 32/5 chasing 179, the pro having figures of 8-6-5-2 when the rains came – thereby sealing the coveted top four spot, once more as runners-up to Heriot's.

The campaign petered out anticlimactically, with defeat to Edinburgh Accies and a losing draw at Stenhousemuir, but Alderman's 43 East League wickets at 13.57 was a decent return, giving him 86 scalps at 11.13 overall. It had been a fruitful summer, one that finished with Watsonians marvelling at Kim Hughes's bravura performance between the showers at the Centenary Test. Brian Adair and his son Robin caught the night sleeper down to London and, over breakfast at the Waldorf, listened to Kim explain how he was going to hit "the Poms" all around Lord's. This he did, winning Player of the Match.

Alderman was back in Australia by then, his place in club affections secured. If not quite as easy-going as Kim had been – "Terry could be quite difficult to manage as a player," recalls Mark Everett, "when things did not go well for him he had a temper and would regularly fall out with opposing players" – Alderman had nonetheless been a popular member of the dressing-room, one who threw himself fully into the ways of club cricket.

One Sunday, blood alcohol level still a little high from the Saturday revelry and with a friendly against Freuchie out in Fifeshire to get to, he handed Jane the keys to their bottle-green Morris Oxford. "Off we went, knowing it would be a 'finish at 7pm, still there at midnight' job," recalls Lockhart. "We also knew we were going to be much stronger than them, so the plan was Terry would keep wicket rather than come down the hill and terrorise some Fife farmers. We batted first and were all out for 90-something, which wasn't part of the plan. So at tea Terry says, 'Look, I'm not going to keep wicket. We need to win. I'm going to bowl.' We bowled them out for 50 or 60; Terry took six or seven wickets. Come about 11 o'clock, as we were starting to think about leaving, we looked around for Terry and eventually found him outside, fast asleep on the bonnet of his car. He was so knackered after two days' bowling and two days' drinking that he had just totally flaked out." Onya, mate.

* * *

Some years later, over dinner in Perth, Alderman told his old Watsonians colleague Jeff Burton and his wife Veronica that the happiest time of his cricketing life was the season he spent in Edinburgh. Perhaps it was simply a congenial line offered to guests who had travelled over 9,000 miles to be there. Perhaps it spoke, obliquely, of the stresses of professional sport. Either way, the sentiments echoed those of Kim Hughes. It is instructive to ask why.

Both men were, for a short period, not far off the best in the world, Hughes topping out at No.3 in the Test rankings, Alderman at No.2. Yet both had major bumps in the road, including the bans that followed those rebel tours to South Africa, which interrupted one international career and ended the other, while Alderman also had a potentially career-threatening injury to overcome and Hughes the torments of his captaincy years. Indeed, so exasperated did Hughes become with those gnarly guardians of Australian cricket's ideological orthodoxies that he eventually refused to do the captain's post-toss interviews with the recently retired Ian Chappell, a dart-blower of extraordinary mercilessness for Channel Nine. Until he was persuaded to U-turn, that is, whereupon Chappelli, having promised his producer he would go a little easier, threw in the following loosener: three months ago you said there were no leg-spinners in the country good enough to play for Australia, so why is Bob Holland in the XI? ("Why did he pick Bob Holland?" muses Lockhart. "He was a fellow Watsonian, that's why!")

Beyond the long shadows cast by these trials and tribulations, Kim's assessment of his Scottish summer was much more about the ambient conviviality of his time there, arriving wide-eyed and full of beans and finding a home to which he has continually returned – a demonstration as good as any of how the overseas-pro experience can enrich the life of both the star cricketer and those who share dressing-room and clubhouse with him.

The first return visit came during the 1977 Ashes tour, when a free weekend allowed him to turn out against Stewart's-Melville. Given the club already had an Australian pro, this was something of a controversial move. "The fact Kim was playing for pleasure rather than pay," reflects Stewart Oliver, "was not an argument which gained much credence – outwith the club itself, naturally!"

Hughes's contribution to the game was a breezy 75, including five sixes and six fours. "They had a good leg-spinner, Ronnie Chisholm, who played for Scotland a number of times," Lockhart recalls. "Kim came down the wicket to me and said he could take care of him but was going to try and keep him on because he would rather face Ronnie than the opening bowler. So he hit one through the covers for four, then picked up a couple of easy twos, and on the fifth and sixth ball patted back half volleys, while announcing 'well bowled' to the bowler. And the captain of course kept him on. This went on for four or five overs."

Having made a Test debut in a dead-rubber at The Oval later that summer, Hughes then joined up with Watsonians on an end-of-season tour to Corfu, bringing along his co-debutant and fellow Western Australian Mick Malone (whose only Test cap it would be, despite match figures of 6/77 from 57 overs and 46 runs from No.10 in his one visit to the crease). It was a setting that fitted Kim's romantic streak like a sweaty inner. Years later, he would remember it wistfully: "Sipping ouzo and coke on the side, twirling your arm over and having a dash: that was life." There on the Spianada in old Corfu Town, an artificial strip flanked on three sides by a car park and the other by a row of tavernas, Kim's dashing blade put on an improv' show, his 78 against Faiax taking Watsonians to a ground-record 203/8 from 33 overs, with a cameo post-ouzo 39 against Gymnastikos the next day.

"Everything came to a standstill when Kim was batting because he was whacking the ball into trees and it was crash-landing on diners' tables," remembers Lockhart. "Back then there were eight clubs on the island and everyone seemed interested in the game. Word had got around, and there must have been about 3,000 people there to watch this Australian international bat." It was a long way from the Australian goldfish bowl, a long way from Dennis Lillee's bumper barrages at nets or Rod Marsh telling anyone who would listen that Kim couldn't skipper his way out of a paper bag.

Hughes also presented the club with a new trophy – a bat autographed by both English and Australian teams from the 1977 Lord's 'Jubilee' Test – which to this day is awarded annually "for consistent batting and a vital or match-winning innings". Just as the club had etched itself into his soul, so he was etching himself into the club's traditions.

He would be back in 1978, too, a quick stopover as he returned home from the Australians' tour of the West Indies, the one-off appearance this time bringing just four runs against Fauldhouse, out second ball. A year later, by which time he was locum Test captain, he was the honorary guest at the Crocks' Supper. He was unable to make it back for a fifth straight year, the itinerary around the Centenary Test not permitting an Edinburgh excursion, although his and Alderman's post-Headingley visit to Myreside the following summer did allow them to catch up with Bob Holland, who was struggling to live up to their exploits, managing 45 wickets at 19.33 with no five-for, along with 264 runs at 13.20 and a solitary fifty. Only one other Test player has since represented the club.

By the time the 1985 Ashes rolled around, Hughes had already made his final appearance in the baggy green, yet whenever he was over doing radio commentary on subsequent Ashes series he would head north for a few days. On one occasion, Jeff Burton took him out to the Old Course at St. Andrews. Golf wasn't Kim's game – he had never had a lesson and played infrequently – but he went round in 83. He was guest speaker at a celebratory dinner in 2006, resplendent in the blazer the club had presented to him 30 years earlier – cream with crimson trim, not too dissimilar to those worn by the attendants in the Lord's pavilion – and ten years later was back as guest of honour to open the new Craiglockhart pavilion on the club's second ground. It was a happy place, as he would explain to the *Scotsman* after cutting the ribbon: "All I knew about Scotland [in 1976] was that it was pretty cold over here and they played a lot of rugby union. However, I should not have been worried because they made me feel at home straight away and the likes of Brian Adair and Donald Scott were great to me. We were also lucky because we had a beautiful summer in terms of weather and the team seemed to come together and play some great cricket – I just remember that I had a ball here."

"Being liked mattered to Kim," asserts Ryan in *Golden Boy*. "Being liked was as important as making runs, maybe even more important, and the wish to be liked never faded, it only ever got stronger." If an explanation is needed, then, for almost 50 years of authentic friendship – a fellowship forged on the fields of his youth but closely nurtured in the intervening years – one only need consider the valediction the club gave him back in September 1976, a few days after his double-hundred in Dundee.

Before sending him on his way to fame and fortune – some 40 Watsonians went along to the airport to bid him farewell – the club held a race night in the clubhouse, a fundraiser that doubled as an opportunity for the double winners to toast their departing conquistador. Brian Adair took care of the formalities. Later, when the hundred or so guests were suitably oiled, not least himself, Donald Scott shushed the room and pulled a sheet of paper from his pocket. On it, he had scribbled a poem, which had taken him "15 minutes to conjure up" – a poem he would last year recite, at the age of 95, with much gusto, to your author. It would bring the packed Myreside pavilion to tears of laughter, perhaps other types of tears. In its content, the sentiments that inspired it and the hearty sincerity of its recitation lie all the explanation needed for the special place Watsonians holds in Kimberley Hughes's heart, and he in theirs.

A Hymn – To Kim

It all goes back to April when Brian gave a ring,
And said another Aussie had come to do his thing,
And knowing the law of averages, I said "he'll be a nit",
And Brian rather casual says, "They say he bats a bit".

In due course Brian's Rover creeps up our stately drive,
And a curly-headed Aryan, looking very much alive,
Jumps out and grabs my spinning fingers, just like a high-powered vice,
By the time I'd finished my First Aid, he'd an arm around my wife.

"I'm Kim," says he, "how are you, mate? They say your digs are beaut,
And skipper here says I'll be right – say, your daughter's kinda cute!"
I little thought this other than a compliment quite bland,
But had I known his way with dames, I'd have shot him out of hand.

But Kim has been a super bloke. He could charm the birds from the trees.
Not everyone dares woo the girls with his kilt below his knees.
But let us not forget that he came here to play at cricket,
And many memorable innings did he give us at the wicket.

Kim leaves us other memories quite difficult to replace,
How he's nearly halfway thro' his meal before I've finished grace,
How he's usually halfway to his ton before I reach Myreside,
And how a gin and tonic makes his eyeballs start to slide.

We wish you all the very best as you go upon your way,
And if you ever would return, you only have to say,
There's always room at Bainfield – Spartan, with floorboards bare,
And I only thank the Lord above I'll be no longer there!

I know these friends around us and they're yours as much as mine
Would convey to you the thoughts expressed in the words of Auld Lang Syne,
There will always be a welcome here no matter where you roam,
We like you for the guy you are – you can leave your bat at home!

4

Richie Richardson
at Thames Ditton, Blackpool, Gateshead Fell, Swansea and Burnmoo

It may not have commanded many column inches or a particularly prominent place in the English cricketing consciousness during that Ashes summer of 2009, but the promotion battle in Division Five of the Surrey Championship was fiercely fought, with Addiscombe, Staines & Laleham and Thames Ditton duking it out for the two top spots, striving to reach the rarefied air of the fifth tier, one step closer to mixing it with the big boys at the top of the pyramid: Wimbledon, Reigate Priory, Sunbury and the rest. Ditton had recruited a player they believed could help them, a 47-year-old overseas amateur with good coaching credentials who was working in London for the Antigua Tourist Board.

The newcomer had missed pre-season friendlies against Shepshed Town, Oxted & Limpsfield and Indian Gymkhana, and was dismissed for two in the final warm-up, a Thursday night T20 against Kingston Student Union. Allaying fears that his eyes might be failing him, a pair of composed unbeaten 40-odds in the opening two league fixtures, both won, gave a glimpse of his promise, only for the trip to Chipstead Couldson & Walcountians to send him tumbling back into single-figure misery, dismissed by the Australian import Jarrod Tait, whose better-known brother Shaun would that summer make a couple of presumably unwelcome guest appearances in Surrey club cricket's sixth tier.

Forced to miss the next two with work commitments, the chap with the Caribbean swagger and a hint of middle-aged paunch found himself run out for 19 on his next appearance, out at Chaldon's charming National Trust-owned ground, where Ditton were unable to take the final, victory-securing wicket. Still, a sprightly 67 contributed to a good win over Wallington and a few midweek runs for Lashings suggested the veteran would be too much for Dorking, but once more he fell in single figures, leaving the lifting to skipper Oliver Turnbull, his sometime business partner in high-summer coaching clinics in moneyed, metropolitan Surrey.

Unavailable once more for the trip to Chertsey, where a much-needed 59-run win was secured thanks to the bowling of Nailson Raj and Buddy Mason, the veteran returned with a little July sun on his back and rattled off scores of 119*, 69*, 1 and 128. The former West Indies skipper, Richie Richardson, was in a good space with his game as the promotion tussle entered its final four rounds. Next up, it was the return game with Chaldon (these days Chaldon CMO, having merged with Croydon Municipal Offices CC).

Situated in the western 'burbs of Greater London between Esher and Surbiton, across the river from Hampton Court and to the east of Sandown Park, Thames Ditton's ground at Giggs Hill Green is a triangular public park open on all sides and flanked by roads, the houses over which are well within range. The hypotenuse is formed by the busy Portsmouth Road, which runs south west, with the club's compact two-storey pavilion located in the north-west corner, just across the Giggs Hill Road, down which the locals might barrel in their SUVs one bright Saturday in the school holidays as they swing the kids down for the long-promised go on the Gruffalo River Ride at Chessington World of Adventures. Anyone starting out on such a journey on 15 August 2009 might have seen, around 2:30pm, a vexed-looking West Indian in a wide-brimmed maroon sun hat, stood there waiting to cross the road and get back to the dressing room – a traffic-enforced moment of decompression ahead of any disgruntled kit-throwing for the world's former No.1 batter after his long walk out to the middle had yielded a first-ball duck, trapped lbw by Chaldon spinner Sunny Sharif. No matter, for after tea Richie chipped in 3/20 to a 109-run win, then 53 a week later as leaders Addiscombe were beaten, followed by 33 as Dorking were trounced to extend the winning streak to four, a 39-point haul that left Thames Ditton two behind Staines & Laleham heading into their final game, and eight behind Addiscombe.

Alas, the visit of already-relegated Chertsey saw Richie bowled by Daniel Shepherd for 27 as Ditton fell 28 short in the chase, although some comfort was drawn over those September ciders as news came in that both rivals had won, rendering their own failure immaterial. It was nevertheless a disappointing end to Richie Richardson's eighth season of league cricket in the British Isles, which saw him represent seven clubs in five competitions, turning out in the South East, South West, North East and North West. Wherever he went, his humility and easy-going Antiguan cheer belied the fierce competitive will of a committed pro and universally admired teammate.

Giggs Hill Green was 13 miles on foot from The Oval, where 14 years earlier he had drawn the curtain on his Test career and 14 years later would referee the second World Test Championship final – 13 miles from The Oval, but light years from the hard-edged northern league cricket that Richie Richardson had played when he was still in his imperious, lidless pomp.

* * *

Seventeen long years before his dotage at Ditton, Richie Rich's previous gig in club cricket had come at Blackpool of the Northern League. This was gnarly, bareknuckle fare, teams who were happy to get in the mud for a brawl – metaphorically speaking – in order to secure local supremacy. Blackpool were comfortably the league's most successful club, with 15 of 40 league titles at that point, and chairman Alvah Haslam was eager to stay ahead of the chasing pack. When the signing was announced in January 1992, he told the *Blackpool Gazette*: "It's not just our intention to be the number one club in our league. We want to be the number one club in the North." Throwing the world's No.2 Test batter into the mix was unlikely to be a hindrance.

Richardson's future Northern League adversaries were afforded a long look at him during the West Indies' tour of England the previous summer, when he churned out three fifties and two hundreds to finish as the series' leading run-scorer – 495 at 55 – just ahead of the world No.1 batter, Graham Gooch's 480. He signed off with 121 in defeat at The Oval, after which, with the simultaneous retirements of Malcolm Marshall, Jeffrey Dujon and skipper Viv Richards, the Antiguan prince ascended to the throne.

Such were the tribulations of Richardson's first assignments – failure to make the final in triangular ODI series in Sharjah and Australia, greeted with voluble criticism back home – that there were doubts as to whether he would take up Blackpool's offer. Reports of a county deal with Essex and murmurings of anxiety about his form added to the uncertainty. On the eve of the World Cup, however, to much relief on the Fylde coast, he agreed. "Blackpool have trawled the waters of world cricket for months to try and land the right man," reported the *Gazette*, "and they have come up with one of the biggest catches around."

Denying that the contract was worth £15,000 (approaching £32,500 in today's money) – a figure that the *Gazette* nevertheless continued to cite – Haslam told the paper that they had sifted through 70 "applicants" for the post after a verbal agreement with the initial target, Chris Cairns, had fallen through when Nottinghamshire decided to take the 20-year-old a year ahead of schedule. The next name to emerge from the rumour mill was Terry Alderman, although Haslam made it clear that the club was "not interested", adding that they were "looking for a young person who wants to make his name in the game". Naturally, they then turned their attention to the 41-year-old Gordon Greenidge, and talks progressed well until Greenock met his terms and he offed himself to Scotland. A dialogue was opened with the 18-year-old Sachin Tendulkar, a young person indeed looking to make his way in the game, who expressed interest until an offer to become Yorkshire's first ever overseas player landed in his in-tray. The West Indies captain it would have to be.

Signing a world-class batter to replace the retiring 50-year-old 'Flat' Jack Simmons made sense. The pitch at Stanley Park was, along with Netherfield's, the truest in the league and bowling sides out was challenging. Better to bank on winning tosses, reckoned skipper Tony Hesketh, and chase down targets in the superstar's slipstream to collect the eight points for a win – or, failing that, bat teams out of the game and pick up three points for a winning draw. Still, home conditions had not prevented Blackpool winning the title in 1988, '89 and 1990, the year they not only landed the second of a trio of Lancashire Cup titles but also registered the Northern League's maiden success in the national knockout.

After a disappointing World Cup campaign, Richardson's final engagement of the winter – his first Test wearing that increasingly heavy crown – was South Africa's emotionally charged return to the Test arena after 22 years of isolation, a thriller in Barbados that saw the visitors head into day five needing 79 runs with eight wickets in hand only to fall 52 short (in Jimmy Adams's version of events, because Brian Lara had got the South Africans blotto in a pub the previous evening). The Stanley Park hierarchy would have been relieved to see a little weight lifted from the new pro's shoulders. However, despite the game finishing just two days before Blackpool's season opener, both Richardson and debutant Kenny Benjamin, a fellow Antiguan also heading to the Northern League, needed special dispensation to arrive late. Ordinarily, reported the *Gazette*, "an overlap with the start of the season on April 25 would have forced Blackpool to abort the arrangement. Professionals are bound by Northern League rules to turn out on the opening day." The potentially self-defeating nature of such puffed-up militancy truly boggles the mind.

The hastily arranged Test and subsequent late arrival not only meant that Richardson was unable to fulfil a heavily promoted speaking function at the Argosy Club in Blackpool with former Liverpool centre-half Tommy Smith and comedian Bernard Manning, but also that a sub pro was needed. They called in Roger Harper, on his way to becoming a behemoth of the Lancashire League across eight seasons with Bacup and two at Nelson that yielded over 10,000 runs at 57 and 796 wickets at 13.5. The locum picked up 4/60 and a hard-hitting 72 as Blackpool despatched visitors Kendal, who would finish the summer as the Northern League's second national knockout finalists, losing at Lord's to Optimists of Bristol.

Harper was not the only tidy West Indian sub pro to turn out in the league that summer, with Fleetwood enjoying the company of BC Lara for three games as a deputy for Indian Test seamer Atul Wassan. "I picked him up at the Tickled Trout in Preston," recalls Fleetwood keeper, John Isles. "He was in the UK watching Dwight Yorke, his best mate, play for Aston Villa. We bowled first and he stood at first slip, chatting away. Nice bloke. Darwen was always a slow, damp wicket and when he batted I saw this huge backlift and thought, 'Oh no, he won't last long if he gets one that shoots along the floor'. I needn't have worried: he made 60-odd not out and took them apart." Lara bought everyone a drink after the game and, after a breezy 38 in his next outing, started making enquiries about a full-time gig for the 1993 season. "He said he wanted £10,000," says

Isles, "and I told him it was a lot of money, and if he came down to £8,000 he would probably find a club. We already had a pro signed for the following year, Richard Staple, who in the end didn't come. Anyway, that winter Brian went to Australia and made his 200-and-whatever and took off. You couldn't have got his shoelaces for eight grand after that."

With Harper having given Blackpool a winning start, everything was primed for Richardson's splashdown. He and Benjamin arrived on Friday, hopped on the Gatwick shuttle and were collected at Manchester airport. That evening, Richie met the *Gazette* at Stanley Park, resplendent in gold-trimmed aviator shades, a navy-and-gold brocade shirt and smart tan bomber jacket, an SS Jumbo slung over the shoulder, the weapon of choice. On Saturday, he made 107* in victory at St Annes; on Sunday, it was 108* against Morecambe in the first round of – deep breath – the Matthew Brown Northern League Theakston's Best Bitter Trophy, the 30 eight-ball over competition played in the first half of the season. He made 73 in the second round, failed in the semis, but in the final, against Benjamin's Netherfield, would carve the standout innings of his season.

After that two-ton introduction came a couple of rare failures – two of only four sub-30 scores in the league – Richie failing to cope with the Darwen stodge where Brian had flourished. The triumphant bowler was 44-year-old seamer David Bonner, who later in the season was singled out for praise – this after Richie had plundered 136* at Stanley Park. "He bowled me one loose ball in 25 overs. At times I've found it easier getting runs in Test cricket than in the league."

That was Richie in a nutshell: not only aware of the lift he could give a humble club cricketer with a few kind and sincere words, but generous spirited enough to offer them. Earlier in the season, he encountered Chorley's 41-year-old legend Keith Eccleshare, a tearaway quick as the club's pro in the early-80s who later mutated into a leg-spinner, combining the two during a spell in the Bolton League at Astley Bridge that saw him go two-and-a-half seasons without being removed from the attack. By the time he was back at Chorley, 'Ecc' was a fully-fledged *wristie*, and after a hard fought 78 at Stanley Park Richie told him he was "the most accurate leg-spinner he had ever faced" and that he could do a job in the international game.

Such respect for the bowling helped Richie's consistency, as he reeled off seven fifties, three tons and a couple of 40-odds from 18 league knocks to finish almost 30 runs-per-innings better than his nearest challenger in the averages. And he did it all with a twinkle in his smile, effortlessly charismatic yet always approachable, perhaps happy to be out of the Caribbean cauldron, having been persistently booed during the ODI against South Africa in Jamaica after describing the two teams' World Cup encounter as "just another game of cricket", a few weeks before a whites-only referendum on ending Apartheid. "He has had such a traumatic time this winter that he may want a while to get over it," said Hesketh. "By the end of the season we will know more about whether he's hard enough to captain West Indies."

The May bank holiday double-header against Fleetwood brought 86 on the Saturday and 42 on Monday, nicked off by leg-spinner Mark Wilkinson, who was known as 'The Crab' on account of his unique, slower-than-slow bowling style. "It was the faintest edge," recalls Isles. "Only me and him knew he'd hit it, but he walked straight off before I even appealed. The umpire said he wouldn't have given it because he didn't hear it. He was a class act. He stayed after the game and had a few drinks, mixing with everyone. A proper nice bloke."

A week later – the first of six frustrating abandonments – he made 79 out of 148/5 against a Leyland team with Kiwi World Cup pinch-hitting star Mark Greatbatch as pro and Geoff Miller playing as an amateur. He followed up with 114* at Netherfield as 205 were chased down and Kenny Benjamin's muscular, chest-on rockets repelled, a prelude to his cup masterpiece. But it had come at a cost, his hands taking a battering from his compatriot. Twenty-four hours later, as Blackpool lost in the Lancashire Cup for the first time in four years, Richie had to sit the game out, watching on as tempers flared – first after Royton tried to roll the pitch again having won the toss and batted, later as one of Blackpool's batters was 'Mankaded'. His hands were still heavily strapped the following weekend when feathering a catch behind against Morecambe for 13, but on Sunday, back in Kendal for the cup final, he was ready to deliver. The four-figure crowd got to witness a shark fight in the Lake District.

Richardson may have been his captain for the Leeward Islands and now West Indies, but KCG Benjamin was not a man to be trifled with, as England's World Cup winning inside centre Will Greenwood discovered during cricket training at Sedbergh School that summer when his larking about had prompted a sharp spell from the coach off two paces. "I had played against Kenny two or three times and he was certainly quick but the spell in the final was something else," recalls Martin Pickles, whose unbeaten hundred in the semi had secured Blackpool's passage. Pickles would have the best view in the house for the early skirmishes. "Netherfield had decided to hold [Benjamin] back for the middle part and end of the innings," he continues. "The first ball of his spell was a rapid bouncer at Richie's throat, which he fended off. It was most certainly 'game on'. The second ball was identical and Richie hooked him for six, straight out of the ground – admittedly, a small ground."

Pickles navigated three deliveries at the end of Benjamin's first over, including another short ball that thudded into his shoulder blade – "thanks for taking that single, Richie" – before slapping a catch to cover off the spinner. Next over, Benjamin needed two balls to burst one through Gavin Wiggans, then scattered Hesketh's stumps for a golden duck: 75/1 had become 76/4 and 'Benji' was smelling blood. At which point, Richardson decided he needed to manage the game and scampered a risky leg-bye. "He just took over," recalls Netherfield's Grahame Clarke, "and didn't let the amateurs face another ball off Kenny. It was incredible."

Sensing what was afoot, Netherfield pulled Benjamin from the attack and held half his allocation back, a dubious tactical gambit with the game there for the taking. By the time he returned, Richie had moved up through a few gears. "He'd played relatively sedately to ensure he was ready for an onslaught at the end, with wickets still in the tent," says Pickles. "The onslaught duly arrived, and he proceeded to play one of the best innings I have ever witnessed at any level."

"The quicker he bowled, the further he hit him," adds Fleetwood skipper Pat King, an awe-struck spectator that day. Richardson had come in at 33/1 in the seventh over and departed at 194/7 with 105 from 86 balls to his name – 78 from his final 40 – including a dozen rasped fours and a quartet of sixes, all of it done in a floppy maroon sunhat with Benjamin bruising the keeper's hands and absolutely no one saying to Richie: I think you best get a lid on, mate. His compatriot's six eight-ball overs had brought 3/50, the most expensive figures in a total of 203/8, which Netherfield failed by 88 runs to chase down. In contrast to the low-bouncing nibblers that invariably bring overseas pros closer to their clubbie colleagues' level, the bouncy surface had exposed the difference for all who were there to see it. If the gap between Richie and his teammates was measured in nanoseconds of reflex time, it was expressed in chasms of poise and possibility.

Holding a celebratory beer, the match-winner was insouciant: "Once I got warmed up and the adrenaline began to pump, I felt great. I haven't felt that good in a long time, not since a Test against Australia over a year ago. I got stuck on 27 for a while and said I was going to have to do something. I got really, really mean. The willow started to talk."

"It was an unbelievable knock," says Clarke. "I knew we were in trouble when Kenny bounced him and he hit it into the middle of the football fields – over the other side of the road!" Hesketh was unequivocal: "It was the greatest innings I ever witnessed in 25 years in the league. He didn't wear a helmet and said afterwards he never made eye contact with Benjamin. He also said the breeze was in his favour. We said, 'What, because it reduced Benjamin's pace?' And he said: 'No, it was to hide the smell of fear!'"

Stellar as it may have been, this was not an innings built on ego. It was perfectly adapted to situation and need. A week later, as he scratched around against Leyland DAF, its true merits would become even more apparent to Pickles: "Richie could have been out twice early on to Dave Makinson, the former Lancashire player, both times to vociferous lbw shouts. I suspect the umpire may have adjudged lesser mortals to have been bang in front, but Richie, as pros often did, got away with it. At the end of the over, he said he wasn't seeing it well and was struggling: 'Martin, you get the runs and I will hang around', or words to that effect." Pickles duly made 94* and the pro a grafter's 50*, happy to play second fiddle. "It was a testament to Richie that he stuck it out, which not all pros would have done, especially as the previous week I had watched him play such an unbelievable knock – the beauty of cricket from one week to the next!"

Blackpool lost to Chorley the following week but were top at halfway. Over the homeward stretch they were undone by their lack of bowling penetration and the appalling weather, with a run of eight games bringing five that either didn't start or finish. Dismissed for 22 in a washout at Lancaster, he hung around to play pool and have his photo taken with kids. When the game at Kendal failed to start, he got involved in an impromptu 11-a-side football match that was feisty enough for Pickles to have to pull out of the league rep XI's semi-final the following day – which makes you wonder what the West Indies cricket board would have made of their skipper skirting about the place with tackles flying in like a 1970s Intercontinental Cup final. Kendal won the football, largely because they were loaned Blackpool keeper Chris Pile, a former youth team goalkeeper at Liverpool who would never make a senior professional appearance, for any club, and only once appeared on the bench – although this was a European Cup final, the infamous game at Heysel in 1985, when Pile was Bruce Grobbelaar's 18-year-old deputy after an injury crisis at the club.

As Blackpool's title hopes ebbed, Richie rolled out scores of 48, 35, 22, and that 136* in defeat to Darwen, then flew back to the Caribbean to select the touring party for Australia, returning to make 83* against leaders Morecambe in a third straight abandonment. The following week Blackpool fell two runs short against Leyland DAF, when victory would have left them three points off top in second with two to play – a game in which Richie lost a battle of the Richardsons, bowled for 51 by Alan, who marched up to him in the bar afterward and asked him to sign the ball. The fading title hopes were mathematically ended by defeat to Chorley in the penultimate game, while the pro's 32 left him six short of four figures. This he sealed in the final game against wooden-spoonists Preston – the only occasion Blackpool bowled out the opposition all year – Richie cruising to 62* in a chase of 117 to finish with 1,056 runs at 88. Only three other players went past 650.

Preston seamer Bob Cuthbertson to this day questions how motivated Richie was by statistical landmarks: "The first game against Blackpool that year was a sporty wicket and I got a few past his edge. Then he had a big wipe at one and as he ran past I called him a 'filthy slogger', and he just laughed. I don't know whether he'd remembered that, but at Preston on the last day I told him my wife and kids had just arrived and said 'I'll have to get you out now, Richie'. He said, 'You want my wicket, man?' I said, 'Yeah, but on my terms'. It always makes me wonder whether he'd have got himself out in a situation where they were obviously going to win. But then it wouldn't have been real, would it?"

No, it would not have been real. But then, many good quality amateurs in other sports might say that not much was real about competing in a meaningful game against the captain of what was still the world's most powerful team. Magical days.

* * *

If the primary batting education of the West Indian greats came on their native Caribbean surfaces – turners in Guyana, flyers at Sabina, roads at the Rec – for many in that lineage a few seasons of English club cricket was an obligatory and complementary summer boot camp, a finishing school to round out the repertoire. Diplomas completed on the glassy sheen of those hard-baked home pitches would be topped up on the grassy green strips across the Atlantic. From George Headley through the three 'W's to Sobers, Kanhai, Lloyd, Richards and Haynes, the majority trod the boards of league cricket early in their journey, and for the teenage Richie Richardson it would be no different.

He arrived for the first time as an 18-year-old after playing for Antigua in the Leewards inter-island tournament, the Heineken Challenge Trophy, heading at the end of June from Nevis to Neath in the South Wales Cricket Association, an established pathway that had brought the likes of Jeff Dujon and Ezra Moseley over to Wales from the Caribbean, playing a little club cricket while representing Glamorgan under-25s and second XI.

Two years later, Richardson's great mentor, IVA Richards, arranged for him to play for Staplegrove in the Somerset League. He had by then made two first-class appearances under the captaincy of Derick Parry – later a friend and professional counterpart in the North East – making a duck and 76 as opener on debut against Barbados at St Kitts, dismissed by Joel Garner in each innings. Richards and Garner were, at the time, the king and prime minister of Somerset respectively, and were good company for young Richie, who lodged with Viv and turned out for the county second XI. Meanwhile, he collected 591 runs at 53.73 as Staplegrove finished just below halfway, and – in what would be a common trope elsewhere – he played for the Somerset League rep XI in the President's Trophy, getting chirped by a teenage Jack Russell against the Western League, launching the former England bowler Ken Shuttleworth for an enormous six onto Mr Kipling's car park during a Player-of-the-Match-winning 76* in the quarter-final against the North Staffs & South Cheshire League, before elimination in the semis against eventual champions, the Shropshire League. They would meet again.

Fifteen months later, still only 21, Richardson made a Test debut in Mumbai, the fourth game in a six-match series won 3-0 by the West Indies. Early the next year, he played all five home Tests against Australia (another 3-0 win), recording his first two hundreds and averaging 81, but he didn't play a Test during West Indies' 1984 tour of England (a 5-0 'Blackwash'), during which word reached Gateshead Fell of the Durham Senior League that Richardson was looking for more club cricket, a chance to further hone his skills with a view to earning an overseas contract with a county. A package making him the most expensive pro in the North East was soon agreed, with the fee covered by sponsors and assorted third parties. The club raised donations from its members, for which they received a maroon sweater and tie emblazoned with the Gateshead Fell crest. "He didn't cost the club a penny," recalls teammate Doug Hudson.

By the time Richie arrived in Gateshead, he had nine more Test caps to his name: a difficult series in Australia (won 3-1) in which he averaged only 26 despite a hundred in Brisbane (nine of his 16 Test tons would come against the Aussies), followed by a four-match home series against the New Zealanders (won 2-0) in which he topped both the runs and averages – good news, undoubtedly, as he rolled into Eastwood Gardens four matches into the DSL campaign, all of them drawn. His CV was taking shape, although this was still a cricketer whose deeds were predominantly known through dark black ink rather than glowing pixels. Time to introduce himself.

"He arrived at 5:30pm and I took him for dinner," recalls his captain, Michael Richardson. "I asked him what sort of food he ate. 'Tropical fish and chicken'. Hmm. We ended up going to an Italian restaurant in Newcastle and he said, 'Skip, you won't have any problems with me. I'll bat wherever you want me to bat, I'll bowl whenever you want me to bowl and I'll field wherever you want me to field.' He was true to his word. I opened the batting with him myself, because I didn't want anyone else running him out. He was a model professional, very driven, who never showed any aggression toward anyone. He felt it was an honour to play for West Indies and that's all he wanted to do."

The eagerly anticipated debut turned into a damp squib, with both games of a mid-May double-header succumbing to inclement weather. This gave Richie plenty of time to settle into his digs, a terraced house over the Tyne in the old mining village of Lemington, on the western fringes of Newcastle, from where he would sometimes make his way into Toon, sipping rum-and-cokes in Bentley's in Bigg Market before hopping onto the Tuxedo Princess, a floating nightclub moored at the foot of the Tyne Bridge. Occasionally, he borrowed his captain's car to visit family in London. Whenever he was around, he practised diligently and demanded others did the same.

Opponents for Richie's belated debut were Sunderland, one of the league's historic powerhouses, winning seven of the first 11 titles, with another six picked up on the way to an unprecedented four in a row in the late 1960s. But it had been 14 years since their most recent success, with hegemony ceded the following decade to Philadelphia, who won six in seven years between 1973 and '79, since when Durham City and Chester-le-Street had shared the 1980s' five DSL championships. It was a strong and storied competition in a county just seven years from its first-class baptism and Richardson took fully 27 minutes to score his first run in it. Thereafter, he adapted quite nicely and cruised on to an unbeaten 106, although the victory charge was held up by local lad Michael Roseberry, who made 57 that day and subsequently over 10,000 first-class runs for Middlesex.

These were timed games with 20 overs in the last hour and no restrictions on how large a chunk the first innings took out of the day. On a drizzly bank holiday Monday at Burnmoor, the Fell were left with just 18 overs to chase down 152. With Richardson slamming a 46-ball 71, it looked on until he was caught in the deep in the penultimate over. The following Saturday, he bashed out another 67, but after his dismissal colleagues settled for a draw in the face of Philadelphia's hefty 236/4.

Nine games in, the Fell were unbeaten. They were also winless. It had been 15 years since the club's solitary DSL title, marching unbeaten through the 1970 campaign, and already it seemed as though they would have to look to the cups for the summer's silver lining. Something had to change, thought all-rounder Hudson, part of that title-winning side, and after Richie's 53* had knocked off Wearmouth's paltry 76, he made a suggestion to his captain: "I said, 'The openers might bowl it quicker but they do nowt with the ball. Richie swings it and I swing it' – him out, me in. I persuaded him to open the bowling with us two."

As difficult as it is to imagine a man who collected a grand total of 13 career first-class wickets operating as the spearhead of any bowling attack, the following winter Richardson did take 5/40 from an unbroken 17-over spell against the English tourists, including Tim Robinson, David Gower and Mike Gatting all clean bowled. True, this wasn't the type of stuff that would elbow Marshall, Garner, Walsh or Ambrose out of the attack, but it proved canny enough in the Senior League and after being elevated to new-ball duties Richie bagged 5/47 and 5/31 as the winning streak was extended to three. "Plan B had become Plan A," says Hudson.

Richie also chipped in 45* and 73* to those wins, bumping his average up to 207 as Gateshead built momentum. Things were shaping up nicely, the pro lifting standards. "He introduced proper warm-ups, which weren't really done at the time," recalls Hudson. "The opposition used to laugh at us jogging round the boundary. I was a 35-year-old who'd started to put on a few pounds but I found it helped a helluva lot. He brought a little bit of professionalism to things."

The final game before halfway took Gateshead and their warm-ups to league leaders Horden, where Derick Parry lay in wait. Hailing from Nevis, Parry was in the fifth season of a legendary 15-year stint at the club, the duration of which not only marks him out as one of the league's greatest ever pros but indicates how well he was able to rub along with colleagues. A brisk, accurate off-spinner good enough to earn 12 Test caps in the era of 100-decibel chin music and a competent enough lower-order batter to pick up three Test fifties, Parry would finish with 994 DSL wickets for Horden at 14 along with 10,736 runs at 45.7, including 15 hundreds. A club that had never won the league when he arrived raised the pennant four times by the time he bade farewell.

Parry had been ostracised from West Indies cricket after touring South Africa with the rebels in January 1983, yet he and Richie remained close friends – which made it all the more important to come out on top. Perhaps the bat handle was being squeezed that little bit too tightly when Richardson, on 18* and nurturing a DSL average of 216, tried to assert himself on things, Parry picking up his friend as the first in a spell of 6/41, although Gateshead hung on, nine down and 50 short of victory, to preserve their unbeaten record. As they would do through the next eight games, which brought a solitary win and seven draws: if you shoved 'em in they didn't leave you many overs to chase; if you batted first, they shut up shop at the first sign of trouble. Richardson's batting remained potent, with scores of 6, 109*, 96, 78, 63, 12, 32 and 60, but his bowling had lost its bite and there was no Plan C.

With five to play, unbeaten Gateshead sat 39 points behind leaders Philadelphia, the next visitors to Eastwood Gardens. The good news was that Phili's pro Suru Nayak, the league's leading wicket-taker, was out with a broken finger. Fell won the toss and inserted. Going was slow, but eventually the visitors were winkled out for 138 in 62 overs, Richardson with 4/28, Hudson 4/47. Plan B was back. They had 29 overs to chase them. Michael Richardson fell for a single, after which Stephen Murray's 41 and Richie's 80* steered them to victory with seven balls to spare. The 20 points left Fell in third, 21 off top.

The following week, as Phili were held to a draw, Wearmouth munched 65 overs for their 132 and again the Fell romped home by eight wickets, Richie's 88* sweeping him past the 1,000-run mark. The August bank holiday then brought a nerve-shredding three-wicket win over South Shields, Richie falling for 21 in a chase of 193, but 61* from Peter Clark kept Gateshead in touch before Clive Lumley arrived at the crease with four needed from one ball and got the job done. The gap was now ten points with two to play.

Eppleton were next, a fortnight after Whitburn pro Max Alleyne's 9/13 had demolished them for 18, although they were unlikely to have been too traumatised about things with a pro as granite-hewn as Stevie Greensword – Player of the Match when Minor Counties champions Durham upset Derbyshire in June and Gateshead pro when they won that 1970 league title, one of seven DSL teams that made him their paid man – and the 41-year-old made a typically over-my-dead-body 96 as the visitors declared, sportingly, at 185/5. Richie was first out for 21, but runs for the skipper, Murray and Hudson saw them home. Phili had drawn. A 39-point gap had been trimmed to two in four rounds of matches. Gateshead remained unbeaten with one to play.

The final-day visitors at Eastwood Gardens were Horden, who were happy to sit around for almost four hours watching it pour down, by which time Philadelphia's game against title outsiders Sunderland had been abandoned. The rain eased and then stopped. There wasn't enough time for a result, but the chance was there to collect a few bonus points: two points to force a playoff, three for the title. "Pretty much all games across the North East were off but our groundsman had covered the whole square," Hudson recalls. "We got on well with Horden. They turned up and Derick Parry said, 'I suppose you'll want us to bat?' Two points was 125 runs or four wickets. They weren't going to give it us but they weren't blocking."

Word reached Philadelphia that a start had been made, and there was alarm when they heard that Gateshead had picked up two early wickets. Envoys were despatched, UN inspectors. The rain returned, growing heavier, but the teams battled on through. "At one point I was running in with my trousers tucked into my socks," says Hudson. "It was bad. The umpires asked Horden if they wanted to go off and they said they were happy to stay on. Eventually, though, it really did get too bad." Too bad, indeed.

Twenty overs play had been possible, and an undefeated season had come within two wickets of forcing a playoff. A shock defeat to Seaham Harbour 24 hours later in the final of the ER Armbrister Memorial Trophy made it a second silver medal, although they did pick up the Savoy Trophy for the fastest team 200 of the year. Still, with the pro having chipped in with 42 league wickets and 1,099 runs at 91.58, they were delighted to have him back in 1986.

Sorrows were drowned and the following morning Richie and Derick headed to Stoke-on-Trent together for the final of the

President's Trophy against the North Staffs & South Cheshire League, wholly dedicated to seeing the job through for their adopted league, whose XI would be without Nayak and Ipswich Town midfielder Nigel Gleghorn. With the two Leewards boys on board, the DSL had seen off local rivals the Durham Coast, Northumberland County and Tyneside Senior leagues before eliminating holders the Bassetlaw League in the quarters and the Manchester Association in the semis, Richardson with the game's best figures and top score: 4/13 and 46. At Longton, the NSSCL batted first and were restricted to 143/9, with Richardson's nine overs bringing 2/23. After tea, in autumnal gloom, he grafted to 34 opening alongside Greensword, whose 57 held things together. With five needed from the final over, Paul Burn hit the first ball for six to seal a third title in the competition's 21 seasons for the Senior League. The following year, they would draw level with the NSSCL and Bassetlaw on four, Richie again flying the flag and burrowing even deeper into local affections.

* * *

"Gateshead Fell are delighted to welcome back as their professional the player who excited millions of television viewers during the winter Test series in the West Indies, the cricket superstar from the Caribbean – Richie Richardson," announced the *Gateshead Post* in early April, a couple of weeks before the grand opening of the first phase of the town's MetroCentre, at the time Europe's largest shopping arcade, built alongside the Tyne at the site of the old Dunston Power Station (owned by Sir John Hall, the future Newcastle United chairman) and partly financed by the Church Commissioners of England. In July, the vast Nissan factory in Sunderland was opened. A region, seemingly, on the up.

In the spirit of things getting bigger and better, Richardson set his sights on breaking the Durham Senior League aggregate record. His 1,099 tally the previous summer was the sixth highest in the league's history – one of only 16 occasions in 71 seasons that the four-figure mark had been breached, six of them by the remarkable Greensword in the 1970s, including three of the top five entries – yet it was still some way short of the 1,284 amassed for Eppleton in 1977 by the hard-hitting NSW opener Steve Small, who later played five

Sheffield Shield finals, in which he averaged 48.2: a canny pro but not quite the same glamour quotient as *wor* Richie, for whom the runs would again flow liberally, although once more with the Fell's title aspirations stymied by an inability to land enough knockout punches with the ball. The season, instead, would take most of its collective high points from the North East's bewildering array of cup competitions, mainly midweek engagements to start with, games in which Richardson was happy and keen to play, albeit not always with the same output as his DSL efforts.

The first cup exit of the season came against Horden in the Armbrister. "They had a guy called Paul Hodder, a New Zealander who played rugby for West Hartlepool," recalls Doug Hudson. "It rained during the interval and he nicked Richie off for a duck and gave him a bit of a send-off: 'Call yourself a Test player!' Two weeks later, in the league, Richie made 111 not out against them and hit Hodder for a six that cleared the rugby club bar and went straight through the goalposts for a conversion." Hudson himself came in at the back end of that run chase, and promptly crunched Hodder through the covers for four. "After I'd hit it, I shouted 'run!' and set off. Richie didn't move. I got to his end and he said, 'When you hit it like that, you don't run, you pose.'"

Richardson missed the Smith Print Trophy loss to Darlington RA, busy making 131* for the DSL rep team against the Durham County League, but was on board for the Northern Invitational exit, a game in which, predicted the *Post*, "the battle between Ramon Shukla, the Thornaby professional, and Fell's own professional, West Indies Test star Richie Richardson, should be worth the 50p admission money alone." Richardson was dismissed by Alan Shutt for an anticlimactic 16, although disappointment was fleeting with another four competitions still up for grabs.

Back-to-back early-July evenings saw the Fell depart at the semifinal stage of both the Tyneside Charity Bowl and Grangetown Florist Bowl, Richardson making a duck against Benwell in the former and a duck against South Shields in the latter. All of which left only the hyper-local Gateshead Metropolitan Borough Council Cup, of which they were holders, and the regional Alcan Trophy, arguably the most prestigious of them all, featuring the top sides from the previous season's Durham Senior, Tyneside Senior and Northumberland

County league campaigns, with a final at the handsome Jesmond ground in Newcastle and a £500 first prize. The Alcan was named after its sponsor, an aluminium smelting concern, but later became the Nike Trophy – the pathway that led the Oregonian shoe and apparel behemoth's branding portfolio from 'Air' Jordan through to Brazil's *seleção* and the Indian cricket team finding an important staging post in the North East's premier 45-over club competition, whose winners got a free pair of trainers each.

While all that was going on, Richie had not taken long to hit his stride in the bread and butter of the league campaign. Absent from the opening two games as West Indies wrapped up a second straight 'Blackwash' – during which he made the only hundreds of the second and third Tests, which may have caused a shudder or two in Durham – he put a disappointing first outing against South Shields behind him, dismissed by Jamaica's Aaron Daley for 15, with a couple of chunky performances: 86 and 7/65 as champions Phili were swatted aside, then 97 and 5/63 in victory at Wearmouth. It would be a false dawn for the Fell, however, with Richardson shouldering too much of the burden.

The bank holiday weekend brought a pair of defeats. Chasing Burnmoor's 159, the Fell fell for just 78 – 41 of them to Richardson before being trapped lbw by Ian Conn, a bowler who would win a record six DSL Player of the Year awards and someone Richie treated with the utmost respect. "He once played out a maiden off Connie and came down and told me it was one of the best sets of six balls he'd ever faced," recalls Mike Richardson. "Richie rated him very highly. He bowled seam up, leg-cutters, off-cutters. He'd dip it away. He could be quite mesmeric, and was sharp enough to bowl a bouncer."

On Monday, Gateshead lost to eventual champions Durham City, who would complete the double over them later in the season. Aside from these three, there were no further defeats but again too many draws, starting with Richie's dismissal for four at Chester-le-Street, a seventh straight innings in all competitions without a fifty. A day later, alongside Burnopfield pro Wasim Akram, Guisborough's Desmond Haynes and a smattering of footballers from Newcastle United and Sunderland, Richardson cut loose during the Live Aid charity game at Burnmoor. Pro's form restored, Gateshead won five of the next six.

The sole drawn game in this sequence was more to do with an inability to take the final Boldon wicket than Richardson's dismissal for six, nicked off by medium-pacer Tony Shields a couple of days after he had made 129* for a NE Select XI against Derbyshire. An engineer at Pyrex Glassware in Sunderland who left Whitburn a couple of years earlier because he wasn't getting a bowl, Shields went to play for Marsden in the Durham Coast League, another competition with no restrictions on first-innings allocation, long memories, and vendettas to make the Camorra's inter-clan squabbles look quaint. Ryhope's seven titles in nine seasons often invited spoilers' sticks in the imperial wheels, and one afternoon Silksworth batted 88 overs and left them a dozen to chase 241. Such bottomless bloody-mindedness would find its *nec plus ultra* in Tony Shields one starchy Saturday at South Hetton.

Marsden had turned up with seven men and home skipper Bobby Steel twice went to the middle for the toss. His opposite number Colin Marshall, busy trying to ascertain where his missing players were, had been out there but the two had not seen each other and the playing area was not visible from the away dressing-rooms. At 1:55, the umpires, who were using the Hetton dressing-room, told Steel that the toss had been defaulted and he duly informed an indignant Marshall that Marsden could bat. Marshall soon had the board rattling along, with a righteous 60 up inside ten overs, after which the tempo changed somewhat, as Jack Chapman describes in *Cream Teas and Nutty Slack*, his wonderful history of league cricket in the county.

"Temperatures rose after an incoming batsman waited almost two minutes before ambling out carrying pads, thigh pad, gloves and bat. Emotional thermometers boiled as Tony Shields blocked for three hours and seven minutes for four runs, the most sterile innings in Durham history. It was no longer a question of 'needle'. It was a stand-off at crazed corral with branding irons at two paces. A dozen adjectives might describe the inertia but where is the word to sum up such driven, blind obstinacy in the name of recreation? Shields suggests 'cussedness'. 'We were not happy with the situation from the start. I've been around a bit and once the abuse started flying I dug in, determined not to get out.' Probably more so when he was batting with his 14-year-old son. Tony Shields and Bobby Steel have not spoken since."

Marsden declared five minutes before the close, having crawled to 136/6 in more than 100 overs, then promptly got changed and went home. They were deducted 15 points and fined £500 for bringing the game into disrepute. Shields quit the league, Marshall was banned for six matches, and one umpire retired. All of which is to say that few teams up here were likely to roll over and have their belly tickled, even by West Indies' No.3 gun, and after the Fell had set them 174 for the win, Boldon stodged their way to 71/9, No.11 Bassett with 18* of them. A day later, Maradona's 'Hand of God' goal in Mexico City eliminated England from the World Cup.

Richardson's contributions to the five wins in that mid-season flurry were a hefty enough 103*, 82, 111*, 95* and 77, the latter against cross-town rivals North Durham, whose pro (and Wasim Akram's flatmate) Mohsin Kamal had pulled up injured earlier in the season, prompting a search for a replacement. "Richie had brought a mate over with him called Edson Brown who, ostensibly, was there to play tennis with him," recalls Hudson. "We fixed them up with free tennis at Gateshead Leisure Centre. Anyway, when Kamal got injured, North Durham decided they'd have Edson as pro. I used to call him 'Bungalow', cos he had nowt upstairs. He bowled a bouncer at Richie in this game who hooked him out of the ground but let go of the bat at the same time and almost killed the square-leg umpire."

The GLC was where Big Daddy held a mid-June glamour bout with 'Belfast Bruiser' and where Richie coached kids on Wednesday mornings through the summer holidays (free for members, 30p if you didn't have a leisure card), before then taking on Edson at tennis or putting his feet up and thinking of the weekend's innings. With a dozen games remaining, the Fell sat just three points behind leaders Durham City in second, but injury and holiday availability hit them hard and they drew the next six to slip back into the pack, the frustrations mounting up. Wearmouth's last pair survived 15 overs; Philadelphia left them 33 overs to chase 260, although 98 from Richie briefly hinted at a miracle; Conn's off-cutter knocked him over for two as Gateshead were left hanging on for a point at 85/9 against Burnmoor; dropped first ball against Whitburn, he cruised to 63 before a once-in-a-lifetime, full-length one-handed caught and bowled from Russell Muse. A slow puncture.

The title tilt was more or less done, but Richie's Sunday programme remained full and a surgical 75 steered Gateshead past Lintz in the Alcan semi-final. "After the game, Richie pulled out a guitar and gave an impromptu jam session," recalls Hudson. "There were 20 or 30 people there till two o'clock in the morning. That was Richie: he was happy and mixed in, a good club man and a great team man. On the field, he was spot on, always geeing you up, although after he batted he'd usually have a snooze."

The next Sunday engagement was the league rep team's semi-final against the Liverpool Competition, for which Richardson warmed up with a lone-hand 56 in that defeat to Durham City. "The Liverpool team had a tall West Indian playing for them who cleaned up the opening bats straight way," recalls Mike Richardson. "It was Curtly Ambrose." The Chester Boughton Hall pro and Richie's future bass-plucking bandmate in Big Bad Dread and the Baldhead finished with 2/26, but the DSL marched serenely on.

The following weekend brought the Alcan final against Horden, into which Richardson came with an easy 56* in a nine-wicket stroll past Chester-le-Street as he closed in on that league aggregate record. The pitch at Jesmond looked tricky, although the two Richardsons gave them a solid start. "County Club had an important league game on bank holiday Monday, so they'd covered that pitch not ours," says Hudson. "We lost a couple of wickets to Derick Parry in the middle and Richie basically decided he wasn't going to bowl at anyone else but him. No one else faced him for about eight overs." A calling card.

Parry worked through his overs for 25 runs, picking up three wickets, but Richie moved in stately fashion to the first ever hundred in an Alcan final, eventually run out for 105 by his counterpart's direct hit from the cover boundary. Chasing 225 to win, Parry's 62 and 72 for Paul Hodder put Horden in control but a niggardly ten-over spell from Dave Young costing just 19 runs swung the game Fell's way and they edged a humdinger by ten runs. The celebrations that evening might have been behind Richie's bank holiday blob against Eppleton the next day, although he was back among the runs the following weekend, stroking 94* against Sunderland in the league and a breezy 35 against Greenside as the Gateshead MBC semi was negotiated. With two weekends left, he needed 71 for the DSL record.

Having already made two hundreds against Horden, he may have fancied reaching the milestone with an innings to spare, but Parry this time got the better of things, sneaking one through a Richardson sweep when he was on 27 and set, a dismissal certain to have been brought up in conversation a day later in front of a heaving crowd at Chester-le-Street, when Parry declined to use Richie's bowling skills as the Shropshire League were restricted to 176/8 from their 45 overs. Starting cautiously with the main job, Richardson was soon pummelling his way to 81 after which Durham City's prolific skipper Graham Hurst brought things home with a composed 53* to give the Senior League back-to-back titles. Two finals down, one to go.

Heading into the final league match, at home to Boldon, Richie needed just those 44 runs to go past Steve Small. There had been five single-figure scores and yet here he was. Given that the summer's previous DSL outings at Eastwood Gardens had brought 86, 41, 103*, 111*, 95*, 35, 68, 56, 56* and 94* – that's 745 runs at 149 – the smart money was on him cruising past it in the canny calypso style, provided he didn't fall over against the left-arm fast-medium swing of Boldon's future one-cap wonder, Simon Brown. But Tony 'Nemesis' Shields had other ideas, a big wet blanket to drop over the fireworks, and for a second time that summer dismissed Richardson for single digits. "I bowled mainly in-swing," says Shields, "and this was a length ball that he tried to hit on the up through the covers, but got a big inside edge onto the stumps. It was incredible to get a great player out twice and I've told the story a few times since, although the young'uns don't seem to know he is."

Meanwhile, up at Whitburn, Graeme Hurst had started the day needing a hefty 131 for the all-time DSL record and had reached 125* when he decided to declare – this with the title already in the bag! Insanity or selflessness, his team won the game in the final over, Hurst finishing with 1,279 runs at 63.95 and the amateur record, while Richardson's 1,250 at 65.78 pipped him in the averages. Twelve months later, Steve Small's record would fall to Indian World Cup winner and Sunderland pro Kirti Azad, who amassed 1,293. "First game of the season against us they were none for two off two balls, Ian Conn on a hat-trick," recalls Burnmoor keeper Graeme Shurben. "Kirti hit his first ball out of the ground and was out in the

13th over for 100, with Sunderland 112 for three! I've never seen another innings like it!!"

Gateshead had finished what had started out as a promising league campaign in fourth place, which just left the final of the Metropolitan Borough Cup against Blaydon, a chance to say his goodbyes to the North East. The chief danger for the Fell in Richie's farewell final was another prolific overseas pro, Mark Harper, brother of Roger, a classical stylist in gold-rimmed spectacles unlucky not to play for the West Indies. He had churned out a record eight hundreds in Blaydon's Tyneside Senior League campaign and another four in the cups, a good chunk toward a staggering final tally of 2,935 for the season. Not even Wasim Akram was spared. In early July, his average peaked at 194.17. So when Doug Hudson slipped one through him at 53, the game seemed as good as won. Blaydon finished with 163/4 and the Fell progressed without problems to 160/0 with the pro on 98 and off strike for the next over. "Richie wanted to sign off with a hundred," says Hudson, "so at the end of that over, after a chat with Michael, he swapped ends and kept the strike. He got to his hundred then gave his wicket away."

"I don't think we purposely did it," clarifies the skipper. "It just happened. We got talking and went to the wrong end. One of the Gateshead supporters spotted it, but the umpires hadn't."

Two trophies, a second inter-league success, a barrelful of runs, 11 not outs in the 18 league victories he was part of across two seasons – it had been quite a stint in the North East and a shot in the arm for the Fell, who six years later would sign a young Damien Martyn as pro and twice in the 1990s emerged victorious from the regional stages of the national knockout, losing a semi to eventual champions Chorley in 1995 and, five years earlier, a last-16 tie to Clydesdale. The pro that year? It was supposed to have been a returning RB Richardson. Basically, for free. But at the 11th hour, the club decided against it.

* * *

Unavailable to commit to the entirety of the 1987 summer, Richardson returned to the south Welsh valleys for a two-month stint at Swansea, playing at the famous St Helen's Ground, with its rugby stands and floodlights on one side, the sea at his back – though no tropical fish, sadly – and the sweep of rickety terracing on the north and eastern flanks, into and over which Garry Sobers famously launched Malcolm Nash for his six sixes back in 1968.

Among the people who coaxed Richardson back down to Glamorgan was the legendary Don Shepherd, the man with the most first-class wickets never to have played an international. His son, Mark, opened the bowling for Swansea, a side also featuring the former Glamorgan all-rounder Geoff Ellis on opening-batting and off-spin duties, as well as a young David Hemp and Robert Croft, although the pair were requisitioned in mid-season for a useful Glamorgan Colts team including Steve James, Steve Watkin, Adrian Dale and Tony Cottey. Colts had won immediate promotion upon entering the league a year earlier and would be the closest challengers to Swansea as Richardson swung into town with another Leewards scholar, Keith Arthurton, in tow.

Richardson, Ellis, Arthurton and Hemp were not only a stiff proposition for the Saturday trundlers of Pontarddulais, Llanelli and Ynysygerwn in West Glamorgan, but also for clubs further east – Cardiff, Newport, Usk, Panteg, St Fagans – who had joined the newly-formed Welsh Cricket Championship, an experimental Sunday 'superleague' backed with £6,000 of sponsorship that had the local cricket establishment scrambling to save plucky pigeons from interloping feline attack. Swansea enjoyed the zesty enterprise – Richardson would make an even 100 against Cardiff, while Arthurton and Hemp put on 246 against Ammanford – but would come second on percentage of points won, the rules re-jigged in mid-season as teams struggled to find space in the calendar to fulfil fixtures.

The Saturday fare of the South Wales Cricket Association competition was no hotbed of overseas pros. Gorseinon signed Indian leggie Laxman Sivaramakrishnan, two-and-a-half years on from a 12/181 haul against England in Mumbai, but he would manage only a quarter of that tally in the three SWCA games he played before making his excuses and heading home. "He found it difficult to acclimatise," said his captain. "The cold weather didn't help him and I don't think he was very happy."

The decade's principal overseas star was Linton Lewis, later chairman and parliamentary candidate for the New Democratic

Party in St Vincent & the Grenadines but back in the 1980s the top *boyo* of south Welsh cricket, slaying all-comers with his big hitting and bustling seamers. Stepping off the train at Pantyffynon station in 1981 as Ammanford's first ever overseas professional – and the market town's only non-white face until an Indian doctor moved in seven years later – Lewis left Carmarthenshire in 1989 having utterly transformed the club's fortunes. The minnows had become a powerhouse.

The deal's inadvertent catalyst was a fire that razed the old pavilion, allowing a new one with a money-spinning bar to rise in its place. It had been brokered by Bill Edwards, who owned a sports shop in Swansea that sold kit throughout the West Indies. Ammanford were languishing in the third tier when the 21-year-old Lewis got there, but immediately won promotion and caused an almighty shock as they landed the Cwpan Cricid Cymru: the Welsh Cup. Lewis made 112* as favourites Gowerton were knocked out in the quarters, was carried from the field after another ton saw off Barry in the semis, and crashed 95 in the final against Swansea in front of a steel band hired for the occasion by sponsors Girobank.

The following year brought another Welsh Cup triumph and another promotion, with Lewis making 989 league runs. No one had ever before made 1,000 runs in a SWCA season. In 1983, as the newcomers won the top division at the first attempt, Lewis blazed his way to 1,543 runs in 16 innings, half of them centuries. He made 1,316 the following year, too, spreading a little sunshine across south Wales as the miners' strike started to bite. "There would be a thousand people in The Park on a Saturday watching Ammanford," recalls SWCA chairman Neil Hobbs, a committee member at the club during Lewis's heyday. "People would phone the club and say 'who's batting first?' You'd tell them 'Neath are in first' and they'd say, 'right, we'll be down after tea'. Some people just came to see him bat. He was fantastic for the club."

Such was the hitting that players on the neighbouring bowling green would turn up in crash helmets, although even that was spun into a positive by the ever politic Lewis, who claimed it taught him to hit straighter, toward the tennis courts, as had been advised by the diehard senior supporters who congregated around the bandstand. Lewis was a good enough player to make 61 for the Windwards against the touring Australians and he took his cultured mayhem to Glamorgan IIs, muscling 211 against Somerset, but was never offered a first-class game for them. Instead he helped Ammanford land a second SWCA title in 1986, collecting 1,145 runs, which they turned into a double by winning the Welsh Cup for a third time. Meanwhile, Lewis had completed a Master's degree in Legal Studies at Bristol University and would later earn a doctorate in Law from Durham, not to mention accountancy qualifications from Gwent College. In 2015, Dr Lewis the multi-millionaire businessman and barrister even found time to release a pop-reggae album called *Peace and Daffodils*, inspired by his long-ago summers in South Wales, and four years after that was a pall bearer for "Aunty Jean" George, the chairman's wife back when the club had opened its arms to him almost 40 years earlier. "The club took a gamble and it paid off," says Hobbs. "It was the making of Ammanford, because to this day they are one of the top Premier League sides in Wales."

By the time Richie Richardson swept into Swansea in late May, Lewis had already won a Player of the Match on the opening day, bludgeoned 160 the week after, then 44 in a second defeat in three for the champions, before contributing 6/61 and 77* as Glamorgan Colts were seen off while Richardson was making his debut 37 at Gowerton. Two days later, against Dafen Welfare, Richie found himself on 88* with eight needed to win. Having already taken 14 from the over's first four balls, he promptly launched back-to-back sixes to bring up what would be his only SWCA hundred. There was a 73 against Pontarddulais but otherwise relatively slim pickings – the St Helen's Ground, laid on a reclaimed sandbank, was fast drying but somewhat fickle in character, particularly when the tide was in.

Openers Ellis and Richardson were back in the shed with a single on the board against Skewen and just five at Ynysygerwn, the pro having been barbecued by his partner. Richie missed the season's sole defeat against Maesteg Celtic, for whom Glamorgan seamer Simon Base took 8/51, but he was there for a run of victories over Llanelli, his old pals Neath (the then five-time champions would finish bottom, relegated for the first time since the league's formation in 1926), Gorseinon and Gowerton, against whom he signed off with a punchy 55, by which time Swansea were the same number of points clear of the chasing pack. After Richie left, they extended the winning streak to eight and wrapped up the title with four games to spare. Keith Arthurton would return in 1989 and score 1,397 runs as a sixth title was won.

At the time of this Swansea sojourn, Richardson was in the middle of a 33-month spell without a Test hundred, encompassing 38 innings. The following summer's tour of England brought few runs (71, with a lower average than Ambrose) and an injury that kept him out of the final two Tests, with debutant Arthurton stepping into his spot. Bounteous series in Australia (528 at 58.66) and at home to India (619 at 88.42) followed, by the end of which Richardson had ascended to No.1 in the ICC rankings. But he wasn't looking for a league gig for 1989 and instead brought a Young Antigua side to the UK. A party featuring future internationals Ridley Jacobs, Stuart Williams, Hamish Anthony and Kenny Benjamin played matches in their manager's old haunts of South Wales and the North East, the latter organised by his friend Michael Richardson, who of course asked his friend about his plans for the following summer. Richie said he wanted to return to Gateshead Fell, so his skipper got the ball rolling.

"I made the arrangement with the club's bankers, who were happy to assist. I organised a car and accommodation," says Richardson. "For whatever reason, the chairman, Godfrey Clarke, said they were going to appoint a local guy from Chester-le-Street and they didn't want Richie, even though it wouldn't have cost them a penny. It was bizarre. If you can have a professional for nothing – a world-class batsman – why wouldn't you? Maybe they thought outsiders were taking over the running of the club. The person they appointed [Iain Young] – there were probably four or five guys in the side who were better players."

Michael told Richie the news and asked if he wanted him to try and find another club. On his next Friday lunchtime catch-up in Newcastle with stalwart Burnmoor wicket-keeper Graeme Shurben, he set out the proposition.

* * *

The Durham Senior League was formed in 1903. By 1990, Burnmoor were the only one of its dozen founding clubs never to have won the title, Horden having broken their own duck two years earlier. "When I started in the late-1970s, we were the whipping boys," says Shurben. Burnmoor had finished fifth in 1988, however, then second in 1989, behind an Eppleton team for whom Jimmy Adams made 1,087 runs at 77.21 (his lowest aggregate in six years of DSL cricket). They were a team on the up. But that last step is always the hardest. A push would be helpful.

Shurben and Richardson talked things through over a glass of wine – £3,500 would have to be found, with the rest of an £18,000 package, thereabouts, covered by the Allied Irish Bank and associated sponsors – and the terms were relayed to the Burnmoor committee. As no-brainers go, a club that had never before won the league being offered the West Indies vice-captain for a relative pittance seemed like a jellyfish jamboree. But there was a snag. Burnmoor already had an agreement in place for first team skipper John Tindale to step into the pro's berth, albeit with no contract yet signed. The 22-year-old had been at the club since he was nine and had lifted two trophies the previous season.

"Originally, the club said that if John said no they wouldn't employ Richie, and they stuck by that," says Shurben. "But alongside all this, John had also been proposed to stay on as captain, which several people in the club felt was a problem, arguing that the pro shouldn't also be the captain. So, David Anderson was put forward by the committee to stand against John. David's knowledge of cricket wasn't brilliant, so I decided to stand as well. Before I put my name forward, I called John and said, 'Look, David Anderson is going to beat you in a vote and I don't think it will be good for the team if he's captain'. John was fine with that. I won the vote and then this situation with Richie came up."

In February, the *Journal* reported that Tindale was unwilling to vacate the pro's position; that he would stay on but leave at the end of the year. Burnmoor were on their way to Cleckheaton for the regional finals of the national six-a-side in early March when another report appeared in the *Journal* claiming that Tindale had been "dismissed after refusing to stand down" and was severing ties. "It wasn't true that he was forced out," claims Shurben. "He'd made his decision and told the papers before he told us. We were as surprised as anyone." Either way, the affair left a sour taste in some mouths. One committee member resigned, while Tindale agreed to join Whitburn as an amateur then changed his mind and joined Chester-le-Street as pro. The deal with Richie was on. "Richie was cheap for who he was," adds Shurben. "What did cost the club money was honouring John's contract even though he was playing for someone else, which they probably shouldn't have done. I'd never heard of a situation like that before or since: paying someone to play for one of your main rivals!"

Richardson and Richardson were joining a powerful batting line-up whose amateurs would contribute a healthy two dozen 50-plus scores over the season: nine for Joe Bittlestone, *Sunday Sun* North East Player of the Year two years earlier when at Ryhope; six and four respectively for teenagers Graeme Weeks and Mark Blunt; two each for Gary Lancaster and Michael Richardson. Richie chucked another seven on the pile, but not a single wicket. "We needed him to bowl, really," says Shurben, "but he decided he was injured. He was also one of the world's best slip fielders but he said he had an injured hand." Instead, the bowling would come from first and second in the league averages the previous year – spurned captaincy candidate Anderson's left-arm swingers and off spinner David Lewins, a solicitor in Sunderland – along with the nagging, ring-field strangulation of Kenny Rudd and spearhead Ian Conn, who, says Shurben, was "a superb player, but was a devil to captain. He used to call you all sorts of names if you took him off. But he made the ball talk and was one of the best local bowlers I ever saw – almost unplayable on certain wickets. He used to get Jimmy Adams out for fun."

Embroiled in a Test series against England that the tourists somehow kept alive until the decider in Antigua, Richie was five games late for the DSL season, Burnmoor having picked up three wins and two draws by the time he arrived. His debut came at Wearmouth, a colliery welfare ground where the square went a year unattended during the miners' strike while the team played the whole season away. It could be capricious to bat on, which Richardson discovered when starting with a duck as Burnmoor crashed to 94 all out, Shurben humping 37* on a pitch he describes as "diabolical" to give them something to bowl at. Conn and Lewins did the rest, Wearmouth crumbling for 60.

Richie had opened the bowling, as he would the following week, when Seaham Harbour racked up 230/3, and that was him done with the ball. After tea, he was knocked over for a dozen, then retired for a customary dressing-room snooze as 70-odds from Bittlestone and Mike Richardson swept Burnmoor past the target and left them in good shape for the derby against Philadelphia, first versus second.

Burnmoor's ground was owned by Lord Lambton and its pavilion was one of the most distinctive buildings in the league, a Grade-Two listed former schoolhouse that looked like a large Methodist chapel, a large space to serve refreshment to the crowds that swelled with the signing of Richardson, although the old timers in 'Critics' Corner' had no trouble making their views heard above the hugger-mugger if things weren't to their liking. There wasn't too much to grouse about in 1990.

The DSL remained timed cricket, with five points for a win and one for a draw, but the first innings had been capped at 55 overs since Richie's previous visit. Phili were shoved in and used all the overs, Greensword batting through for 82* out of a gettable 185/4, even on a large playing area with leg-spinner Peter Graham whirling away. Burnmoor's hitherto prolific top order then crumpled in a heap, as did the middle order. But at 167/7, the home team were still a better than even chance to win, for the man in the maroon sunhat had 136* of them and seemed unstoppable. At which point, the game within his grasp, he slog-swept Graham hard toward deep midwicket where Aussie amateur Dave Tipper took a stupendous catch to deal the mortal blow. A crestfallen Richardson trudged off to a standing ovation. The last two partnerships produced one run, bringing the other ten batters' contribution, minus extras, to 26. Phili had leapfrogged Burnmoor to reclaim top spot. "It was a major disappointment," recalls Shurben. "It felt like we'd crashed down to earth after such a great start."

Entering the June and July jockeying, Burnmoor got back on the horse with a pair of bat-first wins in a double-header: Eppleton were beaten by 84 runs, with Conn (6/34) dismissing Jimmy Adams for three, and Boldon were thrashed by 82 on the Sunday, Richardson smiting 118. By then, the sound of Luciano Pavarotti belting out 'Nessum Dorma' had established itself as the summer soundtrack and Monday evening brought England a nervy 1-1 draw with

Ireland in Cagliari. The following Saturday, the Geordie charmer Bobby Robson's unfancied team were plodding through a scoreless draw with the Netherlands, watched with half-empty glasses by Burnmoor, who had earlier seen off North Durham by eight wickets, Richie rattling off 46. A 1-0 win over Egypt gave England top spot in Group F and a last-16 tie with Belgium. Both Bobby and Burnmoor were looking for a spark. The former got David Platt's otherworldly 119th-minute volley in Bologna, but an anxious Burnmoor would be humped at Horden.

"It wasn't a particularly nice place to play cricket," says Shurben. "Every year they'd move the wicket a little bit so that Derick Parry could bowl into last year's footmarks!" It was with bat, however, that Parry hurt them, stroking his way to 115* as the home team racked up 239/4, after which Stephen Ward's 6/40, including Richardson for 11, sealed a 142-run win and a bucket of cold water to the face. They now trailed Phili by nine. Imposter Syndrome started to form.

Richie made a pair of 54s the following weekend, the second in a win over Chester-le-Street in which he was dismissed by the man whose wages Burnmoor were paying, although 117* from Graeme Weeks orchestrated a 134-run thumping, Tindale making a blob. That night, England rode their luck against Cameroon in Naples to set up a semi-final with West Germany in Turin, a night forever associated, of course, with Robson's two Gateshead-born virtuosos, Paul Gascoigne and Chris Waddle.

Meanwhile, the progression of Richie's old pals at Gateshead Fell to the last 16 of the national knockout meant a two-week postponement of the hotly anticipate reunion. In the interim, Burnmoor picked up two wins and two draws in which the pro was unable to register a half-century, although the fact that they were paying around a fifth of his wages sugared the pill. Come that reunion, and understandably eager to remind the Fell hierarchy of what they were missing – to show his ex that he was very happy in his new relationship, thank you very much – Richie was knocked over for seven by the Fell's new fling, Iain Young, as Burnmoor posted 198/2. The visitors then collapsed to 70/8, at which point came definitive proof of how much the invariably reserved Richardson was invested in things. "There was a slight slope at Burnmoor, so when the ground was hard, the water ran down it," says Shurben. "It started tipping it down and Richie spent the whole delay, about 15 minutes, lying under the covers with a towel trying to stop water getting on the pitch. I'll never forget the image of him lying there."

After the downpour had abated and Burnmoor mopped up, Fell's captain Tony Smare was reluctant to resume, which his opposite number felt was a bit rich given they had agreed to reschedule the match in the first place. Strong views were exchanged. Rare was the opponent who pulled wool over Shurben's eyes. He won the DSL's wicket-keeper of the year award 11 times and in 1990 would add 43 victims to the record 50 from the previous season, although his cussedness at times strained relations with officialdom. "The league put an advert in the *Sunderland Echo* asking whether anyone could find an old scorebook showing a wicket-keeper who had more than 50 dismissals. They never found anyone, so with the league now folded that record will stand forever!" Abrasive he may have been but eventually the umpires intervened and Ian Conn took his figures to 8/40 in a welcome win as these first-time-title aspirants found themselves hitting August with a one-point lead and seven to play. These were uncharted waters.

Equally novel was the weather in Durham during a mini-heatwave that brought a record temperature of 32.5 degrees. Sun on his back, Richie churned out his highest score for eight weeks, run out for 65 just as he was primed to cut loose. It was in fact his sole fifty in an eight-game high-summer streak, followed by another failure in a draw against a resolute Chester-le-Street, the disappointment from which was softened by news of Eppleton beating Philadelphia, over whom they now held a three-point lead as they readied themselves for a trip to Phili, the lion's den, hoping Richardson could find his A-game. "Richie may not have made as many runs as we expected," says Shurben, "but he was very determined in everything he did. Everybody upped their performance with him there. They wanted to show him they could play cricket. He was quiet, but his presence was all that was needed."

Historically, the upkeep of Phili's Bunker Hill ground was paid for by deductions from miners' wages, fuelling the affinity of a partisan support that had revelled as the team rattled off those six titles in the 1970s. Their most recent had been to deny Gateshead in 1985, but with Greensword steering the ship they were confident of seeing off the challenge of the upstart neighbours from a mile-and-a-half down the Chester Road. Shurben won a crucial toss, however, allowing the visitors to control the game. The big wickets were Greensword, as ever, and Paul Burn, a policeman who the previous month had made 47* for the Minor Counties XI against the Indian tourists. "You almost needed a JCB to get Greensword out – particularly after he'd been given out lbw," says Shurben, and the veteran duly dug in for 52 while Burn compiled 78. The pair added 134 for the first wicket, but too slowly, asserted the *Journal*, and Phili only mustered 197/7 in 55 overs amid a flurry of late-order wickets, Shurben picking up three stumpings. The moment of truth was upon them.

Bittlestone fell early but Richie began like a house on fire, punching boundaries against the whitewashed walls that surrounded Phili's compact ground. On 32, however, he feathered county seamer Stephen Peel through to the keeper. "Steve did a lap of honour round the field," recalls Shurben. "I said to Mark Blunt when he was going out, 'Have you seen that? They think they've won the game already'." From the perils of 48/3, in a bear-pit atmosphere with wits pitted against the grizzly Greensword, teenagers Blunt (50*) and Weeks (80*) steered Burnmoor home and into an eight-point lead over both Phili and reigning champions Eppleton with four games left. You can't win anything with kids!

With a pair of eminently winnable games against teams with one victory between them in 44 outings to follow – one of whom Phili were busy rolling out for 47 – Shurben reckoned it vital not to lose to Eppleton in the next outing, although restricting Jimmy Adams to 51 and the visitors to 168 opened the door. Richie was nicked off for single figures, however, and at 23/3 shutters were put up, Shurben stonewalling for 32* and Michael Richardson making 9* in 97 minutes.

Bank holiday Monday brought bottom side Boldon to Burnmoor. On paper, a walk in the park; in reality, a game played with an 87-year-old monkey clambering all over their backs and merrily dropping banana skins as it did so. There was a heaving crowd on, anxiety largely under control if not eliminated entirely. Winless Boldon had made 257/4 against Gateshead on Saturday, and nothing could be taken for granted with Phili now only four points back. Richie had 666 runs at under 40 and owed them a score.

"The fact that he was there meant more than the actual runs he got," reflects Shurben. "On three or four occasions, though, he was absolutely brilliant to watch, just different gravy." This was one such occasion, Critics' Corner purring as the pro delivered to the tune of 140, which was the eventual margin of victory. Phili, meanwhile, were held by Horden. Two to play, four points needed – the sooner, the better with Horden visiting on the final day and memories of the June trouncing they meted out still fresh.

Of all the places to land a long-awaited maiden league title, North Durham in Gateshead would be among the least evocative. "It was the worst ground in the league," says Shurben, unequivocally. "They played rugby on both sides of the square and the outfield was dangerous. The dressing-rooms were disgraceful. The club folded at the end of the season although had they not done so, they might have been kicked out anyway."

Shurben lost the toss, which wasn't the best start to the day. "They only had nine at the ground. Their captain said, 'You can bat. Oh, and can I have some sub fielders?' I said, 'Er, no.'" Burnmoor got their runs as quickly as possible: a ton for Bittlestone and 48 for Richie, whose wife Arlene and son Ari had flown in for the season's last knockings. After tea, they worked frictionlessly through the North Durham batting to win by an even 100 in front of an ecstatic band of travelling supporters who were soon bringing frothing jugs into those dingy dressing-rooms. "I tried to get Ian Conn to take the wicket that won the league but Kenny Rudd bowled the last fella and that was that," says Shurben. The long wait was over. The Richie gamble had changed the club's history.

While Burnmoor carried on the party at HQ, Richardson headed home to his Newcastle digs. The following day was his benefit match, with several West Indies luminaries turning out: Greenidge, Marshall, Ambrose, Walsh, Lara, Hooper, Adams, Simmons, Bishop, WKM Benjamin, as well as Mark Harper, Wasim Raja and Derick Parry from the local pro fraternity. It was Parry who would provide the opposition for Richie's final Durham Senior League appearance, when the Burnmoor faithful had an opportunity to salute their conquering champions and watch some shackles-off pyrotechnics from their departing colossus, their Angel of the North.

"Before the game," recalls Ian Conn, "Richie asked the scorer how many runs he needed for the thousand and was told it was 146." He hadn't made it far up the mountain when he was edging behind off Ward, just as he had at Horden. "The umpire, David Armstrong, was partially deaf, which wasn't ideal," says Shurben. "He had signalled no-ball with his arm but hadn't called it. Richie started walking off and the keeper threw it to Colin Spanton at short leg, who took the bails off. I was on my way onto the pitch because I thought it was poor form, but Horden called him back."

He had eight at the time, but was soon motoring: savage cover drives, bludgeoning pulls when they were foolish enough to drop short, running at Parry with murderous intent, all the more so as wickets tumbled at the other end. "I came in at No.11 when he still needed 50 or 60 and I've never felt so nervous," says David Lewins. "He basically hit Derick Parry out of Burnmoor," adds Shurben. "It had to be seen to be believed. He hit the ball to parts of Burnmoor that it hasn't been hit to before or since." There were six sixes and 23 fours as he romped to 156 out of 216/9, bringing his season's work to 1,010 runs at 56.11, fourth in the averages behind Parry, Sunderland's Gary Brown (whose 1,445 runs was a new league record) and Jimmy Adams on top: 1,213 at 101. "Richie hit Parry over one of the big trees at extra cover," says Conn. "No one ever hit sixes there back then. It was incredible. He walked off with 156 and we thought: has he even been trying for the rest of the season?!"

Horden fell for 188 after tea, Conn with 5/73 to finish as the DSL's leading wicket-taker for a third straight year, whereupon corks were popped on a special end-of-season do as a feeling the club had never before known swept everyone into the night. Richie stayed late, allowing joy to turn into satisfaction as it soaked into the collective bones. A thick-headed team then beat Ushaw Moor in a cup final the following afternoon, Richardson run out for a farewell 63, and a few weeks later he sent Shurben a card with a picture of the West Indies team: "Thank you for a great time. Best wishes, Richie." The feeling was very much mutual.

* * *

Richie may have bid adieu to the North East, but there was plenty of cricket left for him in England. That 1991 Test tour, followed by his year at Blackpool, with the agreement for him to return to Stanley Park scuppered by his signing as Yorkshire's overseas player, apparently on the recommendation of Geoffrey Boycott. It was not a decision met with universal approval by the Headingley hierarchy – not much was back then – with that wallflower triumvirate of Raymond Illingworth, Fred Trueman and Brian Close adamant the club needed a fast bowler, as were, apparently, skipper Martyn Moxon and coach Steve Oldham. Specifically, they wanted KCG Benjamin, not long since smashed all around Netherfield by his Leewards captain, and two years before that terrorising batters in the Yorkshire League for Sheffield Collegiate.

Richardson spent two years at Yorkshire, making one first-class hundred, then toured again in 1995 as West Indies captain, his final act in Test cricket, on which he turned his back at 33. He stayed on for the World Cup the following March, played a season in South Africa that winter, then hung up the sunhat. Three years later, he took it out again to skipper West Indies 'B' in the Busta Cup, and that really was that for Richie in competitive cricket, in the UK or anywhere else. At least, it was until he turned up in the sixth tier of the Surrey Championship in 2009, a strange time of collapsing banks and quantitative easing – a time, also, of a hook-up between the Richie Richardson Cricket Academy and Turnbull Holdings, run by his Thames Ditton skipper, Oliver Turnbull, who the RRCA website claimed "has represented Cornwall at the peak of his cricketing career", which he hadn't.

Still, it was a coup, the second Test-playing Richardson to represent the club after Tom, the England quick of the WG Grace era. "When I first said I was trying to get Richie Richardson, everyone just laughed," Turnbull told the *Esher News*, "but as we got nearer to an agreement people started taking it more seriously. The general reaction is amazement. I am not sure people can believe that Richie Richardson is going to be joining us. He's quite a private guy, who just wants to be Richie Richardson the person rather than Richie Richardson the Test star and have a barbecue and a beer with some mates and relax, which he can at Thames Ditton."

As down-to-earth and easygoing as "Richie Richardson the person" was, it was nonetheless surreal for his teammates to share a dressing-room with a man who had once spent five unbroken years in the top three of the ICC batting rankings. Surreal, too, that August Saturday afternoon for any dreamy young lovers who had wandered down to Giggs Hill Green to find a bench for an hour, any lunchtime drinkers stumbling out of The Angel pub that overlooked the park, any families bundling down Giggs Hill Road and off to Chessington World of Adventures – surreal to have seen a former West Indies captain grappling with his golden duck while waiting to cross the road as Sunny Sharif celebrated with his Chaldon teammates.

If it was a long way from the hard-bitten cricket up in Philadelphia (where it wasn't always sunny), South Shields, Morecambe and Chorley, it was even further from Test matches at the Rec in Antigua (where it was always sunny), with the freaky-dancing Gravy writhing in the stands in a floral dress, pads and wedding trousseau, and the bass bins from Chickie's disco booming out his song:

Who is dat man, flashin' blade in de han',
Beatin' de ball like he playing pouchan,
A livin' nightmare for the opposition,
Richie Rich, Richie Rich, Richie Richardson.

Out first ball for Thames Ditton.

5

Marnus Labuschagne – Steve Smith – Travis Head
at Plymouth, Sandwich – Sevenoaks Vine – Ventnor

If June 2023 promised the most eagerly anticipated Ashes for a decade – Pat Cummins's freshly anointed World Test Championship winners taking on the burgeoning reputation of Ben Stokes's bold adventurers – then the scale of the challenge facing an England team being psychologically reprogrammed to *run toward the danger* could be seen in the ICC Test batting rankings. For the first time in 39 years – when Gordon Greenidge, Clive Lloyd and Larry Gomes were lording it during 1984's 'Blackwash' – the top three positions were occupied by batters from the same team.

In third place was the Player of the Match from that WTC final, the scorer of a match-defining century, as he would be when the Australians upset the hitherto unbeaten phaal-hot favourites India in the ODI World Cup final in Ahmedabad later that year. Sitting in second place – fidgeting, no doubt – was a leftfield genius averaging 60.05 across 97 Tests that had yielded 31 hundreds. And at the top of the pile came a batting barnacle who had locked down the first-drop position to such an extent that 2023 began with him averaging 59.05.

The gold, silver and bronze positions on the long-form batting podium – respectively, Marnus Labuschagne, Steve Smith and Travis Head – comprised such a potentially formidable obstacle and downright nuisance that Stuart Broad even developed a new delivery called an "out-swinger" to combat them. England's outgoing pantomime rabble-rouser was also the player most disposed to, and adept at, coaxing the home crowds from good-natured antipathy into eye-bulging rage (cf. Lord's, day five). All part of the ritual mutual antagonism, of course. Nevertheless, at four clubs dotted across southern England, where partisan passions were conflicted by memories of happy summers with their most celebrated adopted sons, the hard yearning for the Baggy Green to be taken down a back alley and given a Bazball battering sat alongside a sizeable soft spot for the Aussies' famous three-four-five, each of whom left their various clubs awed by their talent and dedication.

Well, not quite all the clubs.

* * *

After reluctantly agreeing to take on first team skippering duties at Grappenhall CC ahead of the 2007 season, Will Sharp still wonders what that third-tier Cheshire County League campaign might have held had the last-minute signing of a 17-year-old leg-spinning prodigy from the Sydney suburbs panned out. The captaincy position had been vacated by the former Lancashire and England under-19s seamer Richard 'Slime' Green, who 12 years earlier had clean bowled Graham Thorpe and Adam Hollioake on his first-class debut but was now busy with other concerns – one of which was persuading his 21-year-old glamour model girlfriend, Katie Greenwood, to sign a contract promising him a threesome "with full and oral sexual relations with him and a girl of his choice" if his bespoke, self-designed website pleasemakethiswork.com received five million hits. When it did, she made good on the arrangement, only then to dump Green – 55 first-class wickets at 41.76 – and strike up a relationship with the *troisième* member of the *ménage*, the dancer and future Mario Balotelli fling, Holly Henderson. Soon the story of the gonzo softcore pictures that "Internet sex gambler" Green had posted on the website were picked up by the *News of the World*, with Miss Greenwood telling the now defunct, compulsively law-breaking tabloid: "It was his idea to have the threesome, but I went along with it to keep him happy and now it's bitten him on the bum. Afterwards he became a nightmare. I couldn't even go to the shop without him following. I turned to Holly as a friend to get me through a difficult patch and things progressed from there." All of which is to say that the start of the 2007 English summer could have been a whole lot weirder for Steven Peter Devereux Smith than it was about to get.

Smith had arrived at Manchester airport fresh off a breakout season at Sutherland CC – once home to the caravan-dwelling country-boy metronome Glenn McGrath – where his exploits had already drawn the attention of the *Sydney Telegraph*, who were excitedly hailing him as "the next Shane Warne: only this one can bat". Smith's clubmate and later New South Wales colleague Phil Jaques had recommended him to Neil Fairbrother, Grappenhall's former England batter who was then just starting out as an agent (his roster would eventually include Stokes, Broad and Joe Root). But Smith would spend only a handful of days up there near sunny Warrington, a mile or so from the Manchester ship canal – and without playing a single game. Instead of Smith, recalls Sharp, Grappenhall's hired help would comprise "a West Indian offie who chucked it, and who claimed to have a British passport even though we called his parents in Barbados and they said they'd never been over to the UK, and a Kiwi seamer, Mark 'Killer' Kilpatrick, who couldn't bowl a hoop down a hill".

Initially, Smith was billeted with Grappenhall committeeman Phil Mills, owner of a construction company whose spacious home overlooked the ground, but a fatality on one of Mills's sites a week earlier meant the new arrival had to lodge with Sharp, who at the time was renting "a small house, five minutes from the ground" with his fiancée. No dramas.

The day after his new lodger touched down, Sharp bundled Smith along to the traditional boozy meet-and-greet at the Mulberry Tree, which, long story short, culminated in violent teenage vomiting. Sickness quickly shaded into homesickness, and the following day this famous cricketing obsessive turned down the chance to go for nets – red flag! – locking himself away in his room instead. Sharp didn't think too much of it – teenagers! – but Smith had already phoned his English mother, Gillian, telling her he wanted to come back to Australia.

"I got back from work on Friday and he'd gone," recalls Sharp. "No note, nothing. The first I knew about it was when Phil Jaques, who was supposed to be looking out for him, called the phone I'd lent Steve, which he'd left in the kitchen. Phil says, 'Where is he?' 'No idea, pal.'"

By then, Smith was 250 miles away in Kent, along with the Woodworm kit Fairbrother had sorted out: "Three thigh pads and a couple of bats that he used for his first couple of seasons with New South Wales," says Sharp. Mum had listened to son's despair and immediately phoned a friend, Tony Ward, best man at her wedding and her old boss. "I wasn't even aware Steve was in the UK," Ward recalls. "The first I knew of it was when Gill phoned. I said, 'Put him on a train. Get him down here. I'll take care of it.'"

Ward scooped Steve up in London and ferried him to the offices of his wax-blending firm, Darent Wax, and from there to the Ward clan's traditional Friday evening rendezvous in the Farm House pub in the village of West Malling, outside Maidstone. Over more moderately gauged libations than had been the case earlier in the week, Ward told his new ward that he would be working over the weekend at Tonbridge RUFC's festival and that cricket talk was forbidden until Monday, at which point his options were spelt out: go home, return to Cheshire and see out his contract, or stay a couple of months with Ward, who would try and fix him up with some cricket in Kent. Having decompressed somewhat, Smith opted to stay put.

After smoothing things over with Grappenhall, Ward – a self-confessed "rugby man with no connection with cricket" – endeavoured to find his lodger some action, first speaking to some lads from the shop floor who played village cricket nearby for Horton Kirby. When credentials were sketched out, they sensed he might be too good for them and pointed Ward to another village team, Allington, who nobly informed Ward that Smith was too good for them as well. They suggested instead one of three Kent Premier League clubs: Bromley in Greater London, St Lawrence & Highland Court near Canterbury, or Sevenoaks Vine, around ten miles west of Ward's home. Thinking about lifts and logistics, about scratching the itch of the boy with ants in his pants and a Woodworm bat that doubled as a teddy bear, Ward called Sevenoaks' chairman, Gavan Burden.

"Tony offered us a free cricketer who, he said, was going to play for Australia one day," recalls Burden with a smile. "The problem was we already had an overseas player, Matt Wallis, also from Sydney, so I told Tony to bring Steve along but we could only offer him second team cricket." Bingo, thought Ward, who didn't see the problem: "Steve would have played in the fourths, done the teas, anything to be around cricket."

And so it was that the man who would become the finest Test batter of the following decade made his debut for 'the Vine' – not Grappenhall or Horton Kirby or Allington or Bromley or St Lawrence

& Highland Court – in a soft-boiled midweek friendly for its veterans side, Old Oaks, against Kent over-50s, in which he slammed 90-odd with such panache that Burden was soon alerting the Kent CCC coaches, including future England No.2 Paul Farbrace, who duly took a long look at him.

"He came home from practising at Canterbury with Kent one day and his fingers were bleeding," recalls Ward. "He mentioned he'd read that Shane Warne used something for it but didn't know what. I told him it'll be surgical spirits and witch hazel. His face glazed over, but we got some and his skin hardened up beautifully."

Smith's second outing on British soil was thus a three-day game for a combined Kent and Middlesex second XI against their Essex and Sussex counterparts, playing alongside a young Irish batter called Eoin Morgan, just back from his country's shock World Cup victory over Pakistan in Jamaica. Smith sent down 63 overs and scored 85 and 39, setting him up nicely for a competitive Sevenoaks debut – for the twos against their Blackheath counterparts in the sixth tier of the Kent League. Not the usual habitat for a 17-year-old emerging genius.

Blackheath racked up 366/4 from their 50 overs – Australian trainee teacher Peter Dean slamming 217* while 102 were chipped in by his unrelated namesake Christian Dean, whose father had been among the protestors who dug up the Headingley pitch in 1975 – an assault that saw the cherubic teenage leggie revert to bowling seamers for the last few overs of his 10-0-72-1. At tea, the visitors were feeling pretty content with their position; three hours later they were less so, having lost by seven wickets with 27 balls to spare, 'Smudge' plundering 185. Suddenly, the Sevenoaks committee had something of a headache on their hands. You didn't need to be fluent in Moneyball to spot Smith's talent. Selectors' heads were duly scratched, but loyalty to Wallis and league rules restricting teams to one overseas player meant Smith would remain with the stiffs. Not for long, however.

"You could see straight away that Steve was a different specimen: the way he fielded, how much time he had when he batted," says Sevenoaks' first team opening bowler Tom Parsons. "In the end, Matt just said, 'Look, this guy's better than me. He should be playing firsts. It's fine, I'll drop down.'"

Bumped up six rungs of the Kent League ladder, Smith began with a golden globe, lbw to Beckenham's Johan Malcolm-Hansen, an erstwhile Loughborough University colleague of Parsons, who claims his mate is "still very much dining out on that!" The following Saturday, there was a glimpse of 'Smudgemode' and a top-scoring 59, albeit in defeat to eventual champions Highland Court. The week then brought what turned out to be a final appearance for Kent second XI, Smith signing off with a blob at No.8, although one nicely landed leg-break provided a 15-year-old Sam Billings with a routine stumping. Murmurings of Smith's freakish abilities – and, of course, his British passport – had crackled along the cricketing grapevine from the Vine to The Oval, and Surrey invited him to play a few games, a sliding-door moment in an alternative history of the Ashes.

Before then, Smith punched out a 44-ball unbeaten 62 on his 18th birthday in victory over Bickley Park, the prelude to at least two or three shandies, while Ward had earlier presented him with a copy of *Wisden* to commemorate the occasion. "He just looked at me blankly. He was so wrapped up in the playing of the game that he didn't seem to know the culture or history. I said, 'Look in the back at the statistics. We expect to see you in there next year.'"

Seven days later he made a second KPL duck in four innings, nicking Gore Court's Kevin Jones into the hands of former Kent skipper Steve Marsh before he had the chance to face Martin McCague, after which came his Surrey IIs debut at Derby, bringing a pair of 46s and 4/100. The chocolate chequebook was readied. "Surrey were very aggressive," recalls Ward. "They wanted to know whether I was his official guardian and, if not, then I could mind my own business. He was far from home, temptation was thrown in his face, and it was the first time in his life he was making his own decisions."

It was still very much on his mind a day later when he plundered an 83-ball 92 for the Duke of Norfolk's XI against Combined Services at Arundel as 339 were comfortably chased down. His Sevenoaks skipper John Bowden, a teammate on the day, recalls Smith being wracked with angst over Surrey's proposition – which is to say, genuinely entertaining the idea of registering as an English-qualified player! – weighing up an offer that provided the sort of professional security that, at the time, could only be attained in Australia through a national contract. It was a thorny dilemma. Ward recalls Smith's parents being "outwardly fairly neutral about where he played, although you know they didn't mean it!" Bowden advised only that he listen to his heart rather than make calculations based on financial security. Smith thus chose the land of his birth.

But Surrey weren't going to give up that easily. Not when they saw him snare 6/14 against Kent IIs a fortnight later, sealing the game by trapping his chauffeur for the day, Tom Parsons, lbw with a googly ("That wasn't a fun journey home," confirms the driver), nor when they saw him launch five sixes in an 18-ball 46 against Essex three weeks after that. He looked handy, and all this midweek cricket translated into scores for the Vine, finishing what turned out to be a 10-game KPL stint with 48, 76, 23 and 41. Still, Bowden, the future all-time KPL leading run-maker, did outscore him in six of his eight games, in which the pair shared four 100-run partnerships.

When not playing, training, watching endless re-runs of *Home Alone* or being obliged by house rules to familiarise himself with the rudiments of domestic self-reliance (signature dish: chilli con carne), Smith would work eight-hour shifts packing boxes in the wax factory, spending some of his earnings "with a young crowd at The Farm House", recalls Ward, "where a young French barmaid took a liking to him, calling him 'Cricket Boy', but it failed to go anywhere". He would hop on Ward's tractor and happily mow his orchards – a more congenial vibe, no doubt, than feeling hungover in Will Sharp's Warrington box room – while also being permitted the occasional chaperoned spin in Ward's Austin Healey. After a hellish start in England, it had become an idyllic few months of gentle self-discovery for the shy and somewhat pampered kid from Sydney, steps toward adulthood made from much closer to his comfort zone.

Such was Smith's adaptation to everyday English life, he even skipped the game against that year's eventual national club champions Bromley (who beat Leicestershire's Kibworth by a single run due to the final ball being mullered straight to deep square leg, accidentally stationed in the wrong position). Instead, he attended his host's annual ten-band, 500-guest, back-garden charity music festival: Wardstock. While Sevenoaks were beating Bromley by 134 runs, Cricket Boy worked the bar all day dressed as a clown, photographic evidence of which remains under tabloidophobic lock and key. (When 'Sandpapergate' blew up, Ward recalls, "I had the *Daily Mirror* knocking on my door, demanding to speak to his grandparents!")

A couple of weeks later, Sevenoaks' serendipitous signing was saying his farewells, off on an Australian Institute for Sport tour of India, Ward having arranged his inoculations and flights. Surrey were aghast, and a representative turned up at Ward's house at eight o'clock on the morning of Smith's departure, contract in hand. "It was a fantastic offer, incredible for an 18-year-old," recalls Ward, "and they pushed quite hard. They even tried to get me out of the room at one stage. I told them it was my house and I'd be staying where I was. I said, 'Let him take it home and talk to his peers. If he likes it, fine.' They said, 'No, no, we'd prefer him to sign it now and if he doesn't like it we can talk about it.' I said, 'Well, it's not really a contract if it's negotiable after it's signed, is it?'"

And with that Smith was gone, contract untouched, head unturned, heart belonging to Australia, Surrey still owing him money, Woodworm bats going nicely. A few days later, the *wunderkind* was offered a three-year deal by New South Wales. After that – spoiler alert! – he pushed on quite nicely. Sevenoaks eventually finished four spots off bottom in seventh, to which Smith had contributed 11 wickets and 309 runs at 44.14, sixth in the KCL averages: a solid A-minus.

"His stats may not look spectacular but they were exceptional for an 18-year-old, first time in the country," says Parsons. "You can just see when someone's got something different about them, and with Steve it was obvious. He had so much time. And he could hit the ball wherever he wanted to, although I don't think any of us thought he was going to turn into a batter who occasionally bowls…"

* * *

The uncanny sensation felt by Smith's Sevenoaks teammates that they had witnessed a fledgling superstar would descend once more seven years later, when another Australian with an ostentatious leave-alone and what Martin Amis once described as "a touch of the severity that all natural ball players have" blew in. Twelve months before boosting the newly promoted Sandwich Town's 2014

Kent Premier League campaign, however, an 18-year-old Marnus Labuschagne had arrived on the Devon coast for a first bite of English club cricket. Plymouth CC's Mount Wise ground was situated on the Royal Navy base, a couple of solid slog-sweeps from waters through which the Pilgrim Fathers had set sail for the 'New World' in 1620 – an apposite piece of symbolism for a fiercely self-starting and adventurous cricketer who was still a long, long way from getting a foot in the professional door.

As anyone who has seen Amazon's fly-on-the-wall documentary *The Test* will know, and anyone who has watched him go about things on the field might guess, Labuschagne is restless bordering on the hyperactive – it wouldn't entirely be a surprise to learn that his parents occasionally used to fire a tranquiliser dart into young Marnus to hurry him off to sleep ("Oooh, Mum, that's a devilishly delicious delivery into the gluuutesssszzzzzzzz") – and sure enough a word-cloud of his Plymouth teammates' reminiscences has "bubbly", "energetic", "infectious" and "livewire" featuring prominently, as well as "dedicated" and "passionate". It is no easy thing for any overseas pro, let alone a teenager, to tip up at a premier league club and immediately set the dressing-room thermostat, yet Labuschagne quickly had the place bouncing to his beat.

"He used to cycle down to the club from his accommodation," recalls teammate Sam Stein, "and if someone asked him to roll the wicket or work behind the bar, there was never any hesitation. He couldn't do enough. He'd sit on the roller for two hours, hit balls for three. He had an incredible work ethic, immaculate standards. He was a class above, even at that age."

"He was the guy who you'd ask, 'Fancy getting to the ground at ten for a net?' and he'd say, 'Let's make it nine,'" adds middle-order batter Jake Luffman. "He was *that* guy. He might as well have built a bed in the changing room."

"He would hit thousands and thousands of balls at training," Stein continues, "but no one could ever get him out! I was our opening bowler and bowled at him for five months and only managed it once, nicked off on a Saturday morning before one of our games. He said, 'What have you done?! You can't get me out before I go and play!!' I said, 'Well, you control that, mate, not me!'"

For a club looking to kick on from their fourth-place Devon League finish in 2012, signing an 18-year-old was "a bit of a risk", adds Stein. Two games into the campaign, however, it looked a reasonably steady punt: Labuschagne began with 126* in a 150-run victory over North Devon, following up with 130* in a 146-run win on a bunsen at Bradninch. Opener James Toms, who scored a hundred of his own in the first game, was dumbfounded. "They were two very different pitches, two completely different styles of batting, same result: unbeaten hundreds. He just looked a different level to everyone."

Sometimes, however, Luffman recalls, Labuschagne's desire to be in the thick of the action was taken to ludicrous extremes. "There was a game against Exeter," he says, "when Marnus clipped one to square leg, who's caught him out, single figures, and he just stood there. Basically, he didn't want to be out, so wasn't moving until the umpire put his finger up!"

Still, this hyper-competitiveness would ultimately serve the team well, never more so than against powerhouses Sidmouth, champions in four of the previous five years. Labuschagne scored a sprightly unbeaten 87 to set up a fighting total of 221 and Plymouth were sitting pretty when the visitors slipped to 148/6 with overs running out, only for No.8 Scott Barlow to launch five sixes in 15 balls. "They needed six or seven off the last over," says Luffman, "and we were looking around for someone to bowl. Marnus always wanted to be involved: bat, ball, in the field, or just chatting bollocks at people. He just said, 'Give me the ball'. He was desperate to bowl. It got down to the last ball, two needed, Anthony Griffiths, an ex-Devon player on strike on 98 not out, and Marnus bowled a dot and went absolutely mental."

Whether Labuschagne's default effervescence was irritating or energising rather depended on which dressing-room you occupied. At Plymouth they adored him, says Stein. "He was so bubbly, always buzzing around, doing his fake throws, never shy of a word, always giving as good as he got. He'd always whizz the ball into the keeper. He just had a massive, massive enthusiasm for the game, and it rubbed off on everyone." In particular, Stein adds, opening bowler Rob Bennett was someone who benefitted from Marnus's chivvying and encouragement, "pushing him along and getting him in shape at the gym. Rob became a very, very good cricketer. He went as a net bowler for Australia at their tour match in Taunton and dismissed the likes of Michael Clarke and Shane Watson."

Occasionally, though, the pro's bulletproof bullishness would get the better of him. Take a now folkloric game in which Plymouth were pumped for a mammoth 366/3 in 50 overs by Budleigh Salterton, the future Surrey batter James Burke making 196 and ex-Gloucestershire all-rounder Bobby Dawson 94. "They were a good side," recalls Toms, "but they had lost every game at that point. They came off thinking they'd finally turned the corner; there was no way they weren't going to win this game. They were quite boisterous in their changing-room and we heard that in ours. Marnus calmly said, 'Guys, there's still a game to be won here.'"

An early wicket brought Labuschagne to the crease, and he cruised serenely to 42. "I'd bumped a couple out to the cover boundary," continues Toms, "and sauntered through for one. Marnus says – not loud or trying to be disrespectful – 'If it goes out there, there's two every time.' Next ball, literally, he pushed out there – 'Yes, two!' – and the guy picks it up and runs him out from the cover boundary. Direct hit. You can imagine their reaction!"

Toms anchored things with 130 – he would soon be scoring a hundred on debut for Devon – and Luffman smoked a 65-ball 115 as Everest was scaled, the Devon League's version of 'The 438 Game' with Marnus in the Jacques 'I think they're 15 short' Kallis role. It was a record total – for three months, at least, until Craig Overton's 154 against Torquay steered North Devon beyond it – and it remains a record run chase. A very lively night was had by all, although Labuschagne didn't really do mandatory post-match intoxication. "He didn't really need to," observes Stein. "Even without a drink, he was more buzzing than anyone else!"

Nevertheless, come fines night, his on-field performances obliged him to partake. "Anyone who'd done well had to neck this lethal punch concoction made by the older guys," explains Luffman. "He obviously had a lot of drinking to do, and we did make him do it! I remember coming upstairs about an hour afterwards and seeing him slumped in the corner holding a bucket, looking very much worse for wear." (He was, after all, there for an education.)

After that electrifying start, Labuschagne's scores inevitably fell away: three more half-centuries, three 40-odds, two 30-odds, and six sub-20 scores, including a couple of ducks. Still, Plymouth finished a creditable fifth and made the semis of both Devon Senior Cup and Twenty20, losing to Sidmouth in each, while Labuschagne managed 730 DCL runs, sixth on the list, at a far from shabby 60.83, to finish second in the league averages (Overton, who also made a 172, came top). There were also 18 wickets at 30.22, a figure just about kept under the luggage allowance by combined home-and-away figures of 8/37 against Bradninch. All in, a sizeable contribution.

Stein believes the teenage Queenslander "exceeded expectations" while Toms is adamant he could barely have done more for the cause: "If you study the stats, I think most of us had our best year that season. That's not a coincidence. That's because of Marnus, who had this infectious desire to pull everyone along. You'd be hard pressed to find anyone with a bad word to say about him in the whole of Plymouth."

* * *

While Marnus was making his waves in Devon, the man with whom he would share a Test debut five years later was busy galvanising another young team, 130 nautical miles or so east along the English Channel. Only, where the uncontracted Labuschagne was still trying to bootstrap his way into the professional game, Travis Head, 14 first-class appearances already under the belt, was cruising along a more green-and-gilded pathway. He had gone to the UK with five colleagues from the Australian Cricket Academy on a short-lived exchange programme for intensive training and occasional games with the Hampshire Academy. There were a smattering of other appearances – among them a couple of three-dayers for the MCC Young Cricketers, an outing for the Isle of Wight Academy, and a game against Kuwait for the league rep side – Head grabbing any opportunity that came up.

The ACA sextet shared a waterside apartment in Southampton and, after a lottery-style draw had assigned them their clubs, played competitive cricket in the local leagues at weekends. Ashton Turner went to Chichester Priory Park in Sussex, following Adam Zampa's stint there the previous season. Zampa took 35 wickets at 16, the fourth best leggie in the league averages behind Michael Munday, Josh Poysden and Mason Crane. Turner's fellow Perth Scorcher Ashton Agar went to Henley-on-Thames in the Home Counties Premier League – and, by July, into the Test side, scoring a world record 98 from No.11 at Trent Bridge. The other four played in the Southern Premier League.

Head had been drawn to play at Ventnor on the Isle of Wight, reputedly the warmest town in Great Britain and once the resort of choice for affluent Victorians seeking a dose of restorative sea air. Uniquely in top-flight English club cricket, this meant him catching a boat to get to his home games – a 30-minute ride across the Solent on the Red Funnel ferry. Unfortunately, these games would not be at Ventnor's charmingly peculiar and hyperliterally named Steephill Road ground – with its short square boundaries and velodrome-shaped outfield; where diminutive bowlers would come *under* the sightscreens – since it failed to meet SPCL standards. Premier League accreditation had thus been withheld, despite the club having produced a number of county cricketers, including Danny Briggs, Adam Hose, Steve Snell and David Griffiths.

Six times in eight years Ventnor had won the first division, and each time they were denied promotion. They were essentially trapped beneath the sort of glass ceiling found at the adjacent botanical gardens, into which Head had launched several sixes on his solitary competitive outing at Steephill, a T20 game in which he crunched a 54-ball 108. "It was carnage," says skipper Ian Hilsum. "There are probably cricket balls still being washed up on the north coast of France."

Ahead of the 2010 season, then, having once more secured their elevation, the club bit the bullet and moved first team home games to the brand new and well-appointed Newclose ground, just outside Newport in the centre of the island. They were immediately relegated, however, although bounced straight back up in 2011. In 2012, the year before 'Trav' arrived, they hoped merely to consolidate, and duly survived by the skin of their teeth. The week before he got there, with the team looking to kick on up the table, they had launched their campaign with victory over Totton & Elling.

Latterly used by Hampshire as an out-ground, the trueness of the Newclose pitch was perfect for Head's aggressive shot-making, and he would finish the season as the SPCL's leading run-scorer, starting with a brisk 44 against St Cross Symondians, albeit in defeat, an innings that impressed opener Olly Mills. "I remember him walking past me when I got out and me thinking, 'I'm a bit nervous for Travis here, his first game in England, he's probably going to be prodding around'. Second or third ball just disappeared over cow corner off Richard Logan, a ten-year county professional. 'Ah, okay, so he's not particularly nervous!' His self-belief really stood out. And his presence, which isn't a particularly tangible quality, but seeing it live you realised this person was going to do things."

A week later, the overseas gun was trapped lbw for a single by Lymington's Ed Freeman amid a pursuit of 175 that subsided from 126/3 to 162/9. However, Ventnor scraped over the line thanks to a pair of fours crunched through extra-cover from last man Mark Holmes – a publican with whom Head would pass many a lively evening – and the islanders set off on a run of four straight wins that took them to the top of the league for the one and only time in their history. Heady stuff. Trav contributed 142* against Bashley; 30 against Bournemouth, for whom his flatmate Alex Keath, soon to become a huge AFL star for Western Bulldogs, scored 116; and after that, in the first of the mid-season bloc of 120-over games, he made 77 in a demolition of Havant, champions in four of the previous six seasons. Before the celebratory *coldie* could be quaffed on any of these, however, Head had homework to complete.

"After every game, he had to fill out an in-depth report on how the game went, then send it back to the Australian Cricket Academy," recalls veteran middle-order batter Neil Westhorpe. "It stripped down batting into ten categories and he'd have to give himself a mark for each, with comments. So before he had a beer, he'd pull out his laptop in the dressing-room and do that. On Wednesday, he would Skype back about the game and how training was going. It was very hands-on and strict."

Ventnor's vertigo from looking down at the rest of the division inevitably saw fantasies of Head-powered glory start to form. Momentum was stalled, however, by a washout against Alton on the weekend of the Isle of Wight Festival, an iconic counter-cultural event played by the likes of Jimi Hendrix and Led Zeppelin in the 1960s and revived in the 2000s (headlined by Travis, of all bands, in 2005, the greatest Ashes summer of them all). "We all went along on the Friday night to see the Stone Roses," recalls Westhorpe, "but Travis stopped drinking quite early and got a taxi to my house, in Cowes. I didn't know he'd gone. We stayed another two or three hours, and I found him later, asleep on my doorstep, readying himself for the game the next day, which was abandoned after two overs, so we all piled into the minibus and back to the festival. That was a big night."

The next two weeks brought further setbacks, with defeats to Hampshire Academy – who winkled Head out for nine and five in their two encounters – and eventual champions South Wilts, where Glenn Maxwell had spent half the previous season, arriving from an IPL campaign with Delhi Daredevils to play T20 for Hampshire, but finding himself at a loose end as he hadn't been registered to play first-class cricket. Hampshire's former South Wilts swing bowler James Tomlinson hooked them up and 'Maxi' was finally rubber-stamped with SPCL registration at midnight on the eve of his debut, which brought a 24-ball 46 against the Academy but only 204 runs at 25.5 overall, grabby pitches and clubby dobbers proving kryptonite for Maxwellball.

Three games without victory had seen Ventnor fall back into the peloton at halfway, although Travis had now hit full stride, unfurling a mid-season sequence of scores that began with 48 (from 48 balls) against South Wilts, followed by 53 (48) in a winning draw against Totton & Elling; 82 (65) in a winning draw at St Cross Symondians; a 65-ball 93* in victory over Lymington, which all his colleagues consider his stand-out knock; 69 (68) in an abandonment at Bashley; and 58 (62) in a second win against Bournemouth. That's a six-game streak yielding 403 runs from 356 balls, at the end of which Ventnor sat in third place on 203 points, 19 behind Havant and 25 behind South Wilts, both of whom had to be faced in the run-in. Game back on.

"That Lymington knock was incredible," reflects Holmes. "Their opening bowler, Matt Metcalfe, is the Southern Premier League's all-time leading wicket-taker. He's a good mate of mine and had met Travis at the festival. Matt came in at tea that day, took off his bowling boots and said, 'That's it, I'm not bowling again. This guy's just too good!'"

"Metcalfe was 70 clicks and nibbled it," adds Mills, "the sort of guy who gets in your head when you try and play him properly. Someone like Travis was like: 'What's this?! This is going in the bush.' And it did."

These long-form games also saw Head's off spin being given lengthy airings – 81 overs in five matches – although not many of his colleagues were particularly convinced by an output that read 21 wickets at 29.9 by the end of the season, despite him later bagging 4/10 in a Galle Test. "I watch him bat in Test cricket and think, 'Fair play, I could see that'," reflects Mills. "But I watch him bowl and think, 'How on earth are you bowling in Test cricket?!' He bowled *runs* in the Southern Premier League!"

"He probably bowled a few more overs than he should have because of his runs, his status, his confidence," adds Westhorpe. "That bought him a few more overs, I think."

With four games left, Ventnor fancied their chances of making history, but an agonising two-run defeat to Havant coupled with a second abandonment against Alton all but mathematically killed their chances. They finished with second defeats of the campaign to both Hampshire Academy and, after Head had departed, South Wilts, which pushed them back to fourth place. Nevertheless, this remains their highest ever SPCL placing, a golden summer for the islanders bringing Head 733 SPCL runs from 14 cavalier innings at a strike rate of 99.59, about which skipper Ian Hilsum, never asked by the AIS for his input, was pretty succinct: "He was the most talented batter I've ever seen. He hit the ball harder, further and cleaner than probably anyone who's ever played in the league."

"Batting with him was great," reflects Mills, whose own Trav-infused mid-summer streak brought scores of 43, 139, 45, 140 and 85. "There was a total lack of micro-management or advice from him, which put you at ease. He totally trusted you and always pumped your tyres up: 'You're a gun and should be playing professionally,' things like that. He knew how to say things at the right times, small things that made you feel a million dollars."

But teammates were equally impressed by Travis the man, the thoughtful, self-deprecating nu-school Aussie whose retro 'tache belies his distance from the macho carapace of bygone eras. There was no posturing, and not much sledging. "He was a salt of the earth bloke," reflects Mills, "as good a mate with people in the fourths as the firsts. No airs or graces. He just saw himself as another member of the club."

"He was a great bloke in the dressing-room," adds Holmes. "The best overseas we've had by a million miles: great personality, played hard when he had to, and the best socially as well. He knew when to do it and when not to. If we'd won a game and there was nothing on the Sunday, he'd come out with us and usually be one of the stayers." But then, it was difficult not to be when home was a ferry ride away.

* * *

By the time Labuschagne returned for a second summer of English club cricket, he was still essentially an amateur targeting a first professional contract with Queensland. Having moved along the south coast to the highly competitive Kent Premier League for the 2014 season, he was thus absolutely determined to squeeze everything out of himself, adopting an ironically gluten-free diet while at Sandwich Town that saw him forego the customary teatime bread-with-filling for nuts and sweet potato. Marginal gains by marginalising grains.

Even someone as implacably chipper as Marnus could not realistically have hoped for as big an instant splash as those two unbeaten tons he had made at Plymouth. As it turned out, however, he trumped it, starting with 127 at Bexley, following up with 203* on home debut against Canterbury, then 83 against eventual champions Sevenoaks Vine. There were no wins to celebrate, but 413 runs in three hits – not to mention 141 and 127 in warm-up games – already had colleagues contemplating the KCL record for most runs in a season, which happened to be the 1,012 scored for Dover in 1992 by one Justin Langer.

Among Labuschagne's new teammates was the 37-year-old 2005 Ashes winner Geraint Jones, hired by Sandwich as player-coach having been displaced at Kent by Sam Billings. Jones was immediately convinced that Marnus was made of the right stuff, even if there were a few doubts about his leg spin. "They were filthy," he says, only half-joking. "The thing was, he just believed he could bowl and would always be badgering to get on. That was Marnus: front and centre. You always knew he was about."

There was the usual manic devotion to practice, too. Rory Smith, a 16-year-old second teamer fresh off his GCSEs, became the designated training partner. Over many long hours of mutual sidearms, Smith got an up-close view of a cricketer who stopped at nothing for a little extra edge. "He lived about five minutes from the ground," says Smith, "so on the way he'd sit down on one of the benches and visualise himself scoring runs that day. Most club cricketers get to the ground an hour before the start, and that's where their game starts. His game started as soon as he woke up."

As had been the case in Plymouth, Labuschagne was soon energising the whole team, even the saltier old dogs. "It was contagious," says Jones. "I loved it. For me, at the latter end of my career, maybe looking to have a quiet Saturday afternoon, having Marnus about, full of beans, was great. He'd also be doing the commentary when batting, the *oohs* and *aahs*. I work in a school now and there are loads of kids who'll do a leave-alone then shout 'No run!!', Marnus-style. They like the way he wears his personality on his sleeve."

Marnus opened the batting all summer with wicket-keeper Ryan Davies, who had recently been an England under-19s colleague of Haseeb Hameed, Matt Parkinson and Saqib Mahmood. The pro's blistering start had left him needing exactly 600 runs from 14 KPL outings to bag the record. The next game stalled the stampede, however, Labuschagne registering his season's solitary duck against eventual runners-up Lordswood, for whom England's Danish-born one-cap wonder Amjad Khan had earlier come in at No.7, at 60/5, and biffed eight sixes in his 100-ball 122, pushing the visitors up to 222, which proved 137 too many. Five fixtures down, no wins: Sandwich were in a dogfight.

Thereafter, Marnus locked into his high-summer groove: 61* against bottom side Bickley Park in a first win of the season; 73 at Blackheath, the following year's national knockout winners; 28 against big-spending Hartley Country Club; 20 against Bromley, poles sent cartwheeling by Dan Christian; 66 at home to Bexley, falling lbw to Shoaib Malik's brother Adeel; 69 in a win over Rob Key and Derek Underwood's *alma mater*, Beckenham; 81 in a two-wicket loss to Sevenoaks; and four at Lordswood in a defeat that plunged Sandwich into the relegation spots with four to play.

Labuschagne needed 198 runs for the record; more importantly, Town needed a win. This they managed against wooden-spoonists Bickley Park, Marnus caressing 50 before chipping a catch to former Surrey spinner Nayan Doshi, and the following week they welcomed leaders Blackheath, who were deprived of their two contracted players, Ivan Thomas and Daniel Bell-Drummond, while all the other sides had theirs available, about which Blackheath skipper Chris Willetts was "absolutely seething. We were top with three to play and ended up fourth!" Marnus made 114 in a crucial 93-run victory that lifted Sandwich out of the drop zone. He was relentless, insatiable.

Still, despite the long hours of Saturday-avo crease occupation, Jones recalls, "trying to get him to understand the etiquette of friendlies was challenging: you know, the idea that when you get to 100 you then have to give your wicket away was totally alien to him and took a bit of time to grasp." One Sunday he was told flat-out he wasn't permitted to bat properly, says Smith, "so he asked if he could bat left-handed and scored a fifty."

The penultimate Saturday brought him an 11th 50-plus score in 15 league innings and with it what remains the Kent League record. He fell for 16 on the last afternoon, but Sandwich had by then picked up the three points needed for safety, finishing one spot above the trapdoor: mission accomplished. The final KCL balance was 1,049 runs, although it's unlikely he bantered too much about it with Langer when he was handed his first Test cap in the UAE four years later – cap number 455, with co-debutant Travis Head given 454 – a Dubai *dayboo* attended by his practice partner from Sandwich, along with two team- and flatmates, Dan Evans and Matt van Poppel, all of whom found themselves in the huddle when the sacred baggy green was presented. Eat your heart out, Jarvo.

"We left work on Friday, flew overnight, spent Saturday exploring, then had dinner with Marnus and his family, even though it was the eve of his Test debut," recalls Smith. "Being there for the cap presentation wasn't intentional, though. There was a delay at the hotel in the morning as they sorted out transport to the ground for Marnus's, Travis Head's and Aaron Finch's families. There was a bit of a panic they wouldn't be there in time. Obviously they're not going to delay the start of the game, so as soon as we arrived, we got shepherded straight from the bus to the pitch. In the chaos, it was almost too much effort to send us somewhere else, so we went and stood in the circle as the three of them were given their baggy green. We watched the day's play, then flew home and I went straight from the airport to work in the morning. 'How was your weekend?' 'Oh, just a quiet one!'"

Marnus remains close friends with Smith, who has spent two stints chez Labuschagne in Queensland. "A couple of years later, after my A-levels, I went out to Australia to play cricket in Townsville," Smith recalls, "but really struggled for the first month, with it being my first time away from home. Marnus said, 'Come down and stay with us for a week' and literally two days later his Mum said, 'You're not going back. You're staying here.' So I lived with the family for five months, the most welcoming people you could ever meet."

Three years after that, Smith became a permanent cast member in Marnus's Instagram cricket reels, having headed back out to Queensland to play football. "My first day there was his first Test hundred, against Pakistan in Brisbane. Then Covid struck in the March and I ended up spending almost a year with him and his wife, mainly playing flick cricket in the house."

The depth of these bonds is testament to a player who left as much at his clubs, if not more, as he took from them. He remains in contact with friends in Devon, too, visiting the club in the lead-up to the 2019 Ashes while bossing things at Glamorgan. It was during that Ashes campaign, of course, that Labuschagne took ownership of the Aussies' No.3 spot, deputising as a concussion sub for his partner in quirk, Smith, who Sevenoaks say is always happy to oblige requests for signed memorabilia or tickets. Head, too, has been back to visit mates on the sleepy Isle of Wight, both prior to that 2019 Ashes and to perk himself up during a lean trot at Sussex a couple of years later.

For Sandwich and Sevenoaks, Plymouth and Ventnor, these were unforgettable summers, seasons to be hewn into the clubs' folklore

– lucking out with hungry young pups on their way to becoming outstanding big dogs of the international game. It says much that the future superstars remain so affectionately connected to those small chapters – those sporting and personal lessons in England's (baggy) green and pleasant land – in what are now their much bigger stories.

6

Mohammad Yousuf
at Bowling Old Lane, Pudsey Congs and Smethwick

On a chilly 11 May 2011, nine months on from the end of a glittering Test career and in the fourth game of a six-match early-season stint with Warwickshire, Mohammad Yousuf skipped out under heavy skies at Edgbaston, past the departing Jonathan Trott, to join Ian Bell at 78/3. It was a derby game, Bears against Pears in Division One of the County Championship, and although the visitors had lost four out of four and Yousuf had made 81 against them three weeks earlier, any sense that runs were there for the taking were tempered by the challenging conditions. Indeed, after winning the game by 218 runs, Warwickshire would be docked eight points for a substandard pitch and on the final afternoon of the season – after Jeetan Patel then Shivnarine Chanderpaul had replaced Yousuf in the overseas chair – they were pipped to the championship by 11 points, drawing at Hampshire as Lancashire chased down 211 in 29 overs at Taunton to end a 77-year wait for the pennant. Difficult as those overhead and underfoot conditions were, Yousuf ground his way to a half-century, then added another from 39 balls, finishing the day unbeaten on 108. Sheer class.

Two months later and five miles north-west, 'MoYo' would be making his Birmingham League bow, one of eight players from that West Midlands derby who turned out in the league that summer, which was not only one of the principal reasons for its strength – along with the Bradford League, arguably the toughest in the country – but also an example of the unique 'porousness' of cricket's strata, its commingling of echelons, routinely throwing international guns together with hardy amateur triers. Yousuf's Smethwick debut saw him dismissed for a single by a future Worcestershire captain, the 20-year-old Joe Leach. Thereafter, the player who five years earlier had scored the most Test runs in a calendar year would be knocked over for under 30 by Tom Lewis,

Paul Wicker, Gareth Williams and Usman Awan, none of whom ever played a first-class match.

Cricket is a space of criss-crossing pathways, unlikely encounters between players from disparate tiers, ocean cruisers passing dinghies in the twilight. One week you're swiping away for the stiffs, the next there's a spate of last-minute holidays and you're called up for the ones, amid whispers the visitors' pro might be quite slippery. While in most cases the intersection of your pathway through the game with that of the legend is from the stands, eyes on, occasionally it will be from the other end, pads on. Herein lies the magic. Legion are the weekend enthusiasts whose cricketing lives have thus come face-to-face with some all-time great or other, who have had their moment in the sun.

Criss-crossing paths through the firmament: greats stepping down, strivers reaching up. While Yousuf made his way to an imperious hundred at Edgbaston, Worcestershire coach Steve 'Bumpy' Rhodes was thinking about how to address his team's batting deficiencies. Watching on alongside him from makeshift changing-rooms at the City End while the new South Stand had its finishing touches added was a batter who had just come on Bumpy's radar and whose leftfield signing would be confirmed on the club's website the following morning, shortly after Yousuf was dismissed by Alan Richardson having added a single to his overnight score. "Worcestershire CCC is delighted to announce the signing of Adrian Shankar," cooed the statement. "The 26-year-old has signed a contract that will keep him at New Road until the end of the 2012 season."

"Adrian came to the club's attention during the winter," the press release quoted Rhodes as having said, "which he spent playing cricket for Colombo in the Sri Lankan Mercantile League. He was the leading run-scorer in the twenty20 tournament with an average of over 52 and also scored three successive hundreds in the longer form of the game. Adrian has the potential to develop further after his recent winter experiences and is keen to make an impact across all forms of the game going forward." It sounded promising, only none of it was true. First, Shankar was 29, not 26. Second, no such tournament had actually taken place. It was pure fiction, the fabrication of someone prepared to stop at nothing to be a professional cricketer. Even fraud.

Shankar had a first-class batting average of 19.2 from a dozen games for Cambridge University, significantly boosted by an innings of 143 against an Oxford attack described by his own coach as "unbelievably bad". The three years after graduation had seen him fail to average 30 for either Bedfordshire in the Minor Counties or Spencer in the Surrey Championship, while making 10, 41, 1*, 1, 2, 13, 6, 5, 14 and 12 in his sporadic county second XI appearances. And yet, ahead of the 2009 season, he signed a two-year deal at Lancashire – who thought he was 23, not 26 – albeit failing to break into the first team before being released. He did, however, write an inadvertently entertaining blog in 2010 for his bat sponsor, Mongoose, who would be major protagonists in the journey that culminated in a smiling Shankar posing for a photo with Rhodes, ink drying upon contract, pear upon his chest.

The previous winter, Mongoose had launched their long-handled, short-bladed MMi3 bat, a radical design for the T20 age, and the big-picture goal, quixotic as it was, was to crack the Indian market, throwing huge endorsement deals at IPL big fish Matthew Hayden and Andrew Symonds to help make it happen. In Shankar, Mongoose CEO Marcus Codrington Fernandez thought he had the perfect marketing vehicle, and duly had him finagled into the IPL auction for 2011. He then emailed Dermot Reeve, assistant coach at Pune Warriors, recommending a "top-order dasher who scored endless runs this year (after a life-changing experience in the spring changed his approach to batting). At Lancs this year, he has developed into a top-order firework display who is an elegant, wristy hitter of Indian descent. With an Indian passport, he can play as a local. He scores lots of big, fast runs, is totally destructive at the crease, looks like a film star, has the brains of a prof (captain of Cambridge Uni for two years) and is thoroughly charming. His stats on Cricinfo are dreadful (from before the life-changing experience) but he has caught the eye of franchises. I think he is the real deal. Name of Adrian Shankar. Read the article below featuring him. I get sent a lot of articles about him." Sincerely held views. Entirely false basis.

The plethora of glowing articles sent to Mongoose were all bogus, all penned by Shankar, documenting his fantasia of criss-crossing cricketing paths. Mongoose, too, were being played. 'Johan van Niekerk' reported on a "pop-up T20 tournament" in Rustenberg in which Shankar "lit up the ground with two scorching half-centuries", smashing Makhaya Ntini and Simon Harmer everywhere with "blurring hand-speed". An IPL auction preview from 'Morne Erasmus' reached them in which "ten picks with x-factor" were singled out, among them Jos Buttler, Eoin Morgan, Faf du Plessis, Dale Steyn and Adrian Shankar, whose "inexperience masks the pulsing raw talent in his grasp". As the auction approached, an article from 'Manoj Ramachandran' was pasted into an email – as always, *sans* link – detailing the branding push being made Adidas, Nike and Reebok to sign up the big Indian stars: "Shankar fits neatly into the mould of [Virat] Kohli and [Murali] Vijay – young, gifted and with an explosive game suited to entertaining the large crowds of the IPL. His brand appeal may be unparalleled, with an almost perfectly scripted combination of cover-model looks, an Indian father and a Cambridge-educated turn of phrase."

Among the few things Shankar shared with Mohammad Yousuf was that neither would ever play in the IPL, albeit for vastly differing reasons. Despite the buzz around him, Shankar and his *perfectly scripted combination* failed to make it through the IPL's rigorous vetting protocols – indeed, invited for trials at Rajasthan Royals, he chose not to attend, lest it *harm* his chances. Overlooked at auction, he headed to Sri Lanka, keeping his eye in on the off chance he might be picked up from the reserve list, lobbying Mongoose hard to this end. Eight days after the auction, an article by 'Johan Conn' reached Codrington Fernandez describing the shock of Shankar going unsold, particularly given "his brand value, which is something other players simply don't offer. Not only does he bat like Virat Kohli, but he would have the same appeal on posters and adverts around India with good looks and an infectious swagger." Meanwhile, 'Vijay Singh' reported on Chennai Super Kings drawing up a list of potential replacements should misfortune at the World Cup deprive them of their stars, with Shankar, apparently, a "ready-made replacement" if Mike Hussey's hamstrings were to go.

When reality dawned that the IPL dream wasn't going to happen, Shankar's efforts turned back to county cricket. Further correspondence reached Mongoose, supposedly from diehard county fans moved to push Shankar's cause, often after chancing upon some off-grid innings or other of his during their winter travels. The sockpuppets always supported counties with Mongoose-sponsored players on the staff, on whom it was suggested the CEO might lean: Marcus Trescothick at Somerset, Jim Allenby at Glamorgan, Gareth Andrew at Worcestershire. From Colombo, Shankar emailed Codrington Fernandez with three pieces of news: first, details of a 121-ball 153 made while losing a kilogram in weight in front of 10,000 spectators in war-torn Jaffna ("believe me there is no such thing as a media centre up there … we changed under a tarpaulin held together by two sticks"); second, rumours that Rajasthan's Paul Collingwood was having a knee operation after the World Cup ("I would have thought I am a like-for-like replacement for Collingwood in many ways, and substantially cheaper"); third, that he had been emailed by Steve Rhodes, "basically asking me what my plans are, etc. He said that a Worcester fan was out in SL watching the World Cup and saw me play and told him good things". Shankar explains the parlous situation of Worcester's finances and asks whether Mongoose could part-subsidise his salary, to help sweeten the deal.

Six weeks later, as Yousuf's blurring hand-speed hurried him to a century on that dicky Edgbaston pitch, his cricketing journey once more brushed past that of Adrian Shankar, who was up in the dressing-room watching the wristy maestro and enthusiastically telling Rhodes about his exploits in the 'Mercantile T20' for 'Colombo Reds', where he had apparently clubbed Rangana Herath for five consecutive sixes. Shankar may even have mentioned to Bumpy that he had played against the then Yousuf Youhana in 2003, making 57 for Cambridge against a Lashings World XI (for whom Sherwin Campbell opened the bowling) after Yousuf had fallen for 27, ct Shankar b Savill. Cruise liners and dinghies.

A day later, as Worcester's acting captain Moeen Ali struggled to 19 off 98 balls, the signing was made public. On day three, Yousuf made a 73-ball 68, the game's second highest score, and Warwickshire wrapped up victory on the Saturday while Shankar was opening the batting with the 16-year-old future Worcester staffer Tom Kohler-Kadmore for Evesham at Bromsgrove in the second tier of the Birmingham League, making four of an opening stand of 26 before nicking off to Mike Wyres. No shame in that. Three days later, Shankar made his Worcestershire debut at Lord's in a televised CB40 game, opening the batting with Moeen and bowled third ball of the match by Tim Murtagh for a duck. No shame in that.

The next morning he was playing against Durham (Collingwood was unfit), in what turned out to be the only County Championship match of this most curious pathway through the cricketing firmament. Almost five sessions were spent in the field as Durham racked up 587/7, after which Steve Harmison roared in to knock over Kidderminster Victoria's Matt Pardoe and Wellington's James Cameron. Vikram Solanki fell next, then Bromsgrove's Alexei Kervezee, and at 50/4 in came Shankar to face a fiery teenager called Ben Stokes. Somehow, he survived, adding 45 with Wolverhampton's Moeen Ali, who then fenced the returning Harmison through to the keeper in the middle of a torrid final half-hour, which Shankar nonetheless navigated alongside his fellow 'Gooser', Gareth Andrew, finishing unbeaten on ten from 60 balls. Here, in full, grisly Technicolor, was an example of that porousness of cricketing strata – only on this occasion it was someone playing way *above* their level, a head that had blagged its way through a hard glass ceiling for a look at the view and quickly succumbed to vertigo. "Harmison was bowling a decent spell," recalls Andrew. "As soon as the Durham boys saw [Shankar's] technique – he did not want to come forward and when he did it went over his head. He just looked so out of his depth. It was a bit scary. It was a bit embarrassing to be at the other end – they just took the piss out of him for half an hour."

It was to be Shankar's final act in first-class cricket. The following morning, he failed to resume his innings, feigning a knee injury during the fielding warm-up, the prospect of more Grievous Bodily Harmison too much to bear. Over the coming week, as a website purporting to cover the fictitious Mercantile T20 suddenly emerged, his story unravelled and the contract was terminated. Three weeks later, however, an email dropped in the Mongoose inbox with a 1,100-word article by 'Fatema Rajkotwala' bearing the headline 'Persecuted Shankar wanted by Kochi, Chennai', which among other things explained that its titular victim "had emerged on the radar when he thumped four sixes off a Shahid Afridi over at Fenner's when Cambridge University took on a star-studded Lashings side", a jazz-hat game in which Shankar had in fact made only 22 in 11 overs, with Yousuf yawning away in the covers and unlikely to have remembered it.

"One of Shankar's biggest problems," continues 'Rajkotwala', "is that his most eye-catching performances have come away from the glare of the media spotlight and official competition. When he was signed to play first-class cricket in Sri Lanka in February, he was suddenly siphoned off into the private Mercantile T20 league, as there was more interest in gauging his suitability for the Sri Lankan Premier League T20 in July. Shankar did not disappoint, but again the statistics have not been made official..." Finishing with a flourish, (s)he adds: "The most telling references come from two titans of the modern game, VVS Laxman and Shiv Chanderpaul, who played with him during his stint at Lancashire," which of course they didn't.

Mohammad Yousuf – who himself made two appearances for Lancashire in 2008, signing off with 205* in a Roses match, a couple of months before Shankar began trialling at Old Trafford – had little need to embellish his CV. His achievements were in the annals for eternity, notably the most prolific year of Test batting ever laid down: 173, 65, 126, 0, 97, 17, 14*, 202, 48, 38, 15, 192, 8, 128, 192, 56, 191, 102, 124. Aside from the obvious issue in the 190s, that's quite the run of scores: a grand total of 1,788 runs at 99.33. He had a Test rating of 933 points at the time, which is the 16th highest in the history of the game.

The week after Steve Harmison had shown Shankar how far out his depth he was swimming, Yousuf faced Durham in his farewell outing for Warwickshire – indeed, his final first-class match. He made a king pair, dismissed by Harmison in the first innings and Stokes in the second. No shame in that. Next stop, after a return to Pakistan for the Faysal Bank Super-Eight T20 Cup, was the Birmingham League. And as Mr Shankar could probably tell him, it would be no walk in the park.

* * *

Smethwick's signing of Yousuf had been arranged by Mohammad Akram, in his younger days a distinctly slippery pace bowler who made nine Test appearances, the last three of them alongside Yousuf, a fellow Punjabi 14 days his senior. Akram's career had wound down on the county circuit with Essex, Sussex and Surrey, and he had played five games for Smethwick at the back end of the previous season, the club's first in the top flight for a decade, helping them out of a relegation pickle.

"Firstly, it was a mission getting Yousuf over," says first team colleague Arif Mahmood. "Even though he was at Warwickshire, it was a different type of visa, so he had to return to Pakistan and then come back. There was quite a delay. Once he was here, he was very good for the club, as it lifted our profile. He was always willing to sign autographs. He was inundated with requests for photos from fans at the ground. Even when we went out to eat. And he was always pestered with the match-fixing questions, as this was the year after the no-balls at Lord's."

Twenty-four hours after Yousuf had completed his king pair against Durham, Smethwick were collecting a fourth defeat from four league outings. A bank holiday washout stopped the bleeding, after which they pulled off a shock win against third-place West Bromwich Dartmouth to give them a straw to clutch at, but by halfway they were rock bottom, 46 points adrift, and every team bar Moseley and Wolverhampton had at least twice as many points. Photos with the fans were great, but what they needed were runs and match-winning performances. Did late-career Yousuf have the appetite for a firefight?

Not according to his skipper, David Banks, a Birmingham League stalwart who had been on the staff at both Bears and Pears but who was now the wrong side of 50 and sitting on the sidelines after a shoulder operation, watching the team get beaten up. "He was a top player, but he didn't really want to play league cricket. He did want to be in UK for the summer, though. I wasn't sure why, but we understood that he needed to be here for some reason. He hardly practised – there was always a reason to be elsewhere – and he definitely didn't enjoy fielding drills. There was more going on than he ever let on."

The last game before the turnaround had brought a haul of -4 points after a six-point penalty for failing to notify the league of the result or submit a captain's report. A week later, Smethwick made it eight defeats from 12, falling to 97 all out after knocking over runners-up Wellington for 118. It was not a particularly buoyant atmosphere to come into – not a dressing-room to energise an ageing introvert who probably didn't want to be there – and Akram was little use as a carrot-wielding motivational go-between, says Banks: "He wouldn't be seen to challenge Yousuf in any way."

His first assignment was against reigning champions Shrewsbury and an attack led by Joe Leach and the elder brothers of ex-Pear, now Bears all-rounder Ed Barnard. "We turned up and there either wasn't a wicket or they'd not put much effort into preparing one," recalls visiting skipper Ed Foster. "Either way, I remember it being cut on the day of the game. It was pretty bad. Yousuf got one from Leachy that took off and he gloved it to the keeper. It wasn't the only ball to misbehave."

The brothers Barnard combined for 8/31 as Smethwick folded for 88 all out and Shrewsbury romped to a nine-wicket win. A week later, the much-vaunted new addition had reached ten when he chipped a return catch to Usman Awan in a 71-run loss at strugglers Moseley that cut them further adrift. Next match, Yousuf inside-edged an airy drive through to the keeper on 20 as Smethwick were rolled for 112, which Himley knocked off one down, with a cameo 33* for the prolific Wasim Jaffer, who had last crossed paths with Yousuf four years earlier, making a double-hundred in Kolkata in what remains the two teams' most recent Test series. The Saturday after that, Yousuf was caught in the covers for 27: another defeat. And in among all this he had managed a half-century in the Staffordshire Cup quarter-final, chipping left-arm spinner Matt Stupples to long on when set. Smethwick posted 227/9, but Stone skipper Richard Harvey's unbeaten hundred took his side home in the last over. "We just told Stupps to bowl as slow as possible, which he did anyway," says Harvey. "I don't think Yousuf had ever seen anything like it in his life."

"He never looked in any trouble but found ways to get out, often soft ways," says Banks. "We had words on a couple of occasions. It wasn't a big thing. I remained very friendly with him and have spoken to him since over food. I simply quizzed him about how motivated he was about playing and suggested that many world-class players had played in the league before him and performed how you'd expect them to. He didn't respond positively and asked one of our mutual friends to ask me not to put him on the spot in front of others."

With the season now in Houdini territory, Smethwick made their highest score of the campaign: 234/6 against West Bromwich Dartmouth, opener Faisal Shahid batting through for 104* and Yousuf making a Birmingham League best of 65. The visitors' openers, future Black Cap Jeet Raval and Kadeer Ali, Moeen's elder brother, made a dent in the target but Smethwick chipped away and the game went down to the last ball, which the No.10 clubbed for four to condemn Smethwick to a ninth straight league defeat. It was almost time to reach for the shotgun and put the ravaged body out of its misery.

Good vibes, then, for Yousuf's 37th birthday – a trip to Wolverhampton exactly one year on from his final Test appearance, *that* game at Lord's – and flickering candles were indeed blown out on another day to forget, Yousuf nicking Western Province quick Johannes Bothma to slip for 14. Moeen picked up 4/36 and a sumptuous 95-ball 100* as the 163-run target was reached without loss. Two days later, Yousuf top-scored with 61 against Knowle & Dorridge, but Smethwick were tumbled out for 142 and the 40-year-old ex-Bear David Hemp's 53* took care of the rest in another nine-wicket thumping. The misery was unabating. Next time out, they lost by 133 against Walsall, Yousuf caught at deep cover for a dozen while trying to whip Paul Wicker over the legside.

Mercifully, heavy rain after tea claimed the penultimate game, with runaway champions Barnt Green having racked up 290, and Yousuf's final act in league cricket was thus to try and smash Kidderminster's Gareth Williams through cover on the up while on five, only to feather another inside edge to the keeper. Having already beaten the outside edge several times, the triumphant bowler followed through with a chirp of "I move it both ways, mate!" Quite the way to bow out for someone whose batting zenith had touched the immortals.

The final ledger was nine defeats and one abandonment, bringing Yousuf 215 runs at 23.88. Mohammad Akram didn't fare any better: nine wickets at 53 as Smethwick finished 141 points adrift of second bottom. "Yousuf was a lovely guy but often just went through the motions," reflects Banks. "We kept on thinking 'today is the day' and, of course, it just didn't happen."

* * *

Put a high-grade touch player happy gliding and glancing and clipping 88mph bowling on Test pitches into the league environment – 22 yards of mint-choc stodge, some hyper-competitive 68mph dobber operating with a top keeper, alert fielders, decent size boundaries and a slow outfield – and throw in the potential challenge to the overseas pro's ego if they fail to dominate as expected, and, effectively, you have dragged an elite combatant on to alien, inhospitable terrain, like the US military in the Vietnam jungle with their rifles jamming in the humidity. This much Yousuf would learn during both spells of league cricket that bookended his mighty career. Not that he was a complete club-cricketing duffer, of course.

Long before the struggles at Smethwick, many years before the high-altitude international feats, Yousuf had spent two summers in the Bradford League, a 21-year-old yet to make a first-class debut brought over to Bowling Old Lane in 1996 by Babar Butt, himself a former pro at Birch Lane. This was a club for whom Yorkshire icons Martyn Moxon, Bill Athey and Darren Gough had played, but one whose glories were far in the rear-view mirror – a most recent title in 1978 and a county cup, the Black Sheep, the year after – a club where the volunteer base was eroding and whose health rested heavily on the shoulders of its "three musketeers": Michael Hope, Brian Clough and Geoff Hanson, who played alongside his two sons, Nigel and Martin, on Yousuf's debut.

Having flown through the night and been dropped off next morning alone at the ground by Babar, who had his own game to get to, the introvert with no spoken English was introduced to teammates ahead of his debut against a Pudsey Congs side led by former Yorkshire skipper Phil Carrick and also including a 19-year-old Matthew Hoggard on new-ball duties, the future ICC umpire Richard Kettleborough in the middle order, with VVS Laxman due to arrive the following week. Wrapped up in three sweaters, the man the *Telegraph and Argus* called "Yousef Yousana" compiled a high-class 117 out of 204/7, Hoggard with 0/42 from eight. Carrick was impressed: just as Laxman had been headhunted the previous year, despite averaging under 30 for a title-winning Hanging Heaton side, so Yousuf would be lined up for the following season.

Bowling Old Lane failed to win the match, however, as they would the nine after that, encompassing a first-round Priestley Cup exit at

Drighlington which brought a third 50-plus score in five innings. Before then, his 75 was not enough for a win against East Bierley and, after, his 126 was not enough to win at Saltaire, although the sparkle of these performances was lapped up by Bowling's hardiest supporters, "Walter and Dennis: two blokes who got many buses to every away game via many, many pubs," recalls the writer and Bradford League stalwart Dan Waddell. "I remember batting at Lightcliffe and saw them appear three fields away, from out of a herd of cows and with a bag full of cans. They started many singalongs, those two – the cows might even have joined in this time."

Those innings, however, were lone skyscrapers amid expansive low-rise suburbs, as Yousuf's Bowling season became one of strikes and gutters: in 24 league appearances, there would be seven single-figure scores and six more in the teens; two thirds of his innings failed to make it past 27. Another of the team's newcomers, Tahir Khan, who had stepped up from the Bradford Central League – "it was absolute chalk and cheese," he says – was run out without facing a ball in that Congs game after a rasping Yousuf straight drive was deflected on to the stumps, but it didn't damage the nascent friendship and the two soon became inseparable. Tahir ferried him to matches in his work van and even found his accommodation, a one-room flat above Shimlas restaurant, from where they would walk down the Great Horton Road toward the city centre to practise on tennis courts at Bradford University, Tahir roping in non-cricketing friends to act as ball fetchers. Yousuf became lifelong friends with Shimlas' owners and on his many free Sundays would tag along and score for the restaurant's team in the Quaid-e-Azam League, for which he was ineligible. The year before his own move to Bowling Old Lane, where he has since served as treasurer for 20 years, Haqueq Siddique scored alongside Yousuf at Brighouse, "and he didn't say a single word in five hours. Not one." With pay at Old Lane modest and his professional salary in Pakistan equally skimpy, the scorer's fee was a welcome top-up, as were his £3 per hour wages at the Royal Kashmir in Cleckheaton, slaving away in the kitchen but guaranteed a free meal.

Yousuf's 126 at Saltaire had nursed Tahir to a maiden Bradford League fifty, but the next four games saw Bowling Old Lane knocked over for 44, 102, 119 and 92, Yousuf's four hits bringing him just 34 runs – 25 of them at Yeadon, where they travelled with a single point in the ledger, which was still enough for them to sit above their hapless opponents in the table. Defending 102, Old Lane had their hosts in the mire at 51/8 only for Andy Marshall and Craig Thornton to haul Yeadon over the line. "He only made 25, but he had so much time it was untrue and you just knew he was going to make it," says Marshall, who added 20* to his 5/35. He wasn't the only bowler to make hay against Bowling: Windhill's nagging left-armer Neil Gill picked up 6/11 including MoYo for a second-ball duck; Yousuf was castled by Rooke for eight against Pudsey St Lawrence; and he feathered a catch to the keeper off Hanging Heaton's lively legend John Carruthers, who sent down 22-12-26-9.

And then, finally, in the middle of June, as Paul Gascoigne was twisting Colin Hendry's blood at Euro '96 en route to that 'Dentist's Chair' celebration, Bowling Old Lane won a game. The vanquished foes were Spen Victoria – four years earlier, home to double-centurion Test debutant Vinod Kambli and his regular training partner at nets, Sachin Tendulkar – who posted a middling 226/6 from 50 overs, with the big wicket of ex-Yorkshire all-rounder Chris Pickles, the league's most feared hitter, snared by another newcomer, Amjid Khan.

In the return match in August, the teenage Amjid – 15 years later the bullish eponymous protagonist of the 'Shabash Khanie, Lad' chapter in Harry Pearson's *Slipless in Settle* – had further success against 'Chris Pick': "I went in and didn't have a care in the world. I hit Pickles for a six into the car park and I just remember Yousuf stood at the other end, smiling. You've just upstaged a future Test player and he wasn't bothered. You've brought over an overseas and paid them the big bucks and some of them might have been taken aback that you've outscored 'em, but Yousuf just gave encouragement."

Back in June, however, still to taste Bradford League victory, Yousuf had his usual tea – a fried egg sandwich lovingly cooked by Howard, who the team knew as "the tea lady" – then headed out to knock off Spen Vic's target, finishing on 128* with Tahir chipping in 47. Joy unbound! Jubilation! But it would be another ten games before the pro raised his bat, another 49 days before Bowling won again – against Saltaire, with Yousuf chipping in 45.

The following week, they knocked over the previous season's runners-up Windhill for 77 and the great escape seemed on, but they could muster only 71 in reply, Mark Bradford picking up the prize Pakistani scalp for 16 in his 8/14. Yousuf then made 110 in a thrashing of rock-bottom Yeadon but the goose was already cooked and by the time of his farewell appearance against Farsley, relegation had been confirmed. Chasing 220, Yousuf was run out for 65 and the Old Lane came up nine runs short, which neatly summed up a season of dependency and despondency. A total of 894 runs at 38.87 left him 15th in the batting averages. Top with 1,253 at 65.95 was VVS Laxman, whose Congs team had let the title slip through their fingers on the final day. Big shoes, then, for Yousuf to fill.

* * *

Pudsey Congs in 1997 were a club still finding their feet in the Bradford League, to which they had been elected ten years earlier after a peripatetic history in various lower-level neighbouring competitions. But they were on the right path, winning £132,000 of lottery funding that summer to improve facilities at the Britannia Ground, where Herbert Sutcliffe had started out. Indeed, the beginning of the 2000s would see them put together the most extraordinary run of success in the league's history, winning five straight titles before the calamity of a runners-up finish in 2005, when they had to content themselves with a third Priestley Cup in four years and a fourth Black Sheep Yorkshire Champions Cup in five. In among it all were two trebles for a team boosted at times by Rana Naved-ul-Hasan and a gaggle of contracted players or ex-pros, including 19-year-old junior product and future Yorkshire, Essex and Northants offie James Middlebrook, Notts' Gareth Clough and Yorkshire's Vic Craven, but whose heartbeat were the "five musketeers": skipper Matthew Doidge, Yousuf's agent Babar Butt, Neil Gill, Andy Bethel and Gary Brook. The sharp end of the Bradford League was a good environment to hothouse the skills of a future great, extremely tough semi-pro cricket, no restrictions on how many were paid and a gaggle of gnarly local legends looking for his scalp.

Of that team, only Middlebrook was at the club when Yousuf arrived, along with Carrick, Kettleborough and Hoggard – a prolonged crossing of paths that would later see them face off eight times in Tests, with Hoggy only once taking Yousuf's wicket, in the last of those games: the forfeiture at the Oval in his *annus mirabilis*, when Yousuf already had 128. Congs were eight rounds into the league campaign by the time Yousuf swept in for a debut at Baildon, now with two first-class appearances under his belt. Three wins, two abandonments, two losing draws and a heavy defeat to cross-town rivals Pudsey St Lawrence – in which Derek Randall had played for Congs, run out for 12 – represented an underwhelming start. After introducing him to his new teammates, Carrick promptly told a flabbergasted Yousuf he was batting No.5. He was skittled for 22 by veteran offie John Marshall, then went up to open on his home debut against Brighouse, caressing a classy 75* in a nine-wicket win. Another victory at Spen Victoria left them sixth at halfway, and Yousuf's 99* next time out prompted a hard push over the second half of the campaign for that elusive maiden title.

The pro's job was simply to make runs. He was seen on match days only, with his accommodation far out of town. "Yousuf was living with his uncle in Colne, in Lancashire, as his uncle wouldn't let him stay in Bradford due to racial tensions," recalls Congs' then secretary, Derrick Reason. "This meant him travelling on match days to Keighley by bus, and I picked him up there along with my friend Michael Knight to make sure he got to the ground for the start of the match. This made life difficult for me and Michael, as the last bus left Keighley at 8:30pm, so we sometimes had to arrange for a taxi if the game overran."

A taxi was needed next game, a tense draw at champions East Bierley, who hung on at 186/9 in pursuit of 229. Earlier, Yousuf had been trapped lbw for 45 by legendary Bradford League all-rounder Murphy Walwyn, who had arrived from St Kitts in 1970, aged 14, soon making a first-team debut alongside Roy Gilchrist, who gave the youngster his first bat, and in 1979 helping the club win the National Village Cup. Walwyn would play in a record 13 Priestley Cup finals and is one of only two men to have taken two 10-fors in the Bradford League (the other is SF Barnes), but it is his fabled smiting that made the biggest ripples, 'Murph' a seven-time winner of the league's coveted fastest-fifty award, the swiftest of them taking 14 minutes.

Congs were in good nick, then, and the next game brought Yousuf 81* in victory over Windhill – for whom Liam Botham's chip-off-the-old-block cameo 25 included 22 in four balls of Carrick – pushing his average up to 111.66 and his team into fourth. A routine win over bottom side Drighlington followed, Congs then skittling new leaders Undercliffe for 93 in another. They were up to third, nine points off top and six behind their lordly neighbours and next opponents Pudsey St Lawrence, the club of Len Hutton (and Bumpy Rhodes), champions seven times in the previous 22 years and, at the time, the Black Sheep's most successful side.

It was a must-win game, decent crowd on, as edgy as it gets, advantages keenly sought. "It was an infamous game," recalls Saints' skipper Chris Gott. "We turned up and their groundsman had doctored the wicket. It was a brand new pitch but there were two holes at each end. They had tried to rough it up for Middlebrook and Fergie [Carrick] but their groundsman had made an arse of it and scraped two big holes on a length. There were words said beforehand and we nearly didn't play."

The 45-year-old Carrick's reputational heft – a former Yorkshire captain with over 1,000 wickets and 10,000 runs in the first-class game – won the day and the game got started, with Hoggard close to unplayable as he decimated the top three, knocking over Ian Priestley for one, Ashley Metcalfe for two and seeing off James Goldthorp for three. "We'd complained that the wicket was unfit," adds Gott, "then Hoggy broke one of Goldthorp's fingers after hitting one of the holes. The umpires bottled bringing us off. I was furious because it was the day before we played the Priestley Cup final."

The rot was stopped by overseas pro Pierre de Bruyn and teenage Yorkshire staffer Gary Fellows, but Carrick nipped them both out to leave Saints in trouble at 60/5, effectively six. They were saved from humiliation by a counter-punching 73 from 80 balls from Gott, a three-time winner of the prestigious Learie Constantine Award for the league's best all-rounder and the man who, six years earlier, became the first and still only Bradford League player to hit six sixes in an over. This '97 summer would also see him, for a fifth straight year, lead the BCL rep XI to Yorkshire's inter-league crown. The steeliest of competitors.

Saints had 172 to defend, but were without 20-year-old spearhead Paul Hutchinson, called up for a Yorkshire debut against Pakistan 'A' and busy collecting match figures of 11/102. He was a big miss, although Congs were without their reliable opening bat, Colin Chapman, keeping wicket in the same game. Carrick opened in his place and was first out at 25, clearing the stage for Yousuf, who made his way serenely to 30. "He looked absolute class," says Gott, "then smashed a straight drive off Pierre de Bruyn, who pulled off a diving stop and threw the stumps down at the batter's end, like Roger Harper did to Graham Gooch." A middle-order wobble offered Saints a sniff at 130/6 but Middlebrook's 52* ensured a huge six points and local bragging rights, untempered by the pitch polemics.

Back-to-back wins against the top two had left Congs level with the neighbours and nine behind Undercliffe, who then lost to Windhill the following week, giving Congs the chance to pull within three with five to play. Without the frippery of bonus points to complicate things – six for a win, four or one for a draw – the pitch at Hanging Heaton was expected to be spicy, particularly with the pacey Carruthers in the middle of a four-year run that brought him 331 wickets, topping the divisional charts each season. Sure enough, Congs were shot out for 110, although the most significant strike came from Scargill, who removed Yousuf for a duck. The 20-year-old Hoggard also found conditions to his liking, however, and snared five cheap wickets. At 54/7 in iffy light, there seemed only one winner, but Gary Scargill and Jason Bird stood firm to condemn Congs to defeat.

The final nail in the coffin came a week later at home to Baildon, when Congs were thumped by nine wickets. Yousuf made a composed 46 but his failure to kick on again exposed the team's vulnerabilities, particularly when the pro offered them nothing with the ball. Set a target of 163, the visitors lost only one wicket thanks to 106* from the free-spirited Richie Robinson, second on the all-time BCL run charts and these days making Headingley's Test pitches as Yorkshire CCC head groundsman. Hoggard's figures were 7-0-60-0. "I just remember Yousuf having so much time and poise," says Robinson, "the complete opposite of my frantic swishing! Hoggy was quite raw at that stage. I told him at tea that I'd have him out of the attack in four overs. I didn't quite manage that, although I did treat Phil Carrick with the respect he deserved!"

Yousuf signed off with 73*, 11 and 23 in three victories as Congs again finished second. A respectable tally of 522 runs at 58 left him top of the league averages and the recipient, as had been Laxman, of the WH Foster Memorial Award. Five months later, he was making five on Test debut against South Africa in Durban. "He tried to drive Allan Donald on the up through cover, first ball, and played and missed," recalls his old comrade, Amjid Khan. "I texted him after the game: 'What on earth were you thinking, Yousuf?!'"

* * *

Since converting to Islam in 2005, Yousuf has been back to Bradford on a number of occasions to give religious lectures, life's path crisscrossing with old acquaintances. He remains friends with the owners at Shimlas and enjoys their famous chicken doner. One summer Saturday in 2019, Amjid was getting a lift home after a match for the Old Lane, making his way up Great Horton Road past Shimlas, when he spotted his old teammate heading to the restaurant, unaware Yousuf was in the UK. He told the driver to swing round the roundabout and double back. They pulled up across the road so that Amjid could say a quick hello before Yousuf embroiled himself in whatever he was doing. Amjid jumped out and skipped across the road, calling his friend's name. The two men clasped hands and hugged, then Amjid noticed that the driver was on his shoulder, eager to meet the legend. "He'd left t'car int middle o' road, he's so excited to see him! He's left t'driver's door open. I said to him: 'What you doing? Get t'car out o' t'road!'"

Among Pakistan's great batters, only Javed Miandad retired with a higher Test average than Yousuf. None came close to his peak ICC rating of 933 (Javed's high watermark of 885 sits next). He was a *bona fide* superstar and the temperamental opposite of Miandad – a low-ego genius who let his wrists do the talking. "With Yousuf," adds Amjid, "it was never 'you come up to me, I'm the big fella here'. No. No matter who he's with or what he's doing, he'll always come straight over and put you at ease. That's what I've always liked about him: his humility and graciousness."

Aside from the odd admonitory text message, the pair lost touch for a few years after that summer at Bowling Old Lane. But Amjid remained friends with Babar Butt and in September 2002 headed out to Lahore with him, visiting family. On his bucket list was a visit to the Gaddafi Stadium, which he had never seen, so he asked Babar if he could arrange it. Across the city they drove to an empty concrete bowl where an overzealous security guard refused to let them pass through the tunnel to have a look at the pitch, the stands, the ghosts of great cricketing feats: Qadir's 9/56 and Inzamam's 329. Babar gave the spoilsport his best spiel. "He said, 'Look, he's a tourist who's come six thousand miles. Give him his memories before he goes back.' So I go through to the edge of the ground and as I'm looking around a car comes through the tunnel and someone gets out. 'Amjid, *bhai*'. I turned round and it were Yousuf. I'd not seen him for six years and was surprised he'd remembered my name."

The pair embraced, Yousuf lightly scolding Babar for not letting him know Amjid was in town. A few days later, Yousuf took Amjid and Babar out for a *desi* dinner at The Village, picking them up from a friend of Babar's where Amjid was upstairs telling the two cricket-fanatic sons that Pakistan's No.4 batter would be round in a few minutes to take them out, none of which was met with much credence. But this was no Johan Conn or Morne Erasmus flight of fancy. "I said to Babar: 'Do us a favour. Text Yousuf and ask him if it's okay to bob inside for five minutes and say hello t'kids.' I told them what was going to happen but they still didn't believe me. When the doorbell rang they answered it and were totally shellshocked. That was Yousuf; things were never too much for him."

A few days earlier, before dinner plans had been hatched, Amjid would be afforded a much better sightseeing tour of the Gaddafi than he had imagined possible. "As it happened," he recalls, "I was dressed in tracksuit bottoms and trainers. Yousuf said, 'Do you fancy having a net?' My eyes lit up. *Come on!* Yousuf sorted everything out with security, then some local club bowlers came down. Young lads. I thought it was just going to be us, then five minutes later I see a big Toyota truck pull up and Wasim Akram gets out. Another car pulls up and it's Inzamam. Then Saeed Anwar turns up, although he wasn't netting. I'm in cuckoo land now. So I end up netting with these legends for a couple of hours on one of the side wickets at the Gaddafi Stadium. Amazing experience."

Yousuf would finish with a Test average at the ground of 93.75, which was almost exactly four times higher than he managed during his half-cocked struggles in the Birmingham League. "I'd seen very good league players, good first-class players and some international players," says Amjid, "so I asked Yousuf what the big difference was: 'how do you take that step up?' He paused, then told me that playing league cricket was harder than international cricket. I was confused. 'What do you mean?' He said the pitches made it harder and often with the bowlers you didn't know what to expect, whereas in international cricket you knew where the ball was going to land."

Perhaps Amjid, then, a good enough bowler to once take 100 wickets in a season for Daisy Hill in the Bolton Association, had an ace up his sleeve as he measured out his run-up at the Gaddafi. Perhaps he fancied his chances. "I'd love to tell you I got him out, but it was 30 degrees and the wicket were an absolute road. Not one ball seamed. Not one ball swung. He middled absolutely everything."

7

Chris Cairns / Ryan Harris
at Bacup / Lowerhouse

An asterisk. A caveat. A qualification. A long shadow cast from the future over the unforgettable glow of a long-ago season in a small Lancashire mill town. Or maybe not, since a reputation is in the eye of the beholder, and for Chris Cairns's teammates at Bacup the memories of that ride through the 2006 summer cannot be reverse-engineered by whatever followed. Whatever followed.

Before the dark clouds rolled in on his life – a name dragged through High Court libel cases in which close friends testified that he had tried to recruit them for match-fixing schemes, then a triple-whammy of health scares within a year: a heart attack, a spinal stroke during surgery leaving him unable to walk, then bowel cancer – Chris Cairns had been the square-jawed, tousle-haired poster boy of New Zealand cricket, an all-action all-rounder known for launching stadium-clearing sixes and, during spells of attitude-streaked briskish fast-medium, sending down a devilish slower ball learnt from Franklyn Stephenson at Nottinghamshire. Had he been born ten years later, with his prime years aboard the Twenty20 juggernaut, he would have left an even mightier on-field legacy. There was plenty of Hollywood about it all, nonetheless.

The big, handsome, charismatic former New Zealand vice-captain played 62 Tests, producing five hundreds and *Tist bist* figures of 7/27. There were 215 ODIs, among them the 2000 Champions Trophy final in Nairobi, the Black Caps propelled to a first ICC tournament success by Cairns's Player of the Match-winning 102 as India's 264 were chased down with two balls to spare. He was a *Wisden* Cricketer of the Year in 2000 – when sitting 11th in the Test batting rankings and eighth in the bowling, indisputably the world's top all-rounder – and five years earlier won the Walter Lawrence Trophy for the English season's fastest hundred, a 65-baller against Cambridge University. When he retired, he had hit more sixes in

Test cricket than anyone else. A scary proposition for club bowlers, no doubt. *Cairns*: his name means 'stones'.

Little wonder, then, that when the 35-year-old agreed to play the 2006 season at Bacup – six months after his final ODI appearance, two years on from bowing out of Test cricket with match figures of 9/185 at Trent Bridge – the Lancashire League website called it the storied old competition's "biggest signing since Allan Donald", who had propelled Rishton to the title ten years earlier. The signing was something of a happy accident, with Bacup's enterprising committeemen reading about his retirement and dropping a speculative line to Notts, whose director of cricket, Mick Newell, visited the town and told them Chris was keen to play some cricket among the civilians. He had spent the 1991 season at Cockfosters in the Middlesex League, and he had watched on as a young boy as his father, Lance, in the midst of accumulating his 43 Test caps, had been a stalwart pro in the North East, representing Durham in the Minor Counties Championship while playing for Whitburn in the Durham Senior League and then Bishop Auckland in the North Yorkshire & South Durham League, using his shoulderless Newbery bat to hit the ball even further than Chris would, if with a little less elegance, not least when winning Player of the Match as the Minor Counties XI won a first ever game in the Benson & Hedges Cup, turning over Mike Procter's Gloucestershire at Chippenham in 1980.

Cairns Jr was following some illustrious company in the pro's seat at Bacup, none more so than Everton Weekes, who adapted so well to club pitches that he churned out 9,069 runs at 91.6 across seven seasons at Lane Head between 1949 and '58 (unavailable in 1950, George Headley deputised). His final year brought the club's fifth outright title, with another following in 1960 courtesy of Roy Gilchrist's 126 wickets. There followed a 40-year drought – taking in eight highly productive years of Roger Harper – which was ended by a run of three straight titles inspired by Australian internationals Adam Dale and Shaun Young, after which, perhaps inevitably, came a downturn, with fourth, fifth and 12th-place finishes leading into the 2006 campaign.

Cairns missed the first game of the season, with his old Notts colleague Charlie Shreck, the genial 6' 7" Cornishman, deputising manfully against Burnley, taking 5/40 in a 46-run victory. It would be June before they won another league game, however – 42 days during which Cairns embedded himself firmly at the heart of things. He was costing the club around £20,000, which teammate Tim Farragher reckons would be "about twice as much as any other pro in the league", although Cairns would go out of his way to put as much back into the club as he could – and not only on the field. He organised Shreck as sub pro; he pulled the shy and retiring Graeme Swann up to Bacup for a sportsman's dinner, with all proceeds going to the club; and he was "always happy to put his hand in his pocket in the bar", recalls the team's 41-year-old keeper-captain John Chapman, "and never frightened of spending his money, unlike a few pros we had, who wouldn't give a door a bang".

Cairns introduced himself to the team at Thursday night nets, among them the 43-year-old all-rounder Terry Lord, who was "ready to retire at the end of the 2005 season, as I'd started to become a hindrance in the field. It was about time I hung my boots up, but after we'd signed Chris I felt a new lease of life." The pair would get on like a house on fire, bonding initially over their shared love of a flutter. Lord took an easy £20 off Cairns over the subject of Don Maclean's 'American Pie' – "I got him to sign the note and kept it in the cabinet" – which was far from the most remunerative wager they cooked up that year. Cairns also leant on Lord for advice about local accommodation. "He said, 'I'm looking to rent a house'. I said, 'Well, what do you want to pay?' He said, '£2,500 a month'. I rang the wife and said, 'Pack your things, we're moving house!'"

In the end, Cairns found a place in Cheadle, just off the southern sweep of Manchester's M60 ring road, about 50 minutes by car, enabling him to attend practice when other commitments allowed, among which was a full programme of games for Lashings and a handful of appearances for MCC. His first formal duty at Bacup was to cut the ribbon on the new two-storey players' pavilion, from the veranda of which his colleagues watched him come perilously close to a debut golden duck against Enfield, inside-edging a ball from Neil Holmes onto his back pad and just past leg stump. He went on to score 51 before being bowled by the former Lancashire stalwart Bernard Reidy, although not before wowing everyone with what would become his calling card: the enormo-six, the sort that prompts thoughts of getting the local glazier on speed dial and beefing up the insurance. "I'd never seen a more effortless six in my life," recalls Farragher, "a little flick and the ball was still rising as it cleared the houses on the other side of Greensnook Lane. It was six on any ground in the world. You realised right then that we had a world-beater."

Indeed they did, although he only managed one wicket as Enfield breezed past the 161 target, the future Proteas opener Alviro Petersen with 86 of them. In fact, it would take Cairns several weeks to get into his stride with the ball, that winless 42 days bringing him only 15 wickets in nine outings – among them a further two defeats in the league, to Todmorden and Ramsbottom; three washed-out league encounters, one without starting, the other two rearranged for later in the season; a two-run loss to Tod in the first round of the Worsley Cup; a win over Crompton of the Central Lancashire League in the first round of the Inter-League Trophy, exited via a bowl-off in the second; and a seven-wicket defeat to Haslingden in the first of four T20 group games, all played in June, all lost.

The reasons behind the early-doors bowling barrenness depend on who you ask. For Chapman, it was a case of "trying to bowl too quick on wickets that weren't going to generate a lot of pace, although he did his homework and changed". Farragher had a different view: "Sometimes he was just too good for players – either too quick or he moved the ball too much. Batsmen often weren't good enough to get edges." When they were, the chances weren't gobbled up with the same efficiency Cairns was used to in the professional game. "No one in the slips could catch the ball," recalls veteran opening bat Peter Thompson, himself part of that beleaguered cordon. "He only came in off six or seven paces, but he was still quick. We were dropping two or three slip catches a game. He ended up bringing these special gloves to practice and we did two hours of slip-fielding practice. It did help, to be fair. That was Chris: always helping out and trying to make us better. He wasn't an 'I don't need to practise' sort of guy. He came up when he could. Even though he was a superstar, he never acted like one."

The wickets might have been relatively scarce yet Cairns put together a consistent run of early-season scores: 47 in the Worsley Cup exit and 83* against Crompton; a top-scoring 36 in the first T20 loss; 51, 51 and 20 in the three league defeats, although his best effort wouldn't count to the finally tally, coming in an abandoned and rescheduled game at Lowerhouse in which one of his four sixes smashed a window in a terraced house behind the scorebox before stumps were pulled with Bacup sitting pretty on 142/1 after 33 overs, Cairns on 52* and Thompson 59* after his partner Paul Gallagher had retired hurt following a blow to "the groin region" from Lowerhouse's unheralded Australian heavy-ball merchant, Ryan Harris, who sent down a dozen whole-hearted yet wicketless overs.

Bacup were second from bottom as the league campaign hit June, although Farragher says the team "weren't too concerned. We knew Chris was a world-class all-rounder who could win a game with bat or ball from almost any scenario, so we did fancy ourselves. We just couldn't find the right formula – batting order, bowling partnerships, slip cordon – but there was always a belief we'd click and get on a roll."

Central to that conviction – with the big Kiwi's pedigree a given – were the all-in attitude and galvanic presence they discovered in those early weeks. "Once we got to know the man," says Chapman, "we realised he wasn't coming for an easy ride. Everyone knew they had to up their game, big time." This was not a message Cairns conveyed through *Any Given Sunday* style rallying cries, says Farragher: "It was more just his demeanour. He expected plenty from us in the same way we expected a lot from him." Things were about to click.

* * *

Ryan James Harris. You may remember him from the time, first ball of an Ashes innings, he sent down to England's redoubtable rock of an opener a delivery so wildly careening that it really ought to have been pulled over by the cops and breathalysed – a delivery that, immediately upon leaving the hand, seemed destined to receive a throaty, tone-setting "areas, Ryno" from the Aussie cordon-chorus as it thwacked into keeper's gloves; a delivery that, halfway into the business part of its journey, began to curve menacingly in toward AN Cook's pads, probing for any small failure in balance, any leaden footwork; a delivery that, upon contact with the cracked-concrete

WACA soil, hit the perfunctory seam on that tomato-red Kookaburra and decided to take a different route to the England captain's oft-impregnable castle, nipping away coquettishly toward the middle stump; a delivery that, already close to unplayable and not yet done with its extravagances, then decided, somewhat gratuitously, to swing even further away from Cook's bat and zero in on the outside part of the off bail, finally breaching the fortress in an act of blitzkrieg insurgency. All at 140kph. *That* Ryan Harris. The brawny Aussie Everyman whose bricklayer physique and no-nonsense approach to the crease – the run-up of a protective uncle barrelling across a suburban street to hurl himself into a sprawling pub brawl started by his now heavily outmanned nephew – belied the delicate tradecraft in those fingers, the artisan reliability of that wrist. The late bloomer whose five commanding years in the baggy green yielded a Test bowling average of 23.52. That fella.

Twelve years before this ballistically improbable offering – cricket's first truly *cubist* delivery – back when he was struggling to stay on the park let alone hold down a place in the South Australia team (indeed, he was on a rolling one-year contract there), Harris had signed for Lowerhouse, founder members of the closed-shop, 14-club Lancashire League and 111 years without winning a single senior trophy, a pain all the more acute for cross-town rivals Burnley's successes (13 league titles and six Worsley Cups, putting them third on the aggregate trophy list behind Nelson's 29 and East Lancashire's 31). Even their inferiority complex had an inferiority complex. By 2003, however, with stalwart ex-batter turned chairman Stan Heaton getting to grips with the junior set-up – eventually yielding a production line of colts with the 'House in their hearts – and Dave Wren taking care of the Moneyball overseas signings, the geological sedimentations were starting to shift.

It was Wren who collected Harris from Manchester Airport on a miserable mid-April evening in 2003, his second stint of English club cricket after a season at Gerrards Cross in the Thames Valley League in 1999, where he scored 600 runs at 75 and took 34 wickets. "I asked Dave how he'd found me," Harris explained to the club's lockdown podcast in 2021, "and he started telling me the research he'd done, the people he'd spoken to, how I'd gone in this game and that game. I said: 'Fuck me, you know more about me than the

South Australia selectors!'" This may not have been too far from the truth: the 23-year-old Harris had played just seven first-class matches for his state and his dozen wickets had cost him over 40 apiece.

Lowerhouse and their new spearhead lost the first three games – New South Welshman Greg Mail taking them for a ton on the opening day, East Lancs scoring 300 a week later, Enfield sub pro Franklyn Rose's 7/40 knocking them over for 89 the day after that – and Harris had picked up a moderately concerning 4/168 across those games. Thankfully, two nerve-unjangling wins followed, Harris's 85 anchoring the chase against Ramsbottom before he then put together an heroic 111* as Todmorden's 140 was hauled in, seven down, with four balls to spare. All in the garden was looking rosier. Well, not quite all: Ryno's combined figures in those two games were 1/101, leaving his Lancashire League bowling average at an ugly 53.8. The batting? That was 94.66, although, recalls teammate Joe Beneduce, "he was a bit of a shit-or-bust merchant when he first came over".

It hadn't taken Harris long to settle into life at Lowerhouse, warming to its underdog yapping, adapting to the clubbie cycle of weekend hair-loosening and chucking a good chunk of change back behind the bar, although he was often eager to spread his wings. "He did love 'The Circuit', as he called it," says Beneduce, "and was always keen to, uh, get out and see what the local area had to offer. With a face and physique like that, plus an Australian accent and Australian confidence, he was often successful in his endeavours..."

Harris was not, by his own admission, the model professional at this stage, certainly not one to observe strict nutritional programmes, and when not hitting Burnley's nightlife, his drinking companions were usually first team skipper Matt Hope and committeeman Tony Woodworth, briefly a professional footballer with Burnley and latterly a policeman who lived a short stumble from the club, which became Harris's regular crash pad. "After matches," says Hope's brother Jez, a veteran seamer in his penultimate year with the first team, "Matt, Ryan and Tony would often be found sitting on the bench at the end of the street at one or two in the morning, eating large doner meat pizzas. Tony even had one named after him at Planet Pizza: the Tony Woodworth special. Sometimes, him and Ryan would go to Planet Pizza, order it, then go home, fall asleep with the door open and the delivery man would walk in the open door and leave it on the table, where they'd find it in the morning."

If this boozy bonhomie wasn't enough to fully endear Harris to the flintier-souled Lowerhouse members, who still dealt in the hard currency of wickets and for whom six poles in six weeks just wasn't going to cut it, then the next match alone would sear him forever into the club's folklore. It was the derby game against Burnley – think Glasgow, with a dash of Istanbul – into which Lowerhouse went with their hopes (Jez, Matt, various prayers for deliverance), their hard-to-shake inferiority complex and their bullocking Aussie quick with zero Burnley baggage. "The Burnley games were our cup finals," says Beneduce. "In previous eras, they'd rubbed our noses in it quite a lot. By the time I'd started playing in the first team in 2000, it was drilled into us that this was a game we had to win."

With the previous few Lowerhouse pros having been batters – Matthew Mott, followed by South African internationals Martin van Jaarsveld, Jon Kent and Jacques Rudolph – they now had someone who could throw a few haymakers. "Even though we didn't win many games with Ryan," adds Beneduce, with a hint of Walter White, "we didn't get bullied. We were the bullies."

The game didn't start too well for Lowerhouse, with Harris, opening, nicking off for two and the two leading amateur batters, Chris Bleazard and Johnny Finch, knocked over for single figures by Burnley pro Pierre Joubert. Thereafter, the innings never got going, stumbling from 31/4 to 60/6 and 95/9, although the last pair managed to chisel out 18 precious runs. Harris then charged in with the new ball, but it was his partner, Kamran Farooq, after a week spent trialling with Kent second XI, who made the breakthrough, gleefully accepting a return catch from Burnley skipper Ben Law. Joubert and the 16-year-old Jonathan Clare, later to play for Derbyshire, steadied the ship, nudging the score up to 29/1, slowly drawing the neighbours' sting, at which point, the game already starting to slip away, Harris intervened.

"Joubert dropped the ball into the gap at midwicket and set off for a single," recalls Beneduce. "Ryan, in his follow through, dashes across in front of the batsman, slides and picks up the ball one-handed, then gets up and spins in the same motion and throws the stumps down at the bowler's end, Joubert a yard short.

It was breathtaking, a ridiculous piece of athleticism for a guy on one leg, although we didn't know that at the time." How's that for commitment from the pro! The cocktail rush of adrenaline and testosterone was so potent that Matt Hope followed the South African all the way off and almost became embroiled in fisticuffs. Meanwhile, out came Andy McLeod, met with a chirp of "he's got a head like a cuckoo clock: it can go off at any minute" from Jez Hope. McLeod's first act was to watch Clare's stumps uprooted by a pumped Harris: 29/3.

It was tense, tetchy, attritional. Bruises were administered, castles defended, anxious laps paced out. At 48/3 Harris punched two more holes in the home batting, a pair of caught-and-bowleds, including McLeod, but Burnley refused to fold and edged up to 72/6, with Matt Hope thinking about giving his pro a breather. "I told him to eff off," recalled Harris, "there was a game to win". And so on he bowled: 12 overs, 14, 16, 18 – "you literally could not get the ball out of his hands," says Beneduce – and still he charged in. "He threw himself into every ball," says Jez Hope. "Our groundsman used to say he'd never seen such deep footmarks on the outfield as with Ryan. They were craters." Ryno by name, rhino by nature.

Another bang-bang for Harris left Burnley in the mire at 78/8, but No.9 Dave Connolly dug in and found an ally in Steve Holden, and at 95/8, 19 needed, the game got squeaky. Holden holed out off Jez Hope, but the last pair took the score on to 109: just five more wanted. Hope had three balls remaining in the 47th over, with No.11 Graham Lalor, on his 18th birthday, off strike and awaiting Harris's last trip to the well, now 24 overs deep. Instead, Connolly went for broke – the six that would win the game – and launched Hope out toward long on, where Bleazard steadied himself under the ball – "it seemed to take an eternity to get there," recalls Beneduce – and safely pouched the catch. Whereupon, some light cavorting may have ensued.

Harris, big heart still pounding, trooped off with his 24-11-39-5 and a place in Lowerhouse legend secure. The post-match was on the rowdy side, understandably. "The wall between the home and away dressing-rooms at Burnley is paper thin," says Beneduce, "and they'd have heard every bit of our celebrations. Every game that we won was heightened because we weren't used to winning much. But we were desperate to get better and desperate to bloody as many noses as we could, so maybe it was that attitude that Ryan liked."

The flipside of an inferiority complex can often be a superiority complex, and once the underlings start refusing to accept their place in things, the psychological shock can take some getting used to. Sleeves kept buttoned down for the routine butcherings can take a while to be rolled up for the brawl. "I think they disliked us more than we disliked them, especially once we started to compete with them," asserts Jez Hope. "They'd enjoyed ridiculing us. The supporters would be on top of us, hundreds and hundreds of people. Once we started to get pros like Ryan, things changed."

A week later, Ryno crashed 75 against Colne, the prelude to another unbroken match-winning spell, initially energised by the sight of the visitors' combative opener, Jeff Ellis, coming out without a helmet. "Everybody in the league knew about Ryan by this stage," says Beneduce. "Somebody said, 'Jeff, are you sure?' He just said, 'Yeah, I don't wear helmets'. So Ryan just went for him. One ball hit him on the inner thigh and knocked him over. The sound he made as it hit him was sickening."

"Ryan built up a real head of steam and hit Jeff on the shoulder," recalls Hope. "He still wouldn't put a helmet on, and got a bit arsey when Ryan suggested he needed to get one on. Ryan turned to me and asked for my thoughts: 'Can I carry on bouncing him?' I didn't see a problem. The next one that hit him flicked off the side of his head and went for four leg byes. Still no helmet. It was one of those moments that was funny, but when you were also hoping he didn't get seriously hurt."

"I did go a bit far," Harris recalled. "Me being young, and a bully, you have to try and hit him in the head, don't you? I said, 'I'm going to fucking kill you'. Coming out without a helmet – it was like him saying: 'I don't respect you'." Ellis was dismissed for eight, caught behind while fending one off his face. Colne skipped up to 104/1 before Harris broke through again, then bulldozed the rest to finish with 8/59 from 20.4 overs. When Lowerhouse crushed Accrington a week later, Bleazard's 106* sweeping him into the league's 10,000-run club, they had five straight wins and a growing belief that 111 years of misery might finally be put behind them. But there was a problem. Harris had only managed 0/31 from nine uncomfortable overs. He went to see a doctor and was diagnosed with osteitis pubis: inflammation of the groin. A session with the physio got him back on the park the following Saturday, but he could only get through a dozen ginger overs, and that was it. Done. "He was absolutely devastated," says Hope.

With their Aussie spearhead back home, Lowerhouse were forced to scrabble around for subs – Marcus North and Asif Mujtaba were among ten deputies – and finished in seventh place. The following year, however, with 'two-metre' Peter Fulton as pro, it finally happened: a first ever trophy, the Worsley Cup. Chasing 310 in the semi, Bleazard made a match-winning 107 off 91 balls using a bat given him by Harris, following up with another ice-veined ton in the final, carried from the field on his teammates' shoulders and into immortality. A year later, with current Australia head coach Andrew MacDonald as the hired help, the 'House won their first Lancashire League title after a 113-year wait. Deliverance.

For Harris, it was bittersweet. "I was filthy that I wasn't there," he reflected. Although delighted for his friends in Burnley, he had desperately wanted to be the guy to end the heartache. There was unfinished business. And when injury kept MacDonald from returning in 2006, Harris jumped at the chance.

**

There's nothing like a derby match to jump-start a spluttering season – provided you win it, of course. For Bacup, heavily fancied for the 2006 title yet sitting above only Burnley in the table after the season's opening skirmishes, the early-June jaunt west down the Rossendale valley – through the gritstone outcrops, the gorse, the light-seeking copses – already felt like the approach to a fork in the road: 'Bacup Road', by the time they reached their destination.

"The away game at Rawtenstall is what every Bacup player looks for first when the fixtures are released," says Tim Farragher. "We call it the Colosseum. There's always a good atmosphere and the crowd feels right on top of you. Bacup are a well-supported club anyway, but spectator numbers were up for Chris. People came from far and wide." It would be a day to remember for Bacup's young batter.

Jesse Ryder and Martyn Evans at New Brighton; an unusually shy Ryder in front of the pavilion; **Rohan Kanhai** at Ashington; **Lance Gibbs** at Whitburn; Kanhai with the Ashington first XI

Watsonians in 1976; **Kim Hughes**, David Bell and **Terry Aderman**, July 1981; Watsonians in 1980, Masterton Trophy winners, with Alderman back left

Richie Richardson with the Durham Senior League XI after the 1985 President's Trophy win; Richardson at Blackpool in 1992

Tynedale chair Bill Charlton catches up with ex-pros Courtney Walsh and Kelvin Williams, joined by Gateshead's **Richie Richardson**; the Blackpool skipper Tony Hesketh welcomes Richardson; Thames Ditton's Oliver Turnbull welcomes the same man almost 20 years later

Marnus Labuschagne with Geraint Jones (*Dover Express*, Brian Green); Labuschagne cuts during his double hundred (*Dover Express*, Will Evenden)

Marnus Labuschagne with Sandwich Town (*Dover Express*);
Steve Smith batting for Sevenoaks Vine on debut;
Smith in the field; enjoying life at Tony Ward's

Travis Head bowling at Ventnor's adopted Newclose home; on the charge at the Steephill ground; Ventnor were early pacesetters (all Dave Reynolds)

BRADFORD LEAGUE: Top trio covered by just one point

Pace duo lead the way in Heaton win

by DAVID MARKHAM
T&A Reporter

Only one point separates the top three clubs as the First Division title race intensified over the weekend.

The only one of the top three to win were Hanging Heaton who had a comfortable eight-wicket home victory against Saltaire.

Pacemen John Carruthers and Dave Watts each took five wickets as Saltaire were dismissed for 111. Opener John Whittle then led the way to victory with an undefeated 56.

This win leaves Hanging Heaton only one point behind joint leaders East Bierley and Windhill. Bierley who were three points ahead at the start of play had to settle for a one-point draw at Bradford and Bingley.

Opener Craig Cockshott (77) and Yorkshire second team batsman Bradley Parker (50) shared a second wicket partnership of 116 as Bingley totalled 219 for seven.

Bierley lost in-form opener Dermot McGrath caught behind off Richard McCarthy for 0 and with all the struggling after opener Graham Higgins and Andrew Bairstow both fell at 36.

Murphy Walwyn (41) and Ryan Robinson (69no) raised their hopes in a fourth wicket stand of 93 but when Walwyn was out Bingley's target proved beyond them.

Windhill drew level with Bierley after taking four points from a drawn match at Pudsey St Lawrence. Neil Nicholson top-scored with 67 in Windhill's total of 214 for seven and Pudsey finished 73 runs short with seven wickets down.

The day's top scorer was Farsley's 19-year-old in-form opener Richard Gould with 140 out of his side's 257 for six at home to Bowling Old Lane who settle for a point at 168 for five.

Elsewhere in the First Division Mark Wakefield scored 82 not out and Glen Yates took six wickets as Idle beat Pudsey Congs while Yorkshire Bank eased their position in the relegation zone with a five-wicket win over fellow strugglers Yeadon.

Baildon consolidated their position at the top of the Second Division with a nine-wicket home win against Keighley thanks to a fine all round performance by Andrew Walker who took five wickets and then scored an unbeaten 61.

Bankfoot moved into equal fourth place with Cleckheaton after beating them by 'eight wickets. Martin Kelly took eight for 34 as Cleckheaton collapsed from 47 for 0 to 122 all out.

TABLES

DIVISION ONE

	P	W	L	D4	D3	D1	Pt
East Bierley	12	7	2	2	0	1	51
Windhill	12	7	2	1	1	1	51
Hanging Heaton	12	8	2	0	0	2	50
Farsley	12	6	2	1	0	3	43
Pudsey St Law	12	5	3	2	0	2	40
Pudsey Congs	12	5	4	1	0	2	38
Idle	12	5	4	1	0	2	36
Saltaire	12	5	4	0	0	3	33
Undercliffe	12	2	2	4	0	4	32
Bfd & Bingley	12	2	4	4	0	2	30
Spen Victoria	12	2	4	3	0	3	27
Yorkshire Bank	12	2	6	0	0	4	16
Bowling Old Lane	12	1	9	0	0	2	8
Yeadon	12	1	10	0	0	1	7

DIVISION TWO

	P	W	L	D4	D3	D1	Pt
Baildon	11	9	0	1	0	1	59
Brighouse	11	8	2	0	0	1	49
Drighlington	10	7	2	2	0	0	47
Cleckheaton	11	6	2	1	0	2	42
Bankfoot	11	6	2	1	0	2	42
Lidget Green	10	3	4	3	0	1	31
Hartshead Moor	11	3	3	2	0	3	29
Lightcliffe	11	3	4	2	0	2	28
Salts	11	3	6	2	0	0	26
Keighley	11	3	5	0	0	3	21
Great Horton	11	1	6	1	0	3	13
Ben Rhydding	11	1	9	0	0	1	7
Mann Mills	12	0	8	0	0	4	4

OFF FORM: Bowling Old Lane's prolific scorer Youssef Yousana could only make 26 in a one-point draw with Farsley

Head and the side before his only appearance at Ventnor's Steephill ground (Dave Reynolds); **Mohammad Yousuf** in the *Telegraph & Argus*, 1996

Ryan Harris in action for Lowerhouse (Nigel Stockley)

Chris Cairns too hot to handle for Bacup (Nigel Stockley)

Cairns celebrating with his Bacup teammates (Nigel Stockley)

Muthiah Muralidaran in the *Leicester Mercury*;
Abdul Qadir with Hanging Heaton in 1982 (*Telegraph & Argus*)

Qadir bats in the Masterton Trophy final as Kirkcaldy 'keeper Steve Watson looks on; **Imran Khan** at Wakefield in 1977

Imran showing his skills for Wakefield

Dennis Lillee with Bryan Knowles; **Joel Garner** at Littleborough in 1976; and at Moorside in 1992; **Mohammad Asif** at his rustic home of Ashcombe Park (*Leek Post & Times*); the Endon players congratulate **Morne Morkel** after his 9-54 at Eccleshall (*Leek Post & Times*)

Endon's Morkel bowls at Ashcombe Park's Asif (*Leek Post & Times*); **Michael Holding** hits out against Burnley at Rishton; **Andy Roberts** meets Holding in the Martini Trophy (with Graham and Barry Knowles in background)

John Chapman won the toss and had a bowl, but the score was 96/1 before Cairns took the first of his four wickets. The run-rate never got away from Bacup, however, and on a compact ground they were happy enough chasing 210, even though Rawtenstall's last pair denied them the two bonus points for bowling out the opposition. The home innings was anchored by 63 from Andrew Payne, once an England under-19s teammate of Michael Vaughan whose promise seemed confirmed by 51* on debut for Somerset as an 18-year-old swing bowler, but only three more first-class appearances followed and he eventually returned to his home club. After Payne knocked over both openers cheaply then the big fish Cairns for four, Bacup were under the pump at 62/4. Up stepped Farragher to play "the innings of my career", an unbeaten 99 as the visitors squeezed home in the last over. It was the start of an 11-game streak that brought eight wins and no defeats. "When Chris gave a goodbye speech at the end of the season," Farragher recalls, "he pinpointed this game as the turning point."

The following weekend Cairns delivered a couple of 'this is why they pay me the big bucks' performances, starting against Church with a first five-for. Farragher's off spin took the other five, a career best 5/29, leaving Bacup a chase of 224. With Paul Gallagher's 74 anchoring things, Cairns came in at 85/2 and smote 93* to secure a maximum 12 points. Rather than drive back to Cheadle, he stopped over for a few fraternal beers and lodged with Peter Thompson, heading to the ground early for the visit of Haslingden, eager to keep the bandwagon rolling. "He energised everyone," Thompson says. "He was fit as a fiddle and such a breath of fresh air."

Haslingden opted to bat first, restricting Cairns to 2/55 from 16 overs as they posted 197/3, the league's 47-year-old all-time leading run-scorer Mike Ingham with 72* and Kiwi pro Tama Canning 46. A middling score looked a very good one at 27/4 with the top four making a PIN of 5453. Out came Terry Lord to join Cairns. "Other pros barely communicated," he recalls, "but Cairnsy talked you through every situation. When I came in, he says: 'Lordy, they're on top now but in a few overs they won't be. I'm going to take the attack to them and get this bowler off.' He must have taken 30 off the next three overs. So then he says, 'Right, we're on top now, the field's back, start pushing singles.' It was incredible. I'd not really experienced that before, when someone's talked you through what was going to happen before it actually did."

Together they compiled a match-swinging partnership of 94, but 121/4 soon became 156/8 as Canning picked up four quick wickets. Out came another veteran, Chapman, and he hung around long enough for Cairns's 111-ball 144* – 16 fours, six huge sixes – to get them home. Lord's 16 was the next highest score. "I've played a lot of cricket, but that Haslingden innings would have to be the best I've ever seen," says Lord. "They must have wondered what happened," adds Farragher. "But for one player, we'd have been soundly beaten. He had a plan for every situation. He upped the gears when he had to. He was in total control. Canning took six for 60 and made 46 and yet looked unfit to lace the opposition pro's boots, that's just how good Chris was."

Among those left awe-struck were Bacup's three most famous (and daftest) supporters, the hyper-partisan and incurably irreverent Roy Marshall, Clive Eastwood, and Chapman's ex-journalist father Gordon – better known throughout the league as Roy of Rossendale, Clive of India and Gordon of Khartoum, whose typical match-day ritual involved a mid-morning departure and pit stops at several pubs before settling in for an afternoon of genial barracking. The stories are legion. "Peter Cockell, a policeman who played for Nelson, dropped a skier on the boundary once," recalls Thompson. "One of them shouts, 'How do you expect to catch criminals when you can't catch cricket balls?' The place erupted with laughter."

The trio had a special fondness for targeting the opposition pros, although this wasn't always appreciated by the Bacup team. On one occasion, Aussie quick Matt Nicholson's pace-bowling credentials were queried at length, sticks of rhubarb mentioned, prompting an extension of the run-up, a bending of the back and James Cunliffe's off stump literally being snapped in half. On another, journeyman Bajan tearaway Jerry Kirton was remorselessly barracked with "Come on Kirton, pull yourself together!" which may or may not have contributed to Bacup losing the game. During a Worsley Cup semi against Haslingden in 1990, they had some fun at the expense of Aussie left-arm paceman Mike Whitney. "Referencing Whitney's curly Afro-style hair they began their wind-ups by calling him 'Whitney Houston'," recalls league historian Brian Heywood. "That was until he dropped a caught and bowled, which inspired the immortal line: 'He's not Whitney Houston, he's Whitney Useless'." Whitney failed to see the funny side.

Interventions were not restricted to the verbal modality. One afternoon, with Bacup's cup tie against Church slipping away, Clive of India commandeered a child's three-wheel scooter and buzzed the ground, zipping straight across the pitch and causing a stoppage that interrupted the momentum of the game, by design or otherwise. Church promptly lost a wicket and never regained control. "They were bonkers, but they were funny with it," adds Thompson. "They never swore and were never abusive. The three amigos. Everyone always asked about them, home and away."

Cairns had been cemented in the affections of Roy, Clive and Gordon by his Haslingden masterpiece. "They worshipped him," says Chapman, "and, to be fair, Chris loved all three of them to bits as well." As much as the string of stellar performances he was to reel off, it was Cairns's attitude that endeared him to everyone at Bacup. He threw himself into the club and, palpably, gave every last drop of effort to the cause. He applied himself with the bat and was aggressive with the ball, happy to get in the opposition's faces, happy to test out the middle of the pitch. 'Go hard or go home' was his mantra. As if to underscore the point, in Bacup's next completed game Cairns took 8/35 as East Lancs were blown away for 78, bouncing out the visitors' sub pro Mohammad Farrouk first ball, after which he headed off on a midweek MCC jolly to the Netherlands, his club teammates already having begun to rev him up for the next game, which promised to be spicy.

Bacup's skipper the previous summer was medium-pacer David Ormerod, whose 18 years at the club had brought him 876 league scalps. He had won the Lancashire League bowling prize for most amateur wickets in the title-winning seasons of 2001 and '02, retaining it in '03 and '04, and eventually finishing with seven awards, the joint record. "He was a great bowler," says Lord, "unplayable on soft wickets. He used to get the pros out for fun." His captaincy had not been universally admired, however – the 2,579 deliveries he sent down for a bottom-three side was over 1,000 more than the rest of the amateurs combined – and midway through the 2005 season he was told by the cricket committee that he would not be kept in his post.

Suspecting political manoeuvrings, Ormerod returned to his first club, Accrington. "He was a great servant of the club but there was a bit of ill feeling when he left," Lord adds. "Cairnsy certainly got himself pumped up for that one." He may have had a helping hand.

Ormerod had told the *Lancashire Telegraph* for its preview that he was "going into the game with some trepidation but I'm certainly looking forward to it… I'm sure there'll be a bit of friendly banter knocking about". Not so much, it turned out, recalls Peter Thompson. "He was one of our legends. We'd won the league with him three years running. He came back and the first ball he faced nearly took his head off." The bowler of that delivery was Cairns, of course, and the score at the time was 53/8. It was soon 53/9, Ormerod gloving a catch behind to his successor. "As he walked off," recalls Chapman, "Chris said, 'I think you picked the wrong fucking team, mate'. He proved later, though, that he hadn't: he captained them to the double!"

Cairns finished with 4/15 as Accrington were hustled out for 63. Everything was going to plan, but dark clouds had started to form. In an effort to beat the rain, Cairns was sent up to open, reaching 28* out of 41/1 before the umpires took the players off. With scores to settle and momentum to nurture, Bacup's travelling contingent grew fretful. A few years earlier, Roy, Clive and Gordon had locked the umpires in their room for an hour after the game in protest at the decision to give skipper Neal Wilkinson out for obstructing the field. On this occasion, however, it was club chairman Colin Shaw who decided to take things up with the officials. It may not have been the savviest move.

"The umpire on the day was a guy called Dave Parkinson," recalls Farragher, "a good bloke, straight as a die, but a big lad who worked as a bouncer in the local clubs. We were watching it drizzle and Colin, who'd had a few too many pints by this stage, goes in to chivvy them along. Thirty seconds later he was being carried out by the scruff of the neck. Dave Parkinson had told him, 'I'm in charge and I'll decide whether it's fit or not'." The day had started with the Cairns accessing bouncer mode, and ended with the umpire doing likewise.

It was one that got away, but Bacup could not be knocked out of their stride and Rishton, with their original pro Vernon Philander having gone home, were unfussily swatted aside, Cairns backing up a cameo 38 with 7/49: five bowled, two lbw. Sunday's game at Haslingden was washed out and Cairns headed off for another full week's cricket – one game for an International XI against the touring Pakistanis, four for Lashings – returning to chip in 4/33 and 42 to a win over Nelson. Next, he top-scored with 74 against East Lancs, following up with 5/44, with Farrouk again bounced out first ball, his second and final innings in the Lancashire League: "Two games, two golden ducks, which must be some sort of record," chuckles Chapman. A day later, Cairns's 6/35 bombed out Accrington for 120, Ormerod again roughed up, after which Cairns put his feet up and watched his teammates knock off the target as they surged up to second place, just four points behind leaders Ramsbottom.

The club was buzzing, the pro delivering, and 24 hours later Cairns showed the Bacupians what they meant to him, rustling up a quorum of Kiwis from county cricket and the club-pro circuit for a T20 exhibition match at Lane Head, with all profits going to the club. "He wasn't asked to do that," clarifies Farragher, "he volunteered. He knew his salary was pretty big and he wanted to do his bit to help out the club." Terry Lord organised a poker tournament for the afternoon, won by Nathan Astle, and by the time the cricket started both Cairns's team and Joe Scuderi's International XI, including one RJ Harris, were not entirely unoiled. The ground was packed, the weather was good, the fun was plentiful – the players operated a self-imposed handicap, fielding everything with their weak hands – and the visiting luminaries stayed "until the early hours of the morning", says Lord, by which time everyone was entirely oiled. For the grand finale, Cairns and Tama Canning led what started out as a semi-naked haka – grainy YouTube footage shows booming Lanky accents shouting "you fat bastard" and higher-pitched screams of "gerr'em off!" – and rumour has it that the pro, ever a crowd-pleaser, went full birthday suit. The event raised "between £7,000 and £8,000", says Lord, around 40 per cent of Cairns's salary.

Yep, the club was buzzing. But the weekend brought serious business: the visit of reigning champions Lowerhouse, who, led by Ryan Harris, were starting to hit an ominous mid-season stride.

* * *

By the time Ryno and his unfinished business returned to Lowerhouse, he was much closer to his fighting pace of 140kph. It began with South Australia head coach Wayne Phillips telling him they had run out of budget and he was going to be released. Two weeks later, however, extra cash was found and they offered him another one-year deal – a lightbulb moment that illuminated the fragility of his chosen career, eventually instilling greater professionalism and, in turn, changes to his run-up that added extra pace (about which no advance email circular was sent on to the Lancashire League's no-lid crew).

He had not made it in time for the season opener, with Lowerhouse engaging another Harris, left-arm spinner Paul (with Chris Harris subbing for Nelson later in the summer, the Lancashire League would thus welcome the full tweed), the feisty South African impressing with 68, 5/68 and a willingness to sledge the opposition about playing for a draw in a win-lose format. Ryan Harris was in town for the victory over Church, before May brought four no-results (three rescheduled) and a nine-wicket hammering from Nelson, for whom another left-arm-spinning Protea, Robin Peterson, added 78* to his 7/41 and comprehensively won the pro-versus-pro game within a game. Meanwhile, Lowerhouse had exited both the Worsley and Inter-league cups. So far, so unromantic for the returning cult hero.

Ryno had six wickets to his name and scores of 5, 11, 11, 6 and 3 heading into the derby, where he was trapped lbw by Mike Kelly, whose career-best 6/37 saw Lowerhouse slide from 97/1 to 135 all out. Needless to say, Harris would be bowling unchanged with such a score to defend. After his new-ball partner Jonny Russell nipped out the openers, Harris took out the next three and at 33/5 Burnley were on the ropes. The inferiority complex was now a memory, Ryno was bowling rockets, and although another Burnley player mustered a career-best, Lowerhouse won by 13 runs. They won the next game, too, Harris taking 96 off Colne, following up with 56, 48, 19*, 87 and 35* but not many wickets. And not many wins, either, for the stumbling champions.

An eight-game streak from early-June to mid-July brought Harris only one five-for and Lowerhouse two wins – both of them courtesy of the Lancashire League Adjusted Target, a local variant on the Duckworth-Lewis-Stern formula. There weren't too many arguments when a downpour curtailed things against Haslingden with Lowerhouse on 150/2 chasing 219 and 23 overs remaining, but an eyebrow or two might have been raised when the LLAT awarded them the win against table-topping Ramsbottom when they were 111/7 chasing 141 with Sunil Joshi – he of the 15 Test caps and 69 ODI appearances for India – sitting on 4/40 and fancying a mopping-up job. As if to prove the point, four weeks later Joshi pocketed himself 4/24 as Lowerhouse were blown away for 52, losing by 146.

Remarkably, however, Lowerhouse were still very much in the hunt for the title at the halfway stage, sitting in joint-sixth with Accrington on 80 points, just six points off top, with Todmorden, in ninth, within one 12-point afternoon (a win plus two points for bowling the opposition out) of overhauling the leaders. Everything to play for, then, as Lowerhouse hit their July double-header with Accy and Tod – provided Ryno didn't hit the circuit too hard.

"The hardest thing was managing the beers on a Saturday night before a Sunday game," Harris would later recall of the challenges he faced as a club cricketer. "I literally had to get straight in my car and drive home, because if I'd stayed for one or two I was going to be wrecked for Sunday." Naturally, this cut down the visits to Planet Pizza, although the ever-conscientious Aussie was also known to tell the treasurer to hold back some of his pay packet when he didn't feel he'd earned it, to which the usual reply was: "Well, you're going to spend it behind the bar anyway."

He would certainly earn it over the next nine games, which brought him 40 wickets at 8.25 apiece. The 137-run win against Accrington was comfortable enough for him not to have to bowl unchanged, operating instead as a high-end battering ram to pick up 3/21 and provide an uncomfortable enough experience for Accy's No.5 Mick Horsfield who, after being hit about the upper body four times in an over, told Harris, "Well, you'll not get me out bowling there". After a sensible Saturday night, Harris then took 5/24 against Todmorden, including the last four wickets for no runs, a useful warm-up for high-flying Bacup on a hot, high-summer day, with Chris Cairns starting to turn on the taps.

Asked to bat first, four of Lowerhouse's top five made it to 24 but none past 31 as neither side were able to land a convincing punch.

The security of 117/3 soon turned into the crisis of 144/8, however, as Lord and Cairns whittled through the middle order, only for the pro to pull up in mid-over and limp out of the attack, after which the last two wickets added 68 runs, with Matt Hope contributing a priceless, top-scoring 36* at No.10.

By the time Cairns and his tight groin were called on to bat, 27/1 had become 27/3 and the visitors' tails were up. Ryno's first ball to Cairns ran away down the slope, beating a heavy-footed poke. The next was full, swinging away, and knocked out the off stump: 27/4. "Nobody in the league troubled Chris, pace-wise," recalls Farragher, "but even he said Harris was quick that day." Next in to face the music was Terry Lord, who battled hard for 11 before being pinned on the foot by another yorker – not only adjudged lbw, but also having to be carried from the field with a broken toe. "Early on, he was really quick," recalls Lord, somewhat ruefully, "but what he did when he was tiring – he bowled two balls flat-out and four when he just put it there." This was one of the first type.

By now, Ryno was on the charge. It was high-octane carnage, a chainsaw rampage through a title-chasing team. In at No.9 walked 'Kipper' Chapman. Without a lid. "Harris said, 'If you don't put a helmet on I'm going to kill you'," Chapman recalls. "We had a bit of a ding-dong. If it had gone on much longer, we'd have finished it round the back of the clubhouse." Part of the reason for the ding-dong's duration was the batter being hit on the gloves in front of his face and the umpire not giving the catch. Still, it would not be too long before his stumps and those of No.11 David Warren were relocated. Harris finished with figures of 13.4-2-35-8 and Lowerhouse were up to third, two points behind Bacup and 16 off Ramsbottom. More importantly, they had their champion strut back. Red-hot Ryno's body of work for July was a scary-good 80.3-23-167-26. Not many were looking forward to their trip to Lowerhouse Lane. *No one bullied us with Ryan. We were the bullies.*

"One thing about Ryan was that he raised his game against the big-name pros," says Jez Hope, by this time retired after a 24-year stint in the first team that had begun in 1981 with him walking out to face Michael Holding, passing an outgoing batter who was retiring hurt with a broken nose. "He always wanted to show them he was as good as them." Sure enough, next time out, another New Zealand

Test player was knocked over for a duck: Nelson's Craig MacMillan, who nonetheless still averaged 95 in his nine-game stint as locum. 'Macca' had come in at 59/0 – opener Danny Kegg having been retired hurt – and little more than an hour later Nelson had been blown away for 107, losing by 133, Harris bagging 5/45. With two lower-profile Kiwis up next, he was smelling blood.

The week took Harris and a few of his Lowerhouse mates down to Old Trafford for the Roses match, where he caught up with his state teammates Jason Gillespie and Darren Lehmann, who listened to his stresses about the rolling one-year deal at South Australia and offered a few hard truths – unwelcome at the time, beneficial in the long run. Harris stormed out of the conversation, saying "I don't have to listen to this. I listen to it all bloody year." Lowerhouse may have seen him as a demigod but the reality was that he was a bloke scrapping for his professional survival, his great autumnal run as a champion quick in the baggy green not yet even showing up in his wildest dreams.

Come the weekend, Tama Canning's 5/19 off 17 had bowled Lowerhouse out for 108 and despite 4/34 from Harris, Haslingden knocked them off for five, halting the four-game winning streak. A week later, they lost again, this time to East Lancs, whose Kiwi pro Mark Orchard had spent the lead-up to the game smashing tennis balls at opening bat Paul Turner from 15 yards, in preparation for the Harris onslaught.

"We would hit them unrealistically fast at each other," Turner told the Lancashire League website's 'My Favourite Game' series, "but it paid off. Harris wasn't scared of whistling it by your nose, but due to the work done during the week, I was able to personally introduce him to Corporation Park a couple of times during my innings. He thanked me wholeheartedly each time and enquired if I'd like to try that against him if we were Down Under. Blackburn was just fine, thanks."

Turner's day in the sun brought him 87* in a chase of 117/1, but Lowerhouse were not yet out of things. The following week, Harris bowled unchanged against Colne, picking up 5/44 before contributing a top-scoring 47 to a ticklish, seven-down chase: a man on a mission. With five to play, Lowerhouse were fourth, 16 off top, and with two of the sides above them, Bacup and Burnley, still to play.

* * *

The elder statesman in the Bacup dressing-room were long enough in the tooth to know that all teams were susceptible to a pro-administered pummelling, that they didn't need to dwell too long over the detonation of Cairns's castle and the rest of the batting by the rampant Harris. Nevertheless, they also knew they needed to bounce back, pronto. The good news on that front was that the pro's exit from the attack with Lowerhouse on the ropes had been precautionary – for he was in the thick of his own purple bowling form, an eight-game run netting 38 wickets at 7.24. That hot-streak average would come down even further as two thumping wins righted the Bacup ship. First, Todmorden were flattened for 85, Cairns taking 5/37; then Rishton fell for 79, Cairns with 7/26. Jitters gone. With seven to play, the gap to Ramsbottom was now just two points, with next opponents Burnley five behind in third.

Inked onto the Burnley teamsheet for a first Lancashire League game in over four years was James Anderson, 24 years old and last seen in whites in March, knocking over Dravid, Tendulkar and Sehwag in England's series-equalling win in the 'Ring of Fire' Test in Mumbai. Anderson was recovering from a stress fracture of the back that would keep him out of almost the entire first-class summer. "There were no sour grapes in Bacup's dressing room about Jimmy playing," says Tim Farragher. "He was Burnley's player. It raised the profile of the Lancashire League even more, which is what everyone wants." Such magnanimity might have been tested had Jimmy been fit to help bowl them to the title – thus taking his spot in quite the hypothetical 2006 Lancashire League XI pace attack: JM Anderson, VD Philander, RJ Harris and CL Cairns – but that was a couple of weeks away yet. The Burnley Lara was there as a batter only.

Alas, rain claimed the entire fixture programme and with an afternoon to kill the Bacup players decided to hit the MFA Bowl for a spot of ten-pin bowling. Two teams were drawn from a hat and Cairns *really* wanted to win. "We were 16 points behind and it was Chris's turn," says Chapman. "We'd had a few pints by this time. He took a 15-yard run-up and released this ball with such ferocity that he went flying down with it and ended up face down, half in the ditch, half in the alley. He got up and the side of his chin was cut and his right arm was cut. All he was bothered about was getting the strike, which he did. That summed him up: 100 per cent commitment." A strike, yes, but also over the line and thus should have been marked as zero.

Either way, the next day was a league game, and another big one: Rawtenstall in the return derby. A good time, then, for Andy Spencer to claim a career-best 5/58, knocking over the top five, before Cairns mopped up with 4/45. The chase was a relatively straightforward 113, but the pitch was treacherous and Bacup were soon going down like skittles, slipping to 25/5. At which point, the pro and his grazed square jaw knuckled down, making an uncharacteristically restrained 40* out of 95 scored while he was out there, shepherding them home and happy into the week. Neither Burnley nor Ramsbottom won, sending Bacup top for the first time with five to play. "Chris was absolutely desperate for us to win the league," says Chapman. "He knew how important that game was and played very sensibly."

The following Saturday Cairns smote 92 against Church and followed up with 6/37 in a frictionless romp to maximum points, setting them up nicely for a trip to Acre Bottom to face a Ramsbottom team on a four-match winless run – also a Ramsbottom team that had proven to be Bacup's kryptonite thus far, in particular Sunil Joshi, who sent down 25-12-41-3 in the league victory at Lane Head and 4-1-8-4 in the T20 win, which he finished with a hat-trick, all stumped.

Rammy batted first and fought their way to a competitive 207/5, the 20-year-old Phil Hayes making 99 and Cairns grunting through 19 overs for 3/64. In addition to the ten points for a win and the two for bowling teams out, the Lancashire League rules provided incentives in the second innings for losing teams: one point if you got within 50 runs of the target (so, 157 in this case) all the way up to five for getting within ten. If the chasing team won, the bowling side could still pick up a point for five wickets, all the way up to five for taking nine. With the table as tight as it was, such things could not be ignored.

Rammy defended the target stoutly. Mike Haslam got through nine overs for 18 and, with Sunil Joshi taking the new ball and racking up the dots, Bacup fell behind the clock. Cairns entered at 43/3 with work to do. He played tight and counter-punched, but no one could stay out there with him for long enough to change the game's direction. Joshi turned the screw. Soon it was 80/5, then 112/6. Roy, Clive and Gordon had fallen silent. Cairns decided to have a dip. "Chris was really fighting for us that day, but we were all getting out around him," recalls Farragher. "They were all over us, but then he hit four sixes in quick succession. One of them knocked someone's beer out of their hand in front of the pavilion. We felt anything could still happen, but in the end he went for one too many and was bowled, slog-sweeping Joshi, who ran down the wicket, celebrating."

At 144/8, Rammy moved in for the kill. Bacup largely shut up shop, although still with half a mind on reaching 157 for the consolation of a batting point, which the skipper secured in the final over, immediately battening down the hatches. With one ball left and Rammy's title challenge on life-support, Joshi produced a beauty to find the edge, where Chapman was caught at slip by Simon Read, a good friend who lived two doors down from him. News filtered in from the Burnley derby. Just ten points now separated Bacup in first from Ramsbottom in fifth.

* * *

If those back-to-back defeats to mid-table Haslingden and East Lancs had knocked some wind from the Lowerhouse sails, the pro's form and a restorative win over Colne maintained the glass just over half-full heading into the August bank holiday weekend double-header. Against Enfield on the Saturday, Harris crafted a measured 88 and followed up with a mind-boggling spell of 12.2-6-8-6 that kept them in touch with the top. Then came a trip to Turf Moor to play a Burnley side that had already lost the T20 final to Rishton and the Worsley Cup final to Nelson. Lowerhouse, naturally, were keen to administer a third dose of poison.

The bad news was that Jimmy Anderson was playing, the good that he still wasn't bowling, and Lowerhouse duly posted a competitive 186 all out, having been asked to bat first. At 45/0 and then 116/3, Burnley twice looked favourites, but Harris ran in as hard as ever and sent down 21-6-39-4, locking down one end. Jonny Russell picked up the final two wickets to secure an 18-run win that saw Lowerhouse leapfrog their arch-rivals in a race thrown wide open with Ramsbottom's last-ball win over Bacup. With three to play, the standings were: Bacup 170, Lowerhouse 165, Burnley 162, Nelson 161, Ramsbottom 160. "I clearly remember thinking after the derby that we were going to win the league again," says rookie skipper Joe Beneduce. "We still had Bacup to play and it seemed like the stars were aligning." As it happened, the star was about to head home to Australia. Not only had his mother's cancer taken a turn for the worse, but the South Australia coaching staff had requested he report early for pre-season training.

The following weekend, scattered showers hit the programme hard. Only two games survived. Bacup played a 27-over thrash, Burnley a 25-over smash in which they restricted Todmorden to 90/9 and knocked them off for none. Second-bottom Colne, meanwhile, were proving a nuisance for Bacup, posting 144 and reducing their hosts to 12/2. A focussed Cairns then plundered five sixes in a 70-ball 74, adding 115 with Farragher to bring the target down to 18, at which point the pro holed out on the boundary off Shaukat Sheraz, who never bowled another over in the league, and an almighty twitch ensued. With 12 needed off 12 balls and six wickets in hand, Bacup conspired to lose four wickets for one run in the penultimate over, including Farragher for 40, leaving the 42-year-old Nick Cronshaw and 18-year-old Scott Thompson – neither of whom had yet faced a ball – to try and salvage things, the helmet-averse Jeff Ellis on bowling duties. A single, a pulled two to midwicket and a dot left eight needed off three. Unbearable tension. Thompson, in the second team until June, found another two and then a precious, precious boundary. The roar rolled all the way into town. With two needed from one, Ellis bustled in and the ball was flicked behind square, those teenage legs bringing Thompson back for two and into the midst of a pitch invasion, Cairns leading his delirious teammates in the charge.

Heading into the final weekend's double-header, the lead over Burnley remained eight points, a dozen over the next opponents, a Ryno-less Lowerhouse. In his stead came Zimbabwean off spinner Gavin Ewing, who Cairns had seen dismiss Astle, Oram and McCullum in a tidy 10-over spell of 3/31 in the Videocon ODI Tri-Series a year earlier. Still, if you were a betting man, you would have fancied some fireworks, particularly with the wicket toward the far edge of the square. And Cairns was very much a betting man.

"One day, early in the season," recalls Terry Lord, "Cairnsy says to me, 'We need a bet. We'll draw a few lads in and take some money off them'. I asked what. He says, 'I reckon I can hit ten sixes in a game'. 'Ten sixes in a game,' I says, 'that's a tough ask'. 'I reckon I can do it,' he says. So we offered even money. There were a lot of £10 bets laid, a few a bit higher. We cleaned up." He left it late, but clean up they did as Cairns pummelled a 56-ball ton including 11 sixes, one of them, says Chapman, "the biggest six I've ever seen on a Lancashire League ground, off Matt Hope. It went over the row of terraced houses by the car park."

"He was regularly clearing the boundary by 30 or 40 yards," adds Farragher. "He kept peppering this one house and somebody came out to complain. We didn't get a couple of balls back. He just shouted, 'You can sod off!' and kept it."

Not satisfied with that, Cairns then ripped out both openers as Lowerhouse fell to 4/2. He returned later to dismiss top-scoring Bleazard, finishing with 4/30 as the home side fell for 172 to lose by 99. Meanwhile, Burnley had beaten Rawtenstall, Anderson getting through six overs, following up his 1/10 with 35* from 27 balls. Bacup needed five points the next day to clinch the title, while Burnley hoped for a slip to claim their first for 27 years.

As for Lowerhouse, 24 hours later they lost to rock-bottom Church and slipped back to sixth, although that wasn't quite the end of the story for RJ Harris at the 'House. The following summer they signed Victoria batter Jon Moss, who pulled out in April, with a last-minute replacement lined up in Aaron O'Brien. Before his visa was approved, Harris filled in for four weekends, averaging 50 with the bat, the highlight of which was a contribution of 144 toward a league-record opening partnership of 257 with Jonny Finch. With the ball, there was a spell of 5/12 in eight overs against Accrington in a game abandoned after an hour and replayed six days later, when he took 5/36. His final Lancashire League stats were 1,253 runs at 43.2 and 99 wickets at 13.21, but beyond the numbers it was the injection of whole-hearted aggression that gives him a cherished place among the club's roll-call of paid men. "He was the most super-human pro, and proper quick," says Beneduce. "I felt we could do or say anything on the field, because Ryan would always sort it out for us, like your hard mate at school."

So long the Cinderella club, Lowerhouse went on to win titles in 2011, 2012 and 2014. The middle year brought a double, with a 15-run win over Church in the Worsley Cup final. Further knockout success followed in 2018 – when Burnley were beaten in a game producing a record gate of £6,469, the 51-year-old Bleazard hitting the winning runs – 2021 and 2024, the no-hopers tag long gone.

* * *

Cairns and Lord left Lowerhouse that September evening with their fistful of tenners, repairing to Bacup for a few steady jars, confident of taking the final step. Once more, the pro stayed over at Peter Thompson's, Bacup's all-time leading run-scorer still avidly supporting the team despite having to stop playing in July with rheumatoid arthritis. Lord had soldiered on with his broken toe, too, but there was bad news for a third member of the forty something fraternity when Chapman woke up on Sunday unable to move his thumb, having taken a blow while standing up to Lord the day before. A fitness test confirmed the worst: it was fractured. Rather than call up the second-team keeper, they opted for a part-timer. "Losing John was a big blow," says Farragher. "He was the captain, the cheerleader, the heartbeat of the team, a useful lower-order batsman and a fantastic keeper. It felt like things were conspiring against us."

Worse was to come when Cairns pulled up with a groin injury in his fourth over. He tried to push on through the discomfort but was forced to limp out of the attack in the middle of his sixth. Still, Enfield had slipped into the troubled waters of 74/5 when, with one Bacup hand on the trophy, Neil Holmes joined the 42-year-old Andy Barker. With no Cairns burst to deal with, they added 79, Barker saving his first fifty of the season for the least convenient moment. "Chris going off took the wind right out of our sails," says Chapman. "They ended up with 187 when they wouldn't have got 120."

Meanwhile, JM Anderson had taken the new ball at Turf Moor, sending down 8-1-17-2 as Haslingden were rolled out for 119, a total then knocked off for four with home-grown pro Jonathon Harvey unbeaten on 55. After which came mainly anxious waiting. Although the early headline news was 'so far, so good'.

Bacup were already 25/3 and deep in the mire when Cairns entered, movement hampered by his injury, the club he had grown to love's hopes resting on his broad shoulders. He hadn't been out there long when the 52-year-old Bernard Reidy, in his final match before retiring, picked up a second wicket, making it 35/4, which the veteran then followed, recalls Farragher, "by a worldie of a one-handed diving catch at slip to dismiss Matt O'Connor. Not long after that, Chris absolutely smashed a low full-toss off Neil Holmes straight to extra cover, who took another unbelievable catch. A yard either side, it was four all the way." Holmes was on his way to his own season's best figures of 6/61. It was becoming a perfect shitstorm.

From the depths of 86/9, however, came hope, as No.8 Andy Spencer and No.11 David Warren – a *bona fide* rabbit, appropriately enough – added 51 to collect a first batting point. Another 40 runs from the final five overs would still mean defeat, true, but also the full five bonus points, and thus the championship. It was the longest of longshots but the last thing to die is hope and *we've got the momentum here lads and Spenner is seeing it well and if he can get the strike and we just get that one really big over and 'keep going, lads!' and you never know, do you, especially as it's getting dark, and stranger things have happened...* And then Burnley received the phonecall they were waiting for, as Warren's now-or-never heave was defeated, as too were Bacup, who were soon huddled in the desolation of the Enfield dressing-rooms, wondering in silence how they hadn't managed to win the title. It was probably the Accrington game, although no one was about to knock on Dave Parkinson's door to have it out with him. If not that, then Ryan bloody Harris.

"It was heartbreaking, one of the biggest disappointments I've had in league cricket," recalls Lord. "We put so much into that season, but everything just went wrong on that last day. We couldn't believe we'd thrown it away having worked so hard to pull it round after a slow start. Chris was quite upset about it."

Ah, the everyday cruelties of sport. The trials and tribulations. Mostly, you don't win. Usually, you don't get close to winning. That's why winning feels special. But it is losing – the response to losing – that most defines a character. Never was this truer than on that strange, sun-dappled evening at Lord's 13 years later when one of Cairns's successors as Black Caps skipper had to find the forbearance to deal with a game – perhaps the biggest game of his life – being stolen from him and his team in the most freakish circumstances imaginable. And so as the shock set in for Bacup and the work of mourning began, Cairns understood that his job as pro was not yet done, although the first steps away from despondency came from an unexpected source.

"Not long after the game," recalls Farragher, "Neal Wilkinson, our second team captain, came into the dressing-room and read out a letter from Dorothy Brassington, a lady in her eighties, the widow of the former president Horace Brassington. It was half a side of A4. She thanked us for all our efforts during the season and the enjoyment we'd given her and the rest of the supporters. This was written before she knew the result of the last game. She just said how good it was to watch us push for the league title and represent the club so well. It was a pretty emotional dressing-room, we were all really down, and this was a really poignant moment. I don't think many of us made eye contact for a couple of minutes. There weren't too many dry eyes in there."

They showered. They changed. The pain started to subside. Just a little. They had a customary visitors' pint then made their way back to Bacup, where the skipper gathered his troops together before the DJ – oblivious to the events of the day – cranked up the party tunes. "We all had a bit of a sit-down and a chat," Chapman recalls. "Chris apologised for pulling up with the groin injury. He was massively disappointed. He wanted to win as much as we did, if not more."

Soon it was time for the captain to address the club as a whole, short and sweet, followed by the departing star, an extrovert who would capture any room he walked into now trying not to look too crestfallen, smearing a dollop of ointment on the collective wounds. "Chris made a fantastic speech," says Farragher. "He thanked the players, the club, the committee, the supporters, and we had a good night in the end. Okay, we didn't win the league, but we received our runners-up trophies. We held our heads high. We were proud of what we'd done over the season, proud of the way we'd carried ourselves."

Cairns had certainly given it his all. In raw numbers, he had taken 87 wickets (joint-top with Canning) at 10.37 (bettered only by RJ Harris of those with more than ten wickets), and at a strike-rate of

22.42 (the best of anyone with over 20 wickets). It would have been a tidy effort on its own. But throw in 953 runs (the third most, and this with feet-up DNBs in three of their wins) at 65.53 (second) and it was a mighty contribution. Without the three abandoned games, he would almost certainly have become just the fifth person in 116 Lancashire League seasons to have completed the double, after Cec Pepper and Vijay Hazare in 1949, Colin Miller in 1990 and, in 1995, Chris Harris, Cairns's replacement as Bacup pro.

He left them with one more memory, too, recalls Thompson. "He didn't just say, 'Right, lads, bye. That's it'. The weekend after, he took us to Suffolk on a mini-tour, a long weekend with a charity game. He didn't have to do that, but he did. We had a great time. He did his bit for Bacup Cricket Club, he really did."

And then it really was farewell – and, after that, the ill-starred ICL, the High Court, the ICU, the land of the long black cloud. Which brings us to that asterisk, and the question of whether subsequent events have smudged the memories of that summer of 2006. Lord is unequivocal: "What he did for the club overrides everything. All the Bacup lads feel the same." Thompson certainly does: "I haven't changed my opinion on Chris at any time. He was brilliant for our club – a total gentleman, on and off the field."

"I don't know the ins and outs of what happened," adds Chapman, "but we all do things we regret in life. None of it detracts from the man we met. He was such a top man. Great with the kids, with the wives, a gentleman in the clubhouse – very funny, very warm, very generous. And obviously a great cricketer, an absolute joy to spend a season with. He's still in touch with Bacup, and he's still in our thoughts."

Human beings are fallible and life is morally complex. Perhaps all we really have to anchor us as we navigate our way through it are the certainties – such as they are – provided by our feelings, our attachments, our memories, our capacity to cling to the best of what we see in others, those bright white brush strokes among the black speckles and shades of grey. The Chris Cairns known to Bacup is the man who gave them whatever he had to give.

"He was a big-name signing and wasn't cheap," says Farragher, "but Chris paid for himself by being Chris. The summer of 2006 will live long in the memory of Bacup Cricket Club, matches and innings that no one will ever forget. I feel very lucky to have been part of it as a Saturday afternoon cricketer, 23 years old at the time. The memories will live with me forever. Absolutely priceless."

No asterisk. No caveat. No qualification.

8

Muthiah Muralidaran
at Leicester Ivanhoe

Word travels fast on the club cricket grapevine, and if no one quite yet knew what Leicester Ivanhoe's new Sri Lankan spinner was called – the *Leicester Mercury* would run through a series of variations, from "Murali Duran" to "Muranlidaran", never quite nailing it, while the *Hinckley Times* opted at first for "Murray Muladuran" – they certainly knew he could bowl, even if they had not much idea *what* he bowled, besides a stock ball that ripped the air like a Chinook helicopter scouting the Vietnamese jungle for lost GIs. But then, initial bafflement at the self-described "wrist-spinning off-spinner" was a common reaction – from Allan Border's remark to Mark Waugh ("You sure he's bowling off spin, mate?") to Ivanhoe's young opener Mike Sutliff: "The day he turned up, because of his wrist action, we genuinely didn't know whether he was an off-spinner or a leg-spinner. There was prodigious turn, but I didn't know whether it was coming out of the front, out of the back, out of the side…"

The trip to Hinckley Town was Muralidaran's third outing in Ivanhoe colours, and after a frustrating opening hour for the visitors he grazed the edge of opener Matt Mettam's bat, the rest taken care of by second team keeper Mark Tebbatt, in for his first game of the season after some alarm at the extras count in Murali's first two games. "I was the last straw to find a wicket-keeper who could stop the ball, pretty or not," Tebbatt recalls. "When I got there, I introduced myself to Murali and he said we should go on the square and have a quick warm-up, so I took the gloves out not really knowing what to expect. His first ball on the outfield landed a metre and a half to my right and went about the same distance to my left. He just smiled."

The challenge for batters was sizeable, yet sage observers at Hinckley knew their punky No.3 – just turned 19 and contracted to

Leicestershire – had something special about him: poise, personality and shots that raised eyebrows, although not too many would have predicted in 1995 that by the time his first-class race was run he would have 591 wickets to chuck in the cupboard with 16,676 runs. If anyone on the ground would have felt confident about handling things that late-spring Sunday in May, it would have been a man who, in his first post-match TV interview as a pro, would pronounce: "If it's in the arc, it's out the park!"

"I still tell this story today," says Darren Stevens. "I walked out to bat after he'd just taken a wicket, and took guard. The first ball pitched on the edge of the strip [outside off stump] and went over leg stump. No word of a lie. I left it after seeing it pitch so wide, and luckily it bounced enough to go over the top. So I walked down to my mate and batting partner Andy Holder, and he said to me, 'Welcome to the dust bowl'. I said, 'Hang on, this is a green seamer!' It was a fresh club pitch, a bit spongy. Andy advised me to bat outside off stump and hit Murali through the leg side. That was our gameplan: if he pitches it outside off stump then we hit him over cow corner. And it worked!"

As is frequently the case in the under-reported realms of the club game, where anecdotes are buffed to a fine sheen down the years, the facts often get muddied, muddled or misremembered – albeit without necessarily changing the essentials. When Stevens entered at 51/1 it was his skipper, Paul Clarke, at the crease, busy eking out 34 valuable runs. Carl Barnett was in at No.4 and made 38, while Andy Holder came in at No.5 and bashed a 31-ball 49, which indeed suggests some eschewal of the posh side, and it could well have been he who advised on the *modus operandi*. As for 'Stevo', he compiled a polished 48 before being run out. "He was able to hit through the ball off Murali," recalls Sutliff, "whereas nobody else in the league really could."

Hinckley were a strong side – three other county staffers turned out for them at various stages: wicket-keeper Phil Whitticase, bleep-test-averse seamer Jimmy Ormond, and left-arm spinner Matthew Brimson, chiefly famous for exposing himself in a LCCC team photo that appeared in *Wisden* – and they would finish the Central League campaign in fourth place. Their total of 234/5 declared was a formidable target. As for Murali, he belatedly worked out he was bowling with the wind in the wrong direction and was removed from the attack for the only time that year, taking 3/75 from 18 overs of toil, his worst figures in a half-season stint in which his wickets cost him 7.81 apiece.

Ivanhoe responded with 172/6 in what proved a tame draw. Murali, no doubt chewing coca leaves for the altitude sickness, came in at No.4 and failed to trouble the scorers. But it didn't take a genius to work out they had a fledgling genius on their hands.

* * *

The story of how Test cricket's future all-time leading wicket-taker – almost certainly in perpetuity, given its present anguishes and infirmities – came to play club cricket in Leicestershire begins in 1967, when a 19-year-old boy from Ceylon enrolled at Blackburn College of Design and Technology. When not busy studying the finer points of textile manufacturing in which he later made his fortune, Sarath Abeysundera played cricket for Whalley in the Ribblesdale League. After that, he headed to Leicester to take the Higher National Diploma, cricket still more than holding its own in the grapple for mental bandwidth even if his talent for the game fell short of his aptitude for business.

'Mr Abey' was soon taking up the managing director's post at Leicester Dyers, where he had been given an initial 25 per cent share of the company, and rustled together a predominantly Asian works cricket team that struggled to convince local clubs to lease them their grounds. The nadir came in 1994 when Abeysundera tried to organise a benefit game for Mohammad Azharuddin in Leicester, which ended up being played in a public park. A fire was lit, he recalls: "I thought: one day I will own my own ground."

Through this period Abeysundera regularly took teams out to Sri Lanka, stitching together the fabric of cricketing connections that would eventually see him host the full 1998 Sri Lankan touring party at the grand opening of the ground he did end up buying in Illston-on-the-Hill, a tiny village four miles east of Leicester with a church, a pub and not much else. Carved out of Leicestershire countryside in the 1950s by Stan Timms, a chicken farmer whose club foot made him no less of a cricket fanatic, the ground's previous tenant had been Clarendon Park CC, where Darren Maddy came through, but by 1996 the club had folded and the place had fallen into disrepair. Abeysundera took a look around and made an offer to the landowner, who confessed to being reluctant to sell it to a Sri Lankan for fear of an 'Asian invasion' in a bastion of Middle-Englishness. So, the ground went to auction, to which Abeysundera sent along his English lawyer as a stalking horse and duly acquired it for £100,000 less than the original bid. Two years later, he bought a hilltop home overlooking the patch of land he would rename Sigiriya Sports Ground, after an ancient fortress situated on a rock near Dambulla, smack bang in the middle of Sri Lanka. "I am the only Sri Lankan in the world to own a private ground," he says, unbidden. The new club was called Illston Abey. One 'b'. No abbeys nearby.

Among Abeysundera's closest connections was Aravinda de Silva, who had stayed with him in Leicester as an 18-year-old in 1984, the year of Sri Lanka's first UK tour as a fully-fledged Test-playing nation, even turning out a couple of times for Ashby Town – the club at which Abeysundera was playing at the time – in one of them coming in at 60/5 in pursuit of 290 and rattling off an unbeaten 150 or so. In April 1995, Aravinda had arrived in England from an historic tour of New Zealand (via the Asia Cup in the UAE), where Sri Lanka had picked up a maiden overseas Test victory in Napier – Murali taking a second-innings 5/64 in the 241-run win, his career best at the time – holding on to claim the series.

Aravinda's next assignment was a summer as Kent's overseas player, deputising for Carl Hooper. It would be a transformative experience – not the first wayfarer to undergo an epiphany in Canterbury – one for which he had arrived with a friend in tow. Unable to find Murali cricket or accommodation in Kent, Aravinda was soon on the phone to Abeysundera, asking if he could help out. Murali headed north.

Initially, Abeysundera deployed his new acquaintance for Ashby Town, where he was captain. And why the hell not! They already had the former Sri Lanka 'A' batter Dileepa Wickramasinghe in the ranks, as well as Suresh Keshwala, a Uganda-born batter who averaged 40-plus for Saurashtra in the Ranji Trophy and West Zone in the Duleep Trophy. Even so, it was not a standard likely to overly tax someone who had just been trying to knock over Sachin and Inzi in Sharjah. After all, the top five clubs in Leicestershire at the time were all playing in the Central League, a geographically quirky 14-team closed shop founded in 1972, the year of Murali's birth, whose members were strewn in the vicinity of the old Roman road, Watling Street: two in Staffordshire (Burton-on-Trent, Lichfield), six in Warwickshire (Bedworth, Blossomfield, Kenilworth Wardens, Nuneaton, Rugby, Water Orton), the Leicestershire five (Ivanhoe, Hinckley, Loughborough Town, Lutterworth, Market Harborough), and Northampton Saints. Beneath (or alongside) this was the Everards Leicestershire County League, a six-division structure whose bigger dogs would have fancied their chances of mixing it with that quintet at the sharp end of the county cup. And then there was the Country Fresh Senior League, where Ashby played. In the second division. The one below Ivanhoe twos.

As sadistically pleasurable as it would have been to see Murali run through Shepshed Messengers, Barkby and Burton-on-the-Wolds, it soon became clear that he needed a tougher assignment. Abeysundera called a friend from cricketing circles, Nigel Dearman, an auctioneer who lived in the same part of Leicester and who was on the Ivanhoe committee. "He said he had three players he could offer me," Dearman recalls. "Marvan Atappattu, Hashan Tillakaratne and Murali. I chose Murali because I felt we needed someone who could bowl sides out rather than bowling them in." The two men shook hands on a package of car plus accommodation, along with "a £100 honorarium" each week.

Dearman immediately called Ivanhoe's president and long-standing former player, Robert Jelley, owner of the Jelson building firm and sometime member of the *Sunday Times*' Rich List. "I told Robert about the negotiations with Mr Abeysundera and he said, 'Right, we better pull our fingers out. This chap sounds useful.' Jelsons had a property they had taken over after buying a plot of land for a development, a two-storey apartment that was sitting empty, quite a decent property, although they were going to knock it down at some point. So me and my wife immediately got that furnished from my auction room, putting curtains and carpets in, and, by chance, a few days later a motor car came into our hands while doing a house clearance and probate on a deceased estate.

It was a Skoda. So, I bought it for a few hundred quid and filled it with petrol. Murali took one look at it and said words to the effect of, 'I don't want that heap of junk'. So Bob Jelley, who also owned a car dealership as one of his other businesses – he fixed him up with a white Renault Mégane."

Murali would make one final Country Fresh Senior League Division Two appearance for Ashby, picking up 6/27 as Ratby were rolled for 68 in pursuit of 243/4. Meanwhile, the Ivanhoe were recording a first win of the season at home to Blossomfield, recovering from 88/5 to chase down 178 without further loss. Twenty-four hours later, a trip to face a strong Market Harborough side, Ivanhoe's attack would have a shiny new Sri Lankan toy, a still unheralded Test cricketer who had appeared as if from nowhere. The wrists from the mists.

* * *

The just-turned-23-year-old "Murali Duran" of May 1995 was nowhere near the 26-year-old bowler who snagged 16/220 at The Oval to inspire Sri Lanka to a first Test victory on English soil. The cricketer being ferried down the A6 that Sunday lunchtime had played 18 Tests and had 63 wickets to his name – 3.5 per game as opposed to the six-per-game ratio he finished with – taken at a cost of 31.53 apiece, against a final career average 22.72, and at a strike rate of 74.9 versus the 55 he would carry into retirement. Sure, his scalps already included Mohammad Azharuddin three times, Martin Crowe twice, Mark Waugh, Mike Gatting, Brian Lara and Carl Hooper once apiece – none of them shabby players of spin – but there were no ten-wicket matches as yet (he would do this 22 times in his remaining 115 Tests) and just four of his eventual haul of 67 five-fors, while none of his 18 Player of the Match awards had yet been pouched. Still, it is inconceivable today that an international cricketer of any repute could turn up for a game of club cricket and nobody would know who they were. Here was a mystery spinner, and no one had a Scooby Doo.

"It's a lovely ground, with a beautiful pavilion," recalls Ivanhoe's young seamer Martin Crowson. "We were sitting outside before the game and were discussing the new Sri Lankan we had coming.

None of us knew who he was. Apparently, we were due to get Hashan Tillakaratne, but I think the deal had fallen through. So this guy Murali turns up and we head over to the nets…"

Skipper John 'Bogey' Beaumont had strapped on a front pad. The team's erstwhile spin twins – Dr Guy Jackson, a slow left-armer and future manager of the ECB's National Performance Centre in Loughborough, and 20-year-old offie Tim Mason, part of the same England under-19s side as Michael Vaughan and Marcus Trescothick, and later to play 20 first-class games for the Foxes and Essex – each rolled their arm over. "It was a mat on a concrete base," says Beaumont. "Neither ball turned more than a couple of inches. Murali bowled his first ball and it went a yard. And these nets were unresponsive to spin. I couldn't believe what I'd just seen."

"The look on John's face was priceless," adds Sutliff. "This was the first ball we'd ever seen him bowl, and on an artificial surface. It went past his left shoulder. We obviously thought: well, this guy seems quite good!"

The other common first impression with Murali tended to be that his action looked suspect. And so it was that shortly after the new overseas player had indicated his surname's preferred orthography to scorer Peter Connolly ("he handed me a slip of paper with his name written on it in block capital letters; at that time, he spelt it MURALIDARAN and, I've subsequently found out that he still prefers it being spelt that way"), Murali found himself bowling at Harborough's No.4 batter, Dave Wenlock, who had spent a couple of years on Leicestershire's books in the early 1980s. "I was fielding at short leg," says Mike Gibson, "as I did for every single ball that Murali bowled for the Ivanhoe – without taking a single catch there! After the first ball he faced, Dave turned to me and said, 'Gibbo, he chucks it'. Murali had the last laugh, though, because he left one that pitched miles outside off and bowled him leg stump."

Ah, the 'chucking' thing. Muralidaran, of course, had the most scrutinised action in the history of cricket, and the first storms would blow in five months after leaving Leicester when, under the intense glare of the Boxing Day Test in Melbourne, Darrell Hair – such a guardian of rectitude that he was later caught stealing $9,000 from a liquor store till – called him for throwing seven times in a three-over spell. Five days into the new year, he was called seven times more by Ross Emerson, standing in his first ODI. Under instruction from his captain, Arjuna Ranatunga, Murali bowled a leg-break, widely considered unthrowable, and was again called by Emerson, thereby exposing the umpire's scattershot judgement and 20 megawatt pre-judgement, ultimately requiring him to leave the field under police escort. Nevertheless, Murali's tour was done and he was sent by Sri Lanka's management for state-of-the-art biomechanical testing at the University of Western Australia where, long story short, three physiological abnormalities were discovered that gave the optical illusion of throwing: first, there was a permanent 38 degree bend at his elbow, meaning it was physically impossible for him to fully straighten his arm; second, his shoulder was flexible to the point of double-jointedness; and third, his wrists were freakishly supple, enabling him to impart the sort of revs usually restricted to particles zapping around the Hadron Collider.

These anatomical quirks were soon evident to his Ivanhoe teammates, not least during the habitual naps Murali would take on journeys to and from away games (the team were reluctant, in the pre-GPS era, to have him make his own way there in the Mégane). "Coming back from one game," recalls Beaumont, "I looked in the rear-view mirror and he was asleep, resting his head on the back of his hand, and the palm was almost touching the inside of his forearm." Still, this didn't stop some of the team nicknaming him 'Chucker' – "most people in the club thought he threw his quicker one," recalls Dearman – although this moniker was confined to the sanctity of the dressing-room. At least, once they'd figured out he could bowl, it was. Crowson recalls Murali being called for throwing by one umpire, although it was quickly explained to the official – with more than a little bending of the truth by Beaumont – that they had had his action videoed and green-lit, and it didn't happen again.

Murali ended up with 5/35 on debut, Jackson 4/36, and Market Harborough – a decent side who would finish third in the league – were rucked for 121. Ivanhoe knocked them off, four down, Gibson with an unbeaten 52. "Duran's five sparks early-season boost for Ivanhoe," trumpeted the *Mercury*'s 'Sports Green' supplement. Hungry like the wolf, Murali had even successfully persuaded the skipper he could bat – the reflex here is to indulge your international star, although fingertip access to the World Wide Web would have been helpful in ascertaining whether there was any substance to the sales pitch – but his entrance at No.4 brought neither runs nor the promise of future runs and he would not remain in that lofty position beyond the following Sunday's duck at Hinckley.

* * *

After that eye-popping start at Market Harborough, the Ivanhoe faithful were keen to see Murali on home turf, which before the Second World War had been the county ground at Grace Road, although in 1947 they moved out to what is now a smart multi-sport complex at Leicester Forest East, not far from the M1 services of the same name. Reigning champions Loughborough Town were the visitors, the pitch sluggish, and what the *Mercury* described as "the leg spin of Murali Duran" toiled away for 4/53 – beating the keeper as often as the batter, it seemed, hence Tebbatt's call-up the next day – while John Coyne, leading from the front, dug in for 66* as 'Boro finished with 182/7. Ivanhoe fell to 50/4 in reply, with early wickets for Dimi Mascarenhas's brother Malintha – known as 'Mints' to his friends, which inevitably became "Mince" in the *Mercury* – before a measured 81* from No.3 Adam McConkey and a "bristling" 22 from fiery opening bowler Mike Gamble saw them to back-to-back wins.

Although unable to make it three from three at Hinckley, it had been a strong start for Ivanhoe, for whom local tipsters had foreseen a season of struggle on the basis that their top three batters from the previous season were no longer around: the former Leicestershire player Russell Cobb, skipper in 1994, had switched to Kibworth in the County League; the overseas pro Luke Marshall stayed in Australia; while Chris Munden had been tragically killed while walking home from the club's bonfire night celebrations. Nevertheless, plenty of batting depth remained. This was amply illustrated in the next game, at home against Water Orton, who batted first and proved it wasn't only the *Mercury* subs who didn't know what to make of Murali as he wheeled his way through 17 overs of unstinting accuracy to snare 5/25. With Tim Mason taking 4/39 in support, the visitors were dismissed for 141. Ivanhoe made a meal of the chase, however, and it required an ice-cold ninth-wicket partnership between Crowson and Mark Challenger, son of the Showaddywaddy drummer Romeo Challenger, to secure the ten points.

Crowson still marvels at the slightly surreal light that is cast on these weeks from the summit of Murali's subsequent achievements. "I still tell people when Murali's name crops up that I played with him," he says. "They're like, 'What, you played against him in a charity game?' I'm like, 'No, he was a teammate.' They're absolutely astonished." (If this was a tale oft-told over a Sunday pint, there was a Sri Lankan flavour to Crowson's ultimate pub story, which involved him taking a hat-trick with the first three balls of the game against Kibworth in 2008, two of them Ivanhoe teammates from The Summer of Murali: Sutliff and Mason. "There's not a person I know who hasn't heard that story at least five times. I strutted around for a while claiming I was the world record holder until someone pointed out that Chaminda Vaas had done it in a World Cup game.")

The following Saturday brought a trip to Lichfield, the city of Dr Samuel Johnson's *bons mots anglais* and Michael Fabricant's BoJo toupee; home, too, of a uniquely triple-spired medieval cathedral, three stumps awaiting their demolition by an iconoclast spinner. "What we hope ever to do with ease, we must first learn to do with diligence." Word up, Big Sam.

In seaming conditions, Gamble and Challenger – a nominatively perfect duo for cracking cases in sleepy cathedral cities – were given seven overs apiece but failed to find any substantial leads, Pritchett making his way to 14 and Peers to 29. Beaumont pushed the Murali button and the wizard was soon making the breakthrough, skipper pouching the catch. He then made another. Then a third. After that, a fourth. Soon, a fifth. And a sixth. When Lloyd Tennant was bowled shouldering arms to a delivery of wildly improbable geometry, thoughts turned to the hallowed ten-for. But Tim Mason, providing the straight-man support act, nipped in with the eighth before Murali polished off the last two for 13.4-5-24-9. Decent.

The run chase was not quite as straightforward as it might have been, however, and even required Murali to come in at No.9, scores level, to hit the winning runs – the apocryphal version of which has him wearing gloves only, no pads, smiting his first ball for four then marching off, although in actual fact he ran out there, fully padded up, because it was starting to drizzle. But yes, it was an ungainly hack, ball leaving the bat face at another improbable angle, before he dashed off to his teammates' acclaim.

Gibson was soon into the psy-ops, telling the *Mercury*: "I don't think people know how to play him. If you block him, you're struggling – and he likes batsmen to have a go at him, too." He wasn't wrong. It was something of a double-pincer, a difficult puzzle for the Central League batters to solve, even if Muralidaran was still honing the finer points of his craft. Indeed, he hadn't even set his eyes on a *doosra* yet – the big reveal would be in Peshawar two months later, Saqlain's debut – let alone have one in the repertoire. The top-spinner was a work in progress. He would develop drift only when Bruce Yardley briefly replaced Dav Whatmore as Sri Lankan coach in 1997, after which the ball would sometimes bend like a Judd Trump deep screw in and out of baulk. He didn't really feel comfortable bowling around the wicket (and in any case, in club cricket, with its at times contentious sightscreen-pushing etiquette, this might depend on teammates' willingness to put their shoulder to the wheel). He dropped in the odd quicker ball, the odd leggie, and he tilted the angle of the seam: sometimes saucered, sometimes scrambled. Mainly, he altered his release point and where the ball pitched, stretching and pulling at the batters' footwork like a breadmaker his dough. There was no post-DRS enlightenment in officials, either, so the line he needed to pitch it when it was ragging big would usually result in the ball being safely kicked away. Most people simply played him on line, as would the Aussies' go-to dead-batting nightwatchman, Jason Gillespie, a little while after Murali had absorbed those lessons from Saqi: "I thought I'd got a read on him: if it was two feet outside off, it was the off-break; if it was straight, the *doosra*. Then he went round the wicket and I was absolutely fucken stuffed!"

* * *

When not chilling with Atappattu and Tillekaratne in his digs on Syston High Street, Murali would usually be found practising somewhere. "He worked very hard," recalls Abeysundera, "going to the nets on his own at four o'clock every day to bowl." Martin Crowson recalls turning up at Ivanhoe one day to see Murali bowling at a single stump on the square, using only one ball: "If he missed it, he'd have to go and fetch it from the boundary. He said it used to help him concentrate, knowing each ball counted."

He popped down to Kent to see Aravinda a couple of times and he dropped into Leicester city centre, invariably parking the Mégane with scant understanding of British road markings, while often scooting there and back with scant regard for the speed limit, which on one occasion led to him spending the night in a police cell – Murali having assumed that having a policeman, Gamble, among his teammates, "would influence things like in Sri Lanka" – before Abeysundera came and straightened things out.

He turned out for Ashby Town in the odd midweek game – the stats I have been cited from which, unverified, are of such *numberwang* dimensions, even for Murali, that they cannot be faithfully reproduced here, although it should be noted that Abeysundera's penchant for ringers would in 2002 see Illston Abey demoted from the Leicestershire Premier League for fielding ineligible players under false names – and he looked forward to his bread-and-butter bamboozlements at the weekend.

Once having got his social bearings, which took about half a game, Murali was the same endlessly garrulous borderline nuisance in the Ivanhoe dressing-room as he would be for Lancashire, Chennai Superkings, Sri Lanka and the rest. He would tell tales from his nascent international career, prompted or otherwise. He would grumble about his position in the batting order. He would toss a ball incessantly, the sound of some hefty tropical insect trying to escape a lampshade. He would observe grown men spraying Deep Heat into the next-but-two batter's box and wonder about his life choices. He would stay for a lemonade, sometimes still tossing a ball, invariably in his cricket clobber: the full-kit banker. "He always turned up in his whites and always went home in them," recalls Chris Tandy, Ivanhoe's sometime opening batter. "In any weather, whether it had been raining or whatever, he always wore trainers, never spikes. And he always played in his Sri Lanka sweater."

With Murali having taken 14/49 in the two games since his relative man-handling at Hinckley, the batters of Burton and

Nuneaton may well have been happy that rain spared them their own Muralidexams. The next outing came at Bedworth, where a pair of grafter's forties from Beaumont and Gibson allowed Ivanhoe to post 179 and enjoy a bullish tea. It was a tough pitch, and they knew they had a sorcerer to unleash. "The whole team would be buzzing – and laughing – when he came on to bowl because the opposition had no idea what was coming next," recalls Tebbatt. "Mind you, as the wicket-keeper, neither did I. I was grateful I was behind the stumps and not in front of them. He had this intense stare and, if I'm honest, I was on the receiving end of more than a few of them."

Bedworth's reply started well, reaching 66/0 at one stage despite the ball jumping from the surface like a tick from a cow's ear. Gaz Loveridge dug in for 56, although would occasionally wince as the big, lbw-precluding lunge invariably meant taking the ball in the ribcage. "He turned round to me a couple of times," says Tebbatt, "and said, 'This *really* hurts when it hits you'. It was coming down so quickly, with so many revs on it." Murali would eventually make the breakthrough, working through another masterful spell of 21-11-33-5, backed up by Mason's 3/44, yet Bedworth hung on to restrict Ivanhoe to five points for the winning draw.

A week later, Ivanhoe welcomed Kenilworth Wardens, the pitch dry and looking *conducive*. Not that this was done at Murali's request – the Kandy Man, scion to a biscuit factory, didn't like it when the surfaces were too crumbly. "He used to complain about pitches at the Ivanhoe," confirms Sutliff, "because, of course, we would prepare things that would spin and when it hit the dry and dusty bits it would turn square. He'd almost prefer to play on a green one, but we wanted these dustbowls because the oppo' wouldn't be able to score."

As if to prove Murali's point, Wardens batted first and proceeded to post the highest score Ivanhoe conceded during the Sri Lankan's stint. Opener Rob Field chipped in with 40, remembering to this day the six he smeared from Murali "after being totally done in the flight", while Jason Pyott made 50 and Saurashtra batter Brij Dutta compiled a commanding 111, those learnèd Indian wrists, feet and eyes defying the 'page one, paragraph one' English dogma about never cutting the offie as he repeatedly pierced the undermanned off-side field. Dutta was unable to return the following summer but recommended his state skipper Shitanshu Kotak, who, despite initial difficulties over a suitable nickname, would stay at Wardens for 20 years, the transliterated first 'h' eventually dropped.

Murali finished with 4/74, Kenilworth with 237 all out – a potentially stiff chase turned to rubble by openers Sutliff and Tim Boon, that year's Leicestershire beneficiary and sometime winter employee of Mr Abeysundera at Leicester Dyers. The pair blitzed their way to 150 inside 25 overs before Boon fell for 94, Sutliff continuing on to 92 as the target was passed with 12 overs to spare. Ivanhoe had moved into second place, in the slipstream of Lutterworth, who were starting to get the sort of breaks assumptive champions get. Against Lichfield, short leg Shafiq Quayyim held a catch between his knees from the game's second-last ball to turn five points into ten. And while Ivanhoe were galloping to victory over Kenilworth, Lutterworth won off the last ball of the match after Northampton Saints' No.11 walked for a gloved catch that the umpire later admitted he would not have given out. Ivanhoe would have been hoping for a similarly charitable attitude when they headed south for their next game, although this was unlikely.

* * *

Northampton Saints had won the Central League nine teams in 12 seasons between 1979 and 1990, the latter part of it under the hard-nosed captaincy of Ray Swann, a PE teacher from Blyth near Newcastle-upon-Tyne who had stayed in the East Midlands after graduating from Loughborough College. Swann joined Saints in 1987, aged 36, after a long spell at Old Northamptonians, where he was the first player to make 1,000 runs in a Northants League season. Two years later he resumed Minor Counties cricket after a 17-year hiatus, now for Bedfordshire having debuted as a teenager for Northumberland against Cheshire in a game shown on Tyne-Tees TV. By the time the Murali Roadshow was rolling into town, he was a still-fiery 44-year-old joined in the team by his 16-year-old son, Graeme, with whom he had been at the crease when the latter made his first senior hundred, diving into the dust at the bowler's end as the 14-year-old called him through for a two that wasn't really on. Confidence was never an issue for the younger cygnet. "The next time, he got his hundred with 30 overs left," recalls Swann *père*. "I told him, 'You could get a monster here', but he hit the next ball straight up, was caught at extra cover and walked off laughing. I batted on and got 148 not out..."

With Central League games stipulating that each team had to provide an umpire, and that failure to do so brought a mandatory points deduction, the 49-year-old Dearman was pulled from the second team and roped in to officiating. He clearly remembers the first words uttered by Ray Swann, in flat Geordie tones, as he stood at the non-striker's end and got his first close-up look at Murali bowl: "Fook'n hell".

Sliding into the middle order after a long spell of seam-up bowling, Ray had arrived at the crease to find Graeme there, grinning from ear to ear. Despite – or perhaps because of – his tender years, Swann Jr was not permitted to bowl in club matches by the hierarchy at Northants – a misguided layer of cotton-wool protection from the Saturday-afternoon swipers, thought father – so had to stand around as Ivanhoe posted 230/8, Sutliff making 89 of them and Gibson 76.

After tea, the player the *Mercury* at this stage knew as "Gary Swann" headed out to open the batting, escaping a vociferous appeal for caught and bowled in Mike Gamble's first over, the square leg umpire adjudicating that the ball hadn't carried. Although still small, the young GP Swann was a precociously talented shot-maker. However, once his future co-star in the 'Rubicon Drinks 50p coin challenge' came on, he dug in and curbed those instincts. "It was spinning *miles*," he recalls. "If he got too straight it was fizzing over my shoulder and the keeper couldn't get anywhere near it. I reckon there were five or six loads of four byes. He just kept fizzing it to the fence!"

The top order came and went, young Swann recalls, none of them getting to grips with the Sri Lankan puzzle. "One of our batsmen, Neil Francis – nickname 'Trevor', of course, a lawyer who played hockey for England – he came in and I said, 'Mate, whatever you do, don't try and hit through the off side against the spin. He's turning it miles.' Trev was like, 'Okay Graeme, we'll see about that.' First ball: big cover drive, bowled leg stump."

By the time dad had joined him, the instructions had not changed: "As I went in, Graeme said, 'He's turning it really big. Even if it's miles outside off stump, don't try scoring off him. Just do what you normally do, Dad, and we'll be alright'. I'd love to say it was comfortable, but it was anything but. Graeme collared him a couple of times, otherwise it was just survival."

That 'collaring' entailed Graeme hitting Murali over the short straight boundary and onto the roof of Cherry Orchard Middle School. In some versions of his account of this day, Swann sheepishly admits, he may have upped the number of sixes to five, although he does now concede that since Murali's figures were 5/30 from 15 overs, number of maidens unknown, this was somewhat improbable – not impossible, technically, but unlikely. By the time he had holed out at deep midwicket for 68, Swann's partnership with paterfamilias had gone a long way to denying Ivanhoe the win. It was a certainly a satisfying experience to imbibe as he pestered one of the seniors to buy him a pint of lager – an educative experience, in fact: "I think that day had quite a lot of influence on me, albeit subconsciously. You just don't see spin like that. I grew up thinking that if you don't spin it hard there's no point bowling spin, which went against everything you're taught in England, where it's all about being accurate first and foremost."

Meanwhile, Lutterworth were picking up ten points without setting foot on the pitch as rock-bottom Rugby failed to put out a team. All of which meant there was little cause for trepidation when Ivanhoe welcomed Rugby the following week, looking for a return to winning ways. Sure enough, Murali bagged 5/39 in a routine eight-wicket victory, setting things up nicely for the top-of-the-table showdown with Lutterworth.

* * *

"It is perhaps too early to talk about championships going on the line," wrote Paul Jones in the *Mercury*, "but today's Lutterworth-Leicester Ivanhoe clash could go a long way toward deciding the Central League title." Over the preceding weeks, Lutterworth's pot-stirring 52-year-old keeper-captain Jeff Baxter had been keen to emphasise that his was a home-grown team, the subtext of which, the cryptological community were saying, was that Ivanhoe were riding on the back of Murali's wizardry, on the subject of whom Jones's preview had this to say: "He can hardly expect any assistance from the groundsman at Coventry Road, who is hardly likely to prepare a dusty track to aid his turn." Not a problem.

Obtuse at the best of times, 'Backo' was being mightily disingenuousness here, for Lutterworth had tried very hard to bring back their overseas pro from the 1993 season, Vaughn 'Hungry' Walsh, a 30-year-old 5' 8" Antiguan tearaway who didn't make his first-class debut for Leeward Islands until the age of 27, but who soon found himself touted by compatriot Andy Roberts as the quickest in the Caribbean, a view with which Michael Atherton came to concur after England's 1994 tour. Needless to say, Walsh sent shivers down spines in Leicestershire's club cricket firmament, where he played initially for Leicester Nomads before moving to Lutterworth and then Barrow Town. In one mythical cup match in 1991, he took 9/2 – eight bowled, one lbw, both runs no-balls – and was denied a crack at all ten because the last man felt that, on balance, he was quite happy not to bat, ta very much.

Still, the fact was that Lutterworth held a 16-point lead, which Baxter required no second invitation to point out placed the pressure squarely on the Ivanhoe, somewhat in the manner of Jose Mourinho one year before a crunch game against Arsène Wenger's Arsenal: "Pressure? What pressure? I look at the table and I see Chelsea leads by five points. The question is: after the match, is the lead two points, five points or eight points? The pressure, *I sink*, belongs to them."

Defeat would be terminal for Ivanhoe's title prospects, yet Baxter was mistaken in thinking that the worst-case scenario would see his team end the day with a six-point lead, because by evening 12 points had been trimmed from it, Lutterworth having been deducted two points for slow over rate as Ivanhoe put together a massive 261/9, with half-centuries for McConkey, Sutliff and Gibson. In reply, Murali was restricted to a measly three wickets for only the second time that summer – albeit this was 3/14 off 13 overs as the hosts crashed to 84 all out. The Ivanhoe had won by 177 runs.

Eight days later, after a restorative victory had kept the Lutterworth nose in front, Baxter was telling the *Sunday Mercury* that "no one can stop us". The only explanation for such a proclamation – other than delusion – was that Baxter had learnt already that Murali was leaving. The Sri Lankan board insisted that players report home a month in advance of overseas tours – they were heading to Pakistan at the end of August – so there would be no Hollywood ending here, no shoulder-mounted ride from Ivanhoe turf and into the sunset, glories delivered. The story is of a future all-time great turning up out of the blue, doing very well for half a season, then disappearing into the night, en route to cricketing immortality. Baxter was thus proven correct, the title would be theirs, Ivanhoe coming in second, but not before Murali had signed off with 5/8 in a 170-run trouncing of Blossomfield, who were shot out for "a sad 44".

The 18/91 Murali had snared in his final four outings suggest he was getting the hang of things – that he might have gone okay for the remainder of the campaign, might have been a handful on the late-July and August bunsens. The final ledger read 53 wickets at 7.81, top of the averages by a distance, with a strike rate of 20.05 balls per wicket and an economy rate of 2.34. With the bat, there was a less impressive 67 runs at 11.17 – although, insofar as this figure is higher than his bowling average, it qualifies him as the all-rounder he always claimed to be!

"If Murali had stayed we'd have won the league, I'm absolutely certain of that," asserts Gibson, no stranger himself to a little press-assisted pot-stirring. "I told the *Mercury* that we were trying to sign him for 1996, but I was being tongue-in-cheek, putting it out there to get a reaction. It was never going to happen. We all knew he was going on to bigger and better things. I was just trying to wind the other clubs up."

After the tour of Pakistan came those Hairy problems in Australia before the ICC cleared his action, allowing him to play a key part in Sri Lanka's shock World Cup win in March 1996, Murali sending down 10-0-31-1, the most economical figures in the final, before Aravinda's lordly 107* steered them past Australia's 241 – all of which was a long way from that debut at Market Harborough, the memories of which remain vivid today, adds Gibson. "We'd all played a pretty decent level but to have someone like that in the team was just an amazing thing. It's something that always comes up when any of us get together. I'm sure for the people who faced him it's the same – the all-time leading wicket-taker in Test cricket playing in Leicestershire club cricket. It's hard to believe it really happened."

To remind them of it all, Ivanhoe have Murali's Lancashire shirt from a dozen years later framed and mounted on the pavilion wall. There was no glorious ending, no first Central League title, but they will always have their unbeaten half-season with the 800-wicket wizard, in whose honour they adapted the team's traditional victory song:

Row, row, row the boat, gently down the stream,
Murali, Murali, Murali, Murali, life is such a dream.

9

Abdul Qadir (and Imran Khan)
at Hanging Heaton and Stenhousemuir (and Wakefield)

Deep in the dustiest dungeons of YouTube lurks a grainy and soundless ten-minute film of a club cricket match in Scotland from 1985 – Holy Cross Academicals against Stenhousemuir in the quarter-final of the Masterton Trophy, since you ask – a video that was posted on 17 April 2009 and which, at the time of writing, has been viewed just 343 times. The film's chief point of interest is the identity of the bowler, a squat fellow with weightlifter's thighs and yacht-rock mullet who happens to be one of the greatest leg-spinners ever to draw breath.

Despite the smudgy, lo-res pixellations, the idiosyncrasies of the bowler's approach are immediately recognisable: the licked fingertips, flicked ball fizzing on the palm; the strutting steps, elbows jutting into a praying-mantis gather and tongue presumably protruding as he completes this *tour de torque*. Yes, prancing in obliquely to the crease for 'Stenny' on this overcast Edinburgh evening is Abdul Qadir, 27 years old and 33 games into a 67-Test career ultimately bringing him 236 wickets at 32.81 and what was at the time the fifth – and remains the eighth – best bowling analysis in Test history: 37-13-56-9 against Mike Gatting's vexed England in Lahore, a couple of years after his tormenting of the perplexed Holy Cross swipers – baffled batters aiming wholly 'cross the line as they try and counter the trickster's repertoire.

Short leg is garbed in the old style – melon unprotected, shinnies still a glint in the kitman's eye, unmentionables securely stowed – and, worst of all, is fielding not in the regular position (i.e. square on to the putative forward stride, terminus for the spitting wrong'un that travels via glove and thigh to bread basket) but at a 45-degree angle to the striker's wicket: which is to say, right in the mooing arc. The bowler might not be bounding in with quite the whirligig verve of, say, his famous Faisalabad evisceration of Viv and the Gang, or any of the four ten-wicket games he reeled off against England, yet it is imperative for the safety of the short-leg fielder, Tommy Dickson, that he stays mindful of the dangers. Indeed, one of the film's Comic Sans captions is soon proclaiming 'Steve Mather Almost Hits Qadir for 6', before we then see an erroneous umpire's corrected signal deprive the lanky larruper of what would be the oratorical *coup de grace* of a brandy-soaked and frequently aired anecdote. "Did I ever mention the time I hit Abdul Qadir for six?" (Once or twice, Steve. Once or twice.)

Five-and-a-half minutes in, another caption: 'Abdul persuades Sandy that Vishnu was bowled'. That "persuades" is doing some heavy lifting here, implying perhaps that the batter had *not* been bowled and that the act of convincing the umpire was another of the sorcerer's tricks. Alas, the delivery was one of the few for which the cameraman had decided to tighten in the focus at the bowler's end. We thus see Abdul send up the loopiest of 'lollipops' – Dickson having been moved out of Boot Hill – then immediately dash toward short midwicket in anticipation of a return catch clunked or spooned in that general area, giving it the air of a slapstick ruse from a Charlie Chaplin flick. Two or three scurrying steps' ground are made before whatever happens at the business end of the pitch happens – an event beyond our perception and seemingly the umpire's, too – after which the wizard appears to *appeal for a bowled decision* against the unmoved batter. The aforesaid Sandy obliges, and Vishnu Chetty has little choice but to troop off, not the only one to be comprehensively defeated by the Pakistani that season.

Qadir may be toying with them – as with those viral videos of toddlers who have fallen into the gorilla enclosure at a busy Japanese zoo, only to be absent-mindedly and tenderly pawed by the silverback patriarch as crowds look on aghast – yet there is a prevailing sense that he could assert himself more assiduously over the unholy cross-batters should he so wish, that he could bomb rather than bluff them out. If he were stretched. But the point of him being in Stenhousemuir was that he wouldn't be unduly stretched, wouldn't be flogged through 40-over days on Trent Bridge featherbeds by some unsympathetic county skipper; that he would have the opportunity up there in Scottish club cricket – principled professional cricketer though he may be – to lark about some.

Take, for instance, the friendly at Forfarshire's Forthill ground in Dundee some four chilly weeks earlier, 24 hours after a steely Glaswegian by the name of Alex Ferguson had led his Aberdeen team to a third Scottish Football League title in six years (only two clubs have won it since: guess which). Stenhousemuir batted first and Qadir slid up the re-jigged order to biff a quick 29 before slipping into a chauffeur-driven car that had arrived to ferry him the half-hour ride over to the Gleneagles Hotel, where the Pakistani ambassador was waiting to take tea in one of those stately rooms in which, back in June 1977, the eponymous agreement was reached by Commonwealth heads of state to impose sanctions on Apartheid South Africa.

A couple of hours or so after buzzing off to hob-nob with His Excellency Ali Arshad, Abdul was back in Dundee to take 2/19 from 11 probing overs as Stenhousemuir kept the engine oiled following three wins from their opening three East League games. It is unlikely Qadir would have vamoosed for two hours mid-game had this trip to Forfarshire been a league match, high tea invite with the high commissioner or not. Still, it wasn't entirely unusual for him to slip off the field for refreshment, particularly in the early weeks as the biting Scottish winds chilled those Punjabi bones. "Abdul cultivated the tea ladies," chuckles Dickson. "They adopted him, waiting on him with coffee and vegetarian snacks and sandwiches. In the cold, he'd bowl an over then wander off for a swallow of coffee, then re-emerge. I don't think the umpires were always absolutely on the money about when he was allowed to bowl. The rest of us were less privileged with the tea ladies."

Abdul couldn't always be guaranteed to be found on the field, but then everyone spent a lot of time sheltering from the elements that year, which remains the worst Scottish summer on record – these dating back to 1910 – with 455.6mm of rainfall between June 1 and August 31. Avoiding getting *drookit* meant a glut of dressing-room cricket. Surprisingly, Qadir wasn't much cop. "Whilst he was keen to play and was undoubtedly the man who resurrected leg-spin bowling," says Dickson, "he was crap at indoor cricket. The habit was for a small cohort of us to use a stump, a tennis ball and a bin as the wickets. There were local rules, and the legal action was underarm. He couldn't play the spinning tennis ball and never mastered the wrist and finger action that were needed to be a success. I think Jack Iverson would have been unplayable."

Nevertheless, in amongst the drizzly Macbethian atmospherics there was plenty of hocus-pocus for his teammates to savour – plenty of "double, double, toil and trouble, fire burn and cauldron bubble". But the bigger question here is how the only full season of cricket played on British shores by Abdul Qadir – one of the sport's genuine superstars (in 1984 John Arlott proclaimed him to have replaced DK Lillee as "the cult figure of the game") and a name-your-price desirable as a county overseas pro – came to be in one of what the acerbic English architecture critic Jonathan Meades referred to in the title of the final episode of *Off-Kilter*, his three-part BBC documentary series on Scottish urbanism, as 'The Football Pools Towns'.

* * *

It was the sole *full* season, but not the only club cricket Abdul Qadir played in the British Isles. There had been a wee dabble three years earlier, when he was still very much a literal 'mystery spinner' – no one in the UK having yet seen him bowl on television – and had signed up for what turned out to be a short stint at Hanging Heaton on the edge of Dewsbury in West Yorkshire, who in 1982 were about to embark on just a third year of Bradford League cricket. David Garner's men had cruised undefeated through the second division in 1980, Jamaican-born Ronnie Hudson becoming the first man ever to record a BCL double-hundred as he chucked 1,210 runs into the promotion push, and they had finished their second season third in the top flight, with left-arm spinner Roger Braithwaite winning the first of three BCL Bowler of the Year prizes in six years. The cake was baked; Abdul just needed to provide the icing.

Qadir had been brought over by the Gujarat-born businessman Solly Adam, owner of a Dewsbury sports shop and a chain of local grocers, Pick 'n' Pay. Adam was also a well-known 'middle man' fixing up south Asian cricketers in Yorkshire, the most famous of which would be the deal that made Sachin Tendulkar the county's first overseas player in 1992.

Adam was initially beguiled by Qadir while watching him bowl at Habib Bank's nets in December 1981, and later that day asked him whether he fancied a year in the English leagues. Once back in the UK, Adam called Hanging Heaton chairman Brian Wilkinson to tell him he might have a player for him. Qadir had just eight Test caps and 22 wickets at the time, but Adam was adamant he would cut it: "I told Brian that if he didn't take more wickets than Iqbal Qasim [the Pakistan Test left-arm spinner, pro at his own club, Spen Victoria, in 1980], I'd pay him myself and find them another pro."

This was tough cricket, however, certainly one of the top leagues in the country, one to which the Yorkshire-contracted players would gravitate for a weekend earner when the schedules permitted, one in which clubs could legally brown-envelope four players if they wished, thus providing something of a honeypot for the *crème de la* club-cricketing *crème* from the many nearby leagues clustered either side of the Pennines. They often had the coffers to do so, too, back when pubs were forced to close between 3pm and 5:30pm on Saturdays and from 2:30pm to 7pm on Sundays, whereas the social clubs could stay open – provided they served food – through those long, thirsty afternoons. Kerching! Gnarly, nous-filled and granite-hewn, the Bradford League was thus a competition that Pakistan's brand new Test skipper, Imran Khan – planning for a three-Test series against the post-Botham's-Ashes England – felt would provide useful acclimatisation for a star leg-spinner who had never before played in the country. Not that Hanging Heaton knew for certain when they signed him that he would soon be spirited away.

The teenage Imran had himself played half-seasons of Birmingham League cricket for Stourbridge in 1971 and '72 while at Royal Grammar School Worcester, the 18-year-old even appearing for the BDCL rep XI in the final of the '71 President's Trophy against the Bassetlaw League, a couple of months after being thrown in the deep end at Edgbaston for his Test debut. He was no stranger to league cricket in West Yorkshire, either, having spent a short spell at Wakefield in the Central Yorkshire League in 1977 while waiting impatiently for his transfer from Worcestershire to Sussex to go through.

The Wakefield gig had been arranged by Philip Hodson, a Cambridge Blue and Imran's 1973 Varsity opponent. Hodson had met and married Tony Greig's sister, Sally Ann, on one of his winter trips to Western Transvaal and was asked by Greigy, the Sussex skipper, if he could find Imran some cricket to keep him ticking over. Hodson was himself playing for York, in a different league, but since his father pulled most of the strings at Wakefield CC, this seemed an ideal placement. Imran was signed up for a month-long CYL stint, encompassing ten games, before making his Sussex bow at the end of July (coincidentally, Garth le Roux, his equally fearsome new-ball partner at Hove the following summer, was himself playing club cricket a short hop away at Lascelles Hall on the edge of Huddersfield in 1977). Imran's weekends were thus spent at Solly Adam's house in Dewsbury, weekdays in London. "He told me he had left Worcester because it was dead," Adam recalls with a chuckle. "He said: 'There are no girls, no autographs!'"

Imran was by this stage a long way from those puppyish Stourbridge sorties. The Pashtun playboy had spent the non-nocturnal part of his time up at Oxford deconstructing and re-engineering his action so that he could upgrade from 'purveyor of heavy ball' to 'blimey, that's *quiiiiick*'. If not yet quite carrying the full regal bearing of the statesmanlike cricketer and cricketing statesman he became, there was nonetheless an eagle mindset that saw him soar above the clammy patchwork of parochial passions. Indeed, Adam recalls Imran turning down a sizeable collection one day after scoring a fifty in front of "a big, big crowd" at Liversedge. "He said, 'What's this?' Both hats were full. So I explained this tradition to him. He said, 'What am I, a beggar? Give it back.' So in the end they put it behind the bar, which made him very popular!"

"I think Imran just wanted a net to keep himself relatively fit and wasn't really interested in the team or the league," reflects Hodson. "He brought a lot of publicity to the club, but little else. He didn't take many wickets or score too many runs, so the gamble of signing him failed. Obviously, he should have bowled a full length; but no, he bowled a county length."

Or, if you riled him, he was more than happy switching to throat-threatening length, as was the case when Wakefield visited the decidedly compact surrounds of Hanging Heaton, still then in the CYL. Hodson went along to watch and remembers Heaton No.3 Alex Jackson taking evasive action from one Imran rocket, the ball ricocheting from bat handle into the car park of the Fox & Hounds at fine leg, while another bumper apparently sailed clean over the boundary, teaching the future MCC president that the Laws did not allow for six byes to be awarded. Ronnie Hudson, meanwhile, recalls being caught behind by Wakefield keeper Allan Broadhead, "who was standing no more than five or six yards from the rope". Spicy.

A couple of weeks later, Wakefield were at Ossett in the Heavy Woollen Cup – named after the epicentre of the textile industry and the oldest organised knockout competition in the UK, pre-dating the formation of even the most venerable leagues – the qualification criterion for which was the club sitting within eight miles of Batley Town Hall. Not someone who could ever be described as meek, Imran was once again irked into giving the batter an impromptu sniff test, leading to an altercation with Ossett skipper Dave Ward – who, along with Geoff Beck, became one of two men whose bones he broke that afternoon.

"Imran bowled a quick bouncer and Ward, the non-striker, turned round and swore at him and called him something very bad," recalls Adam, confirming that it was, allegedly, the P-word, which is wrong in at least two main ways: moral and strategic. "So Imran says, 'Okay, let's wait until you get to the other end. We will see how you play me.' First ball hits him straight on the forearm and breaks it. Imran then showed him where the dressing-room was."

Ahead of the 1982 tour, then, Imran was well aware that the spunky, spikey Tykes would not be standing on ceremony. Abdul touched down in Manchester and was taken by Brian Wilkinson straight to his welcome party – which is to say, a specially organised net for them to run the rule over their shiny new bauble, with Hudson the guinea pig in pads trying to operate Googly Translate. Two days later, the pro got into his match-day work, starting with 3/38 from 17 tidy overs against Bowling Old Lane, who nevertheless hung on eight down. Solid start.

Seven days later, Qadir returned 8-0-51-0 against a strong Farsley side who romped past their 270 target thanks to a top three who would go on to make 218, 216 and 248 first-class appearances respectively: 70 runs coming from the bat of Kevin Sharp, 100 from Ashley Metcalfe and 26 from Tim Boon. (Raymond Illingworth, unretired and back in the county game with Yorkshire at 49 after a four-year hiatus, also turned out a few times that summer for his boyhood club, which adds another 787 first-class games to the pot.) It was the first day of May, the Punjabi pinkies were cold and unresponsive in the Baltic conditions – "it was absolutely *freezing* and Abdul must have had four or five jumpers on", chuckles Hudson, "I kid you not!" – and the Hanging Heaton hardcore were keeping as firm a grip of their views on the new overseas as the folklore says a Yorkshireman does of his £10 notes.

Imran was keeping close tabs on things, too, calling Solly every Saturday night for an update. Adam reported back that Wilkinson's feet were getting as cold as Qadir's fingers. He even had to petition Hanging Heaton to give it two more weeks of try-before-you-buy, after which, if they were still unhappy, he would accept the unwanted goods. Over the next four games, all doubts were laid to rest, the naysayers swayed by cricket's universal bottom line: numbers.

First, on the day the Pakistani touring party was announced, Abdul bounced in and bounced back with 6/56 against eventual champions Bingley, whose 186 nevertheless proved seven runs too many. The following day, against Spen Victoria in the Priestley Cup, it was 6-2-10-5, and Hudson is "pretty sure four of those runs came off the thigh-pad and should have been leg byes". The next league game saw Qadir jam out all the big tunes in a spell of 15-6-22-6 against Eccleshill, although Heaton once more failed to knock off the runs. And a week later, at home to Yeadon, the maestro really began to flex, completely upstaging the visitors' none-too-shabby spin attack: offie Geoff Cope, who had made his England bow in the same Lahore Test in which Qadir had debuted, and an 18-year-old Richard Illingworth, in the foothills of a long career that took him all the way to the 1992 World Cup final. Hanging Heaton raced to 257/5 from 45 overs – Hudson biffing a 60-minute ton as Illingworth was spanked for 1/82 off 11, Cope taking 0/47 off 11 – with Yeadon then crawling to 89/8 from 52 overs in reply, Qadir whirling merrily through 20-10-35-7 on a mild, late-spring day. Trees blossomed, bluebells bloomed and salacious West Yorkshire smiles burst forth, the sort that say: *good luck facing this stuff, pal.*

Then everything went tits up.

It was the second round of the Priestley Cup, at home to Undercliffe, whose attack was spearheaded by Peter Hartley – en route to 232 first-class appearances and the ICC umpiring panel – while the overseas pro was Haroon Rasheed, scorer of centuries in each of Qadir's first two Tests. Abdul had a maximum of three more West Yorkshire weekends before having to join up with the Pakistan squad, and was in a pretty good place with his bowling. It was coming out okay. As per the Khan Plan, cobwebs had been tickle-sticked away. Indeed, it is conceivable that Abdul would have reasoned that his recent form for Hanging Heaton – 24 wickets at 5.5 apiece, striking every 15 balls while going at 2.2 runs per over – would be enough to guarantee him choice of ends. But that was not so.

"Roger Braithwaite always bowled at the Club End," explains Hudson. "Against Undercliffe, David Garner brought Abdul on from that end after David Peel's opening spell. Strategically, it was a mistake because he needed Roger to bowl in tandem with him, and Roger had never bowled from the Fox End. So David was obliged to ask Abdul to change ends. And Abdul said no. David came over and told me what had happened. I said, 'Ask him again'. He did, and Abdul still refused to change ends. The Fox End is five or six metres shorter; it's slightly uphill and slightly into the prevailing wind. The slope that goes across the ground doesn't affect the wicket. He could have handled it, no problem. I can't think why Abdul was so adamant."

My guess – and this is pure speculation – would be that, despite Braithwaite being the reigning WH Foster Bradford League Bowler of the Year, Abdul *bhai* probably felt that the 60-20-132-24 he had sent down over the preceding four matches allowed him to regard himself as first fiddle, top of the pecking order, prima ballerina. Moreover, with an international colleague looking on from the opposition ranks, it's possible that Qadir didn't really see himself having to fit around local bowlers. No, no, no. Braithwaite wasn't going to be offered the Fox End, either, while impending defeat wasn't enough to prompt a U-turn from the Hanging Heaton hierarchy and give Abdul the end he wanted. Ergo, with figures of 1-0-1-0, that was the pro's shift done for the day. Actually, the season.

"David had consulted me," continues Hudson, outlining his firmly-held red lines, "and my view was that if the captain asks you to bowl from a certain end, whoever you are, then you bowl from that end. There's no discussion. So I said, 'If he's got to go, then he's got to go'. There was no question of giving in to Abdul. Doing that just to win a game? That's a nonsense. But he didn't storm off. He stuck around for the rest of the game and by the time we got into the bar it had become quite funny."

"I was looking forward to facing him, a world-class bowler," adds Undercliffe opener Dave Crossland, who had watched the six balls sent down at Haroon with especially keen interest, "but on the other hand I was also quite pleased he wouldn't be bowling as we had a cup match to win!"

Abdul did not play for Hanging Heaton again, kicking his heels in Dewsbury for a couple of weeks before rendezvousing in London with the Pakistan squad. The touring party headed from there up to Scotland for a low-key, sponsor-glad-handing warm-up for the warm-ups against the Noor Mahal President's XI in Partick on June 20, where embryonic contacts were made and faint future possibilities laid down by fate, like a civil engineer speculatively drawing the line of a potential rail track across a dusty plain. *If you will it, it is no dream.*

* * *

"To the 91.6 per cent of Britons who don't live in Scotland and to many of the 8.4 per cent who do," remarks Meades in his by turns affectionate and unapologetically supercilious scoot through 'The Football Pools Towns' of post-industrial Scotland, such places as Stenhousemuir, Cowdenbeath, Dunfermline, Alloa and so forth "have no existence other than as components of a Saturday afternoon rite. They're merely names on a football pools coupon." It is certainly unlikely that Abdul Qadir knew much about the place prior to 1985.

Stenhousemuir may have been off the beaten cricketing path, but it wasn't a total backwater. This was the club that bequeathed Brian Hardie to the game – scorer of 29 first-class hundreds as the methodical and Presbyterian wingman to Graham Gooch through Essex's golden 1980s, when ten major trophies found their way to Chelmsford. Hardie's mentors at Stenhousemuir were the former Essex wicket-keeper Bob Paterson and the adhesive ex-Scotland opening bat Morison Zuill, an accountant who had played against Bobby Simpson's 1964 Australians and who, aged 48 when Qadir arrived in Stirlingshire, was entering his 28th straight season as first-team captain. He would serve 31 in total, handing his lucky coin over to son Douglas for the next 20.

Taking on the job in 1958, AM Zuill was in situ for the 1965, '68, '71 and '79 Masterton Trophy wins, the Eastern region's midweek knockout competition. In 1974 and '75, he had steered the team through the regional phase of the William Haig Trophy, British club cricket's blue riband knockout event, where they eventually fell, respectively, to Sunderland in the last 16 and York in the last eight. And he had been part of the East League successes of 1955, '56, '58, '62, '68, '71 and '73 – a glorious year in which he also hoisted aloft the club's maiden Scottish Cup, scoring a POTM-winning 65 in victory over Perthshire in the final. But they had not won the league title since that golden summer, forced to watch on as Heriot's Former Pupils, Royal High, Watsonians, Heriot's FP, Heriot's FP, Heriot's FP, Heriot's FP, Heriot's FP, Heriot's FP, Heriot's FP and Kirkcaldy rode off with the spoils. In 1984, the year before Abdul arrived, they had finished second with the nominatively apt services of Derek Stirling – the New Zealand Test seamer once pummelled for 28 in an over by IT Botham – losing by ten wickets to Heriot's on the final day and thereby pipped by Kirkcaldy. The itch was becoming unbearable. So Zuill decided he would push the recruitment boat out and chance his arm with the world's greatest leg-spinner, who was being courted by both Surrey and Essex but had no doubt intuited that he would have been worked like a diamond-encrusted dog on the county treadmill.

"We found out during the winter that he might be available and we worked very hard to get him," Zuill told John Mann of the *Scottish Daily Express* for his article 'Hail Abdul, the Tartan Tweaker'. "We made the right approaches and had a bit of help from his fellow countryman Salahuddin, who played here as a pro with West of Scotland and with Ayr."

Zuill would in fact call Lahore on more than a dozen occasions, each time reassuring his prospective charge that he would be well looked after, that needs would be met, comforts assured, cricket stimulating – everything bar the weather guaranteed. Qadir pondered and mulled, hummed and hawed, then stuck a finger in the air to feel the cosmic vibrations and told Zuill that yes, he would come and play cricket in Stenhousemuir. It was a happy man who placed down the receiver that evening.

"Qadir himself," continued Mann, "is unsure about his reasons for coming to play at the club. 'When they phoned me at first I declined,' he explained. 'But they phoned me again and the captain Mr Zuill just seemed so honest and friendly about what the club had to offer that I decided I'd give it a go.'" *If you will it...*

Another important if less glamorous recruit was 26-year-old top-order batter Iain Philip, future winner of 135 Scotland caps (three of them in the 1999 World Cup) and four B&H gold awards when the likes of RJ Hadlee and CEL Ambrose were in the opposition. Another protégé of Bob Paterson, Philip was born and raised in Stenhousemuir, but at the age of 12 his father won the football pools – true story – and the family emigrated to Western Australia, where he played first-grade cricket in Perth with the likes of Barry Richards. "He was a fabulous batsman," says Dickson, "a destroyer of attacks when he was in. He would just murder mediocrity."

Abdul was clearly the headline act, though, having had his moments in that 1982 Test series and shone in the 1983 World Cup back on English soil. By the time he arrived in April 1985, he was the ICC's 12th-ranked Test bowler and starting to approach his mesmeric peak. Indeed, as the season unfolded, both the Stirlingshire and Scottish press would carry anguished features discussing whether these high-profile pros were "mercenaries" distorting the fairness of the competition. That was all further down the line, though.

Qadir lodged about 200 metres from the club with the man he called "Mr George", a.k.a. George Runciman, a hockey player at the nearby ICI Grangemouth club who, says Dickson, "may not have totally understood the concept of halal. Abdul would often ask John Goodall, our opening bowler, to get him a chicken that was properly killed." Not that Abdul was ever left wanting for anything, adds Stenhousemuir match secretary Duncan Walker: "There was no problem providing for him as he was so revered among the Asian community that regular deliveries of food would arrive on the doorstep."

A couple of months before touching down in Scotland, Qadir had been kicked off Pakistan's tour of New Zealand, accused by management, including skipper Zaheer Abbas, of not trying in the field. Initially, he was fined, but when he refused to pay and then complained to the press, he was bundled on a plane home. 'Stenny' could thus have been forgiven for harbouring some trepidation about a potentially difficult character – particularly if Zuill's due diligence had taken in Abdul's huffing Hanging Heaton exit – but there wasn't a trace of diva behaviour, says Goodall. "My memory of him is that he was a good team guy, very warm, very approachable, always giving tips. Despite being world famous, he was just one of the lads. He stuck around after the match. There was no big-headedness or prima donna behaviour. Nothing like that."

"He was a very proud cricketer and always gave of his best," emphasises Walker, shortly before issuing a gentle rebuke under the Misuse of Nomenclature Act. Apparently, 'Stenny' – as in *The Stenny Boys*, the history of the club written by John MacNeil – was an abbreviation coined by the *Scottish Sun* in the wake of a notable victory for the football club. "'Stenny' is a term much disliked by older members but is common among the young. In our heyday, we were known as 'the Muir' or 'Muiries'."

Indeed, *'Muir* is the preferred term of the *Falkirk Herald*, principal newspaper of the adjacent town a couple of miles south, where "in the late nineteenth century", explained Meades on BBC4, "the Barr family of cork cutters established a fizzy drinks business which would eventually produce an enduring masterpiece: Irn-Bru". Meades also noted that this famous Scottish beverage worked as a tanning agent, "romancing the pores", although there would not be too many sunbathing opportunities amid the near-constant rains of 1985. Still, despite the weather's inclemency, Qadir threw himself into things with both alacrity and humility, which wasn't the case for all new arrivals from the subcontinent.

* * *

Speak to any of Qadir's Stenhousemuir teammates and the story they most readily recall is the one that sounds like the title of the majority of noughties Booker Prize nominees: *The Bamboozlement of Mr Prabhakar*. It was a heist in two acts, the first played out on the opening day of the East League season on home soil at the Tryst, during which Qadir experienced something of an overseas-pro-in-the-UK rite of passage, certainly anywhere north of Manchester: a game dusted with (and pushing on through) light snowfall. Abdul was wrapped up in skipper Zuill's smart, cable-knit Scotland sweater, commandeered for the entirety of this 'summer' at 56 degrees north, a royal blue thistle adorning this occasionally spiky competitor's season. Even with fingers like frostbitten carrots, he managed to give it a rip.

The visitors were Leith Franklin, who had signed the Indian swing-bowling all-rounder Manoj Prabhakar as pro. He had played the first two of his 39 Tests against England the previous December, even opening the batting in the second innings on debut in Delhi, his hometown. Two months before that, in a Rothman's Asia Cup game in Sharjah, he had had a brief look at the Qadir wiles, which was enough for him to figure out the optimal gameplan, recalls Dickson. "John Goodall and I bowled the first half-dozen overs, Abdul trotting off twice to have a coffee and warm up his hands, at which point I was taken off, the shine having sufficiently gone, and the ball was tossed to Abdul. He was treated very carefully by Prabhakar, who pretty much left the Leith players to fathom him out for themselves."

Prabhakar made 70 out of the first 101, dismissed not by Qadir but off-spinner Willie Taylor, a gravedigger from a humble background who "was taught to use a knife and fork by the tea ladies when he came to the club", says Dickson. "He had a terrible stutter and was a quiet man, but he, like me, could swear well. He gave it a bit of a run-up, like Ronnie Barker in *Open All Hours*. Willie was a good bowler and a really prodigious spinner of the ball."

Leith were eventually knocked over for 155, the AQ Artistry Quotient bagging 5/52, followed up with a punchy and professional 64* to salvage a potentially ticklish situation. A good start to the campaign. It certainly providing an interesting prelude to the return game, when top-of-the-table 'Muir headed to Leith Links, a short hop across Irvine Welsh country from Hibernian FC.

Nine games in, Zuill hadn't yet lost a toss in the league, and this time he opted to bat first. Stenny were dismissed for 175, Qadir making 54 and Philip 57, while Prabhakar's zippy, skidding swingers – a sandpaper bowler in India, a tricky customer with juice in the pitch – bagged an evidently exhausting 5/35, for he declined on this occasion to take up his usual position at the top of the batting order.

If Qadir was offering passion and inspiration to the Stenny Boys, the effect 'Manoj the Motivator' was having on his own troops

– beyond 400 runs and 35 wickets in eight competitive outings – was less easily gauged. Some clues were nonetheless provided by an interview he gave to the esteemed WH Kemp before the game, which appeared in the following Wednesday's edition of the *Scotsman* under the headline 'A far cry from Delhi to Leith Links', Kemp describing "a cold damp wind blowing off the harbour" and Prabhakar in "his sunhat, but a sou'wester might have been more appropriate. And that on one of the better days of the summer."

Long enough was spent in Prabhakar's company for Kemp to ascertain "an outspoken attitude which is sometimes misconstrued", while venturing that captain David Cowper had "quite a delicate task" on his hands to marshall his star man. Subtext: he's an A-grade diva, certainly a man whose degree course at Delhi University was unlikely to have been in Public Relations. Leith, as you might expect, had no media manager sitting beside Manoj, snipping verbs from the shadows or smudging Vaseline onto the more strident adjectives. Thus it was, with Manoj having explained that, as a youngster, he had wanted to play international badminton but abandoned that path because the competition was too fierce, taking up cricket instead, he meditated briefly on Leith's strengths and weaknesses: "I've got to do everything, bowl, bat and field, and if I can't do anything … Franklin have no chance." Warming to his theme, Prabhakar observed that "it has been an interesting experience playing in Leith. The standard of cricket is not too good but the experience of playing on soft wickets has been worthwhile." Where Qadir would remark that he had "noticed some outstanding young talent in Scotland", Prabhakar was unequivocal about the local cricketing crop: "I haven't seen any very good Scottish cricketers." Something lost in translation, perhaps. Hang fire on the honorary citizenship.

There was certainly no great effort being made here to endear himself to the local cricketing firmament or to pump colleagues' tyres up, but then Prabhakar would go on to develop a fairly solid reputation as an awkward personality in Lancastrian league cricket – an 'arsehole', in the vulgar vernacular; 'wally' or 'prat' at the more Methodist end. Two years later, at Tonge of the Bolton League, he came second in the bowling averages and sixth in the batting – outperforming fellow all-rounders FD Stephenson, PV Simmons and CL King as Tonge landed the Hamer Cup – but late chairman Frank

Baldwin's well-thumbed after-dinner recollection of the season always had him waving the pro off at Manchester airport with V-signs and a tenuous synonym for *bon voyage*. It was a similar tale in the Central Lancashire League, at Norden in 1988 and Oldham in '89, as it was at Lowerhouse in the Lancashire League in 1991, where novice skipper Jez Hope recalls a remote, occasionally recalcitrant figure who had no interest in socialising, who would lie under the covers at training, and who incurred a ban for scratching up the ball against Roger Harper's Bacup. File under 'difficult' – no: 'abrasive'.

"Woe betide anyone who lets him down badly," mused Kemp, capturing the diva streak and diplomatic deficiencies of the Delhi man. "Some of his idiosyncrasies create confusion, such as last week against Stenhousemuir when, having taken five for 35 in helping to dismiss the opponents, he felt he could not open the batting. Franklin were caught on the hop." With more than a little artistic licence, Kemp adds that Prabhakar came in only minutes later, "still munching his tea" (no doubt having failed to rouse his colleagues into run-chase heroism). At which point came the legendary legerdemain, the jiggery-pokery, Abdul Copperfield's act of misdirection.

"It was the highlight of the season," says wicket-keeper Alan Smith. "Leith is a small and narrow ground and it's easy to hit boundaries, sideways at least. Prabhakar was one of the five-foot-six Indian fast bowlers of those days, but he could bat. When he came in Abdul stopped everything and took his time setting the field: eventually, eight on the off side, one on the leg. 'Stand wherever you like!' he said to the fellow on the leg side."

"It was majestic," adds Dickson. "At first, he carefully and obviously changed the field to show favour for the googly, moving me as a second short leg, then changed his mind and put me back in the gully."

"Prabhakar must have thought the same as me and everyone else," continues Smith. "But when Abdul came up to bowl, I thought: 'hold on, that's not a leg-break'. Prabhakar played no shot and, as he shouldered arms, his middle stump came out of the ground." Hook, line, sinker.

Kemp's *Scotsman* profile fails to record whether the Indian had fully swallowed his cheese and pickle butties by the time he was trooping off, but a golden duck for the pro led to 22 all out for Leith, thereby supporting the Prabhakar postulate (indeed, the following week Franklin racked up 285, of which Prabhakar made 182*, and a week later they were 36 all out). Meanwhile, Qadir finished with 6/12 and Goodall 4/6, the pair dovetailing beautifully. "I got a lot of bounce from my height, even on a Scottish wicket, and picked up wickets because they went after him," says Goodall, although he didn't always appreciate bowling at the other end to the wizard.

"John was a very good bowler and accomplished bringer of cheer with his jokes and one-liners, which kept us all in high spirits," says Dickson. "He bowled off about 15 paces and, prior to Abdul's arrival, would often bowl 15 to 20 overs on the trot. Not when Abdul was at the other end. John got one of the supporters to time Abdul's overs. It took him around one minute and 40 seconds to bowl a maiden over, and there were quite a few of those."

"I would still be huffing and puffing at long leg when I had to bowl again," Goodall adds. "There was one occasion when I hadn't even got my sweater back on by the time I had to go again."

Perhaps the speed with which Abdul rushed through things was attributable to a specific energy source, speculates Smith. "He was famous for what he called his *digadigs*, wee 'garden seeds' that he'd take before the game. We thought, 'what on earth are these?' So Morison asked him and Abdul gave him one. Morison didn't stop running for a day. He had so much energy. It was obviously some sort of stimulant, maybe a tablet to keep you awake. Anyway, these were what kept Abdul going."

If the first Prabhakar bout had been a split decision, the second was an emphatic knockout, shots fired across the Attari-Wagah border crossing, Pakistan 1 India 0, Stenny's lead at the top of the table consolidated. League standings were decided on percentage of possible points won – a counterweight to vagaries of weather or disparities in ground-drying equipment – and the *Scotsman* had been quick to install Stenhousemuir as East League favourites, Qadir having followed the opening day victory over Leith with 6/61 against Watsonians, whose 99 were knocked off after a mini-wobble at 70/6.

'Muir kept things at 100 per cent in the third game as Fauldhouse folded for 72, Kenyan World Cup batter and owner of the Kenyan General Store in Shotts, Abdul Rehman, top-scoring with 18. The game was disposed of in two hours and 21 minutes, albeit with a sprightly

43.1 overs being bowled on what the newspaper described as "a slow wicket which really didn't help Qadir", which might explain him having to settle for figures of 13-4-23-8. He was four-fifths of the way to all ten wickets when Goodall dropped one off his own bowling onto the stumps at the non-striker's end, after which Abdul took a catch at mid on that may otherwise have been strategically fumbled. The runs were then spanked off without loss thanks to a "rumbustious" unbeaten 47 from Eddie Pollock, a prop forward for Stirling County and the only rugby union player in Scotland who had turned out in all seven divisions. He was also, says Dickson, "a hell of a hitter of a cricket ball".

Three weeks in, Bob Spalding in the *Scotsman* was already convinced the Abdul-cadabra would reach out and grab the title: "Stenhousemuir might be forgiven for echoing Walter Hagen's immortal phrase: who's going to be second?" Not least because the expectation was for firmer wickets, assuming the Atlantic systems had a wee break. But that didn't happen, and the following day's friendly in Dundee was the last cricket he played for 18 days during that sombre sporting May of the Bradford stadium fire and Heysel disaster. The trip to Forfarshire was, as we have seen, a game that went down in folklore, a game vividly – if also at times erroneously, mythopoeically – recollected.

"When [Qadir] died," says Richard Bowman, "I was interviewed by a UK-based Pakistani news channel because I was at Forthill when he played there in 1985. They cut out of the interview [the bit] when I told them he batted, smacked Jim Morrison off the face of the pavilion, put another into the tennis court behind it, then buggered off to Gleneagles for afternoon tea with the Pakistani High Commissioner and didn't bother bowling. Apparently too cold for that."

Just as well it was snipped, according to Forfarshire player Bruce Dyer. "I played in that game at Forthill," he responds. "You're right that he batted and then left but he came back and bowled. Facing his first ball I played forward and the ball spun over my right shoulder, taken by Alan Smith who said 'well bowled, Abdul'. In the Stenny innings, it was Iain Philip who put JD Morrison over the clubhouse. It was some hit. The only other person known to have done that was Kim Hughes when he was at Watsonians. He went on to make 218 not out."

* * *

Whoever it was that put Jim Morrison over the pavilion, Stenhousemuir's players had to ride out a storm for the rest of May as back-to-back rounds of the Ryden East League were totally washed out. With Qadir ineligible, they exited the (English, or British) National Club Championship, too, a competition in which no Scottish team has ever made the last four (although 1985 happened to be the year Freuchie won the National Village Knockout at Lord's, returning as heroes to Fifeshire where their coach paraded through the rain-lashed village behind a 28-piece brass band and ahead of a gaggle of beaming locals huddled under umbrellas). But Stenny did manage to slip past Grange in the second round of the Masterton, Qadir adding five wickets to the 4/18 he had snared in the first round against Penicuik, the club at which, 18 years later, Misbah-ul-Haq would sub-pro for five games, scoring 99 runs and taking 11 very medium-paced wickets.

If nothing else, the cricket-less weekends gave local batters plenty of time to think, to recalibrate, to wrangle up some sort of gameplan. Thus, when June arrived and league action returned, Qadir recorded his worst figures of the year in front of a sizable Edinburgh crowd at Grange Loan, home of Carlton – coincidentally, the name of the Australian club at which Qadir would play 13 years later, a 43-year-old chasing down and breaking the record for most wickets in a season of Victoria Premier Cricket. "At spectator-less playing fields all over Melbourne," wrote Christian Ryan, "the ranks of the befuddled grew: at Windy Hill, at Arden Street, at Ringwood's Jubilee Park."

The architect of Abdul's taming was Steve Alleyne, a North Londoner of Bajan heritage who ventured north to study Actuarial Science at Heriot Watt University. This is of course a profession devoted, precisely, to measuring and managing risk. The actuary's calculations, thus applied at Grange Loan, would have been: how long can the slog-swiping come off, factoring in a few dropped catches? If you can't read the spin, then the smart move is to have a hack, no? "I think they just shut their eyes and swung the bat," says Goodall. "He went for a few that day."

Alleyne biffed his way to a *gallus* 106* out of 200/4 as Qadir, struggling with the undulations and slope of the run-ups, lacked the usual vim and zip, recording chastening figures of 1/110 from

25 overs. "He always took great pride in his personal performance," recalls Smith. "If he was hit for four or six he would be really annoyed. This was a very annoying day for him."

Vexed he may have been but he was not cowed, and after apologising to teammates he vowed to make amends. "He came in at the interval and said he'd make a hundred," recalls Walker. Qadir was a good enough batter to crack a century in his second first-class game and in a 1987 World Cup thriller famous for Courtney Walsh refusing to 'Mankad' No.11 Saleem Jaffar with two needed from the final ball, he had belted the Jamaican for six earlier in the over to set up a famous heist. Here, focussing fiercely, he steered 'Muir away from the perils of 93/5, eventually chiselling his way to 94* with four runs needed, whereupon he launched one high toward the boundary only for it to bounce a few feet short of the rope. The 98* from 116 balls would be his highest score of a fruitful campaign with the bat, the perfect exemplar of his commitment to the cause, his determination to bring the title back to the Tryst and a smile to Morison Zuill's face.

But he still wasn't quite back in his devastating groove with the ball, and the following week against Royal High – home, three years later, to a young Jimmy Adams – he again proved expensive, bagging 4/96 as the Hamilton brothers made half-centuries apiece ("hackers who got away with it," snorts Smith). The game was abandoned seven overs from the end, with 'Muir on 135/6 chasing 177 and Abdul unable to perform the rescue act with bat. Stenhousemuir's PPP thus dropped to 93 per cent, but they remained top for the visit of Holy Cross, who started well, reported the *Scotsman*, with "Anil Haththotvegwama adding 50 with George More for the first wicket before the Sri Lankan with the unpronounceable name was caught by Tom Ferrier off Abdul Qadir for 21".

Haththotvegwama was the first of Qadir's 8/50 as Holy Cross fell for 134, although they couldn't be accused of repeating the timorous mistakes of the Masterton Trophy game (and future YouTube classic), nor of failing to think outside the box. "One guy's way of playing Abdul," recalls Smith, "was to stand about ten feet outside his crease, practically in the middle of the wicket. When Abdul ran up to bowl, the guy ran backwards, obviously trying to put him off. It was original but it didnae work."

Qadir then stroked a serene 59* as the runs were knocked off, setting the 'Muir up nicely for the trip across the Firth of Forth to Kirkcaldy, home not only of Raith Rovers FC, Jocky Wilson and Scotland's linoleum industry, but also, for the summer, Indian Test batter and counter-punching middle-order fulcrum of the 1983 World Cup shock, Sandeep Patil, a charismatic sometime Bollywood star who had, it turned out, played the last of his 29 Tests against England that winter. He had seen plenty of Qadir in recent times, too: nine of his final 13 Tests were against Pakistan, including a score of 127 at Faisalabad the previous October in a series truncated by the assassination of Indira Gandhi. This was a big-ticket sizzler, an opportunity for the humble clubbies of Stenny and Kirkcaldy to see two very fine cricketers go *mano a mano*. Or it would have been. Alas, the visit to Bennochy saw a third league game out of nine succumb to the weather, but the two big-name imports would soon have the chance to go head-to-head in a cup final.

* * *

Having begun the East League run for home by demolishing Leith for 22, the Stenhousemuir focus then turned to winning a first Masterton Trophy since 1979. A first Scottish Cup since 1980 would be welcome, too, but that first league title since 1973 was the principal target. Abdul had the added distraction of arranging his benefit match for the back end of July, although he remained sufficiently attuned to the day job to back up his Leith performance with 4/54 in a 121-run trouncing of Watsonians.

The Masterton final the following Thursday did not go to plan, however, 'Muir mustering a disappointing 107/7 from 25 overs as they aimed for a record fifth win in the competition. Worse, Qadir could only bowl two overs, straining a leg muscle and having to leave the field to receive treatment. Young Graham Gardner removed Patil with his second ball to give Stenny a sniff at 60/4, but that was as wide as the door opened.

The pro was still unfit 48 hours later, a "nasty stomach complaint" having been added to the list of ailments. As Live Aid unfolded at Wembley, Fauldhouse mustered just 53 in what became a game of landmarks. Smith claimed his 1,000th victim for the club – the first man in Scottish cricket to reach the milestone – courtesy of a stumping off Willie Taylor, whose 6/15 did the damage, after which an easy chase saw captain Zuill score his 26,000th Stenhousemuir run. By the time he retired there would be 27,558, still a record for Scottish club cricket, a tally including 18 hundreds, all but two of them red-inkers. An accountant's career, right enough.

Qadir skipped Sunday's Scottish Cup pool game against Northern Counties in Inverness, sat on his *bahookie* at Mr George's while teammates made the scenic six-hour schlep over the Highlands and back. Meanwhile, a storm began to brew in the East League teacup. In the *Edinburgh Evening News*' double-page splash on the overseas pro situation – 'Professionals or Mercenaries?' – there was a spicy line from Fauldhouse secretary George Francis, who claimed his club had declined the services of Mudassar Nazar – not because the fee was too high but because "it wouldn't be in the spirit of the league to introduce a player of that standing". (After the season, incidentally, Fauldhouse were docked points for fielding an ineligible player and "concealing his identity", which led to their relegation, after which they won an appeal, which was subsequently overturned on a vote.)

In a season that saw Scottish club cricket host a then-record 31 overseas pros, other ten penn'orths were proffered on the situation. "Fears are being expressed that the reliance on overseas pros is getting out of hand, to the detriment of emergent talent in Scotland," wrote Bill Lothian, neglecting to mention that it was Willie Taylor who had destroyed Fauldhouse, not Qadir. For his part, Morison Zuill took the opportunity – with six league games left – to underscore the fact that top pros give local players a unique experience, while providing "no guarantee of success". Meanwhile, skipper at Stenhousemuir's title rivals Heriot's FP, Hamish More, said he welcomed the imports, a claim just about audible over the caveats: "I have no objection to a paid overseas player at a club, but he should be helping and influencing other players. At the moment there are total mercenaries around." It's not entirely clear how Mr More would have known what any other club's pros were getting up to on, say, a Tuesday evening, although Duncan Walker does note that Qadir "was never desperate to practise in the cold and would sit at home working on different grips and wrist movements with an orange".

There was, then, an undeniable gnashing of teeth if not clutching of pearls abroad, a sense of playing fields requiring a spirit level. After all, some clubs' constitutions expressly prohibited the hiring of professionals, while others' grounds were flanked by public pathways, which legally prevented them from charging admission to recoup any putative outlay.

Back on the park, Stenny visited Edinburgh Academicals, where Iain Philip – who would not have been eligible under stricter residency rules, wrote Lothian – crashed a 95-ball hundred out of 201/3 declared. Accies then hung on at 106/9 thanks to Willie Tait's 55, with Qadir settling for 6/46 as Tom Dickson felt the paradoxical perils of fielding at short leg: which is to say, the worse the batter, the greater the danger. "Very many of the club players tried to play him by swinging across the line," he says. "We didn't have helmets then so I was wary. One Accies player middled it and it ricocheted off my knee back to Abdul, who dropped the catch. Neither he nor Morison were concerned about the knee, just the drop."

Indifferent to his close catchers' welfare he may have been, but one thing Abdul was concerned about was his benefit game, a welcome money-spinning opportunity (if the weather played ball) long pencilled in for July 28, ostensibly the high summer. Star names were floated to the press – a rotating assembly that at times included the glamour of Imran Khan, Ravi Shastri, Mohinder Amarnath, Mohsin Khan and Franklyn Stephenson, none of whom made it – with apologetic backtracking made in the same pages. Who knows what influence Allah brings to bear on the Caledonian climate, yet as the day approached so did the gunmetal skies through which the occasion's lustre had to struggle. The show must go on, however, and two sides were cobbled together. Sponsorship was provided by Glasgow's Castle Cash & Carry (a.k.a. Castle Warehouse, a.k.a. Castle Wines), and the Stenny denizens dribbled in under the drizzle. Castle chairman Yaqub Ali was snapped with the beneficiary, as was his 15-year-old son, the recipient of some paternally-conjured prize of dubious credentials. On the field, the International XI made 197/5, Qasim Omar dazzling with a half-century in the rains, before Scottish stoicism was finally vanquished, players admitted defeat and everyone headed indoors, where they remained. Later, King Qadir took the visiting guests for a complimentary banquet at his local haunt, the Gulnar in Larbert.

Either side of the benefit came another pair of East League abandonments. The first of these was a top-of-the-table cash with Heriot's, into which Qadir headed not only with 48 wickets but also the league's top batting average (64.80). Alas, for a second time that summer, Hamish More's troops were denied the one-season-only opportunity to pit wits against the Pakistani maestro. Seven days later, at home to Carlton, a fifth game from 15 was totally washed out, although 24 hours later the same team returned to the Tryst to dump Stenny out of the Scottish Cup, bowling out their hosts for a paltry 66 before ex-'Muir batter David Ponniah saw them past the target. Qadir had made 28 of those 66 runs, a warrior raging against the tides. All eggs were now in one basket.

With three to play, Stenhousemuir required 33 points from 60, assuming Heriot's picked up a maximum haul. After 20 days without a league game, the trip to 'Auld Reekie' to play Royal High loomed like black ice on a Highland road. The week's preparation included a savage Thursday afternoon run out against a touring side, clearly demonstrating that business was meant. "Morison had this thing where he never called off," says Goodall. "Even for midweek friendlies, we always had a pretty strong team out. You played every game for the club; that was the expectation. Friendlies were played hard."

The visitors were the Malahide club from Dublin, a lovely trans-Irish Sea encounter: play fair, share a beverage, cement ties. Or something like that. The Scottish and Irish have been known to beef – most notably, over the spelling of whisky/whiskey, plus some occasional religious quibbling – but it seems a little walnut/sledgehammer to allow your world-class Pakistani leggie to roll through the touring oppo' to the tune of 8/47, before then helping biff off the 96 target, two down. The blarney! The craic!

Suitably primed, Qadir took 6/31 at Jock's Lodge, passing 100 wickets in all cricket as Royal High were swept away for 52. Runs were knocked merrily off and all headed back to get pissed at the Tryst, during which Dickson – the team's other teetotaller besides Abdul – ferried "six or seven very well refreshed teammates" down to the Gulnar. "With Abdul in tow we always got far better service," he chuckles. "The waiters were rolling over themselves to be helpful."

In the end, almost inevitably, the title was sealed while watching rains fall from the shelter of a clubhouse. A *wee keek oot the windae* revealed to Abdul that there would be no Bollywood culmination to his story, no final act of derring-do. Given that he was forced to fly home the following week to visit his sickly mother, missing the final game against Kirkcaldy – which saw Stenhousemuir suffer a sole league defeat: 58 all out, knocked off for six – it was more fitting to win it in slightly anticlimactic circumstances with the pro present. Abdul stuck around for the evening, sipping Coca-Cola, soaking up the joy, the relief, the bonhomie. "Celebrations in the Tryst continued late into the night," reported the *Herald*. "Needless to say the champagne was flowing and it has been heard that Eddie Pollock and Tommy Dickson are likely to play the ugly sisters in the Larbert Operatic Society's Christmas pantomime."

Stenny's prize for winning the title was £100. Prabhakar won £50 for the fastest fifty in Division One, while Qadir won the WJ Green Memorial Trophy as leading wicket-taker, finishing with 54 (at 9.91) from ten outings – which is 97 pro rata, without six games succumbing to weather and two he didn't play. There were 104 wickets for the club overall, along with 743 runs at 41.3 in all cricket. He failed to win Sports Personality of the Year at the Falkirk District Sports Awards – former WBA and WBC lightweight world champion Ken Buchanan handed the gong to David Hannah of Polmont, "Scotland's fastest ever road racing cyclist at no fewer than five separate distances", while the SPOTY runner-up was "attractive redhead Anne Anderson whose sport is tae kwon do" – although the team did pick up the Club of the Year prize. *Braw*.

For Zuill, all those winter calls to Lahore had paid off handsomely. The drought received its metaphorical rains and the league embraced its superstar. "It is as if a footballer of the standard of Europe's finest, Michel Platini, had decided to come on loan to Haddington Athletic," wrote Hugh Keevins in the *Scotsman* in early August, a feature bearing the headline 'Abdul Qadir: A Missionary for Cricket'. He turned 30 four short weeks after his final game in Morison's Scotland jumper, and headed off with 34 of his 67 Tests still to play and exactly half his wickets to take. His replacement was Omar Henry, South Africa's first ever non-white cricketer, who had won a trophy in each of five seasons at Poloc in the Western Union. Stenhousemuir retained their title.

Before Qadir left, however, he told Keevins that for him cricket was "a principled game" – hence being impressed by the straight-talking Zuill, "a good human being" – and he offered a few observations on Caledonian cricket that would perhaps have resonated with Jonathan Meades, although the deep-fried Mars bar was still a decade yet from its conception in Stonehaven. "I have noticed some outstanding young talent in Scotland, but they do not want to work hard. Too many smoke and drink. When they learn to do what is good for sportsmen of any type, standards will improve in spite of cricket not being the national game, and although you have a climate which does not help either."

10

Dennis Lillee
at Haslingden

FA Cup final day 1971 at the home of Haslingden CC president John Entwistle was, as usual, an afternoon of unfussy ritual dotted with hearty hospitality, on this occasion laid on for the club's 21-year-old Australian fast-bowling pro and his 18-year-old wife, Helen. Cups of tea poured forth through the slow build-up to kick-off, an epic televisual pre-amble taking in Arsenal and Liverpool's passage to the final, the freshly minted team songs and runic reports on what had been consumed for breakfast at the respective hotels. By half time, Mrs Entwistle was serving meat pies and mushy peas – as hors d'oeuvres, you understand, although the guests had assumed they were the main event and thus failed to leave quite enough room for the full roast dinner that followed the match, which saw the Gunners prevail 2-1 after extra time, quintessential 1970s maverick Charlie George netting the winner. Three weeks into Dennis Keith Lillee's first trip to the UK, here was a proper Lancashire welcome, a metaphorical clasp to the bosom of town and club, a *mi casa, su casa*, an 'any problems, get on th'blower'. It therefore came as something of a surprise several months later for DK Lillee to learn that the president's notes in the 1972 yearbook – looking back on the previous summer's body of work by Test cricket's future leading wicket-taker, a man whose deeds would secure him a statue outside the WACA and a berth in Richie Benaud's All-Time Test XI – described the Australian as "the worst pro we have ever had in terms of figures". *Another pie, Dennis?*

'Deeks' didn't have a dog in the FA Cup fight – it was in fact the first "soccer" match he had ever watched – which makes it even more certain that he would have preferred to be having a Saturday gallop. However, cup final day had been cricketless for a while in these parts. Lancashire League officials – not many of whom could be said to underestimate their own importance as wardens of this world-renowned club competition – had in 1954 written to the Football Association enquiring as to whether the custodians of the national sport might consider moving their somewhat inconvenient showpiece game to an earlier kick-off time so as to allow the normal course of sporting events to unfold in the east Lancashire mill towns – which is to say, they wrote to Lancaster Gate concerned about the effect on Lancashire League gates – but their solicitations were not so much rebuffed as ignored. The committee responded in 1962 by permitting Sunday fixtures – which, generally, drew bigger crowds – and in 1963 they abandoned cup final Saturday altogether, begrudgingly accepting their place in the grand scheme of things. Ever since, it had been a day for practice, pastry appetisers and pub-crawls, not that DK was knocking back much grog back then, in the days before close-of-play schooners became *de rigueur*.

The following afternoon, still full of belly, Lillee was pounding across the spongy turf at Acre Bottom, home ground of Ramsbottom CC, five miles down the Rossendale valley, bagging 5/38 from an unbroken stint of 16 eight-ball overs – 1971 was the first year the league had adopted limited-overs cricket after 80 summers of timed matches – but it wasn't enough to prevent their neighbours winning in the final over, eight down, as a skimpy target of 79 was passed. Lillee had earlier been run out for eight – the first of a vaguely scandalous six run-out dismissals that year in 17 innings – which was a slight improvement on his debut blob in defeat to Burnley the previous week, the first of five in an underwhelming batting effort in the league.

Lillee finished the campaign with 207 runs at 12.17 – not as grisly a stat as it sounds, given that none of his colleagues broke the 20 barrier – while there were 69 wickets at 13.65 on the main line, which placed him seventh in the overall wicket charts and 19th in the averages, beneath eight of his 13 fellow pros. Such middling numbers would bracket him with a clutch of Australian right-arm medium-fast men who had pro'd in the league in the 1960s – Frank Misson, Grahame Corling, Laurie Mayne, Graham Watson, Dave Renneberg – all of whom were capped at least five times, none of whom made it to double figures. Here in Lancashire, where robust opinions are boldly proffered, it would have taken a sagacious soul to see that this wasn't Lillee's true level, to have avoided filing him under 'No Great Shakes'. But then, this was still a prototype, a man whose rough edges were mirrored in the Hawkwind hair, the billowing shirt whose buttons lay largely unused, and in the raggedy beard he sported throughout the summer, facial hair not yet trimmed back to the terror-'tache of that mid-'70s warhead, with its brisk, duck-footed taxi back to his mark before the roar of the engines, the awesome projectile forces.

Over and above his relative callowness (24 first-class appearances), the reasons for Lillee's lack of wickets – which is to say, the reasons for Mr Entwistle's subsequent I-tell-it-like-it-is frankness – were the fairly standard ones encountered by uncomfortably quick quicks in league cricket. First, the deathly slow pitches, be that through nature or nurture. Second, the damp footholes, often the result of curious, *X-Files*-ish ultra-microclimates. Third, the calamitous slip fielding – "almost every snick went for four," lamented Lillee in one of his autobiographies, *Menace* – although one can imagine a few pointed recommendations, chuntered or bellowed, to *bowl at th'bloody stumps, lad*. Fourth, the pro being too slow to adjust his L&L to the LL realities, reluctant to come down to the locals' level. Asking Lillee to blow sides away in such circumstances was like handing Hendrix a guitar with broken strings and expecting 'Purple Haze'. Still, for all the frustrating inability to dominate, important future lessons were being absorbed, both on the field and off.

"I was aware of being a professional cricketer for the first time in my life," he later observed, although straight after cup final weekend he headed to his job at the local quarry, where he earned £1 a day for ticketing trucks on the weighbridge (Helen, meanwhile, was being paid £15 a week as a secretary at the venerable local haulage company, Benjamin Barnes & Sons). Already an avid trainer, Lillee spent long, inactive days at the quarry eating sandwiches and putting on timber that needed to be jogged off later. It is doubtful whether his colleagues were particularly impressed that their new workmate was an international sportsman, Lillee having in January and February that year played the first two Tests of what would turn into one of the all-time great careers. It is equally questionable whether there would have been any more effusiveness at the quarry a decade later, when he overtook Lance Gibbs to become Test cricket's leading wicket-taker.

Lillee's baggy-green bow had come during the same series as the *dayboos* of his two brothers-in-arms, Rod Marsh and Greg Chappell – fittingly, all three would retire together in 1984 – with a first gallop in the sixth and seventh (sic) Tests of that winter's Ashes, which Australia lost 2-0 to Ray Illingworth's cussed tourists (the next time England visited would be a different story, of course, with the fabled 'Lillian Thomson' as twin terrorisers). On debut in Melbourne, Lillee had shared the new ball with Thomson – the lesser-spotted Alan, not slingshot Jeff – and taken 5/84 in his first innings, impressing Geoffrey Boycott, with whom he struck up a friendship. Eager for cricket in the northern hemisphere summer, Dennis asked 'Boycs' whether he could fix him up with a gig on the county circuit (not at Yorkshire, obviously). Boycott asked around, even wrote letters on his behalf, but there were no takers for the tyro tearaway and so Lillee ended up in the Lancashire League as Haslingden's first ever Australian pro, on a contract worth £1,400 (around £17,000 in today's money). He would soon conclude that the club had had "rather the better of negotiations".

It seems astonishing from our historical vantage point that Lillee was not yet a full-time pro – the Packer revolution that eventually brought this about was still more than six years away – and so had to request six months' unpaid leave from his job at the Commonwealth Bank in Perth in order to embark on his club cricket adventure. For Helen, it was a first trip outside Western Australia, while the furthest Dennis had ever been was New Zealand. They shared their first intercontinental flight with three of Lillee's WA colleagues: Bob Massie (playing at Kilmarnock), Bruce Yardley (also heading to Scotland, from one Perth to another) and Tony Mann (a second campaign along the Rossendale Valley at Bacup), the latter two accompanied by their wives.

It was during two-day stopovers in Hong Kong and Zurich that Lillee learnt he had been moderately stiffed on his deal. While he was stumping for his own airfare, accommodation and automobile, the others were not only getting those extras comped but also receiving heftier basic salaries, something for DK to ponder on the trains from Heathrow to Euston and on up to Manchester Piccadilly, where he was met by club secretary Tom Lees and taken to the semi-detached digs he was paying for out of his own pocket – digs that he soon discovered had no heating, no working fridge (butter and cheese could be safely kept in the larder), and a decrepit old bed that collapsed underneath them the first time they sat on it. Lillee called Lees to explain the situation and was met with a prolonged silence, prompting thoughts that Haslingdonian tongues might soon be wagging with florid tales of the newcomers' bedroom antics.

There were enough potential irritations with the contract and the cricket for Lillee to have spent the summer in a softly simmering funk, but he threw himself vigorously into things and was consistently effusive about the warmth of the welcome he was given and the manner in which he was looked after. Chief among the support structure were Jos and Joan Knowles, at whose house Helen would do the Lillees' weekly laundry and where the antipodean bed-breakers would often have 'tea', served at 5pm on the dot, before Jos then coaxed 'Blue' along the road for a fish-and-chip supper at 9pm. Usually, the chippy run would include Knowles's son Bryan, a 22-year-old top-order batter who was starting to make an impression in the first team having been a bit-part apprentice as Clive Lloyd, Haslingden's pro in 1967 and '68, did his languorous, hot-dangorous thing.

The night after his arrival, Lillee headed down to Bentgate for training. It had been a mild spring and the practice pitch cut on the end of the square was uncharacteristically firm (Lancashire firm, not Western Australia firm). Hassy's opener, Jack Austin, father of future Lancs limited-overs kingpin Ian 'Bully' Austin, was the probe-head tasked with the first 22-yard perusal of the new Aussie quick. "In ten minutes' batting," recalls Knowles Jr, "Dennis must have bowled him six or seven times. The wickets were flying all over the place. We were all rubbing our hands, going: 'Bloody hell, this is going to be great. We're going to clean up!' But it was a damp summer, which meant Dennis, with his long run-up, could hardly stand up some games."

Twenty-four hours later, at the club's customary 'Meet the Pro' night, Lillee expressed hopes that he might take 100 wickets, while new skipper Tony Holden told his new charge that "we have one of the happiest clubs in the league and with your help we could win the league", which was not a view shared by many. Haslingden had finished joint-bottom the previous year and were a long way from the powerhouse they became, later landing seven titles in 11 years, initially under Knowles's captaincy. Heading into that 1971 campaign, they had won only three of the 80 Lancashire League championships contested, the most recent coming in 1953 with Vinoo Mankad as pro. But still, there's no point playing sport if at some level you don't allow outlandish dreams of against-the-odds glory to run freely about the back garden, without warning them too much of the statistical likelihood of bruised knees, cut elbows and dented pride. Start with the fantasies, then play it by ear as reality makes its presence felt.

With an opening-day washout at Enfield followed by those defeats to Burnley and Ramsbottom in which they were skittled for a measly 67 and 78, Haslingden finally got the engine started up at Colne, a game in which DK bagged what would turn out to be his best figures of the season, prompted by the overwhelming stench that drifted across the ground when the doors to the sheds of the neighbouring chicken farm were opened. Having got things rolling in the first over of the game by trapping Derek Harker lbw – when the fingered batter lingered, Dennis informed him in unambiguous monosyllables that he needed to vacate the crease as per the rules of the game, to which Harker replied: "I would, but I think you've broken my bloody leg" – Lillee ended up with 7/45 in a ten-wicket win, earning him one of just two collections that summer (pros had to take six wickets for 30 runs or fewer, or seven or more at any cost in order to get the coins jangling). It came in at £70 – split with wicket-keeper Maurice Lawson, who pouched six catches – which was quite the boon given his daily pay at the quarry. With the decimal system having been adopted in February, there were no confusing crowns or farthings for him to sift through.

Haslingden came back to earth with a bang the next day, a strapping 17-year-old by the name of Bernard Reidy, later to play 107 perm-heavy first-class games for Lancashire, steering Enfield home after the hosts had been knocked over for just 109. And herein lay the problem, over and above Lillee's underwhelming wicket return (or perhaps in some roundabout way *causing* it): only twice in the entire league campaign did Haslingden score over 150 runs, and one of those was a demob happy last-day outing against second-bottom Lowerhouse. Their other totals when batting first were 78, 109, 89, 103/6, 91, 142/7, 135/7 and 140/9, derisory efforts that allowed opposing batters to sit on the pro and milk the other end, albeit where a useful foil was provided by the left-arm swing of Rupert Jackman, a late-'50s Windrush arrival from Barbados who worked in JH Birtwistle's mill in town. In fact, Jackman finished top of both bowling and batting averages for Haslingden that year, while Malcolm Grindrod was leading run-scorer with a paltry 291, including 57* in the return game with Colne that constituted Haslingden's highest individual score of the season and one of only two half-centuries they mustered between them. Bowler-friendly pitches or not, these were slim pickings, a sign of just how difficult it was to free oneself from the stranglehold of even the non-superstar bowling pros.

Take the chief protagonist in that loss to Enfield: Suleiman 'Dik' Abed, a so-called 'Cape Coloured' from Durban via Cape Town's District Six who had been recommended by Basil D'Oliveira ahead of the 1967 season. The following year, adaptation to turf complete, his medium-fast seamers snared 120 wickets at 8.76 as Enfield won a first title for 25 years, while the 1971 campaign would bring him another 101 at 7.96 as a second title was pocketed. Dik Abed may not be the biggest name to have graced the league – reputationally rather than orthographically – but he was among its most productive: ten years at Dill Hall Lane yielded 885 wickets at under 11 apiece, along with 5271 runs at 27.17. He was without doubt one of the best cricketers never to have played a first-class match (let alone any international cricket, a few late-career ICC Trophy games for Netherlands aside). He was also among the notorious beneficiaries of the aforesaid ultra-microclimate. "It were always piss wet through for Dik at one end up there," explains Knowles, "and dry as a bone at t'other."

The problem for Dennis was not so much that he wasn't receiving the same sort of track-doctoring assistance from Haslingden, but that *the exact opposite* was happening. Having observed the Bentgate wicket being shaved and repeatedly rolled one day, the greenhorn Lillee was solemnly informed that this was the way to inject pace into a surface. The dubious local knowledge had been proffered by his 44-year-old teammate John Ingham, a rake-thin, dry-witted schoolteacher who had been Haslingden pro in 1958, not to mention fulfilling paid engagements at six other clubs in neighbouring leagues. Canny chap. Ingham also happened to be an off-spinner with a well-honed and perhaps somewhat blinkered desire to tend to his own stats.

The penny only dropped for Lillee that his teammate was ordering wickets to suit himself when they travelled to East Lancashire CC and found the ball zipping through off a hard green pitch for former Australia all-rounder Neil Hawke, who had by then played the last of his 27 Tests and settled in the UK, having married a girl from Leeds: "Suddenly it dawned on me – Ingham, an old hand in the leagues, had been getting into the groundsman's ear and ordering the sort of wicket that he personally wanted, and never mind about the professional! I fronted the groundsman, who coughed up the plot and we finally struck a compromise. He would shave the wicket at one end for John and leave plenty of grass at the other for me."

It wasn't the only lesson young Lillee was taught by his experienced compatriot, either, with Hawke having to explain that the floaty half volley he served up to get Dennis off the mark was supposed to be pushed for a single not clubbed for six, and that it was part of a mutual back-scratching etiquette that definitely did not include the nose-tickling bumper from DK that had put him on his backside. Fair go.

Having taken 5/46 in a one-wicket win at home against East Lancs seven days earlier, Lillee followed up with 23* from No.10 in the return game – earning him a promotion to No.5, where he reeled off scores of 0, 0, 2 and 0 – yet Haslingden fell nine short, the first of eight straight losses that definitively killed Holden's crack-pipe dreams of going from basement to penthouse.

The two-tone pitches at Bentgate certainly raised a few eyebrows, although the Haslingden players had few problems brass-necking their way through any indignant chuntering, which always had a hollow air given how rife such antics were. Indeed, the systemic pitch chicanery was further underlined over back-to-back Sundays against neighbours Rawtenstall, whose pro was leg-spinner and future mentor to Shane Warne, Terry Jenner – the man whose spattered blood Lillee had found upon arriving at the crease at the SCG three months earlier, 'TJ' having been felled by a bouncer from John Snow, who was subsequently pelted by bottles, tinnies and half-eaten pies at fine leg, leading Illingworth to march his troops from the field. Things could occasionally get spicy in this Rossendale derby, the grounds barely a mile apart, but it was unlikely Lillee would need a helmet at fine leg.

The first game was played in front of Bentgate's biggest crowd of the season, who had to endure watching Haslingden fold for 89 – Lillee one of five home ducks as George Croisdale took 4/0 in ten balls – a target knocked off with over 100 balls to spare. Annual bragging rights were pencilled in. Yet Lillee had bowled briskly for his 4/40, giving the visitors something of a shake-up despite the six-wicket cruise, and so seven sunny days later it was little surprise to find sopping-wet wicket ends at Rawtenstall, where the steep banking on the northern flank made it arguably the most atmospheric ground in the league and an ample early-June crowd brought a season's best gate of £66.30 (around £800 in today's money). Padding gingerly through the crease, Lillee took just 1/62 in Rawtenstall's 161, then managed two singles before hoicking one into the deep off Jenner, who picked up a first five-for of the campaign to set up a 16-run win amid raucous scenes. With Haslingden having lost to Ramsbottom 24 hours earlier, that made it four Rossendale derby defeats from four played. A sense of mid-season gloom started to descend.

Despite the poor results, and whatever his thoughts on the pace-nullifying pitch preparations, Lillee lapped up the parochialism of the Lancashire League crowds, writing in *Menace* that it was "nothing like Perth, where the players were fanatical but there weren't enough spectators to be that way inclined". Chief among the Hassy hardcore was Donald Nally, a blind supporter ferried about by a handful of obliging club members, who would then sit beside him and commentate on the game – which is to say, provide the raw material from which Nally launched into regular tirades outlining why the opposition's pro, or sometimes their own, wasn't much cop. "He could tell what they were doing wrong, even though he couldn't see what was happening," chuckles John Ingham's son, Michael, then a promising 14-year-old, later the Lancashire League's all-time leading run-scorer. Nally's ten penn'orths – as much provocation as observation – would later be stitched into something more cogent and all-encompassing at the AGM, where the Any Other Business section was his invitation to hold forth as to where the team was falling short and how they might improve.

Another part of the Haslingden furniture was Dave McWade, a gentle-souled and avuncular sexagenarian who by day worked the signal box at Helmshore, the village-cum-suburb where the Lillees' fridge-less home was situated. In his spare time, McWade was Haslingden's kit man, zealously guarding the communal pads, bats and balls used at practice nights (or on match days, for those who needed it). All summer he looked after a bat for Lillee, sanding and oiling it in the hope that the pro might soar to as-yet-unimagined heights. Above all, though, McWade treated the club's practice balls like a squirrel treats its nuts.

"You could *never* get a ball off Dave," recalls Ingham Jr. "He was so protective of them. Every time a ball was hit over the wall, he went mad and rushed off to find it. He wasn't a fan of the big-hitting pros. You'd ask him for a ball and he'd say, 'I haven't got one', and then you'd say, 'Well, I need one for t'pro to bowl with' and he'd suddenly pull a nice hard shiny one out of his pocket, like a rabbit's head."

McWade's net-ball catastrophising was not the only problem with practice nights. The main problem with practice nights was that very few people turned up to practise – and if they did, Lillee discovered, there was little appetite for fitness work or fielding drills, which he didn't push on them as he was anxious not to come across as too keen. He also found it strange to do notional 6:30 to 9pm sessions rather than the 5pm-to-7:30-then-dinner he had been used to in Perth. This was an old-school 'hit a few, sling a few' then into the bar, with no one except Dennis bothering to shower. Still, it was part of Lillee's duties to attend these Tuesday and Thursday night sessions, although he was granted a week off in mid-season when he and Helen headed to Scotland in the cranky £100 Ford Anglia they had bought, which would also take them on jaunts to North Wales, Sherwood Forest, London and the Lakes. After spending two days with the Yardleys in Perth, the four then headed to Kilmarnock for Bob Massie's wedding to local lass Nancy Coulthard. There they rendezvoused with Tony Mann and barracked for the groom-to-be in a midweek cup match, little reminders of home that helped keep the Australians' spirits up.

By the time Lillee's Haslingden met Mann's Bacup in back-to-back mid-July fixtures, they had won just two of 14 league games. They were out of the Worsley Cup, too, victory over league wooden-spoonists Nelson in the first round followed by a calamitous one-wicket loss to East Lancs, who found themselves 93/8 and 128/9 in pursuit of 155, yet scraped home thanks to the heroics of No.8 Ian Houston, who clubbed 52* including two big straight sixes off Lillee.

Heaven knows what Donald Nally made of that indignity, yet the upshot was that the two Bacup games, the third pair of derby fixtures, were already primarily about local one-upmanship rather than any wider goals – about asserting oneself in a rivalry that pre-dated the formation of the Lancashire League by several decades, with matches of two innings in the mid-Victorian era organised primarily for gambling purposes and frequently attracting crowds of over 4,000. The mill owners who founded Haslingden CC – gentlemen of means who would allow working men to bowl at members but not play for the club – were known to engage as many as five itinerant professionals for such occasions. It was alongside this 150-year-old feud, occasionally brought back to the boil, that the Western Australian sub-plot played out: a rising superstar against a stalwart state player later elevated to Club Baggy Green during the World Series Cricket years, even making a Test century as nightwatchman.

The first game, at Haslingden, saw both men pass the 50-wicket mark for the season, Lillee cleaning up Mann in single digits en route to figures of 6/30 and a second collection of the campaign. Chasing 101, he then clubbed Mann's leggies over the ropes to seal the win. The following Saturday, the eve of Lillee's 22nd birthday, the pitch at Bacup, unsurprisingly, was a little less congenial for the Lillee rockets, and he managed only 2/70 off 13 but did contribute 29* as 158 were knocked off, again taking Mann for the winning runs as a gloating rumble was sent barrelling down the valley.

With ten games left there was little to play for save pride, collections and perhaps the honour in finishing above the three Rossendale rivals. Frustratingly, four of the next seven games were abandoned, including both fixtures against Rishton, whose 34-year-old pro Ken Higgs – he of the 71 wickets at 20.73 in 15 Test outings – was about to return to the professional game for nine more seasons. Haslingden did record a pair of wins over fourth-place Accrington, however, whose pro, the fringe Lancashire batter David Bailey, managed an unbeaten 50 in the first game. "He was very kind to me in the bar afterwards," Bailey recalls, "and somewhat surprisingly remembered meeting me when I paid a visit to the Aussie dressing-room during the Old Trafford Test the following year, when I was doing 12th man for England".

Haslingden nonetheless remained a brittle team, as illustrated by them losing to rock-bottom Nelson in the next game, with 19-year-old No.11 Roger Tattersall – called up by Lancashire two months earlier for the only two County Championship appearances of his life – scrambling a single off the last ball after Dik Abed's brother Goolam had made 40 of the 141 required. A campaign that had begun with Lillee sizzling his way to 34 scalps in eight innings – putting him on track, pro rata, for that 100-wicket target – had by the penultimate weekend fizzled into a run of just 25 wickets in the subsequent 14 fixtures – that's more than half a season – which wouldn't have stacked up particularly favourably in the minds of supporters with the recent fast-bowling reference point of Charlie Griffith's 144 wickets at 5.21 for Burnley seven years earlier. Slippery he undoubtedly was, yet Dennis had not been as much of a menace as was hoped. But then, Lancashire League cricket could be a difficult beast to tame, as Lillee's Test captain Ian Chappell had found out during a season as a 21-year-old at Ramsbottom in 1963, in which he scraped together just 510 runs at 24.28 from 24 knocks.

Nevertheless, Lillee would have been desperate to salvage something from the final three games of the season – a signature performance, a smile on the faces of the Hassy ultras, a few quid to spend on his post-season sightseeing trip to London – and duly began with 4/24 in victory at Lowerhouse, with Jackman's 6/27 earning the day's sole collection. Twenty-four hours later, Church's last man was dropped then run out from the same Lillee delivery, consigning him to figures of 5/30 (which could well have cost him a trip to Madame Tussauds) in an eight-run win.

Heading into the final game, Lowerhouse's visit to Bentgate, Dave McWade promised Dennis that the bat he had looked after all year – allowing no one else to touch let alone use it – was his for keeps if he could manage 30 or more runs. Coming in at No.6, Lillee dug in against the strapping South African journeyman seamer Des

Sparks (who worked at Main Gas in Padiham during the week, a nominative-determinism accident waiting to happen), and registered Haslingden's joint-third best knock of the season, run out four short of a half-century. A happy-ish ending.

"It was hard work adjusting to the slower wickets and there were times I would have given a lot to have been able to pack it all in and go home," Lillee reflected in another autobiography, *Back to the Mark*, before concluding that "it was a wonderful experience playing in the league and I learnt a lot." He departed Lancashire with £30 to his name, while the club made both a £556.11 loss and a friend for life, Lillee donating a trophy that is still given to Haslingden's best performing junior cricketer. Sometimes it isn't immediately obvious exactly what you have paid for, what the benefits of an investment might be.

"The engagement of the Australian Test cricketer Dennis Lillee prompted considerable optimism at the outset of the season," wrote Tom Lees in the 1972 handbook. "The Professional certainly contributed a great deal to the spirit and enthusiasm which prevailed throughout the team, and he displayed no lack of effort and endeavour in striving for success. We were perhaps slow to adjust to the demands of limited-over cricket … and it must be admitted that the Professional was not as effective as generally expected."

Be that as it may, the rocket-burners were slowly firing up. Exactly three months after the 46 against Lowerhouse, in an unofficial Test against a World XI that had replaced the cancelled South Africa series, Lillee shrugged off the debilitating effects of a virus to send down a career-making spell of 7.1-3-29-8, including five wickets in nine balls, the last six for no runs, as a line-up including Sunil Gavaskar, Rohan Kanhai, Zaheer Abbas, Clive Lloyd, Tony Greig, Garry Sobers and, uh, Richard Hutton were routed for 59. It was perhaps around this time that John Entwistle, having secured the last remaining quarter-page ads for that 1972 handbook, began jotting down his notes.

Lillee stayed in touch with the Haslingdonians, remaining tight friends with the Knowles and Ingham clans. The following summer's Ashes tour – perhaps best remembered for Bob Massie's curvaceous debut 16/137 at Lord's – brought a few boozy reunions with old teammates, as well as an impressive 31 Test wickets at 17.67 for

Lillee, providing unambiguous confirmation that he was a special bowler. The 15-year-old Mike Ingham became the first recipient of Haslingden's Dennis Lillee Trophy that year, and seven years later his dad flew to Australia for Lillee's appearance on *This Is Your Life*.

Three counties had approached Lillee on that 1972 tour but he was already afflicted by back pain and 'Chappelli' counselled against the indentured rigours of county cricket. Only in 1988, aged 39 and emerging from a three-year mothballing, did he give it a go, playing a summer at Northants that yielded a serious ankle injury, a few bruises to his reputation, and some lonesome, late-night reckonings of the soul. In early September, having just turned out for Michael Parkinson's XI against an MCC side containing seven of his Northants colleagues, Dennis was asked if he fancied a game in the Lancashire League – sub pro in second-placed Rishton's last match of the season, at home to Rawtenstall, as they sought to pip leaders Haslingden to the championship.

Perhaps he thought about a collection on the drive up, although by 1988 the crowds had dwindled still further from their immediate post-war peak. And perhaps that was for the best, for the legend sent down a creaky 19-2-86-0 in a ten-run defeat, so disappointed with his efforts that he gave some of his fee back to Rishton. It was a final indignity for an all-time great bowler who, at his peak, in Christian Ryan's memorable formulation, "bowled faster than anyone who could bowl better and better than anyone who ever bowled faster" – a bowler whose tearaway-trimming refinements were emulated by Richard Hadlee, and whose mid-'70s intimidation was aped by Clive Lloyd's mean machine.

"It was a real shame," recalls one of Rishton's starstruck opponents, "but his pace had gone. Our lads climbed into him. He shrugged his shoulders in the bar: 'Sometimes you have bad days, and this is one of my bad days.'" Still, Dennis had finally played a small part in securing Haslingden a trophy.

11

Joel Garner

at Littleborough, Moorside and Glastonbury

The competition rules for the Lancashire & Cheshire League's venerable Walkden Cup were clear: substitute professionals were allowed, but the deputies must be "of equal calibre" to the players they were replacing, the tacit understanding being that a batter should be replaced with a batter, like for like, insofar as this were possible. It thus came as something of a shock to Denton St Lawrence skipper Tony Lancake in the tense minutes prior to their 1978 Walkden semi-final with Moorside when his counterpart Nigel Heap, having won the toss and invited Lancake's men to bat, told him that their pro, Chris O'Rourke, a wicket-keeper from Widnes with one first-class appearance for Warwickshire against Scotland ten years earlier, had broken a finger the day before and thus that Moorside, after a frantic evening on the phone, had engaged an emergency deputy, whereupon a 6' 8" Bajan lumbered out of his compact complimentary car and prepared for a light afternoon's work. After the surprise reveal – *ta-da!!* – a fretful Lancake turned to Heap to protest: "You can't do this. It's not on." Heap's response was to shrug his shoulders and look over toward the Big Bird, giving him the universal hand gesture – Kit-Kat fingers, away shape, extra bounce – for 'we're having a bowl'.

The Joel Garner who had arrived at the beginning of the 1976 season to take up the pro's berth at nearby Littleborough of the Central Lancashire League was a 23-year-old late developer with only two first-class appearances to his name. The Joel Garner who sidled into the Moorside dressing-room for this locum pro-ing gig was no longer an unknown quantity. Quite apart from a terrifying body of work across two-and-a-half seasons in the CLL, all faithfully and occasionally gruesomely recorded in the local (Rochdale and Oldham) and regional (Greater Manchester) press, he had seven Test caps to his name – all of them played at home and thus none shown on British television, thereby depriving them of their full, nightmarish dimensions.

For the 1977 and '78 seasons, Littleborough had loaned out their star man to Somerset, too, some of the oeuvre indeed making its way to the telly – his 4/27 against Middlesex in the previous season's Gillette Cup semi, for instance – thus penetrating the English cricketing psyche as readily as a Garner yorker bursts through a tentative tail-ender's defences. Three days after this Walkden Cup semi-final Garner would play the second round of the Gillette, sending down 6-4-5-1 in a comfortable victory over Glamorgan, while in the quarters, against Kent a fortnight later, it would be 9-6-5-1. Even accounting for the pre-pinch-hitting passivity of the era, these high-summer PIN analyses hint strongly at the difficulties of scoring off the big fella. And that's for full-time pros. The Denton St Lawrence boys would therefore have been justified in surmising that Garner represented a significantly greater obstacle to the club's passage to a potentially money-spinning cup final than 33-year-old gloveman O'Rourke.

With legitimate fears of a battering starting to percolate, Lancake called his troops together for a meeting, delaying the start by half an hour. "We had a vote and the feeling was that we should not play," Lancake told the *Manchester Evening News* in the aftermath of the game. "But for the sake of the league we decided to go out. I am completely nauseated. I am disgusted and ready to chuck everything in. They have pulled a stroke which I did not think was possible."

With Saints having begrudgingly decided to get the game on, Garner stretched out those long limbs, marked out his run and got into his work. Back then, the various Lancashire competitions' knockout formats had no flim-flam such as maximum over-allocations – crowds would come to see the pros, and pros they were going to see – so there was no chance of toughing out someone's eight, nine or ten overs, ducking a few, squirting a few, and getting your runs elsewhere. It was going to be Big Joel all innings, no hiding place. You just had to grin and wear it.

The game was predictably one-sided, Garner snaring 9/44 and following up with an unbeaten 56 as Moorside romped past the eventual league champions. A few days later, Denton St Lawrence held an EGM and wrote "a letter of the strongest possible complaint" to the league. "We are asking for the tie to be declared null and void and that it should be replayed," explained Lancake to the *MEN*. "Moorside have bent every loophole in the book. I don't mind admitting I was frightened to death facing him. He is a Test bowler and players wear helmets against men of his pace."

Moorside's chairman, Nigel Lord, explained that they had faced an emergency situation – 18 hours to find a pro who wasn't cup-tied – and, butter chilling nicely upon the tongue, duly countered: "We don't think we cheated anybody and we entered the game in the right spirit." The Lancashire & Cheshire League committee disagreed. Instead of a replay, they kicked Moorside out of the cup, and Denton progressed to the final, where they lost to Hyde.

* * *

Thirteen years later, with a legendary career in the back pocket – the third lowest Test average (20.97) among bowlers with 200 wickets (behind Jasprit Bumrah and Malcolm Marshall) and still the lowest ODI average (18.84) among bowlers from what used to be called the ICC's 'full members' – the 38-year old Big Bird swooped back in for two years as Moorside's pro, by which time the club with the highest ground in England had begun a third stint in the Saddleworth & District League. On the fields of Uppermill, Friarmere, Droylsden and Stayley, and those of Heyside, Austerlands, Micklehurst and Flowery Field, Garner lumbered slightly stiffly into the popping crease to cast a long reputational shadow down those proddable Pennine pitches, albeit failing to help the Tanner Cup holders land fresh silverware. He headed the league bowling averages in 1991 with 92 wickets at 10.1 apiece and an economy rate of 1.85, yet Moorside came a distant second to Delph & Dobcross. There were another 69 at 13.2 in 1992, this time bumping him down to second in the averages, Moorside finishing fifth.

And that seemed as though it might be that for Garner in club cricket until Las Latty, a Jamaican entrepreneur and jazz aficionado who had married a girl from Somerset, proposed a return to his old South-West stomping ground. Las and Liz were running the bar at Glastonbury CC, formerly Morlands, and once Garner had put pen to paper, first teamers Dave Beal and Rich Burt went up and down the high street persuading businesses to stump up sponsorship money. Having Somerset legend Garner down in Glasto was a rare coup. He may no longer have been headlining the main stage but was still a formidable proposition ambling in off seven paces. So formidable, in fact, that while those 40-year-old limbs could not quite propel Big Bird to the crease with the same wingèd majesty as before, there was still whingeing that it was a travesty.

"Disgruntled village batsmen skittled out by former West Indies Test star Joel Garner have been told to pipe down or head for the pavilion," trumpeted the *North Somerset Times* in a piece bearing the headline: 'It's not cricket, say lads bowled by Joel'. "Mr Terry Mockridge, secretary of the Avco Trust Somerset League," continued the *Times*, "said it was by no means unique to have a former first-class player move down a level. 'Grant Flower, Zimbabwe's opening bat in the World Cup, scored 1,200 runs for Winscombe in our league and nobody complained at that,' he said. 'It is just when good bowlers take wickets that batsmen start to complain because they don't score as many runs as they are used to.'"

And with that statement a universal truth seemed to have been alighted upon: being monstered by a *batter* playing below his level is one thing, but even an over-the-hill Garner carried the threat of more than mere humiliation – in theory, anyway, although in practice Beal likens Garner to a benign old patriarch, pawing playfully with his foes and very much keeping it pitched up: "The first game was a damp pitch and you could have thrown a beer towel over the indentations."

The Walkden Cup rumpus from 15 years earlier had shown that such indignation was not exclusively a southern phenomenon, for the north was no monoculture of hard-nosed, bring-it-on bravado. Rather, there was a patchwork of leagues with differing views about the merits of overseas pros, differing takes on the ethos of introducing heavy-hitters to the recreational game. Nevertheless, the culture shock was more pronounced down in *Zummerzet*, a greater disturbance of the old amateur codes of wholesome fairness – facades though these occasionally may have been – certainly when compared to the scrape-out-their-eyeballs competitions at the sharper end of things up there in the Rugby League Belt and beyond. The young Garner's stint at Littleborough was thus par for the course, a challenge to be stoically faced in the knowledge that it would only have to be twice endured (unless he signed for three years, of course).

Storm Teacup's first ripples on the still waters of the Avco Trust Somerset League were felt when Garner long-levered his way to 62 against wooden-spoonists Watchet, including 32 from the final two overs, following up with 7/12. Next game, it was 6/15 against Chard. The week after that, 5/40 and a breezy 34 against Taunton. At which point came the cider-stewed chuntering from the good men of Joel's old manor. Not everyone was down with the Fire in Avalon – even if it was considerably less fiery than when he had been propelling the county to the first five trophies in its history (and still over half the honours they have won) – although Ilminster's Craig Rice provided a dissenting voice. "I'm really looking forward to it," he told the *Times*. "I know people have been complaining about Joel but I think it's good to see the league getting some publicity." That's the spirit!

The profile-buffing brought by Big Bird saw TV crews from Sky, ITN and HTV descend on The Thorns for the visit of Bridgwater, although Garner took just one wicket in a tied game (187/8 apiece), while current Millfield prep school director of cricket Beal pouched 7/58. "Our chairman at the time was in France," says Beal, who a couple of years earlier had played three first-class games for Somerset, bowling Sanath Jayasuriya in one of them, "and he saw it on the news, me doing a Freddie Flintoff pose when the last wicket was taken."

Twenty years after young Viv had turned out for Lansdown CC in Bath, the county's other West Indian icon provided a memorable club-cricketing bookend for the period. The bald numbers saw Garner finish third in the bowling averages with 67 wickets at 12.14 – Somerset's future stalwart all-rounder Keith Parsons was top, with Milverton's Dorset leggie Vyv Pike's 74 wickets leading the way on that front – and he came third with the bat, collecting 488 runs at 44.63. Indeed, his batting presented as much danger as his bowling, with one fiercely clubbed shot skimming from the outfield and straight through the clubhouse window, striking one of the club's crown green bowlers in the face as she was having lunch.

It all added up to a golden year in Glastonbury. With Big Joel on board, the team moved up from the previous year's ninth-place finish to be crowned champions for the first time in their history – the Somerset League was still a pre-pubescent 11 years old, mind – pipping Parsons's Taunton St Andrews at the top of the pyramid. Meanwhile, a couple of miles down the road, the famous Pyramid Stage was headlined by Lenny Kravitz and The Black Crowes. *Mama, he's sure hard to handle now.*

* * *

Littleborough firsts were embroiled in a derby match at arch-rivals Rochdale on 23 June 1979. Even had the rains not swept in before tea to terminate things, the 'Boro boys would have had more than half an eye on events at Lord's, where West Indies were hurried to a second straight World Cup triumph by the man who had worn Littleborough colours for the previous three Central Lancashire League campaigns, arriving there as a fluffy-feathered fledgling and leaving as the soaring Big Bird who would habitually work the vice-tightening second shift after Holding and Roberts had done their thing up front, the early birds making you squirm. Those Littleborough colleagues, more than anyone, had seen Joel Garner – young, hungry, merciless – cause the kind of wreckage about to unfold on the grandest of stages.

Despite a Brearley-Boycott nudgeathon of 129/0 in 38 overs in pursuit of 286 from 60, the match was not yet entirely unwinnable for England. Graham Gooch, batting in his Essex helmet, had just started to wield the sleeper, but then up hopped Garner to bag what remains the best figures in a World Cup final, yorking Gooch for 32 then knocking over Gower, Larkins, Old and Taylor for ducks, a burst of 5/1 that blew out the hosts' faintly flickering candle. Yes, the 'Boro men had seen the bespoke Garner trigonometry many times over, that savage yorker gradient of his – the ball from side-on sent barrelling down that steep hypotenuse and into the timbers; or, from the batter's perspective, a delivery descending from the ionosphere and into the blind spot by the tootsies before setting poles a-dancing.

There were other teams besides Littleborough in the folds and crannies of those Lancashire moorlands to have caught a glimpse of it all, too. Some 377 days before that World Cup final, Garner had made his solitary Lancashire League appearance, for Burnley, deputising as pro for Pakistani Test batter Shafiq Ahmed and blitzing Haslingden with a spell of 8/37 in an eight-wicket stroll. "He was coming over the sightscreens and out of the slate roofs of the terraced housing at the Burnley Road end," recalls the then 21-year-old Mike Ingham, who made 41 of Haslingden's 89 all out and that morning had packed the bright red canoe helmet he had used in Venture Scouts when he heard Garner would be playing, although declined to use it for fear of the stick he'd get. "After a few overs, I remember John Dyson, our Australian Test player, saying: 'You look like you're handling Joel okay so you take him and I'll take the amateur.' I politely reminded him that he was the paid man and that he should take Joel and I'd sort the amateurs out! But it was a great experience. I was looking good for a collection until he nipped one back that brushed something on the way through – not my bat – and it was given, last man out."

The man who had initially brought Garner to Lancashire was his more than useful new-ball partner Duncan Carter, an officer in the Barbados Police Force who made a single first-class appearance for the island in February 1965. Carter landed the pro's job at Burnley that summer as a late replacement for Charlie Griffith, who had taken a record 144 wickets the previous season but had been threatened with legal action for breach of contract when he informed the club he would be several weeks late for the new season due to West Indies' home series against Australia running into May. Carter took 94 wickets in 1965, was kept on for '66, and when Griffiths returned to Turf Moor in 1967 he moved to Littleborough as pro, spending the next five years there, taking over 100 wickets in each of his final four years without being able to steer them remotely close to a CLL title they had last won in 1936. That most recent triumph was Littleborough's fourth in five years, their tenth overall from 45 championships, at the time second only to the dozen won by their grand old neighbours from down the valley, Rochdale, who would soon be adding a further seven to the pile but who themselves hadn't won it since 1956, the last of six titles in seven years. Not so much the Auld Firm, these teetering neighbours were the Auld Infirm.

After a second spell in the Lancashire League, Carter rejoined a Littleborough team that had ended a 31-year trophy drought by winning the 1973 Wood Cup, which they retained in '74. Heading into the 1975 season, Carter helped entice a compatriot to Hare Hill, a player by the name of Garfield Sobers – at 38 years old, a year younger than the title drought – who, along with Roger Bannister, Charlie Chaplin and PG Wodehouse had been knighted in the Queen's New Year's honours and thus became league cricket's first active knight of the realm, although he would remain "Garry" to his teammates. Sobers back in the Central Lancs, where he had spent the first five years of his twenties with Radcliffe – surely now the championship pennant would be flying again over Hare Hill.

A few months before the season, Sir Garry appeared on *This Is Your Life*, with Eamonn Andrews informing the audience that he would be spending the summer at Littleborough (a decent promo opportunity), whereupon club president and benefactor John Ashworth, a partner in a law firm, got to his feet to say how happy they were to have him. He didn't come cheap, however. Ashworth told the *Manchester Evening News* that the club had to shell out "more than twice what we have ever paid for a pro" to secure the great man's services – an unspecified figure the *MEN* put at £3,000 (around £22,270 in today's money), which they speculated would make him "probably the highest paid club pro in history" – debatable at the time as a gross figure, and certainly short of Learie Constantine's inflation-adjusted salary at Nelson in the 1930s. The *MEN* called it "a tremendous gamble" – an interesting description of signing the greatest Swiss-army-knife cricketer of all time – while admitting that Littleborough were now "most people's idea of likely champions". Most people, yes, but not Milnrow or Werneth, both of whom would finish ahead of the 'Boro.

The investment seemed a sound one – certainly in terms of those intangible currencies of glamour and prestige – when the Granada TV cameras and 2,500 spectators turned up for Sobers's debut at home to Rochdale, producing a club-record gate of £200 (£1,450 in today's money). Littleborough batted first, Sir Garry coming in at 31/1 and grafting out a nuggety 56 – a big crowd meant a big collection, so flamboyance was eschewed for something a little more sure and sober – but the crowd were happy and the coins rattled in to the tune of more than £40, a tidy little sum to hand over to that season's flunky, Ray Hill.

"I was the kid who used to go and put his bets on for him," Hill recalls. "To say I was star-struck would be an understatement, although I think it's fair to say that Garry was more interested in the horse racing than the cricket by that stage. The most excited I ever saw him was when a Yankee [five-bet accumulator] came up for him when we were playing at Heywood."

Other young teammates were roped into the Sobers retinue. Roger Lord had broken a leg playing football in March, putting him out of the entire cricket season, but his detail was to have a whisky awaiting the pro in the dressing-room: always after an innings, occasionally before. Meanwhile, when Hill missed the return match with Rochdale ("the day they took the flamin' team photo, would you believe!"), the bookie-run became 17-year-old rookie Chris Dearden's job. It was the men's singles final at Wimbledon. Sobers had stuck £100 on Arthur Ashe, and thus required continual updates on the score, duly provided by Dearden from third man. Ashe beat Jimmy Connors in four sets – drinks all round.

Littleborough weren't quite able to force victory on Sobers's debut, with Rochdale declining to play obliging patsies. Everyone had started to troop off at 81/9, thinking the game won, only for Stan Smith – Rochdale's last man, not the Wimbledon No.7 seed – to emerge from the pavilion nursing an injured eye from earlier in the day, whereupon he stonewalled through the last four overs alongside ex-Lancashire stalwart Ken Grieves. Twenty-four hours later, Sobers was at Quaglino's, off Piccadilly in London, receiving the Walter Lawrence Trophy for the previous season's fastest first-class hundred, a sign that the old powers, ebbing as they were, had not yet been snuffed out. Indeed, a condition of Sobers signing for Littleborough was that they release him for the inaugural World Cup in June, and he was duly named in the West Indies' provisional Prudential Trophy squad, which meant a warm-up against his old comrades at Notts on June 4.

Alas, the weekend before joining up with Clive Lloyd and the gang, Sobers tweaked a groin against Middleton and was forced to miss the tournament. Two weeks later, as Alvin Kallicharran was flaying ten consecutive balls from DK Lillee at The Oval for 35 runs to get the jamboree cooking, Sobers caressed a season's best 137 against Castleton Moor, his sole hundred for the 'Boro. "This was one of the few occasions I batted with him," recalls Hill. "He was about 60 not out when he said to me, 'Man, I'm not running any more' and just proceeded to hit fours and sixes."

There would be nine fifties, too, as he finished with 1,152 runs at 57.6 – top of the averages, second to Walsden's Trevor Chappell on runs – to go with a moderately disappointing 68 wickets at 12.59, which was second in the averages yet behind six other pros in the wicket charts, including Chappell, who became the first player to do the CLL double of 1,000 runs and 100 wickets since Sobers had achieved it for Radcliffe in 1961, the season he inspired them to a league and Wood Cup double.

However, this is to reduce to mere numbers what was, for many, a priceless and unforgettable experience. Royton's John Punchard, who became one of the league's legendary locals, took a half-century off Sobers and went into the away dressing-room to have him sign the bat, which he still cherishes to this day. "He then invited myself and Bob Kelsall, our pro at the time, to the Littleborough pavilion for a special screening of a film of his 254 for the Rest of the World against Australia in 1972, something I will never forget."

Royton took £150 on the gate that day, and Sobers proved a boon for all the clubs he visited, with the chance to watch at close quarters arguably the greatest cricketer who ever drew breath proving irresistible. "Everyone wanted a piece of Garry," Hill affirms, "but he always had time for everyone. In the bar, he would give everyone a couple of minutes. He was always very generous in that respect."

The common touch he might have had, but not the Midas touch. Littleborough finished third, 11 points behind champions Milnrow. Sobers had turned 39 in July, and after lengthy consideration declined the offer to return, with even weekend cricket now too much as the dusk fell on a great career – too much for a body gravitating ever more toward golf, gala dinners, gambling and gallivanting.

* * *

What to do if you're in a four-decade league title drought that not even Garry Sobers had been able to end? Without too many affordable established world stars on the club-pro market, Littleborough needed to find raw potential, hidden value, a Moneyball option *avant la lettre*. Felicitously, ripples had made their way from Barbados to Duncan Carter. One can imagine the tip-off: "Well, there's this guy, a big, strapping fellow. Made his debut for Barbados a few weeks after he'd turned 23. Sent down 10-4-11-3 on a spinner's pitch in Roseau against Combined Leeward and Windward Islands. Might be worth a look…?"

On the face of it, if anything was a "tremendous gamble" it was this, not Sobers, although trusting the thrusting ambition of those with plenty of testosterone in the tank is often the better bet when it comes to overseas pros than opting for players with several journeys around the block. Either way, judging a cricketer is a perilous business. Indeed, when Littleborough referred Garner to Lancashire for trials later in that sweltering summer of '76, the Old Trafford hierarchy's verdict was that he was "too tall" to be a fast bowler.

Garner's first outing for Littleborough came in a pre-season friendly at Church of the Lancashire League, with signs being sought and runes read for the likelihood or otherwise of that 40-year wait being over. Making his debut the same day was Derrick Knight, who vividly recalls the anxious anticipation around the Big Bird's capabilities – the northern leagues, after all, are littered with journeymen West Indian pros unable to quite cut it. The consensus that the big fella might do them a job would be instantaneous.

"I've never seen so many open mouths after his first ball," Knight recalls. "We'd never seen pace and bounce like it. Everybody in the slip cordon just smiled, shook their heads and couldn't stop giggling." They were a sleeping giant, fuzzy-headed from too long in slumberland, but Garner appeared as a triple-espresso caffeine injection. "We started looking at each other, going: how good is this guy?!" adds Dearden. "We knew there and then that he was going to be something special."

A relatively subdued CLL debut followed a day later, Garner taking 3/54 and Carter 7/25 at home to Heywood, leading the *Rochdale Observer* to muse: "On the eve of the season, Littleborough's claim was that they were not going to be a 'soft touch' for anybody this season. By that, the club meant that when it has a side on the rack then they are going to move in for the kill and the Heywood batsmen had difficulty coping with Garner more often than not […] Gerry Heywood will probably testify to Garner's power and accuracy. He can't have seen the ball which yorked him and scattered the stumps." An interesting read come Wednesday for those within the postcode.

A week later, at Royton, the first major shock waves were felt through local batting bones, with undoubtedly the grisliest of several Garner-induced CLL retired hurts. Cliff Burton's 8/30 had rolled Littleborough for 76 in 20.3 of their 35 eight-ball overs, skipper Jack Hunter making 40 of those on what was evidently not a road. Then it was over to Bird, who "got down to business and frightened the life out of the Paddock side with a terrifying display of pace and bumper bowling," reported the *Observer*. "Garner showed no mercy even with the tail-enders and Royton professional Bob Kelsall will testify to the venom in Garner's bowling. Kelsall had to be taken to hospital for stitches in a nasty mouth wound after a ball from Garner had risen viciously off a length and crashed into his face. That blow seemed to knock the heart and stomach out of Royton's men."

They weren't the only affected stomachs – at least, not according to Dearden's folkloric version of events, which had forward short leg Ray Hill throwing up on a length as he saw the 6' 5" Kelsall spitting blood and teeth through two split lips. "Good story, but not true," says Hill, while counter-claiming that Dearden fainted on the spot, also denied. "Bob gets hit in the mouth and is spitting teeth out," Hill elaborates. "Unbeknown to me, he had dentures. So when I went around picking his teeth up and one set were attached to a piece of gum – that was the time I nearly threw up. 'It's knocked his effing gum out here!' Bob was in no position to tell me it was from his dentures, which he did after the game, so that's what made my stomach churn."

It turns out, in fact, that there was both vomitus spilled and a lie-down needed, but not on the Littleborough side of things. The casualty was Royton's Mike Dunkerley, padded up and due in next-but-one, who came onto the field to escort the stricken Kelsall off, whereupon he threw up on the boundary edge and again in the dressing-room before taking a moment to restore his equilibrium and, says teammate Dave Cooper, "go around like Corporal Jones – 'don't panic!' – asking for everyone's blood group".

Another who could have been excused a speedy evacuation of his stomach was next man in, John Punchard, who had to stand and wait for over ten minutes as blood and dentures were cleaned up.

Middle and leg, please, umps! After taking one in the chest that sent a button flying from his shirt – for a moment, teammates feared this was yet more teeth – 'Punchy' promptly popped one up to short leg and Royton were soon routed for 35. It was quite a way for Joel to have announced himself.

* * *

For anyone unfamiliar with the bone-chilling oeuvre of Clive Lloyd's West Indies, it might be worth checking in at YouTube to familiarise yourself with the specific examination that Joel Garner posed for international-class players, let alone the taxi drivers, taxidermists and tax inspectors of the CLL. It was a challenge to rival the north face of the Eiger, which was not much steeper than Big Bird's back-of-a-length staples.

The run-up was regularly described as "loping", which calls to mind a gentle diplodocus following those ravenous new-ball tyrannosaurs, but this would be a misconception. Garner could hit the crease at a tidy lick when the mood took him, loading up into the highest of gathers and from there snapping into that cargo-crane delivery of his with the alacrity of a much wirier figure, before then taking a sharp left off the track in follow-through, like a break-dancer or *capoeirista* preparing for a spin. At Hare Hill he would rumble in slightly down bank from the Higgins End, and he would invariably bowl all day. "I was skipper when Andy Roberts was pro in 1982," says Hill. "You couldn't have got him bowling straight through from one end. But then again Joel was at the very start of his career when he came to us and Andy was near the end."

A week after Bob Kelsall's unscheduled dental appointment, 'Boro fell one short chasing Werneth's 92, then reeled off five straight wins to surge to the top of the table, igniting hopes that where Sobers had failed Garner might prevail. Duncan Carter did most of the damage as his protégé settled for three- and four-bags while acclimatising to the strange properties of the Lancashire soil, an on-field education accelerated by living with Carter and his wife over in Swinton, although Garner still hadn't yet got the grasp of running between the wickets with his shorter-limbed colleagues. Three hardcore supporters, Kenny Lambert, Donald Hill and Phil

Flinders, eventually took bets on how often Garner would run out the 5' 8" Ray Hill. "My wife found it hilarious when we got together in the middle of the pitch to discuss things," says Hill. "She used to say, 'You look like a long mop and bucket.'"

Hill wasn't the only one to suffer from Garner's dubious calling. Against Walsden, the fourth of that five-game early-season winning streak, when Garner took his first five-for of the season – five men clean bowled in a spell of 6/36 – he had earlier managed to run Derrick Knight out for the first of four times in the season. "As a young pup," Knight recalls, "I was under orders to obey the pro: 'If Joel says jump in the canal, you jump in the canal.' His running was suicidal, which was okay for him; it only took him four strides to complete the run. After the fourth time it happened, my dad told me, 'Next time, send the lanky beggar back'. So, next time I did and ran him out. On my return to the pavilion, I was given the biggest 'telling-off' of my life from Jack Hunter. Different era, the '70s. Know your place, young man!"

With seven wins from eight outings and Bird starting to spread his wings, the Garner-Carter double act looked certain to sweep 'Boro to the title. However, the day after the ex-pro's 6/39 knocked over Castleton Moor for 79 – the sixth time in eight games Littleborough's opponents had failed to reach three figures – the CLL Player of the Month for May damaged tendons in his arm while bowling for the league rep side. With Carter playing as a batter only, the team lost five of the next six, a drop-off that invited renewed chat about 'shamateurism' and speculation about just how amateur the 'Boro overseas amateur was.

"No one knew exactly what was going on, but Duncan was presumably getting a retainer from the president," says Roger Lord. "It was all hearsay. Anyway, the day before we played Heywood we went to Ashton and I took three of the lads in my car but we broke down en route. I phoned the club secretary and asked him what to do. He told us to get a taxi and he would give us the money back later. The next day, the Heywood lads in the bar were saying, 'Come on, come clean: who's paying Duncan?' Just as we were talking about it, the club secretary came out of his office and handed me a small brown envelope. I opened the top, flicked through the pound notes, and put it in my pocket. The looks on their faces: Jesus Christ, they're even paying you! Perfect timing. To this day, I never let on to them."

Without Carter locking down the other end, the CLL batters suddenly had some respite and duly grew in confidence, despite the pitches starting to bake hard in this hottest of *Fire in Babylon* summers – although the removal of jumpers would bring the arrival of bumpers. Nor was it only on the field where temperatures were rising. Rochdale may have been the longstanding fiefdom of the vastly corpulent (and prolifically sex-offending) Liberal MP Cyril Smith, yet the National Front were becoming increasingly active there and mid-June saw the petrol-bombing of a local mosque. Lord spent more time with Garner than anyone that year, and he insists his mate was never subjected to discrimination: "I can't remember anybody having a pop at him or him getting any racial abuse. Everybody respected him. He would purposefully walk around the ground and chat to everybody. He was well known in virtually every pub and club we went in, although we didn't go that far afield."

Still, Knight recalls Oldham's Rhodesian pro Trevor Townshend calling Garner a 'kaffir', prompting a mini-barrage and "square-ups at the end of each over, and very nearly a fistfight when he walked off. Magic!" Garner finished the game with 7/71 and a new two-year deal – a Bird in the hand, as they say – yet Oldham won by 79 runs to nudge Littleborough into that mid-season slump. The visitors' match-winner was Gary Crossley, a policeman who had dug in admirably for 73 of Oldham's 149, yet the amateur who played Garner best that debut season was Heywood's Ralph Farmer, a Windrusher famed in those parts for his powerful arm. "They used to have a competition in Saddleworth at Easter where you tried to throw a potato over the railway viaduct," explains Hill. "A great Lancashire tradition. Ralph used to win it every year."

Farmer was also the man with the fastest CLL hundred since Learie Constantine's effort for Rochdale in 1938, and there was the occasional agricultural flourish as he met fireball with fire, hooking Garner with merry abandon to launch three fours and a six off one over, and this on the league's biggest ground. The Big Bird had his wings clipped to the tune of 9-1-54-0.

The following week – at about the same time as an archipelago of bruises was left on Brian Close's right flank at Old Trafford during that infamously ferocious spell of band-leader Michael Holding, a four-piece Garner would soon be joining as they settled on the classic line-up – Bob Kelsall appeared back in the cross-hairs, gutsing his way to 44. Dave Cooper recalls him "wrapping himself in massive beach towels secured with safety pins, over which he put a couple of thick woollen sweaters. He looked like the Michelin Man going out there."

Kelsall, Crossley and Farmer's successes indicated, perhaps, that the locals were getting the measure of things, and two weeks later Garner went wicketless at Werneth, finishing with 0/51 against opponents who had gone top at halfway thanks to a contentious win over Rochdale, whose secretary Mike Butterworth glossed the matter with one of the great equivocatory euphemisms: "We felt the umpires were not quite as unbiased as they might have been."

Two weeks after that, Garner again returned 0/51, this time at Milnrow, who, due to the quirks of the fixture list, didn't face Littleborough until August 1, which meant an awful lot of Joel-shaped horror stories crackling along the jungle telegraph before the feverish imaginings encountered flesh-and-blood reality. Openers Stuart Wales and Kevin Power were unperturbed, though, adding 191 without so much as a wicket being taken across the innings, Power finishing with 83* and Wales 92*, although Littleborough felt the pair were more concerned with breaking records on a featherbed than pushing home a promising position, scoring only 51 in the final 12 overs. "There's still a photo in the clubhouse at Milnrow of those two standing in front of the scoreboard," chuckles Hill. "What the caption doesn't say is that Littleborough won the game. Quite easily, I might add."

* * *

Littleborough's mid-season wobble was partially arrested by the signing of Jack Dyson from Middleton, 20 years after a golden summer that saw him capped by Lancashire not long after scoring for Manchester City in the FA Cup final in which Bert Trautmann famously played on with a broken neck. Dyson made 72* in the victory over Stockport that helped stem the 'Boro bleeding, and although the team would win eight, draw two and lose two of their final dozen league games, they were too far off the pace to put serious pressure on the top two and instead settled for a cup run.

After a first-round bye, they headed to Crompton for the quarter-final, a team twice beaten in early May league games. Having top-scored with 43 of Littleborough's 140, Garner then roared in to snare 7/28 as Crompton were blitzed out for 67, last man Les Whittle being laughed all the way to the crease as he shuffled out in a bright yellow hard-hat from construction firm Wimpey. He subsequently charged at Garner – while backing away – to be dismissed stumped, and was promptly laughed all the way back to the pavilion. The CLL beaks were not amused and handed Whittle a fine and a ban. "Les Whittle, the man who invented the batting helmet!" jokes Knight.

The semi-final against Ashton saw Garner pick up another seven-for as Littleborough's 156 proved 52 too many. In the final, against Radcliffe at Heywood, Garner's 30 and 42 from Jack Hunter nudged 'Boro up to 152/9 from their 40 overs, before Carter's 6/36 secured an ultimately comfortable 38-run win, a third Wood Cup in four years, and a party for the village. "It seemed like they were all at the game," recalls Knight, "and I remember having kids coming up to me asking for my autograph. Unbelievable!"

Knight missed the evening's celebrations as he headed off on holiday to the exotic climes of Lytham St Annes, although as a 16-year-old he had in any case developed a habit of trying to avoid the post-match shenanigans. "I'd never had a proper girlfriend in my life," he says, "but had to run the gauntlet of Joel and Roger Lord every game saying 'come to Manchester with us, Greggy…' – my 1976 nickname, after Tony Greig – '…and we will help you *break dee ice*'. Bird's words. Scary!"

Instead, it was down to wingman Lord to keep Garner company on lively jaunts to the Caribbean Club in Oldham or treks to The Top Brink pub above Todmorden and The Ladybarn at Milnrow, an establishment whose name is difficult to say in anything other than an Alan Partridge voice. "The ladies looked after him," confirms Lord. "Some in more ways than others, but we won't go into that…"

Littleborough signed off in the league with four straight wins in which Garner gave notice of the enhanced threat an ever more streamlined and experienced cricketer would pose the following year. Six days after beating them in the Wood Cup final came a spell of 6/61 against Radcliffe. Against Milnrow, batting at No.3 with title chances gone, he made a maiden half-century, then went through the 100-wicket barrier after retiring Stuart Wales with a blow on the head that ultimately left him deaf in the right ear. "He was quite poorly with it for a while," says Lord. "The joke when they met up later was, 'You think you're a big fast bowler but I was actually through the shot!'"

He followed up with a brutal century against Ashton as Littleborough knocked off 140 in 12.5 overs, demolishing his opposite number, Derek Parker, a man described as "trendy professional" by the *Observer*. "He was a bit of a hippy-type, who looked like Jesus," elaborates Hill. "But no one had a clue what he bowled. Mystery spin. Although when Bird made his first ton he kept putting him onto the railway line at Ashton." Mystery solved.

"People often struggled with Derek," adds Dearden, "yet Bird's height allowed him just to stick his leg down and *twomp* it on the half volley or the full, and the ball kept disappearing out of the ground. Huge hits!"

Finally, before the September sayonaras, Garner's 4/45 steered Littleborough to a braggadocious nine-run derby win over Rochdale, giving him a final tally of 110 wickets at 12.97, third in the averages behind Parker and Colin Lever, Peter's brother, the pro at champions Heywood. It was, by any measure, a tidy haul, yet this was still not quite an apex predator. By the time Garner returned the following spring he was a Test cricketer with five caps and 25 wickets against a strong Pakistan side to his name. Finally, the club felt, its 41-year itch might get scratched.

***

For Roger Lord, the turning point prior to the turning point in Littleborough's modern history, the event that compelled them to rebuild and renew, was the fire that burnt down the old pavilion in 1966, the year Indian batter Sher Mohammad was pro and tragically lost his 4-year-old son, run over by the heavy roller at Stockport. "The fire changed everything," Lord insists. "I don't know whether the insurance gave them some money to get decent professionals, but it just lifted the club out of the doldrums."

It would be fair to say that Joel Garner was the most important of those star professionals, and in 1977 the burden to deliver was even greater without his new-ball partner and landlord. Duncan Carter had stayed home to become a detective in the Barbados Police Force – and, later, chairman of the National Sports Council and a member of parliament for the Labour Party – and in his stead as overseas amateur came a Western Australian wicket-keeper, John Garrity. Garner was now lodging with Jack Hunter's son, David, an arrangement permitting him a little more late-night latitude. Lord once more was his shepherd. And vice versa, of course.

"One Friday night we went to Bamford squash club in Heywood," Lord recalls. "I'd got chatting to a young lady and we were all over each other. I was a bit of a blond Adonis at the time. All of a sudden, Joel comes over and tells me we're going. I try and protest, but he grabs me and drags me outside. I never thought any more about it but the next day we played Crompton and I found out she was their skipper's wife! I said to Joel, 'I think you saved my life, mate'."

Crompton were expected to be Littleborough's chief rivals, having picked themselves up no fewer than three overseas amateurs – one of them the future Australian chairman of selectors and Test leg-spinner Trevor Hohns – to complement the pro, former Kiwi Test seamer Bob Blair, known best for his courageous innings in the 1953 Boxing Day Test against South Africa in Johannesburg, two days after losing his fiancée among the 151 killed in the Tangiwai rail disaster. In the end, though, the main challenges came from Middleton and Ashton, the latter propelled by DV Parker, the 'hippy' schoolteacher who went on to write several books, among them the fictional tale of a failed league professional, *The Pained Willow*.

Six games in, however, 'Boro were spluttering. Garner had missed the first game, a defeat to Werneth, after which came a draw, an abandonment and an astonishing damp-deck tussle with Heywood under smudgy early May skies. Littleborough were knocked over for 57, with Kenny Stephens, a Freddie Mercury, Elvis and Roy Orbison impersonator from the local club circuit returning once-in-a-lifetime figures of 10.2-6-15-10. Still, as that old cricketing nostrum has it, you always have a chance with a 6' 8" future great of the game in your ranks, and soon enough Heywood's wickets started to tumble, although Tyrone Knight, hailing from a mile along the Barbados coast from Garner, stood firm. When Big Bird finally trapped his compatriot lbw for 29, Heywood were 55/9 and the Great Escape was on, but Bob Dearden was then dropped at midwicket by Ray Hill – "an absolute bloody dolly," recalls the offending fielder – and Littleborough's moment was gone.

They responded with a 190-run win over Castleton Moor, Garner sending down 7-2-9-5 as the hosts were levelled for 25, then lost again to Heywood, for whom 'tater chucker Ralph Farmer clubbed another 50 after 'Boro were skittled for 77. It was too early yet to reach for the panic button, but one win in six was far from ideal, a title race started with a tortoise crawl by the boys from Hare Hill.

That week, Garner got away from the 'Boro bubble's squeaking anxieties, heading down to Taunton with club chairman Fred Hamer to make his Somerset debut, contributing 4/66 and 2/71 to the county's first ever victory – likely now to remain the only one, given touring schedules – over the (Packer-addled) Australians. Joel was signed up for the rest of the summer, fitting games around his principal commitment in Lancashire, where he celebrated with 7/40 against Oldham. Victories over Radcliffe and Rochdale sandwiched another against title rivals Ashton, whom Garner biffed for a second CLL ton. Momentum was then stalled by another abandonment – fortuitous, given Littleborough were 44/6 batting first, although they may well have fancied it with another 20 runs – followed by a draw with Stockport, Garner going wicketless having decimated Glamorgan with 8/31 in the week. Nevertheless, victory over Crompton took the team top at the halfway mark, a position consolidated by two further wins as they headed into a top-of-the-table clash with Middleton that would sent 250 volts of confidence crackling through the 'Boro dressing-room.

Garner, bowling unchanged, had taken a comparatively pricey 5/78 as Middleton put together 177/8 from their 35 overs, after which Littleborough's chase ebbed and flowed in the classic style. With two overs left, 26 were required, seven wickets down, Lord and Garrity at the crease. Nine were scampered from the penultimate over to leave 17 off the final eight balls, Colin Boucher to bowl. Garrity took a pair of twos and a three; Lord returned the strike: nine off four. Garrity then clubbed a four and a huge six into Higgins Field to send the home crowd into throes of delirium and the team eight points clear at the top – outwardly: 'we're just taking it a game at a time'; inwardly: 'we are indomitable lions!'

Convincing wins over Walsden and Castleton Moor extended their lead to ten points, yet just when those giddy feelings of Garner-undergirded invincibility started to bed down, the Wood Cup holders were dumped out at the semi-final stage, with another schoolteacher-pro, John Hemstalk, adding 50* to his 6/44 to send Werneth through. The disappointment of the cup exit was not allowed to linger, however. Skipper Jack Hunter was a veteran of several CLL championships from his Rochdale years in the 1950s and was quick to ensure the 'Boro boys refocused ahead of the following weekend's league double-header. Oldham were duly trounced by 109 runs, Bird taking 5/12, followed by a 110-run victory over Royton to which Garner chipped in handily with 71 and 8/37.

With six games left and the Littleborough juggernaut on a run of 13 wins and an abandonment from the previous 14 league games, those long-awaited laurels now seemed a formality. At which point came back-to-back defeats to Radcliffe (by 45 runs) and Ashton (by 30), for whom DV Parker picked up 6/36 en route to an astonishing season's haul of 130 wickets at 8.84 apiece, 25 more scalps than Garner, albeit pipped in the averages. "Derek used to just amble up and launch them like rag puddings," says Lord. "He was one of those annoying bowlers where you think 'I can hit this bugger' and the next thing you know it's drifted in and you're on your way back."

With four to play, the lead was back to two points, and apocalyptic scenarios readied themselves for a dance across the collective psyche – if not for the youngsters in the team then certainly among the longer-suffering long-in-the-tooth members, the more pessimistic among whom would already have been starting to chunter something like: "If they can't win it with this guy…" (the subject pronoun invariably shifts from *we* to *they* in such instances) "…then they may as well pack it in." These, then, are the moments an overseas pro earns his corn. Dreams have to be delivered. All eyes on you. Hundred-wicket seasons are all well and good, but the game is about glory and you are the person expected to pave the road there, the person to orchestrate the grandest chapters in a club's history, kicking down the door to Elysium in your size-17 boots.

Alas, Garner would fail to add to his season's total of ten CLL 'Michelle Pfeiffers' over the final four matches, the last of which was washed out. Mind you, over those three clutch games he did send down a moderately tidy 47.2-15-74-10 – and again, these are eight-ball overs, giving him an economy rate, in new money, of 1.17 runs per over – as three straightforward victories were completed by eight, five and eight wickets, Garner chipping in a 47* and 45* for good measure. And with that, the champagne corks popped on four decades of frustration. The legend was sealed. Big Bird, now and ever more, would be an adopted son of Littleborough.

* * *

After the highly promising courtship in 1977, the hierarchy in Taunton were naturally keen to move in with Joel full time – to get a dog and look at mortgages. The snag, however, was that he had a year left on his deal at Hare Hill, where the appetite for the CLL crown had not been remotely sated – where, if they cared to explore their baser, darker motives, 41 years of well-marinated revenge fantasies now had the perfect instrument for their realisation: *Knock 'is bloody 'ead off, Jawl*. The club were therefore delighted when, rather than angling for an exit, Bird told the Somerset brass that he would be continuing as before, seeing out his contract with Littleborough and only making himself available for county cricket around his club's needs, the sort of loyalty that cements an already deep affection. In the end, that extra-curricular with Somerset amounted to another four Championship appearances (22 wickets at under 16) and a run to the Gillette Cup final.

Title or not, Joel had become a local legend in Littleborough, a village celebrity, a weapon of mass destruction all of their own. Teams were going to cop it, and cop it hard. By the time he flew back in on the big bird, the league had adopted six-ball overs and he had another couple of Test caps against Australia to his name (13 wickets at 15), along with a season of World Series Cricket in which he'd knocked over Greg Chappell on eight occasions, neatly encapsulating the scale of the challenge up there on the north-eastern fringes of Greater Manchester. The streamlined Bird of his second CLL season – 105 wickets at 8.54 – was now an even more fearsome proposition.

Still, he made a relatively slow start with the ball, picking up 1/33 against Heywood on the opening day of the campaign, although he did then club three huge sixes in a 51-ball 62 ("Garner, not noted for his caution…" observed the *Observer*). He was soon into his bowling work, however, with 6/50 against Royton, whose pro was fellow Bajan and future international umpire John Holder. Next, defending 130 against Werneth, of which Garner had made 51, it was 18.1-10-16-8. After that came a double-header: 7/24 off 13 as Middleton were routed for 71, followed by a spell of 13.2-3-26-6 defending 120 against Crompton, whose top six mustered 13 runs between them, the whole team just 54.

Undoubtedly, it was quite the ordeal for these doughty club cricketers, helmetless and in some cases hopeless. Even when events are recollected today, almost 50 years on, it can be difficult to ascertain the level of jelly-legged apprehension that clamped its claws into body and mind. The tough-guy gameface endures down the decades, fronts still have to be maintained. Nevertheless, it is reasonable to suppose that however much courage was shown, not many of them genuinely looked forward to it all, which is obviously a curious headspace for a *recreational* sportsman to occupy.

Five games in, Littleborough had 23 points from 25. Just behind them on 20 points sat both Oldham and their next opponents Walsden, whose nuggety opener Albert Ross lost the battle of the big birds as Garner nipped in with 5/13. The following day Littleborough survived a Wood Cup nail-biter against Werneth, who, batting first, crawled to 97/7 from their 48 overs before six wickets from Cheshire seamer Ian Gemmill caused a few flutters and earnt him a £25 collection, although 'Boro eventually scraped home, eight down.

Garner had earlier bowled unchanged for 4/43, with the snapper sent along by the *Observer* successfully capturing the big fella's hostility in a couple of photos of bouncers that scudded past those voluminous (and highly flammable) 1970s barnets, reproduced in hair-raising detail in Wednesday's paper. "David Marsh must have been hit on the body many times," proffered the match report, "but he stuck to his task and provided a backbone to the Werneth innings." Later that season, Marsh wrote to the league asking for clarification about what constitutes 'intimidatory bowling', citing Garner by name and mentioning that two players had stated they would only face him while wearing crash helmets (one of them may have been Andy Wood, hit in the face by Garner during that cup match).

This wasn't the only hoo-ha about the alleged chin music pumping out of Garner's ghetto-blaster amid a growing air of bumper fatigue, a note of floundering souls asking for respite. An op-ed from Bob Cull in the *Manchester Evening News* appeared under the headline: COME ON, GARNER, PITCH 'EM UP:

Although cricket is essentially a team game, few Hare Hill supporters would argue about the impact 'Big Bird' Joel Garner has made on the club over the past two years. He played a major role in their championship success last season, and this year – following a successful winter series with the West Indies against Australia – he appears to exert even more influence.

He came into the Central Lancashire League as a raw recruit unused to the overcast skies, biting winds and damp wickets. That soon altered. He had batsmen throughout the league wincing in anticipation while the old timers at Littleborough sat back and rubbed their hands with glee. And why not. They had seen some of the greatest, and none more brilliant than Garry Sobers. But this was something different, an explosive talent they could help mould in the fearsome Roy Gilchrist image: blinding speed and aggressive spirit and the ability to send down his last over as fast as the first.

And that's why it's a pity he seems to be using fear rather than skill as his major weapon this season. Reports have been coming through about repeatedly short bowling – ask the Werneth batsmen how they felt after the Wood Cup clash last Sunday – and there seems to be an increasing number of bouncers.

One man feeling black and blue this week must be Werneth No.3 David Marsh. He took repeated blows on the body but stuck to his guns in an effort to wear the bowler down. Earlier this season Middleton skipper Paul Rocca suffered the same.

"The only way to counteract those short deliveries was to run down the wicket at him. It hurt, but it was safer than staying back and risking a blow on the head," said Paul.

It all seems so pointless. Garner is a world-class player. He doesn't need to intimidate and his returns proved the point. When he bowls to a length his sheer pace and movement guarantee him a bagful of wickets. So come on Joel ... pitch 'em up!

It is an extraordinary rebuke, about which a few things might be said. First, one person's bouncer is another's back-of-a-length-ball-that-got-big, although we can probably agree that leg gully was mostly in the game for Joel. Second, any KC worth their salt would argue that the effectiveness of the length ball, m'lud, is directly connected to the use (implied or actual) of the short ball, and thus that any batter feeling certain there wouldn't be any of these in the pipeline would have acquired an advantage. Third, Garner was being paid to win matches for Littleborough and if an overly comfortable batter was getting in the way of that then surely it is legitimate to drop in a short ball. Fourth, Garner's teammates broadly refute the idea that he bowled more than a smattering of genuine bouncers – and these only at top-order players – let alone being a practitioner of intimidatory bowling. "He didn't try and hit anyone, ever," asserts Dearden. "The lift he got from a good length was phenomenal. He didn't need to bowl short, and anyway it wasn't in his personality to do it at club level. That was just the way he was as a bloke. He wouldn't want to be seen as a bully, picking on people who are not of the same standard."

Notwithstanding the fact that pitches aren't exactly Perth-hard in the Pennine *piedmont*, the photographic evidence refutes this *never-bowled-'em-guv* defence. Which is not to say Garner overdid it, merely that he didn't deny himself an occasional dabble. (Perhaps it was simply the zeitgeist – there was, after all, a certain wildness in the CLL air, for along with several acts of streaking, that year's Wood Cup final at Heywood saw a ten-man punch-up outside the pavilion.)

"I honestly don't remember Joel being the aggressive type," elaborates Hill, "although 'Noddy' [Dearden] used to stand there saying, 'Get him off that front foot, Bird. Get him off that front foot!' When you're six-foot-eight, pretty quick and can bowl probably the best yorker that anyone's ever seen, you don't need to bowl short that much. One or two people did wind him up, though. Paul Rocca would have been one of them, the way he ran down the pitch at him. There was only one instance I can think of where *we* might have revved Joel up. I worked in the Inland Revenue and Joel had a bit of a problem with the taxman when he came over. Nothing untoward. Papers went missing and he wasn't getting his proper tax code. Middleton at the time had a top batting line-up. Somebody said to Bird, 'You know these top four all work for the taxman?' He bowled pretty quick that day!"

* * *

In 1976, the 23-year-old Garner had it all to prove and very little pedigree. In 1977, he was a Test cricketer but still with rough edges. By 1978, he had become a precision-engineered devastation machine and no matter how, conceptually, one parsed 'bouncer' from 'throat-seeker' it was going to be a tough afternoon of batting.

Littleborough duly made it 33 out of 35 points when Garner's 6/40 set up victory over Castleton Moor. Next came Oldham, whose pro was a 25-year-old Queenslander who later went on to coach the Australians to two World Cup wins. John Buchanan's 6' 5" frame would at least mean a little more effort required for Garner to jam out the jaw jazz. In the end, it was another low-scoring affair – Oldham 65 all out chasing 132 – in which Garner's 4/24 from 17 overs was decisive. Radcliffe were the next team to be skittled for under 100, Garner's 8/42 a fairly major factor. The following Saturday Ashton fell for 87, Garner with 5/34. This was relentless match-winning, a world-class operator moving toward his peak.

A small fly had flung itself into the ointment, however. While on Somerset duty, Garner had been warned by umpire David Evans for bouncing Sussex tail-ender Giles Cheatle, news of which would have added fuel to those festering CLL grievances further north, bringing the circling wagons tighter.

Littleborough were then dumped out of the Wood Cup by Radcliffe, going down by 121 runs on a corpse of a pitch at the Racecourse. Worse, Garner picked up a niggle, forcing chairman Fred Hamer and president John Ashworth to scour around for sub pros for the following weekend's double-header. Paper talk about John Snow failed to pan out, although in the end it mattered not as the derby with Rochdale was rained off. On Sunday, they roped in Blackpool pro Mushtaq Mohammed – his nephew Shoaib would play for Littleborough in 1981 – who scored 76 out of 140/2 from a rain-reduced 28 overs then took 4/47 as Stockport hung on, nine down, leaving Littleborough with a 12-point lead at halfway, Garner having taken 60 wickets at 6.06.

He was back in situ for the 13-game homeward stretch, the first three of which brought comprehensive victories: Heywood skittled for 105, Stockport for 95, Royton for 112, Garner picking up 6/32, 5/45 and 6/34 from first change, Jack Hunter not dallying too long before launching the Big Bird. It was becoming a procession: Joel the juggernaut, a Notting Hill carnival float with ten happy teammates cavorting on his back.

With Garner creating such a slipstream, it became easier to blood the next generation of future Littleborough stalwarts – the self-styled 'Cream Kiddies' – all of them helped along by the stewardship of coaches Bob Thew and Tommy Greenhough, the Rochdale-born leg-spinner who had taken 5/35 against India on Test debut at Lord's in 1959. In came the 15-year-old Philip Deakin, joining the 17-year-old seamer Mike Farrar – who had played a few games for Lancashire's second XI that year and later became CEO of the NHS Confederation, for which he was awarded the CBE – and the 20-year-old Chris Dearden, who made his maiden first team half-century in the next game, a three-point win over Werneth, who came within two runs of becoming the first and only team to take 200 off Garner's Littleborough across three seasons. Deakin and Dearden are still going strong, representing England over-60s in 2024's World Cup in Chennai.

When Garner mangled Middleton for 68 in the next match with a spell of 14-7-15-5 – including the wicket of overseas amateur Andrew Hilditch, future Australia Test opener and Hohns's successor as head selector – Littleborough's lead stood at 17 points, the league seemingly done and dusted by mid-July, eight games left. But Joel was in no mood to take his foot off the gas.

Twenty-four hours later, against Milnrow, he was finally warned for intimidatory bowling as Littleborough failed to defend 104. The ever-plucky Stuart Wales made 32, while a cameo 23 from 11 balls by one of Garner's West Indies teammates, Derick Parry, and 29 from the 19-year-old Pete Abrahams, younger brother of Lancashire's John, consigned 'Boro to a first league defeat of the season. They lost the next one, too – Walsden's Albert Ross and

Rod Lawrence adding 103 for the first wicket – before avenging the Milnrow defeat thanks to Garner's freebie-free 24-10-24-5.

Fifteen points clear with five games left, Garner headed off to play the televised Gillette Cup quarter-final against Kent, winning Player of the Match for that spell of 9-6-5-1 – an enjoyable watch for the plucky nudgers of the Central Lancashire League – after which came the habitual phone call to Roger Lord. "He used to drive back from wherever they were playing during the week," Lord recollects, "calling me up from somewhere and saying, 'I'll be home in two hours. Call at the chippy and get some fish and chips in. I'm starving.' I used to meet him at his place with them. One time he'd obviously won Man of the Match and had this huge bottle of champagne. So there we were, drinking mugs of champagne and eating fish and chips in his front room on a Friday night."

After the battered cod came more embattled prods, Garner ensuring there would be no home-stretch shakiness, starting with 17-7-22-7 as Castleton Moor were routed for 57. He followed up with 6/38 against Oldham then 6/23 at home to Radcliffe, whose 103 all out was knocked off nine down, thereby confirming Littleborough's second straight championship, won from gun to tape.

The penultimate game, the Big Bird's farewell appearance, was lost to Ashton, with DV Parker bagging another 6/36, including Joel, to finish with 103 wickets for the season and 336 at 10.98 across Garner's three summers. For 'Boro's final game, a day after Bird's Somerset had been defeated by Sussex in the Gillette final, Collis King appeared as sub pro and thus on the team's championship photo. Too tall he may have been for Lancashire, but Garner had taken 115 league wickets at 6.7 in 22 innings, bringing his final tally for the club to 334 in three seasons at 9.34. The impact still resonates today.

* * *

Sitting among the Littleborough boys in June 1979 as Garner rattled through England's middle order to seal the World Cup was another Bajan novice on his first UK jaunt. Franklyn Stephenson wasn't able to bring any silverware to the club but did become one of the best overseas pros in various leagues of Lancashire before productive spells at Notts and Sussex.

Three years later, the 31-year-old Anderson Montgomery Everton Roberts strolled into the village, an old gunslinger with his best battles already fought. "John Ashworth had offered him an incentive to win either the cup or the league," recalls his skipper, Ray Hill. "Roberts said to me, 'How many games to win the league?' I said 30. 'And how many games to win the cup?' 'Four.' 'Okay, we'll win the cup then,' which we did." Splitting his time between Littleborough and Leicestershire, Roberts delivered to the tune of 8/25 against Royton in the final, six of them caught at short leg and leg gully.

Three years after Roberts came Ezra Alphonsa Moseley, the deceptively quick and relentlessly hostile Bajan who was the only West Indies rebel to play international cricket after touring South Africa, and who famously broke Graham Gooch's hand on Test debut in Trinidad. Moseley's five years at Hare Hill brought 100-plus wickets every season, 613 at 10.52 all in, as well as a couple of 1,000-run campaigns, two league titles and one double. While Ezra was busy doing all that, a familiar figure *loped* back through the Littleborough gates. Only this time he headed for the away dressing-room.

They thought they'd seen the last of him, on the field at least, but in 1987, after he had been unceremoniously cut by Somerset and a month after playing the last of his 58 Tests, Garner was back in the CLL. While Viv headed to Rishton in a helicopter, Bird was unable to return to the old nest, occupied as it was by Ezra, so signed instead for Oldham. Friends reunited, smiles all round, lovely stuff. Until he had the ball in his hand. "I remember Ezra bowling them out for 80 on a poor wicket at Oldham," recalls wicket-keeper Billy Taylor. "We felt quite comfortable at tea but not after Joel's first over, the score being 1/3 with David Schofield, Philip Deakin and Chris Dearden all yorked inside six balls."

Although his pace had dropped from that late-1970s prime, Garner took home a bag of 9/37 that day – the joint-best analysis in the CLL that year, along with his own 9/37 against Castleton Moor – and finished with 90 wickets at 9.59, topping the averages ahead of Moseley, Carl Hooper and Curtly Ambrose. Boot on the other foot, 'Boro finished seventh, Oldham third. But no hard feelings. "He was a character who got right into the club and still comes to see us," says Dearden, "so it was pretty strange to face him. I didn't play against him at Littleborough but at Oldham he bowled me first ball. Yorker. I knew it was coming as well!"

After Oldham came those stints at Moorside and Glastonbury, where he became a club patron, but Littleborough is the place where it all started for Bird, the place that gave him a leg-up, the club he repaid by deferring his Somerset ascension. "He obviously holds Littleborough very dear to his heart," says Hill, "purely by virtue of him coming down to the club every time he's in the UK. He remembers a lot of the games, too, which for a guy who has played cricket at the level that he has, all around the world, is absolutely incredible. Forty-odd years ago!"

In particular, he has remained friends with Roger Lord – bodies brought together through cricket and whose older bones settle straight back into still vivid memories of their youthful mischief and merriment. "We used to go to The Ladybarn on a Friday and Saturday night," says Lord. "There were a few young ladies that worked behind the bar there and after their shift we used to take them to the local club: the Nordic Club or Tiffany's in Rochdale. I took a fancy to one of these barmaids and we went out together for a while, nothing serious, always in a crowd. We lost contact with each other after Joel went to Somerset. Anyway, a couple of years ago, my wife sadly passed away with cancer. I'd moved up to Morecambe to retire, so I came back to be closer to my family and got a little flat in Littleborough. Not long after, I bumped into Rita, the girl I used to go out with back in 1977 and '78, and, long story short, we now live together. Talk about life going full circle! Joel came over for two months in 2023 and met her, so they were reminiscing about old times, too, and we're going out to Barbados soon, our first visit to the Caribbean." A club revived, lives interwined – it is quite a legacy.

These days, the air over Hare Hill is ruffled by a platoon of wind turbines sitting atop the mounds and bumps of the encircling moorlands like long-limbed invaders, an alien appearance belying their function as benign energy harnessers – much as the mills in these valleys had once been, only taller. Much taller: a Garner following a Carter. For all the shock-and-awe with which the long-limbed Joel presented opponents at the time – the sense of something unremittingly hostile, a force beyond the ordinary scale of things – the buzz was ultimately worth it.

12

Morne Morkel / Mohammad Asif
at Endon / Ashcombe Park

For the cricket lovers of the Staffordshire Moorlands, up there where the wallabies roam (or so local legend has it), the afternoon of Saturday, 2 August 2003 provided several options for their leather-on-willow fix. On the TV – Channel Four, no less – there were the masochistic pleasures of England's attempt to salvage the second Test against South Africa, whose greenhorn skipper Graeme Smith had backed up scores of 277 and 85 in Birmingham with the small matter of 259 at Lord's to establish a narrow 509-run lead on first innings – three knocks over the course of which he had treated England's swing-bowling tyro James Anderson, just turned 21, with such cuffing disdain that it seemed unlikely he would ever recover.

Closer to home, in Leek – a small industrial town and antiques centre known as the 'Queen of the Moorlands' – there was an intriguing North Staffordshire & South Cheshire League Premier Division relegation encounter bringing together two Pakistani Test cricketers: opening batter and part-time leggie Imran Farhat, busy making frustrating cameos for Porthill Park, would pit wits against the middle-order carnage, leg-spin lasers and part-time lunacy of Shahid Afridi, Leek's deputy for injured professional Albie Morkel, who had flown home mid-way through his second season at Highfield with a groin strain.

Four miles down the road in Cheddleton was the hipster's choice: another relegation battle – this time in the North Staffordshire & District League Senior 'A', the region's third tier – a Moorlands derby between Ashcombe Park, who sat in tenth position on 120 points, and Endon, who were ninth with 121. The principal reason for attending, these savvy clairvoyants would have known, was that it brought together, in fledgling form, two of the most challenging bowlers of their generation: a gangly 18-year-old from Vereeniging duking it out with a skinny 20-year-old from Sheikhupura.

Exactly seven years later, Mohammad Asif would have a career-high ICC rating of 818, the 88th best in the history of the game. He was ranked No.2 in the world. By the end of the month, amid sport-shaking scandal – when the man with a fondness for overstepping the line overstepped it once too often, but not as much as it was overstepped by Mohammad Amir, who nevertheless was deemed not to have overstepped it as far – Asif's international career would be done. The loosest of cannons he assuredly was, but the boy could bowl. Kevin Pietersen and Hashim Amla both rate him the best seamer they faced.

There were one or two in the international game that struggled with Morné Morkel, too, who would himself rise to No.3 in the world, finishing with over 300 Test wickets. 'Morras' first learnt his trade with Shaun Pollock and Makhaya Ntini as mentors before settling into a team that went 3,278 days without losing an away Test series, Morkel the splice-splintering 147kph straight man to the two jaffa merchants: Dale Steyn's jet-propelled snakers and Vernon Philander's asphyxiating alleyway of jag and nibble.

Morné had been seconded to Endon by his father, Albert, who had heard how much Albie enjoyed the previous summer at Leek and wanted to find his younger son a club in the vicinity, initially contacting Ashcombe Park. "I was at work one evening when I got a random call out of the blue," recalls Dave Goodwin, a first team player and *ex officio* committee member responsible for pros. "It was Morné's dad. Someone had given him my number. He explained how he wanted 'somewhere for my boy to gain experience in English conditions' and we had been recommended. However, by then we'd already done a deal for Asif to be our pro." Eventually, Papa Morkel found Endon, who paid Morné £70 per week and covered his portion of the rent on the town-centre flat in Leek he shared with Albie on Haywood Street, opposite Leek Oatcakes.

The 20-year-old Albie had in 2002 joined a team that had won an unprecedented treble of NSSCL title, Talbot Cup and Staffordshire Cup the previous summer with the talismanic, charismatic Ottis Gibson as pro, a difficult act to follow for a natural introvert. Nevertheless, Johannes Albertus contributed 848 runs at 60.57 (second on both counts) and 56 wickets at 14.07 (sixth in first category, ninth in the second) as the team finished fourth, and his enjoyment of the season could not be tarnished by a *faux pas* at Leek's inaugural summer ball, his *de facto* 21st birthday party, at which, with the room hushed and the benedictions flowing, the chairman presented the squirming pro with a blow-up sex-doll, ostensibly to help combat his homesickness and loneliness. The prank's architect, Albie's 20-year-old teammate David Fairbanks, had even selected 'Ebony' from the respective drop-down menu, adding another patina of cringe to things, but by season's end he had worked his way back into the good books sufficiently well to accompany Albie back to South Africa for a winter's club cricket, there befriending over Morkel family *braai* "a lanky 'Dutchie' who hardly spoke a word of the Queen's" with whom he would become firm friends.

Albie and Morné were a couple of weeks late arriving for their respective north Staffordshire assignments in 2003, and the *Leek Post & Times* reported that Leek were trying to sign Waqar Younis as a short-term locum, although this was apparently scuppered by "visa problems and cash". Once ensconced in Leek, it would be fair to say that brothers steeped in the zeal and diligence of their Afrikaaner father's Calvinist work ethic were not hell-raising habitués of the town's multitude of drinking establishments – it is one of several towns to have laid claim to having more public houses per capita than any other in the country (or maybe, more people per capita than any other town in the country claiming it has more pubs per capita than any other town in the country) – unlike the unlikely oat soda aficionado from down the road, Mohammad Asif. Nevertheless, Fairbanks and his future brother-in-law Andrew Johnson were regular Saturday-night stopovers in Haywood Street – the Englishmen boozing while the Saffers were snoozing – where the never-hungover Morné would rise from a bed that was too short for him to find Albie knocking up an improv' breakfast comprising the local delicacy of Staffordshire oatcakes filled with leftover kebab meat, cheese and strawberry jam. "I'm telling you, I found a taste sensation!" insisted Albie. It was *Men Behaving Not Particularly Badly*, although Morné was once pulled by the police for cycling the wrong way up a one-way street.

Morné's principal aim for the summer was to gain experience and physical strength. It became difficult to do this on the field, however, as Endon – competing in a division with good quality sub-continental first-class players and the odd international, often bowling unchanged from one end – had unwittingly signed an overseas pro restricted to a maximum of seven overs per spell and no more than 18 per game, bound as he was as an 18-year-old by the ECB's fast-bowling directive. Whoops. The club wrote to the ECB, querying whether its jurisdiction applied to a South African national. Yes, came the reply, for they had a duty of care to all cricketers playing under their auspices. On the other hand, Endon could have slotted him into their under-18s team, although this option was never exercised.

Still, there were other ways of beefing up, one of which involved labouring for the family building firm of Leek CC stalwart and Staffordshire CCC legend Dave Cartledge, whose 76-year-old father Joe was a regular on site, invariably out-muscling Morné and Albie on the wheelbarrows until one day he overdid the pecking-order posturing and fell head-first into the skip with his 'barrow. Trying quite hard not to laugh, young Morkel rushed to his aid, finding Cartledge Snr in a state of disarray atop a heap of topsoil from which, dusting himself down, he issued a simple instruction to the now convulsing junior labourer: "Fetch me mi fucking pipe!"

* * *

It may come as a surprise to learn that Morné Morkel's two-and-a-bit seasons in English club cricket were more successful with bat in hand than ball. A bowler who often had Alastair Cook, Andrew Strauss and Mike Hussey in his pocket – you can see him now, can't you, making 92mph throat balls scud into grilles, or leap from back-of-a-length and dart away from round the wicket – such a bowler, you may think, would blow teams away in the third tier of north Staffordshire cricket, but this would happen only occasionally: a story of slow pitches, searching for an unnatural length and, mostly, an understandable callowness of experience and a lack of snap and stability in those long heron's legs.

As for the batting exploits, although Morkel did twice make 40 in Test cricket, 22 of his 81 completed innings were ducks, seven more produced a solitary run, and another seven yielded only two, with

18 more single-figure efforts in there, including a streak of 13 in a row. Graeme Pollock, he was not. Indeed, his calamities with the willow are perhaps best summed up by him walking from the crease straight into the groundsman's garage at The Oval in 2008, caught at short leg off the top of the bat handle while trying to upper-cut Stuart Broad over the slips. Five years earlier, he would complete a first NSDL campaign with just 29 wickets at 23.03, finishing 13th in the divisional averages. Meanwhile, there were 583 runs at 38.87 – eighth in the averages, seventh in the runs – including a couple of hundreds. Club colleagues felt he might become a genuine all-rounder.

Neither batting nor bowling potential were particularly auspicious in Morkel's first full game, however, at home to Hem Heath, a colliery team widely fancied to win the division, which they did. Their pro, Amir Wasim, a chain-smoking 42-year-old left-arm spinner who played like it was a life-or-death game in the streets of Sialkot, would head the league averages with 72 wickets at 8.53. Here, initially bowling seamers, he sent down 11.3-5-16-3 as Endon were hustled out for 94, while Morkel fell for a second-ball duck, caught-and-bowled one-handed by Steve Atkinson.

Still, many an early-season game has been salvaged when defending such a score. Especially if the pro gets it right. Sets the tone. Strong start. Couple of early wickets. Gets in amongst them. Or, in this case, sends down a 12-ball opening over including six of what eventually became 15 no-balls in a first spell on English soil that produced figures of 5-0-59-0. The issue of Morné's restriction to seven-over spells was distinctly moot as the runs were blitzed off in 12.3 overs, Dean Hodson carving his way to 38* from 26 balls.

"With it being a small target, we said we should try and attack it," Hodson recalls. "I remember square-cutting him for six over point towards the dressing-room at Endon and cowing him a couple of times, which he didn't like. He then bowled me a couple of bouncers, which I hit for fours, one a big top-edge over the keeper, which annoyed him even more. You look at what he did in his career – it was a long way from his league debut against a pit team from Stoke!"

It was not a first outing to engender a great deal of collective confidence in the Endon dressing-room. Indeed, Morkel's propensity for overstepping not only further curtailed his bowling allocation – the NSDL had just introduced strict penalties for tardy over rates – but also failed to instil much appetite for nets, which had become extremely hazardous. "He was literally bowling off 18 yards," shudders skipper Darren Dutton, who also pooh-poohs the anecdotal accounts of Endon's compact Post Lane ground being too small for Morkel's run-up – however poorly measured out this was, however much he seemed to prioritise that superstitious quirk of turning through 360 degrees at the top of his run over hitting his mark and/or getting some part of those size-15 speedboats behind the paint. Besides, even when the bowling (and the run-up) clicked, opposition teams knew the new-ball onslaught would last for seven overs, maximum. "Some weeks you were getting opening batsmen dropping themselves down the order to avoid Morné's [first] spell," says Dutton. "Or they'd pitch a tent at the other end. It was embarrassing."

Nevertheless, Morkel inevitably picked up after his debut – with the bat, that is, where 40-odds against Silverdale and Scot Hay were the prelude to 118* against Hanford (who, to be fair, lost 17 of 22 games that year, winning none). There was 35 in a win at Oakamoor and 51 in victory at Weston, but no five-fors by August when, after a washed-out first encounter, it was time to face the flopping fringe and fiendish fingers of Asif *bhai*.

* * *

If Morné Morkel was all discipline, dedication and drive in this formative stage in his career, 'Iffy', as his teammates came to know him – presumably as a diminutive of Asif – was more old-school: supping Budweiser and chugging Marlboros, while haughtily commanding some involuntary *ashtray wallah* to do the necessary. And that was on his first day at the club, where he had arrived on a damp April afternoon as a relative unknown, the agent having sold him as "a good young lad who's going to be the next Shoaib Akhtar", which of course not only didn't pan out for Asif's bowling style but is also somewhat ironic given that Shoaib Akhtar almost stopped Asif becoming the next Shoaib Akhtar by clouting him with a cricket bat. "This six-foot-four skinny guy walked through customs," recalls

Ashcombe gloveman Steve Proffitt, "and we wondered at first what we'd got. He didn't look like your typical fast bowler." Mohammad Asif wasn't your typical anything.

It is unlikely Asif would have paid much attention to the club's potted history at his meet-and-greet. He was their first overseas pro since Sonny Ramadhin, with whom they won NSDL titles in 1960 – pipping Frank Worrell's Norton – and 1961, before finishing bottom in 1962. Unfortunately, this was the year a dozen clubs broke away to form the closed-shop NSSCL, so Ashcombe missed the party. They eventually came in 21 years later, not long after the first expansion, and by 1991 found themselves sitting top of the table with two to play, in a three-way dogfight with Stone, the next opponents, and Caverswall. Determined to close the door on a rival, Ashcombe batted for 83.4 overs, leaving Stone 29 to chase 230. It was not all that well received. The draw kept Stone behind them – mission accomplished – but allowed Caverswall to sneak into top spot. Ashcombe now needed a favour – from Stone! – and after taking care of business against Knypersley seven days later, they slipped down the A53 to watch the denouement of Caverswall's floundering pursuit of 225/8, where the cheery arrival of the previous week's spoilers prompted an abrupt switch in tactics from Stone: from pushing hard for the win to rolling out the red carpet for their hosts as 'the Park' watched on, seething. Sweepers were eschewed, whoops-a-daisy wides were bowled, tail-enders went unpressurised, and Caverswall took the title. A year later, however, Ashcombe would prevail, but after that came decline, gradual at first, before they eventually slipped through the trapdoor in 2000 and back out to the NSDL, up from which came just one team per year, subject to the approval of facilities. Asif's job was to get them through that narrow skylight.

They had signed him from Ainsdale, situated near the links golf courses and vast beaches below Southport and playing in the Merseyside Competition, the area's second-tier league, which they won on the final afternoon. He took bags of wickets, including a couple of nine-fors. He got the ball reversing on lush green pitches, slipped in the odd beamer after losing his cool, suffered a bout of shingles, and had his eyes opened to the independence of women in the West (interest piqued, it was a hobby he would bring with him to Staffordshire).

After the initial hellos were done, Proffitt dropped Asif at his lodgings in Cheddleton, a one-bedroom flat next door to the post office. "We didn't want him in Shelton [six miles away in Stoke-on-Trent]. We wanted him close by so he could help out with training. He couldn't drive, so I had to ferry him about everywhere, including down to Pak Stores in Shelton! He always used to text me: 'What time you pick me?'"

Asif was soon making himself at home in the Staffordshire Moorlands. In fact, says Proffitt, he soon made a few other cricketers at home in the Staffordshire Moorlands: "Two or three moved in. There was Zulqarnain Haider, Waqas Ahmed and some leggie whose name I forget. They were pro-ing in different parts of the country and would somehow get to Stoke station for their games. Iffy liked people around him because he made them do all the cooking, washing and cleaning." The lodgers certainly made for interesting midweek practice at Ashcombe, which at least partially filled the mischievous Asif's plentiful downtime.

"After a couple of weeks in the country he said he was a bit bored and wanted to get a job in the week to get more cash," recalls Dave Goodwin. "I went with him to Kerrygold in Leek and managed to sort him a job: six in the morning till two in the afternoon, packing butter. He realised there was no bus at that time so borrowed my bike to get him to work on time. He lasted three days before deciding professional cricketers don't get up at that time in the morning. I got him another job through a visit we made to Thornbury Hall [a high-end South Asian restaurant]. He started at their operation at Alton Towers. I think he lasted two days before I got the call: 'Goody, can you come and pick me.'"

Asif's early season form was somewhat more promising than Morné's: 12-2-13-4 against Blythe in his first gallop; 9-4-8-3 at home to Barlaston in the Staffordshire Cup the next day; then 12-5-18-6 at Newcastle, whose 76 all out, in which six wickets fell for no runs, were knocked off for nine. "He could really make the ball talk, with amazing control and accuracy," observes Goodwin. The early look at the Asif skill-set certainly made that escape hatch back to the NSSCL seem attainable. But then, figures of 13/39 from 33 overs were always going to be difficult to sustain – ball sometimes talking far too garrulously for the Senior 'A' snicks – and he went wicketless against second-placed Silverdale, given a bit of treatment by his compatriot Tahir Mughal, after which came 1/66 against third-placed Wood Lane and 2/36 against no-hopers Hanford. Ashcombe had by then gone seven without a win in the league, nine in all.

Frustration would frequently get the better of Asif, as it did during a spell of 5/66 in a draw at Scot Hay. "He got involved in some verbals with one of their batsmen," Goodwin recalls, "and turned to me and said, 'I think I can bowl the beamer'. I thought he was joking, but he wasn't. The next ball missed the batsman but left him lying in a heap after taking cover. Lots of bat waving ensued." The primary source of Iffy's irritation was James Collett, architect of a rescue operation from the perils of 28/5 to 199/9 after having his stumps comprehensively rearranged first ball of the game, a no-ball. Unintentional, of course. When it happened again later, greeted by a huge roar from the partisan home support, Asif's head went, to use the technical term. Thus the extension of his run-up to within feet of the boundary; thus also the beamers. Collett eventually fell for 90, bowled Asif.

Scot Hay was something of a bear pit at which Morkel had also been riled. His antagonist was Ian Porter, who during a gutsy 80* was offering unsolicited, free-at-the-point-of-use advice as to a suitable length for conditions, while ball after back-of-a-length ball flew through to the keeper and 'Po' loudly counted down the remaining deliveries in Morkel's spell until his mandatory removal from the attack. "Ian played him brilliantly and baited him a lot," says Robin Hollins, busy making 56* at the other end. "A couple of years later I suspect we would have been having a hospital visit or had our stumps all over the place. Morkel was quickish then, but Asif was noticeably sharper at the time."

There were plenty of other days when Asif performed well, only to be let down by colleagues. He bowled briskly to bag 6/34 at Oakamoor, yet Ashcombe were knocked over for 78 chasing 87, rotund left-arm leggie Alan Palmer taking 8/19. He took 4/21 to threaten a Staffordshire Cup shock against that year's NSSCL champions Longton, yet Ashcombe were knocked over cheaply and bundled out. He followed up with a season's best 74* against Oulton – a surprisingly high score for a man who averaged 5.64 in Tests and whose chief association with the bat was the Akhtar incident – yet once again these efforts failed to produce a victory, which had a little to do with Proffitt dropping his elder brother Dave off Asif and a lot to do with Asif ambling in off four paces having felt a twinge in his knee in the game's first over. "We also had Dave caught behind and the bugger didn't walk," recalls Proff Jr. "He said it was because Iffy didn't when he was batting. And they say blood's thicker than water…"

Asif missed three of July's four league games with that niggling knee injury, contributing 6/37 and 56 in defeat to Blythe in the one he did manage, by which time Ashcombe were reconciled to a relegation scrap. Nevertheless, for all the sketchy results, the club were delighted with their new pro, who had not only paraded those prodigious bowling skills but integrated well into the culture of both dressing-room and wider community. "His spoken English wasn't that great at first but he could understand more than he could say, and he had a great sense of humour and an infectious laugh," recalls first-team scorer Martin Ball. "He was tall and good looking, and soon had some of the ladies at the club eating out of his hand, wanting to mother him more than anything else – I think! There was an air of a little boy lost about him sometimes, perhaps when it suited. Steve Proff's mum did a lot of his laundry for him, if not all. On occasional nights out in Leek, along with me and most of the players, he was good company with an eye for a pretty girl. He could get a curry down him faster than you could say onion bhaji, all washed down with a drink and a smoke."

* * *

Whether it was Asif's diligent training regimen that got his dodgy knee limber enough for the relegation clash with Endon is a question best left for the medical professionals, although it is perhaps more likely that financial considerations prompted the self-administered green light ("Even back then he was totally motivated by cash!" says Goodwin). It did not go well, as the *Leek Post* would spell out in a report carrying the headline: MORNE-ING GLORY. "Ashcombe Park paid the price last Saturday for going into the match with a half-fit professional as visitors Endon completely outplayed the home side, cruising to a seven-wicket victory. The Ashcombe batsmen struggled to make headway early on against the opening attack of Morné Morkel and Kevin Cockerton and the early runs came from the continual no-balling of Morkel."

Given that headline, it would be a little hard on Morné to kvetch again about his lack of penetration, although figures of 1/37 from 14 were upstanding enough. The damage for Endon was done by leg-spinner Nick Goldstraw's 5/46 as Ashcombe were dismissed for 177, after which, with Asif limping and the rest of the attack limp, what might have been a stiff target was stroked off without undue alarm, although Neil Sellars's stumps were sent cartwheeling second ball of the innings. Asif then collided with Phil Clowes while taking a steepling catch at mid on to leave Endon at 57/2, after which Morné plundered 67* and "assaulted the ball as if trying to hit it into Derbyshire". Asif finished with 2/55 off 11 half-cocked overs and bore much of the brunt, recalls Dutton, as "Morné kept pulling him for four or six over midwicket, probably his best shot". Morkel 1 Asif 0.

If this wasn't exactly what Endon thought they were getting, they liked it all the same, especially when he followed up with 104 and 4/45 in victory over Newcastle. Suddenly they were in the top half, although there would be no further wins as they slipped back to an eighth-place finish.

Meanwhile, the injured Asif sat out the next two, neither of them won, but returned to the relegation fray to play four in a row – three wins and a draw – the first of them against Hanford, whose stonewalling earlier in the season had brought sarcastic slow-handclapping from the Ashcombe team and thus a sprinkling of spice to the return game, which Asif took care of in a spell of 9.3-5-9-8, the eight wickets falling in 18 deliveries of carnage. At one stage Hanford had been 46/0; the last nine men faced 27 balls between them. THERE'S NOTHING IFFY ABOUT MOHAMMAD trumpeted the *Post*, whose defective crystal ball failed to reveal to them two subsequent positive tests for Nandrolone, an attempt to take a wrap of cocaine through customs at Dubai that was explained away as unsolicited medicine from a witch-doctor, and a seven-year ban for match-fixing, along with a year at Her Majesty's pleasure.

A week later, contract still to play for, Asif bagged 6/35 at home to Oakamoor and, after a rain-truncated game at Oulton, signed off with 5/51 and 24* in victory over high-flying Wood Lane that lifted Ashcombe into the top half of the table, whereupon he put ink to a fresh one-year deal. The club may not have improved their league position, but the new professional's presence had bumped bar takings from £14,000 to £26,000, hipsters and loyalists alike enjoying the exotic fare on offer. Asif had finished second in the league averages with 58 wickets at 9.36 to Morkel's 29 at 23.03, and chipped in 232 runs at 21.09 compared to Morkel's 583 at 38.87: honours even.

Morné had long since been re-signed for the 2004 campaign, although with Albie not returning to Leek there was some speculation that he might step in as his replacement. In reality, those were not Premier League numbers, and Leek opted instead for Alfonso Thomas, who left for an 'A' tour in mid-season and was replaced by Vasbert Drakes.

By the time young Morkel was back at Endon, this time on £120 per week, his career had taken a significant step forward in the shape of a first-class debut for Easterns against the West Indians in Benoni. Figures of 5-0-54-0, including 17 no-balls, were a marginal improvement on the rough treatment handed out by Hem Heath, but he did make 44* at No.10 as Albie, batting two spots above him, compiled 132 to drag Easterns back into the game, the brothers adding 141. Morné then knocked over Ramnaresh Sarwan as a maiden first-class wicket, while chipping 6.55 rpo off the first-innings economy rate. There were another three SuperSport Series outings – and 39 no-balls – before he was back in the Moorlands.

With Albie no longer around, Morné's living arrangements became more complicated – not quite sofa-surfing, but moving between teammates' spare rooms, an apartment in nearby Milton owned by a colleague, and a countryside B&B run by another member of the club. He got around on a pushbike, did a lot of running, a lot of gym-work and some more bricklaying, throwing himself into the slow labour of transforming his body into something eventually capable of making the world's finest players hop about.

When journeys required alternative forms of transport, he invariably called Anthony Bunn, who he had personally head-hunted after being impressed by a gritty and accomplished 40-odd on a wet one at Oakamoor – "basically on the outfield, with me getting stick from some lad at short leg who'd never made a run in his life despite me only playing-and-missing at one ball", chuckles Bunn. While Bunn thought the teenage Morkel "was never *quick* quick", he did regret taking him along to a coaching session at Biddulph Valley Leisure Centre, where the combination of a rock-hard, lightning-fast indoor surface, a 6' 5" man's 12 o'clock release point, a total indifference to the sanctity of the popping crease and a desire to show up 'Sir' in front of his students led to a hairy "15 minutes diving out of the way of it". More pleasurable, recalls Bunn, an avid Stoke City supporter and co-creator of the much-loved fanzine *DUCK Magazine*, were excursions to what was then still called the Britannia Stadium, with Morné roped into hawking *DUCK*'s precursor, the magnificently named *A View to a Kiln,* before a July pre-season friendly with Valencia. "This big lad with a thick South African accent – no one could understand a word he was saying. I think he sold about six. But he was enthusiastic! He threw himself into it, as he did everything else."

Two years older than Morkel, two years closer to ripening, Asif had played 11 first-class games over the 2003-04 winter, five in the Patron's Trophy and six in the Quaid-e-Azam, where he finished with the fifth most wickets. Despite the busy schedule, he arrived on time for his second NSDL campaign. "This was a big surprise to everyone," recalls Martin Ball, "not least the guy who had gone to Manchester airport to collect him, as Iffy had somehow landed at Heathrow. Unbeknownst to all, he had changed his flights in Dubai without telling anyone, and then rang up from London complaining that there was no one there!"

For his second summer, Asif was upgraded to a two-bedroom flat above a barber's shop in Leek. "I used to get my hair cut there and he would tell me when Iffy had been round town till one o'clock," recalls Steve Proffitt. "But on the field he never let us down, so I wasn't bothered what he got up to. He still couldn't drive by then, but he got about. He'd get the bus into Stoke, get trains here and there. Nowadays, with the UK Border Authority regulations, you have to have a lot more control of where they are, so it probably couldn't happen." Such stringency would not necessarily be a bad thing with someone like Asif, whose first playing assignment in 2004 was a trip to Endon to see the fellow who'd pumped him far over the mid-wicket boundary a couple of times the previous August.

Alas, there would be no early-morning tumescence for Morné this time as a docile April wicket permitted little scope for pushing batters back from back-of-a-length. Nor did a bowler who, Bunn asserts, "usually cranked it up against the opposition pros, especially when they were fast bowlers" get a shot at Asif, who wasn't required as Ashcombe posted 230/2 declared, Morkel toiling hard for 1/44 from 18 overs. In reply, Morkel came in at No.3 and immediately punched Asif back down the ground for four, only to cloth a pull-shot to square leg next ball, to the bowler's evident delight. The jetlagged Asif finished with 4/57 from 20 tidy overs, although Endon ground out the draw on 174/7, Bunn making 85 of them. A points win for Asif: 1-1.

* * *

Lacking the consistency of his more battle-hardened peers among the division's professional ranks, the 19-year-old Morkel nevertheless showed regular glimpses of the cricketer he was becoming – or rather, of the talent he possessed, since many of his headline performances again came with bat in hand. A week after the Ashcombe opener, he blitzed 133* on the Blythe postage stamp as 214 were knocked off, seven down, that gigantic stride and the opposition's obvious reluctance to pepper him once more proving advantageous.

The next away game was the featured match in the *Sentinel* and finally brought a prototype version of the monster bowler he would become, blasting through promoted Eccleshall with 9/54, before Bunn and Darren Dutton knocked off the 125 without loss. The team's soft underbelly was exposed over the following five games, however – a draw and four comfortable defeats to the teams that would occupy the top four spots, Morkel managing just four wickets against the top three – after which came a visit from the other promoted side, Sandyford, who had decided to play without a pro when their initial signing had pulled out at the 11th hour.

"Somewhere at the club there's a team-sheet with MS Dhoni's name on it," says Stephan Shemilt, back then Sandyford's opening batter and these days the BBC's chief cricket writer. "Longy and

Spyder sorted it [agent Darren Long, bat-maker Gary Stanyer, both ex-Sandyford]. Spyder had almost signed him for Kidsgrove two years earlier, but I don't think he had a passport and, anyway, his employers were reluctant to let him leave for six months. We signed him not knowing he was a wicket-keeper. They said he whacks it but we thought he'd be opening the bowling. Ultimately, he didn't come because he was picked for an India 'A' tour [to Zimbabwe and Kenya in July and August], but we did get to a stage where we thought he was coming and picked him for the Saturday, hence the team-sheet. Just imagine, you could have had Morné Morkel, Mohammad Asif and MS Dhoni playing in the same division – the third tier of north Staffs cricket!"

It was a wet early-June day at Endon and the game started late. Freed from the ECB's red tape, Morkel bowled unchanged to take 5/49 from 19.2 overs as Sandyford were dismissed for 110, of which Shemilt made 74, the next highest contribution just six. With rain about, Morkel was sent up to open with Bunn. Mark Leese had taken the new ball from the Post Lane end, his medium-paced out-swingers solid enough to earn him a third over, which he went into with 0/10 and came out of with 0/40. "They were young and chopsy," says Bunn, "and Morné just went berserk."

"It was a short boundary straight and leg-side to Morné," adds Shemilt, "and he just kept launching 'Ken' over midwicket and onto the football field. Laurie Thomas kept on having to go and fetch it, and after the third one he shouted from the middle of the football pitch: 'Shall I just stay out here?'" Thomas did return to the mid-wicket boundary, and the next ball sailed over him, too: all in, five sixes in the over, Morkel a blitzkrieg 51 and Endon victors by nine wickets.

A week later, the last before the turnaround, they went down by the same margin at struggling Weston, having posted 195/9. Home pro Saad Wasim then rode his luck to compile 123*, adding 162 for the first wicket with Mike Chester, who made 48. At which point, the game as good as won, No.3 Simon Barratt came in, *sans* lid.

"Their professional walked up to him and said, 'It's a quick bowler, you'll need a helmet', to which the guy said, 'No, no, I'll be fine'," recalled Endon keeper Neil Sellars. "He had a slash at a few, got a few thick edges and scored a few quick, flukey runs. It was the first time I saw Morné get slightly angry. A few words were said, the batsman said a few words back, and he carried on playing the same way. Suddenly he just bowled this bouncer that was a few miles per hour quicker and it hit him smack in the forehead. Everybody thought, 'Oh, that'll hurt'. He had a cut right across his forehead, staggered off and went to hospital for stitches."

At the halfway mark, Endon languished in ninth position, Ashcombe in seventh. Asif had been slow to get going, taking just 15 wickets at almost 21 apiece in the opening seven league games, only one of which had been won. Ashcombe had also exited the Staffordshire Cup at the first round stage despite the pro's 9-4-14-5, a day at Fordhouses near Wolverhampton that did not appear overly enjoyable if the *Leek Post*'s acerbic report was anything to go by.

"A surprise awaited them on arrival as a large, luxurious pavilion gave way to playing facilities that were substandard to say the very least," declaimed the byline-free piece (sources indicate the author had an Ashcombe connection, and usually took several pens to the game). "The square, badly in need of a roller (or better still, a plough), boasted a lone dandelion in full flower at the side of the cut strip and the recently mown outfield would have benefited considerably from the loan of a local farmer's baler. With dressing-rooms well out of sight of the field of play and with no scorebox, players and scorers sat in the open in autumnal temperatures and an occasional invigorating drizzle. With the clubhouse suddenly closed due to a bingo session, it became easy to see where the priorities lay. Added to that, with what sounded like the all-comers motorcycle scrambling championship taking place in the next field, an interesting afternoon was guaranteed." Good day then, yeah?

Still, exiting the Staffs Cup put them into the Staffs Plate spin-off comp', where they made the semi-final before coming unstuck at Old Hill, Asif sending down 8-0-53-0 amid a volley of verbals and beamers. It was a delivery to which he had once more demonstrated himself partial in the league campaign's first home game, against a strong Wood Lane side that would go unbeaten through the season. Their Kiwi No.3 Shane Wills recalls "having a fairly short and concise conversation with Asif mid-pitch at Ashcombe Park that mentioned 'my bat' and 'his head' if he repeated his experiment. He'd bowled me a huge no-ball beamer that felt like it was off about 16 yards, as the previous ball I had dispatched into a horse trailer in the adjacent paddock to the ground."

By mid-June, Park had bowled out only one side and no one had a five-for to their name, despite the attack being bolstered by the increased availability of the former Staffordshire player Dave Clowes, back from Australia, and the return of ex-pro Ian Pearson from Leek, a diabetic who died tragically while out walking his dog on Christmas Day a few years later, and who had once taken a top-flight 10/47 while sharing the new ball with Ottis Gibson, the Bajan realising two overs into his spell that he'd chosen the wrong end but gallantly running into the wind as 'Peo' already had three in the bag by that stage. Suddenly, however, Asif clicked – the reasons for which as unfathomable as everything else in the life of this rakeish, rake-thin enigma. He took 9/24 as Weston were demolished for 46, following up with 5/62 against Eccleshall, then 7/56 against Oakamoor, all three games won, Iffy making a club-best 75* in the third of those games to primp him nicely for the visit of Endon.

* * *

MS Dhoni may have been the superstar who slipped through the NSDL net – although not without a group of Sandyford lads pranking skipper Dave Moors one evening, sometime after the club had decided to spend the cash on new net facilities, leaving him a voicemail from the back of a boozy cab in which they pretended to be Dhoni, just touched down at Heathrow, then forgetting about the prank and being convinced he had in fact arrived – but the third tier of north Staffordshire cricket seemed to attract an unusually high number of well-credentialed overseas players through the noughties, be that actual or future.

It is arguable that Morkel and Asif, the 2004 versions at any rate, were not even among the division's top three that summer, those being: Newcastle's pacey Pakistani Tanvir Ahmed, who would make a Test debut six years later; Wood Lane's gentle giant Abey Kuruvilla, who had played ten Tests for India and spent six successful years in the Liverpool Competition, five with Southport & Birkdale and one at Fleetwood Hesketh, his on-a-string-and-both-ways seamers topping the wicket charts in five of those years, including the 111 at 8.47 in his debut season that propelled Southport to a first title in 17 years; and best-adapted of all to the club game was Silverdale all-rounder Tahir Mughal, who topped both Senior 'A' batting and bowling averages in 2004 (1,207 at 100.55 and 81 at 10.10), and was called up as a one-off locum overseas pro for Durham in early May.

The obvious reason for this concentration of firepower in the third tier was the desire to sneak through that slender skylight into the NSSCL, and the ensuing arms race it provoked. By 2006, the NSSCL had subsumed the NSDL into a pyramid, making promotion easier and, perhaps, further incentivising ambitious clubs to spend big. That summer alone brought three outstanding tri-format Pakistani internationals to what was then NSSCL Division 2A, its third tier.

Abdur Rehman, whose darted left-arm spin would earn him 22 Test caps, once swindling a game against Andy Flower's England in 2011, was back at Caverswall, for whom he had bagged 82 wickets in 2005. A larrikin with scant regard for the recently introduced indoor smoking ban, Rehman also sub-pro'd for Ashcombe a few years later, and Steve Proffitt recalls him having "the quickest arm ball I've ever seen. You're thinking: if he [the batter] edges this I'm gonna get killed. He had the signal – a little tap on his elbow – and you'd be looking for it. When you saw it, it was: 'Oh no!'"

Besides Rehman, there were a couple of players who would turn out in the inaugural T20 World Cup final the following September. Sohail Tanvir lived in a flat attached to Haslington's smart new pavilion, financed by Mike Trevor, a cheese magnate who built the club from scratch, moving it to its current location in the Cheshire countryside, where he was buried on site. Tanvir was a generally quiet presence, although on occasion would crank up his decidedly lively, wrong-footed left-arm swing bowling. In one game against Oulton, he made 116 then took 8/59, hitting one batter and knocking him onto the stumps. Another opponent, Chris Beech, then a 14-year-old first-team debutant for Blythe, laughs at being "asked to open because no one else fancied it, then being stuck down his end for seven overs, about two balls of which were at the stumps. I was hit twice on the grille, got off strike, and was then cleaned up by a dobber, by which time Tanvir found his yorker and broke the captain's brother's foot."

On another occasion, however, Tanvir found himself travelling to the tune of 11-0-79-1, whipped off after three overs and returning to bowl spin. His destroyer was Imran Nazir, a free spirit with Bollywood looks and good spoken English who certainly took to the compact dimensions at J&G Meakin CC, hemmed in as it was on two sides by the Caldon Canal. Sat permanently on the towpath was a long aluminium pole with a scooping device on the end, a much-used gizmo that summer with Nazir's first seven scores at home being: 227 (19 fours, 18 sixes) – this contributing to 397/3 declared against Haslington, who replied with 389/7 before coming off for bad light with two overs left – then 9, 21, 149 (16 fours, 10 sixes), 134* (10 fours, 12 sixes), 59 (eight fours, one six) and 168 (21 fours, 13 sixes). There was also a 100 and 97 on the road, and with five games of the season left he had 1,153 runs and Aakash Chopra's league record aggregate of 1,415 firmly in his sights. As it turned out, he failed to add to those 1,153 runs: two abandonments, two blobs (one golden, yorked first ball by student Rob Spruce) and home a week early. More importantly, Meakins finished just one place above the relegation spots, so in 2007 went for a quick-bowling option: the 21-year-old Wahab Riaz.

Wahab used to catch the bus down from Manchester on Saturday morning and, although at times extremely fast – with 35-yard boundaries at both ends, there wasn't much real estate behind the cordon – he was also somewhat disappointing in the season's opening couple of months, not least because he had a tendency to run in with arms stretched out, mimicking an aeroplane, juvenile and disrespectful antics that his captain James Menzies soon drummed out of him. However, a two-week break to attend a Pakistan 'A' training camp along with the arrival of his parents and a mid-season renegotiation of his contract, including a wicket bonus, flicked the switch. He signed off with seven straight five-fors – 77 wickets at 13.66 all in – to earn Meakins promotion, and was promptly offered a five-year deal, which his ascendant star prevented him from taking up.

Throw in the likes of Asif, Abdur Razzaq, Azhar Mahmood, Shahid Afridi and a host of lesser lights, and at times in the 2000s there were amateur cricketers from north Staffs – posties, parkies, sparkies, chippies – who had played with or against half of any given Pakistan team. For Asif and Morkel, then, the desire to best their direct counterpart was a not insignificant aspect of the experience, something to sharpen the mind and elevate their game – and, thereby, the contest. Not least their final league encounter.

Morné was certainly ready for business, each week an imperceptible step closer to smashing out of his chrysalis, each day tightening up his pitchmap to find a length threatening these English castles. Twice in his first over and four times in his opening five Ashcombe timber was struck, bringing Asif to the wicket at 25/5, helmet eschewed for a green Pakistan cap. With the innings circling the drain, Asif mixed dogged defence with the occasional rustic heave, profiting as Morkel, bowling an unbroken 24-over spell, began to tire. He finished with a 110-ball 69 out of 119 all out, Morné with 7/46.

As the heavy black clouds closed in during tea, Ashcombe more than fancied their chances, particularly when Bunn – who would compile 977 league runs that year, second only to Mughal – was bounced out in Asif's first over. This became 25/4 from 13 overs, Clowes producing a jaffa to bowl Morkel for nine, but by then steady Moorlands drizzle had become a downpour and the players, once having trooped off, never got back out, a score draw in the head-to-head making it Morkel 2 Asif 2. Consensus was that the Park were strong favourites, a sentiment subtly hinted at in the *Post*'s headline: RAIN CHEATS ASHCOMBE PACE ATTACK.

* * *

It is perhaps surprising – although maybe not, given that one career headed abruptly south as the other moved inexorably north – that Asif and Morkel never played a *bona fide* international fixture against each other. The only time they met after this gloomy July joust in the Staffordshire Moorlands was the three-match Afro-Asia Cup in June 2007, three ODIs in five days between the Asian Cricket Council XI and an African XI – both men taking their team's first over, both occupying the No.11 spot. Asif wasn't required to bat, but did dismiss AB de Villiers in two of the three games, caught by Sandyford's Dhoni in the second. Morkel was dismissed once, by Asif, and claimed among his tournament-topping eight wickets the scalps of Jayasuriya, Sehwag, Ganguly, Jayawardene, Yuvraj and Mohammad Yousuf. He was by then a different species from the coltish teenager who ran as though his limbs were being controlled by a puppeteer's strings, a long way from the bowler carted all around Endon by self-employed tiler Dean Hodson four years earlier.

Asif's gritty *soixante-neuf* against Endon formed one of the high peaks of an unlikely month-long batting apogee – innings of 75*, 69, 3, 1, 60, 72 and 26 – that would have been difficult to foresee as he made ten single-figure contributions in 17 hits the previous year (it would be 39 in 44 Test innings). With ball in hand, he largely ran hot for the rest of the summer, barring a mauling from Mughal, who bludgeoned 143* at Ashcombe. The August warmth brought Iffy 8/38 against Bagnall, 6/49 at Newcastle, a remarkable spell of 21-13-19-6 against Sandyford, who nevertheless hung on for a draw amid a barrage of beamers at Laurie Thomas, and finally – before an early-September 7/44 at Eccleshall continued the purple patch – an afternoon that would have been bizarre even for someone who frequently dragged around a cloud of incipient chaos.

Ashcombe arrived at Weston to find a troop of Travellers camped on the outfield: a dozen or more caravans along with a menagerie of animals and assorted kids rutting up the outfield on a pony and trap. Initial negotiations had floundered after the Travellers accepted a cash payment only then to decide that, actually, they didn't want to leave, thank you very much. After further discussion, the three caravans on the square were relocated beyond the boundary, leaving one more at short third man whose owner, apparently, "was away doing a bit of business", eventually returning in a Nissan pick-up to set out his position on things, his smallprint T's & C's.

"It was an awful day," recalls Proffitt, "and I felt really sad for Weston. One of the Travellers had a caravan rammed full of power tools which he was trying to sell to our groundsman. There was a donkey tethered up in the corner, hens, goats, all sorts. Then the guy comes back – the one who owns the camper that's still on the pitch. 'Would you mind moving it, mate?' 'I will, but if that red ball hits it then that brick building over there [the Weston CC pavilion] will be burnt to the ground by the morning'. 'Okay lads, shall we call the game off…?'" (The fixture was rescheduled for the Sunday after the last match, Weston beating the Asif-less Ashcombe – who nonetheless engaged a sub pro to ensure the integrity of the competition – thereby surviving the drop and ultimately relegating Bagnall, the unfortunate collateral damage in the sorry episode.)

However, just as it seemed Ashcombe's season was winding down to an underwhelming fifth-place finish, they suddenly had the final of the league knockout to look forward to, having been reinstated after losing a semi-final to Oulton, who were kicked out for fielding an ineligible player. The ringer was Ian Austin, Lancashire's erstwhile death-bowling maestro, who clobbered 92* and sent down 5-1-7-0 in a 101-run win, playing as an amateur alongside regular pro, leg-spinner Mo Fayyaz. Austin had registered as a playing member at Oulton via a connection with his employer, Thwaites Brewery, but his availability was limited by virtue of him, uh, pro-ing for another club in Lancashire. Nevertheless, he had a free Sunday on the day of the semi and Oulton threw him in. Then the league threw *them* out. Which meant Ashcombe facing Silverdale in the final, although there would be no silverware as they came up 11 runs short, the last three-quarters of an hour played in rain so torrential that they held the trophy ceremony inside the pavilion.

Morné, meanwhile, followed his farewell encounter with Asif by bumping up against another South Asian finding life in the Moorlands to his liking, Sohail Rauf square-cutting his way to 130 at Oakamoor as the thrum of Alton Towers' rollercoasters rumbled down the Churnet Valley. Thereafter, Morkel locked into the early model of a now-familiar groove, producing an August every bit as purple as Asif's. First he took his season's figures against Eccleshall to 16/81 with a spell of 7/27 (Asif managed 12/106 against the wooden-spoonists), having earlier clubbed 105. A week later it was 5/49 against leaders Wood Lane, although Endon fell in a heap chasing 129. Next, he pocketed 5/57, including the key wicket of Mughal, as third-placed Silverdale were tipped up. And then it was 5/48 in defeat to runners-up Oulton: 22 wickets at 8.23 in the month. There was one more outing before his farewells, a game that brought, recalls Bunn, "one of the few times I ever saw him go at anyone verbally".

Endon batted first and racked up 280/4, to which Bunn contributed 168* and Morkel nought, cleaned up by Tanvir Ahmed and promptly given the sort of dressing-room directions he could have used at The Oval four years later. Come Tanvir's turn to bat, out he strode in a

Pakistan shirt, Pepsi logo and all, despite not yet having represented his country. "It was a red rag to a bull," adds Bunn. "Morné bowled a very quick spell at him. He kept following through, saying: 'You need to earn the right to wear that badge'. It was a proper ding-dong. 'You don't deserve the shirt. You don't deserve the shirt.'"

Tanvir dug in for 48, Morkel signed off with 4/59, and Endon again came in eighth. Morné had finished his second season with a much-improved 65 wickets at 14.34, leaving him seventh in the averages, four spots above Tanvir and four below Asif's 76 at 11.45. He again edged the batting honours, with 533 runs at 33, finishing 18th in the averages and eight spots above Asif, who chipped in 372 at 26.57. A score draw on the stats front, too.

A matter of months after what turned out to be his final appearance for Ashcombe Park and just turned 23, Asif was debuting for Pakistan in the New Year's Test in Sydney – where there were no Winnebagos on the wicket, no beamers hurled through the air – trying to outfox Ricky Ponting and Matty Hayden where he had failed against Laurie Thomas and Matty Hagan. Ashcombe had initially tried to re-engage him for the 2005 season, only to be gazumped by first division Barlaston, although a freshly minted PCB central contract ensured he would never take the field for them. Ashcombe turned their attention to a big South African lad playing three miles west, with Dave Goodwin and skipper Dave Beswick meeting Morné at The Plough in Endon. "We got the contract sorted with him but it wasn't to be," laments Goodwin. "He broke his ankle in South Africa and was unfit to come over."

Asif then signed for Leicestershire in 2006, by which time he was able to drive, popping up to Ashcombe in a "big, blacked-out BMW" to visit old friends and new pro, Najaf Shah, a colleague on the previous year's Pakistan 'A' jaunts to Sri Lanka and Zimbabwe. Najaf had given the club a mid-season heads-up that he was going to miss the final two months, and Goodwin was quick to line up his replacement. "Morné was arranged, the paperwork completed, at which point Najaf announced he was staying! So for Ashcombe Park and Morné it was never to be."

That would not be the end of Morkel's story in Staffordshire club cricket, however. At a loose end once more after the Najaf U-turn and firing up the Xbox in Pretoria, those twiddling thumbs were soon fielding a call from his old mate Dave Fairbanks, who was now at Audley and explaining to him that their pro, Alfonso Thomas, was heading off for a month on an 'A' tour, inviting Morné to deputise. "He said yes straight away," recalls Fairbanks. "He just wanted his flights covered. We didn't even pay him for playing!"

* * *

The 21-year-old Morné Morkel who jetted into Heathrow in July 2006 had by then worked his way up through the pace-bowling adjectives from 2003's 'lively' and 2004's 'sharp' to sit now at 'slippery' while fast approaching 'horrible' – although these things are, up to a point, relative. Yet there remained some bad old habits that he had failed to shake off, as Audley discovered on his debut at Meir Heath.

"First game, he must have bowled 20 no-balls," chuckles Andrew 'Tracker' Johnson, who had accompanied Fairbanks to Vereeniging in late-2002, giving Morkel a lift to the airport for a Gauteng under-19s fixture only for Morné to realise they had gone a day early. "At least 20," he continues, "and he'd even brought a tape-measure with him to mark out his run. He worked out later that he'd had it upside down and was using the wrong side!"

Morkel's figures that day were an ugly 8-0-58-0. Given that Audley were defending 104 – Imran Tahir having run through them with 7/32 from 21 overs of sorcery – this cannot be considered an unqualified success. But he did get it through; about that, everyone was in agreement.

The best seat in the house for the new, bulked-up Morné was to be had by wicket-keeper David Whitehurst, signed as the long-term replacement for Audley's legendary former skipper Alan 'Frinty' Griffiths, an impish tactical wizard who played over 100 games for Staffordshire, as well as for the Minor Counties XI against the '82 Pakistanis and mighty 1984 West Indians. A short guy with bright eyes and fast hands who kept wicket in big, loosely buckled batting pads that flapped about like an elephant's ears, Frinty was a charismatic, canny ringmaster who could read the runes and see the game before it happened. He could also be pessimistic if the tea leaves spelt trouble. Never more so than those occasions when his pencil-thin, military-medium yet devilishly effective 6' 5" left-arm opening bowler Gary Latham – the half-speed Bruce Reid, if you will – failed to make his first delivery with new ball curve back in at the pads as desired, at which point Frint would gather the ball – the unwelcome slant-acrosser – and toss it to first slip, before pronouncing, *sotto voce* but succinct as ever: "We're fucked."

If more given to understatement, 'Whitey' was just as laconic, and just as keen to see Morné v2.0 up close, particularly after the tape-measure rigmarole. And so in Morkel charged after the interval, whereupon his first offering duly elicited an "ooh, that's quick" from the keeper. "Which," clarifies Fairbanks, "was Whitey for 'Fuck me, that's rapid'."

Arguably the worst seat in the house belonged to Richard Stonier, effervescent future fitness trainer to the Bangladesh national team: "Morné rocks up, tape measure out, spray, the works. First ball to me: 'No-ball!' It hit me flush on the forearm. I never even saw it. Half my players on the sideline turned away laughing, as if to say, 'Oh my god, how quick is this?!' I managed to get one away through covers, only for two though because Nicky Locker didn't come back for three. I don't think he really fancied it. I think the first over was an 11-baller, with something like five no-balls. Part of me wanted the umpire to stop calling them! It was absolutely rapid. It was unbelievable how far back the slips and keeper were. Good experience, though."

Meir Heath knocked off for three with a lot of balls flying over gully, and within 24 hours Morkel's cumulative figures would sit at 12-0-96-0 after a heavy defeat to treble-winning Stone in the T20 semi-final round-robin at Porthill. But he was quick; about that, everyone was in agreement. Not least Brian Sims, who saw Morkel's round-the-wicket approach to his leftie opening partner Phil Cheadle and might have assumed he would come back over the wicket to him, a right-hander. "Cheesy kept running him down to third man and because it was wet on the other side he stayed round to me, basically trying to put a hole in my armpit. He certainly wasn't slow!" While Sims's 46* anchored the chase, the impetus was provided by Shaun Jenkinson's breezy 54, whose chief memory of the day is "Dave Fairbanks standing at mid off laughing his bollocks off after repeatedly telling Morné to bounce me". As you would.

Audley lost the day's other game, to hosts Porthill, girthsome *bon viveur* Matt Hole clubbing a 65-ball 124, and soon Fairbanks's unilateral recruitment of the sub pro was being queried. "He comes for free, just wants his flights paid for, to be fed and spend some time with his mates," grouses Fairbanks, "but our old club secretary, John Tryner, says to me: 'We know why we've signed him, because he's your mate! And if he plays for South Africa I'll swim the Atlantic!'"

Morkel would be a Test cricketer within six months, of course, but even he wasn't entirely convinced he would make it, recalls his skipper, 'Big' Dan O'Callaghan: "He was so humble. I remember him asking me, 'Do you think I'm good enough?' 'Well, you're six-foot-five and bowl 90 miles per hour, so you've got a chance!'"

Neither Tryner's scepticism nor Morné self-belief would have changed too much after the following week's home double-header, when a bowler who would later become accustomed to impala-bounding-across-the-savannah carry watched the ball scuttling apologetically through on the lifeless surface at Kent Hills ("Our groundsman, Hinksy, used to roll the shit out of it," observes Fairbanks, archly). Nor did the wicket-keeper particularly appreciate taking 140kph rockets on the second bounce, and on Sunday Morkel broke Whitehurst's thumb, putting him out for the season. Still, there were runs to be had on the featherbed at Audleyabad, and in Saturday's bore-draw with Leek, Morkel made 67 before being run out by centurion Fairbanks. Twenty-four hours later, having gone wicketless as Moddershall racked up 258/7, Morkel's 105* marshalled a tricky chase home, steering Audley into a Staffs Cup semi-final.

The free accommodation part of the Morkel package was taken care of by Tracker's brother and teammate, 'Ticker' – known to his mother as Paul – whose grandma brought round rice pudding whenever the South African made his puppy-dog eyes. Morné also managed to convince two separate groups of people on two separate days that it was his birthday, ensuring a liberal flow of free refreshments, all to the astonishment then admiration of Fairbanks: "I think he's the only person I know bar the Queen who has two birthdays!"

Meanwhile, Morkel spent his weeks grafting, picked up in the morning by Tracker and taken along with Big Dan to lay driveways out west, an unconventional way to build up his core strength. "He always had a spring in his step and had the gift of the gab," recalls O'Callaghan. "There was an elderly couple in Wem who were asking him questions about their forthcoming job, and me and Track were in the van worried Morné might be caught out with his lack of knowledge and experience. But he talked them through it like an old pro, as though he'd been doing it 20 years, not two weeks!" Driveways, yes; fanzines, no.

While his runs were welcome, what Audley most needed from Morkel as they drifted further from the fringes of the title race were a few wickets, and three whose distinct form and feel presaged later adventures – good pace, big bounce, ball flying to slips stationed in a neighbouring voting district – would come in a resounding win at basement-dwelling Little Stoke, where a proto-Bazballian 128 from Sean Price allowed O'Callaghan to declare at 284/5 before Morkel tore in from the Farm End and Tracker's calloused labourer's hands proved useful in clinging on to a trio of catches at second slip, one of them from opposing pro Richard Harvey, Staffs skipper and Alfonso Thomas's brother-in-law. "I nicked it and turned round, and everything seemed in slow motion as it sailed to Tracker, who was absolutely miles back," Harvey recalls. "Honestly," says Johnson, who bagged 6/62 in the Morkel slipstream, "me and Big Dan were about five yards off the boundary."

Things were looking good for back-to-back league wins when Audley reached 171/4 at home to Knypersley the following Saturday, but after Morkel was bowled sweeping Qaiser Abbas they folded to 175 all out. The visitors' opening pair, Jon Cumberbatch and Ross Salmon, then drew the South African's sting as they ground out 65 runs from a combined 155 balls, setting up a six-wicket victory. Morkel signed off the next day with 69 and 2/27 in a Talbot Cup quarter-final romp past Oulton, leaving him with figures of 9/277 from six long-form outings: an average of 30.78. He was still around the following Saturday, though, cursing as he watched Alfonso bag 8/93 on a pacey pitch at Moddershall before then heading off on his ascent to the bright lights of international cricket, where his maiden Test victim was Sandyford's MS Dhoni. "If someone had said to me when he finished at Endon in '04 that he'd play Test cricket," reflects Bunn, "I'd have said no chance.

I just didn't see that extra pace coming. It just shows you how single-minded he was and how hard he must have worked."

* * *

After that December debut against India, Morkel sat out the following month's home engagement with Pakistan, although he may well have told Messrs. Smith, Amla, Kallis and de Villiers how he'd pumped the series' leading wicket-taker (19 at 18.47) all around Ashcombe three years earlier. He was still carrying the drinks when South Africa visited Pakistan later in 2007 – these two famous oversteppers destined never again to tango – but by the summer of 2008 had shuffled his Sideshow Bob feet under the Proteas' fast-bowling table. "I was in Birmingham selling a driveway," recalls O'Callaghan, "and a South African answered the door with a Proteas cricket cap on. In the background Morné was bowling against England in a Test match, live on the TV. That's how quickly it all happened for him. I said to the guy, 'Morné was working for us on the drives the year before last' and he just looked at me like I was some kind of a lunatic."

Pakistan and South Africa's next tussle came in November 2010, by which time a lot of water had passed under the bridge. Making his debut in Abu Dhabi – a direct consequence of Asif's misdemeanours in St John's Wood – was Tanvir Ahmed, finally earning the right to wear the badge and duly taking the venue's slim window of opportunity for conventional lateral movement by knocking over Alviro Petersen, Smith and Amla in his first spell in Test cricket, before de Villiers put together a career-best 278*, adding an unbroken 107 for the final wicket with one Morné Morkel, who made 35*. Morras was ranked a career-high third at the time, behind only Dale Steyn and Graeme Swann, but would finish the match with one wicket only: Tanvir's.

Almost a year to the day later, Asif was in Southwark Crown Court awaiting sentencing. Earlier that summer, in the UK on bail, he had dropped in to see old friends at Basford Bridge Lane, even posing for a photograph with Steve Proffitt, who was handing him a £20 note – an awkward, tender moment, the club reconciling the egregiousness of the act with their affection for an old teammate.

"He was a loveable rogue," says Proffitt, "a great lad in the dressing-room. He was a future Pakistan Test player but he played like an English village cricketer. When he was in his zone he wanted to knock people's heads off, as fast bowlers generally do, but after the match he just wanted to have a Marlboro, a bottle of Budweiser and join in the craic with the lads. He was always such a joker. I just don't think he realised the seriousness of what he'd done – until he was convicted."

He had visited in 2010, too, shortly before the spot-fixing scandal had engulfed Pakistan's tour, Dave Goodwin arranging to watch him strut his stuff in one of the Tests. "The actual weekend of the infamous Lord's game," Goodwin explains, "I was down in London to watch Stoke play Chelsea on the Saturday and Iffy had invited me and my 11-year-old son to Lord's on the Sunday. Tickets were to be left for me. On the Saturday evening, I'd been trying to contact him, to no avail. I got up the next morning to see the headlines about the no-balls and that his phone had been taken from him – with about 50 missed calls from me on it! I never got to see him that day, but we managed to get in the ground and obviously the rest is history. In fact, while his trial was being organised I got a call from his barrister, asking me about his bank account. I'd arranged to open it with him as I had contacts at NatWest Bank in Cannock and they made things easier to sort out. It had been alleged that the people offering the bungs to the players had opened special bank accounts for the money to be paid into. Iffy's reply had been, 'No, Goody open my account!' I had to make a statement for the Old Bailey trial to that effect!"

Once Asif had served his prison time and ICC ban, Ashcombe spoke to him about returning as pro, 15 years after originally signing him. A deal was done in 2018 to bring back the prodigal son, only for visa issues to scupper things. "I'm convinced people would have travelled to watch him play," says Proffitt, ruefully.

"If I had to sum him up," adds Goodwin, "he was an amazing player on the pitch, a proper character off it. It was just great to say you had played in a game at Ashcombe Park when there was a world-class bowler playing for each team. They were great times, personally and for the club, and will live long in the memory."

13

Michael Holding / Andy Roberts
at Rishton / Haslingden

Saturday, 15 August 1981 and the birds are already busy in Rossendale when Bryan Knowles rolls himself out of bed at 6am and straight into his weekend routine. Grabbing a perfunctory breakfast, he slides into his van then drives the 40 miles to Ormskirk market, where he lays out the bathroom towels, the flannels, the duvet covers, the pillow cases, the blankets, sheets, throws and tea towels on his market stall, finds himself a brew and a bacon buttie, and waits for punters with household textile needs to roll in.

Around 10:45am, the sun now fully stretching out its limbs, he switches on his transistor radio for *Test Match Special*, comforting ambient noise amid the eager thrum of bargain hunters. England, somehow 2-1 up in the Ashes and looking to seal things at Old Trafford, are 70/1 in their second innings, a lead of 171, with Chris Tavaré still in the foothills of his 289-ball 78 and a storm called Ian Botham – feeling pretty good about things, all in all – awaiting on the balcony. Bryan, too, is feeling good about his cricket. His last few scores for Haslingden, in the thick of a Lancashire League title chase, have been a string of captainly contributions: 26*, 41, 68, 33, 77 and 33, bringing six wins out of seven and leaving 'Hassy' – without a championship for 28 years – in second place with six to play. It was a potentially decisive double-header weekend: today, Colne away; on Sunday, Rishton at home, for which there should be a few on.

Shortly after 11, his wife Ann arrives in the family car, two sons in tow, and takes over the running of things. Bryan's thoughts turn to the game. Scooping up the boys, he scoots back to Haslingden and picks up the club pro, Anderson Montgomery Everton Roberts, rented out to Leicestershire for the week and arriving late back to Lancashire the previous night after a three-day County Championship match at The Oval had wound up just as London's weekend bustle started to gurgle onto the streets.

It hadn't been a spectacular summer for 'Fruits' with the Foxes: 19 games into the season, seven of them in the Champo, he was yet to pick up a five-bag. The wrong side of 30 now, he's no longer the bowler who, five years earlier and fired by Greig's "grovel" *faux pas*, had roughed up England's fortysomething cannon fodder, Closey and Edrich, on that X-rated Old Trafford pitch, match figures of 9/59 propelling him to No.1 in the world rankings; no longer the bowler who, later that same year, was clocked at 98.1mph at the WACA – on rudimentary equipment and in non-match conditions, true, but decidedly slippery all the same. Even so, Haslingden might reasonably have assumed, he ought probably still be good enough for the Lancashire League's finest. Yet even there, 20 games deep by the time he was not saying much in the car as it wended its way up through the moorlands to Colne, he had managed just the three five-fors and only one bowling collection. "Back then, it wasn't easy to get a bowling collection for a pro," says Knowles. "You had to get six for less than 30. It was five for less than 40 for an amateur. It was probably easier for him to get a collection for a fifty."

Perhaps today will be the day, the Antiguan's teammates were no doubt hoping after he had knocked over the first three Colne wickets cheaply, but that would be his lot as Trevor Lonsdale's 70 nudged the home team up to 161/6 from 34 eight-ball overs. Roberts then joined his captain at 54/2, Knowles making 49 to take his tally to 750 for the season, while the pro clubbed five sixes in a free-wheeling 72* as Haslingden cantered to victory, pyrotechnics that were indeed enough to earn him a second batting collection for the season, none of which went into the team kitty. "You didn't get much out of Andy in the bar," says Knowles. "He wouldn't spend much more than £5 all year. Peter Swart [Haslingden's pro from 1974 to '77] used to go out on a Friday night, have 15 pints of lager, smoke about 60 cigarettes, three women, then turn up on a Saturday and get 70 or 80 and six wickets."

While Haslingden were beating Colne, Franklyn Stephenson's 5/32 led third-place Rawtenstall to victory over erstwhile leaders Burnley, meaning Hassy had gone top – by a point – for the first time that season. Knowles and crew repaired to HQ to celebrate the win, although not Andy, who trundled back to his handsome terraced house a mile or so away in Raby Street, Rawtenstall, to spend the evening with his wife, Janet. Sunday brought a welcome lie-in for Bryan after the previous evening's pints. A substantial breakfast in the tank, he then drove the 200 yards to Bentgate, hit a few, observed Andy fraternising with his opposite number, lost the toss, strapped them on and, eventually, took strike, as he always did. Rishton's pro marked out his run, about half its usual, hardcore length, for Michael Andrew Holding was feeling his way back from a nagging back injury. Twenty-four hours earlier, he had collected a relatively profligate 4/79 in defeat to Accrington. The coming Wednesday he will be playing for Lancashire in the NatWest Trophy semi-final at Northampton. Maybe a good time to be facing him.

Certainly better than five months earlier in Barbados, when West Indies skipper Clive Lloyd told Mikey for the very first time that he, not Andy, would have first dibs on ends. In deference to his great comrade and mentor, Holding replied that he would have "whichever end Andy doesn't want" and duly took the second over. And *what* an over it was – mythical now, of course. The unfortunate batter taking strike was Geoffrey Boycott, master technician but recently turned 40 years old. After being speed-roasted in five fireball deliveries – Holding at his rhythmical apex, running in purposefully yet smoothly, a cheetah prepared to pursue its quarry over miles of savannah – the sixth sent Boycott's off stump into a series of Simone Biles floor-routine cartwheels and the crowd into a frenzy of limbs, an iconically brutal moment from the snuff-movie showreel of one of cricket's most unforgiving teams. Penny for your thoughts, Bryan?

Within a couple of hours, Knowles would be bunting Holding back over his head for a one-bounce four – giving him membership of a very, very exclusive club, one would imagine – en route to 96 out of 205 all out, the Jamaican finishing with 5/68 from 17 unchanged eight-ball overs, including AME Roberts for six. "I wouldn't say it was easy batting against him," Knowles deadpans, "but having bowled his initial spell with a leg slip, three slips and two gullies, any time you got bat on ball was runs."

There was also a sizeable stroke of luck when Knowles feathered one to Rishton wicket-keeper Frank Martindale on 46. Not that there was ever any question of him walking, even though everyone knew by then from Holding's columns in the *Lancashire Evening Telegraph* that his twin bug bears were doctored wicket ends and batters who didn't take the decision out of the umpires' hands when they had scratched one through. That was never going to happen, no matter how many towels and tablecloths had been shifted that week. It was not the code. So he slapped on a poker face, got the desired head-shake, and prepared for the incoming storm.

In Mikey's code, bouncers in club cricket to amateurs were usually to be scorned, except in certain special circumstances. Here was one of those asterisk occasions. It was time to have a look upstairs. Bespectacled and lidless, Knowles took him on, hooking and pulling a handful of fours, a couple of them even working some rarely used muscles in the Roberts mush: "He didn't smile too often, didn't Andy, but every now and then there'd be a little grin when you hit Michael for four." With a hundred in touching distance, Knowles fell as he "tried to hit an amateur who was bowling little in-swinging floaters out of the ground and got caught on the edge. There was quite a bit of time left, too, but I thought: if it's in my half, it's going!" Knowles trousered a tidy £55 from his collection, over £200 in today's money.

In reply, Rishton were soon up the creek at 67/8 – MA Holding lbw Roberts 1 – and with the four points safely bagged (barring a miracle), the only question was whether Hassy could pick up the bonus for bowling the opposition out. In the end, a late-order rearguard from the still bristling Martindale saw Rishton hang on at 101/9. With four games left, Haslingden were joint-top with Burnley, Rawtenstall two points back, while Knowles needed 154 more runs for the mythical Lancashire League 1,000, which at the time had been reached only twice by amateurs, and not for 62 long years. See you at Rishton next Sunday, Mr Holding.

* * *

To paraphrase Bishop Berkeley's famous empiricist thought-experiment: if a legendary over is bowled in a game that isn't televised, did it really happen? The answer is: Yes, Bish, it happened. In fact, Boycs still remembers punching a 150kph throat ball toward Garner in the gully. But unless you happened to have been watching Tony Francis's two-minute despatch on ITN's *News at Ten* on Saturday 14 March, it would have slipped past your attention that Rishton's new pro had relocated Geoffrey's off stump 20 yards nearer the press box. Which, on reflection, might not be a bad thing to have slipped your attention.

Nevertheless, if the Lancashire League's top-order batters hadn't seen the recent Barbados bombardment, they will have had vivid memories of Andy and especially Mikey's Old Trafford brutalism from five years earlier: Holding roaring in off the boundary, the 45-year-old Brian Close now jerking his comb-over away at the last second from the hard red missile like a stuntman avoiding a punch, now chesting it away to point like Niall Quinn playing in Kevin Phillips after a long diagonal from full-back, eventually walking off with a torso resembling a Rorschach Test – heavily bruised, yes, but not out.

"Closey got one run in 59 minutes and had the shit knocked out of him," recalls Pat Pocock. "He was in a terrible state when he came in. I had got in as nightwatchman in the first innings [on day one] and I didn't get out that night. Next morning, I'm walking out with John Edrich and he asked me, 'Which end do you fancy?' I told him I'd have Andy Roberts's end as he was a bit of light relief. John pisses himself laughing: 'I tell you now, if Andy Roberts is light relief then we've got problems.'" Yep, the 1981 season promised to be a challenge for the hardy amateurs of east Lancashire's mill towns.

So much so, in fact, that Ian Bell, the 21-year-old opening bat at Ramsbottom, Rishton's first opponents, decided to retire on the eve of the season, calling the hiring of Roberts and Holding "a retrograde step" – this in a league with a lineage of West Indian speedsters (not to mention Ray Lindwall, Dennis Lillee, Frank Tyson and others), running from Learie Constantine and Manny Martindale through Roy Gilchrist, Chester Watson, Wes Hall and Charlie Griffith, who in 1964, en route to a league-record 144 wickets for Burnley, was rumoured to have sent 37 people to hospital. When Rishton played them in the Worsley Cup final that year, a jar of laxative tablets was found in their dressing-room, which they promptly launched out of the window before going on to win the game. "I just don't fancy playing against such as Holding and Roberts," Bell told the *Lancashire Telegraph*. "I will be getting married in the summer and I have other responsibilities in addition to playing cricket. I want to feel that I will be at work every Monday morning in a fit condition."

Fair to say there a few nerves jangling about on Easter Sunday – a few prayers as Ramsbottom opener Peter Ashworth scratched out his guard and looked up into the distance to see the lean and mean 27-year-old Jamaican standing at the top of his run and preparing to send down his first ball in Lancashire League cricket. His partner, Mick Everett, a police sergeant in Bury who had knocked off from his night shift at 5am, was glad to be getting a look at one. Hallelujah!

Adding to the air of anxiety was the Ramsbottom committee's unprecedented investment in three brand new plum-coloured helmets, along with assorted padding, which could either be seen as confidence-building tools or as starkly tactile reminders of the impending physical jeopardy. The procurement of these various bone protectors formed the main through-line in Saturday's *Rossendale Free Press* – the weekly newspaper covering Rammy, Haslingden, Rawtenstall and Bacup – which ran its preview under the headline: 'Enter the Tin-Hat Brigade'. After noting the purchase of the new £50 helmets, the correspondent observed that "there will be a number of well concealed chest and thigh pads among the equipment. Some players could find it difficult just walking to the crease! But now the talking has to stop. The action is about to start. And, to be fair to these world-class cricketers, let's just give them a chance to get on with the job that they're being paid (handsomely) to do. It is so easy to pre-judge. Surely, players of their calibre have no need to stoop to any intimidatory tactics? Flying deliveries won't get many wickets but they could result in one or two sore heads. Captains and umpires will, hopefully, keep a close watch on the situation." The tone was wary – the fears and pre-emptive bargaining of a village that had spotted hordes of barbarian invaders on the horizon.

Four days earlier, Holding had been playing the final day of the Jamaica Test in 32 degrees Celsius. He flew into London with the England squad on the Friday, from where he was collected the next day by Wilf Woodhouse, owner of a shop on Rishton High Street that rented TVs and top-loading video recorders. The Rishton chairman, evidently, was a gifted salesman, coaxing Holding to the village for a summer's work when he was near the top of many counties' shopping lists.

Woodhouse had approached his man during the previous summer's Old Trafford Test, impressing with his passion and energy, as Holding would later recount in his autobiography, *No Holding Back*: "Wilf was very enthusiastic; I liked that. He told me that the standard of cricket was good and I would not find it a chore. He said that Rishton would pay me £5,000 for the summer. In those days that was a lot of money, especially for playing at weekends only. After discussing it further I thought, why not?" Holding left his job in the Central Data Processing Unit of the Jamaican government and took his "first venture into professional cricket outside West Indies".

Woodhouse would also loan Holding to Lancashire for what turned out to be seven first-class and seven List 'A' matches that summer. They had tried to sign Holding in 1977, only for him to return to Jamaica to complete his degree, and would pay Rishton a fee for his services as well as provide insurance coverage should he pick up an injury on county duty – although the chances of this were diminished by having his West Indies skipper, Clive Lloyd, in the captain's chair at Old Trafford. The loan fee wasn't the only benefit of the arrangement, either. Barrie Hill, the Rishton dobber whose "little floaters" would, come August, account for Knowles on 96, was carrying over a troublesome shoulder injury from the previous summer and as a deal-sweetener he would receive free treatment from the Lancashire physio.

When Woodhouse and Holding pulled onto Rishton's Blackburn Road ground that Sunday lunchtime there were already around 2,000 spectators there, the biggest crowd since the days of Hall and Griffith almost 20 years earlier and ten times the average of the previous few seasons. But then, this was the fastest bowler in the world – an action that was pure liquid, the most sublime cricketing spectacle of the age – and he was at the peak of his powers. Of course they flocked in. Besides, the pubs shut at 2pm, whereas the cricket club didn't.

The gate of £850 (around £3,175 in today's money) already meant that 20 per cent of Rishton's outlay had been chalked off. Canny bit of business, Wilf. Membership had almost doubled to 700, which was very welcome with work ongoing on a new £60,000 clubhouse. Holding Fever had arrived, so much so that the 1,200 meat pies the club had bought in for the day were gone before the tea interval, forcing club secretary Harry Crabtree to head off in search of more. "We'll need a lot of meat and potato pie nights to pay for yon lad," observed one Rishton ultra. The pie consumption might have been connected to the nippy April weather, a chilly 12 Celsius, with spectators hunkered under blankets, which wasn't the case at Sabina Park earlier in the week.

Cold or not, Holding Fever had also drawn film crews from the BBC and Granada TV, who busily conducted their David-and-Goliath interviews with the Ramsbottom players. A phalanx of national press were there, too – *Telegraph*, *Times*, *Sunday People* – and the previous evening Woodhouse had told the *Guardian* that "a man of Holding's abilities should find this a piece of cake. But he will be under pressure to get us the wickets. Rishton have been third these last three years. We want to win the league and the cup, so we went for the best." Lemon squeezy.

Rishton lost the toss and Rammy opted not to get stuck straight into the batting, hoping the temperature might drop another muscle-stiffening degree or two before their turn came. The pitch had spent three Sisyphean weeks under covers and the winds were biting, but the hum of excitement could not be muffled. Alas, the home side's batting was unable to rise to the challenge of the grand tour's opening night, and Holding's 26 – featuring one six out of the ground, which became something of a motif – was the top score in a disappointing effort. His wicket was taken by Andy Taylor, a private in the Royal Transportation Corps in Hull, back home on leave for the weekend and fresh from football in the morning. No send-off was proffered. Rishton subsided from 98/5 to 108 all out. And then it was time. How's your ticker?

"He did not start his run-up across the main road or on Rishton Station as some comedians in the clubhouse had suggested," observed the *Lancashire Telegraph*. "He took 17 giant strides from the sightscreen and several times tried a shorter run." Peter Ashworth survived physically intact, but contributed just three to a run-chase in which Holding's figures after an eight-over opening burst – four off the longer run – were 0/21. The *Sunday People* described him as "hampered by jet-lag, two sweaters, a bitter wind, no proper total to bowl at, and stiffness from his winter chore of cleaning out Boycott and Gooch."

On the eve of the match, Sergeant Everett had told the *Guardian* that his aim was simply to "pick up one four off the meat of the bat", and this he did as he and Mark Price took the score to 58/1 before the latter was run out for 23 by a direct hit from Holding at cover. At 70/2 the game looked as good as won, but Holding returned to clean up Everett up for a valiant 30, made over what he called "ninety wonderful minutes" and at the cost of one thumbnail. Holding had needed 70 deliveries to take his first Lancashire League wicket, 19 more than his Test strike rate, and when it came he raised his hands to the heavens in salutation.

Runs thereafter were dragged from the depths of Rammy's doggedness and, despite a wobble from 93/4 to 94/7, they managed to scramble over the line. Maurice Haslam struck the winning four off Mikey, a moment taking pride of place on the mental mantelpiece. "Holding, though very fast, was never vicious," reported the *Lancashire Telegraph*. "He bowled fairly and won respect and admiration when he did not allow the pressure to drive him to send down bumpers."

Price reflected on "the best day of my cricketing life" (there are 23s and 23s) while Everett told the *Bolton News*: "It is something you cannot describe. I set my stall out just to survive and help the team win. When I first went out my nerves were really bad but once at the wicket I just concentrated on batting. He was nippy, particularly early on." Nippy indeed – though not as nippy as he might have been had it not been quite so nippy – Mikey had finished with 3/48 on a wicket lacking some of the zip of Bridgetown.

Ever keen to take the sensationalist line, the *Sunday People* was having none of the "respect and admiration" stuff, none of this bowling fairly. It was red meat all the way, as they saw it, a rhetorical flurry that was as much projection as reporting: "Rishton, home of 7,000 cricket maniacs, wants to win something after three years of finishing among the bridesmaids. That's why Holding is being paid nearly £200 a match. That's why the ground was packed for his debut. They won't be coming back if he insists on being the first gentleman of speed. They want someone pinned to the sightscreen. And somewhere in his engagement of 26 matches Holding will feel obliged to satisfy them."

Whether Holding would crank things up and/or abandon his full length as circumstances (and conditions) changed was a question for down the track, so to speak. However, if anyone thought having the world's quickest bowler in Rishton's ranks would simply mean other teams folding, Rammy had shown them to be sorely mistaken, not least because the league was littered with international pros, including five players who would take part in the World Cup final a couple of years later. Besides Holding and Roberts, there was Lowerhouse's Mohinder Amarnath (Player of the Match, of course, in India's shock win at Lord's), Enfield's Madan Lal (a trophy in each of his first three seasons at Dill Hall Lane, 1,087 runs at 78 in his fourth), and Nelson's newcomer Kapil Dev, who sat at No.4 in the ICC bowling rankings, three spots above Mikey, ten above Andy. Those illustrious West Indian sleeves would need to be rolled up. Weather permitting, naturally.

* * *

Roberts had missed the season opener, waylaid in Antigua after the England series. With the Lancashire League mandarins sharply focussed on providing box-office entertainment, his tardiness incurred a £200 fine for Haslingden, voted through 12-0 by the other clubs, with one abstention.

He may well have assumed he wouldn't be donning the whites that first weekend after arriving, either, having awoken on Saturday – eve of the match, first full day in Lancashire – to two feet of snow in the Rossendale Valley, which was enough for Bryan Knowles to abandon his trip to Ormskirk market. When the doorbell rang on Sunday morning, Roberts opened the upstairs sash window to see social committee chairman Ernie Taylor, hot breath creating plumes against the Christmas card backdrop. Taylor told him he'd pick him up in an hour, the game was on. East Lancashire CC's low-lying Alexandra Meadows had extensive covering for the square and an army of busy volunteers. The show must go on. It was the first time Andy had ever even seen snow. "If we set off early," Taylor explained, "we'll be in time to follow the snowplough."

"I dropped in at East Lancs the day before and never thought in a million years we'd be playing," says Roberts's teammate, Mike Ingham. "We rocked up at our ground and they called and said, 'Game's on, you'd better get over.' Andy's shaking his head. Couldn't believe it. But then he was a big draw, a chance for East Lancs to make a few quid."

Thirty-six hours earlier, 'Fruits' had boarded his flight at VC Bird International Airport in a *guayabera* shirt and here he now was being ferried over heavily gritted moorland roads to Blackburn, where he stepped out to see the snowfall had been banked up at the boundary edge. Rishton's game at Colne had been abandoned, as had two others. Ramsbottom and Todmorden's game had lasted two balls before snow started falling again. Enfield and Lowerhouse felt the pitch for their game was fit, but the captains decided the wind was too strong and the temperature too low. A mile or so south-west of there, Bacup beat Church over a full 34 overs apiece, as would Burnley against Accrington up at Turf Moor. Four miles west of Church, Roberts was probably still trying to work out if it was all a cheese dream or whether in fact these lunatics were actually expecting him to run in and bowl. Meanwhile, word reached Holding that his mate's game was on, and he was soon being picked up by Woodhouse, who lent him a long winter coat and pair of thick, wool-lined gloves. They didn't pack a picnic.

By 1981, Roberts and Holding were long-standing roommates from West Indies tours and World Series Cricket, plotting and scheming many a batter's downfall using only memory and diagrams. They were tight. Holding was best man at Roberts's wedding and Roberts at Holding's first, to Cherine, who had given birth that Wednesday in Blackburn's Queen's Park hospital to Holding's first son, Ryan Marc – by all accounts, a quick delivery. Amigos or not, their Lancashire League encounters would be competitive – within the ground rules of the Fast Bowlers' Union, naturally – but before then it was all comradely sympathy as Mikey watched his pal trying to bowl in long johns and several pullovers to combat the near-freezing temperatures. "Andy commandeered everyone's sweaters out of their bags," chuckles Ingham. "He must have had four or five on. He just rolled his arm over, which is all he could really do with that many sweaters on."

Knowles nevertheless made sure he got the full shift of 17 eight-ball overs out of the pro, in which he picked up 1/50. Indeed, across 23 bowling innings in the league, there were only 34 overs Roberts might have sent down that he didn't. Fourteen times, he bowled unchanged; on six occasions that meant the full 17 (or 22.4 six-ball overs, pro rata). Rare were the circumstances in which a genuinely fiery spell bubbled through this combination of mulish workload, pace-pacifying pitches and reluctance to tap into the upper gears.

At tea, Holding went into the dressing-room to commiserate with Roberts, the pair of them huddled together by a one-bar gas heater. Shivering Death.

Haslingden had 155 to chase and were going along nicely, Ingham moving steadily toward a half-century, when the heavily-swaddled Roberts entered at No.4, salivating after watching a few overs' loopy leg-spin sent down by Brian Bowling. "He couldn't wait to get in," says Ingham (who was later given out by the umpire, then recalled by the East Lancs captain, only to be told to get on his bike by the same official). "But Brian was very experienced, very canny, throwing these 'pies' up, as Andy thought. I said, 'Don't take him for granted, he can bowl.' He hit a couple of big sixes then got out. For 12. 'We told you so,' we said." They did indeed tell him, but the Roberts batting method – similarly violent to the Holding batting MO – would not change too much as the season warmed up and wore on. Still, Haslingden snuck home in the final over, nine down, and their title tilt was up and running.

It had been just your run-of-the-mill April game in the Lancashire League – the world's fastest bowler watching on from the pavilion as his new-ball partner for the last five years, the erstwhile world's second fastest bowler (behind Thommo), was stumped by at least a yard off a 49-year-old leg-spinner sending down moon balls with snow banked up around the ground. The tearaways' main takeaway from the day was surely that cricket up here was going to be decidedly un-Caribbean. Welcome to Lancashire, Andy! Enjoy the summer, Mikey!

* * *

Holding had packed away the gloves and sheepskin by the following Saturday, bagging 3/18 in a 60-run win over Rawtenstall that would bely the two teams' later trajectories – a season in which Franklyn Stephenson outperformed two of his fast-bowling heroes thanks in large part to the superpower of his fabled slower ball, developed over the previous two years at Littleborough and Royton of the Central Lancashire League.

A day later, Rishton's trip to East Lancs' Snowbowl didn't survive the weather – all seven games were abandoned – and by the time

Holding was next in action, at home to Church & Oswaldtwistle, he had played four straight days' cricket for Lancashire: three in Northampton (match figures 5/105) and a B&H Cup loss to Warwickshire at Old Trafford. It seemed as good a time as any to be facing him – glass half-full, he'd be weary rather than grooved – a good day for the let's-get-this-over-with, the breakfast you can barely swallow.

Once again, the pitch at Rishton was sodden. Covers were removed and a new strip was cut, on which the wicket ends would eventually resemble a chocolate gateau attacked by three hungry Labradors, conditions that were just fine for Church's 46-year-old medium-pacer Jack Houldsworth – who would pick up 6/44 en route to a 1,000th Lancashire League wicket later that year as Rishton fell for 127 – if less so for Mikey. Indeed, by the end of the game, Church's skipper, Ian Osborne, a 30-year-old IT manager, had made 56 and entered an even more exclusive club than would Bryan Knowles later in the summer. "Nobody has ever hit four sixes off me before," confirmed Holding in his first *Lancashire Evening Telegraph* column of the year.

"It was a very wet day," recalls Osborne, "and there was a reasonably short leg-side boundary. Michael would say that he wasn't bowling at full pace, but he was still pretty quick. He was at the height of his powers at the time. He wasn't coming over as a has-been. He was 'The Man'. Anyway, the first six I top-edged, and it hit the sightscreen behind me. Clearly, he wasn't slow. There were two over square leg, front foot pulls, and the other was a pick-up over midwicket."

The innings earned Osborne the highlight of his cricketing life along with a £36 collection (approximately £135 in today's money), and Church's sole win in the opening 11 rounds, Holding slipping and sliding his way to figures of 1/59. Osborne even made the national press, with the *Daily Star* running a half-page on his exploits. "It was the original 15 minutes of fame," he says, "the sort of thing that is never going to happen in your life. It was quite, quite strange."

"So far," Holding's column went on, laying out his initial observations, "I have noticed that the first four or five batsmen all play very straight and tend to come on to the front foot a lot and like to drive, which is alright on the wickets we've had in the opening weeks. It might be a different matter when the pitches get harder."

You didn't need to be Wittgenstein to read between the lines with that one, the velvet glove of an innocuous cricketing truism covering the iron fist of its subtext. "You could say I'm really looking forward to the return game against Church," he added. Gulp.

The temptation for the acclaimed superstar when suffering such minor indignities would indeed have been to have come off the full run, to go full Mikey. But the Lancashire weather wasn't going to make that easy. And even when it was dry, it was wet – away, anyway. "I remember turning up for an away game once," he wrote in *No Holding Back*, "and for the entire week before the weekend it had been nice and sunny. I thought, finally I'd get a dry pitch, but when I got there the square was soaking wet. Now Lancashire is not such a wet county that the rain comes from under your feet, so I think someone must have said, 'Hey, that Holding's here on Saturday – get the sprinklers out.'" Columbo had cracked the case.

Other factors militating against Holding accessing those scary upper gears were his workload and, recalls Frank Martindale, his general reluctance to go as hard at recreational players as he might, say, at Brian Close: "Michael said, 'I won't bowl at full pace against the amateurs. These guys have to go to work on Monday morning to earn money to feed their wives and kids. I wouldn't feel right hurting them.' A couple of times, he really let it go against the professionals. And some of the amateurs said he bowled quick at them, and he might have done, but not as quick as it could have been…"

Ahead of Holding's next gallop, away at Enfield, any batters heartened by Osborne's exploits were given pause for thought while perusing the week's County Championship scorecards, where they would have noted that he had twice knocked over Vivian Richards at Old Trafford, picking up 5/37 from 20 second innings overs. A day later, it was 5/36 as Enfield fell for 118, giving Rishton a target readjusted after a brief teatime shower to 112 off 32 overs. Despite an opening stand of 55 and a top-scoring 32 from local cardboard-packaging tycoon Eric Whalley – chairman of Accrington Stanley when they returned to the Football League in 2006, back in the side after a brain haemorrhage three months earlier – Rishton came up two runs short.

The next two games brought Rishton a pair of much needed wins, however, sneaking them into the top half at the end of May.

Holding contributed 5/35 and a whirlwind 47* (six sixes) against bottom side Colne, then 7/51 and 33 (four sixes) at Ramsbottom, arriving seven minutes late after getting lost on the way. It was the first time he had bowled without a sweater, although he would note archly in the following week's column that "the square was surprisingly very wet while the outfield was very dry". Clearly, he could not be *entirely* neutralised.

If those Rishton wins engendered a smattering of belief that they might make good on Wilf Woodhouse's early-season hopes, the next two months brought just two league victories from 11 outings for a team increasingly resembling North Korea: impressive warhead, not that robust otherwise. That being said, the early weeks of June were exceptionally wet. Six teams had four straight no-results over two double-header weekends. For Rishton, it was three out of four. In one of the abandoned games, Osborne added 33* to take his career average against Holding to 99, although the umpires dragged everyone off one over shy of the required minimum of 20 to constitute a match, with Church needing 30 runs from eight balls to go ahead on run-rate, much to Holding's growing frustration. The four points would have left them within a victory of the leaders.

Despite the iffy weather, the game produced a £214 gate (just over £800 today) for the Church coffers. A week later, it was £223 for East Lancs at home – Holding taking 4/29 before the rains became too persistent – although Woodhouse reckoned this derby fixture alone could have brought in £800 with better weather. Overall, Rishton figured they were around £2,000 down on expected takings by the middle of June, while Haslingden's estimated shortfall was in the region of £1,500. Signing players of the West Indians' ilk was a gamble predicated on recouping the money at the gate.

The one early-June game Rishton played to a finish, away at Rawtenstall, came after another delayed start. With prospects looking bleak, Holding accosted his opposite number to find out where the nearest bookie was. Franklyn Stephenson in turn asked his teammates, he writes in *My Song Shall Be Cricket*, then accompanied Holding on "what was my first experience of a betting shop. After a short while inside, which felt like ages, I asked if we shouldn't check on the conditions of play. Michael's response was to assure me that no play would be possible with all the rain that had fallen. I left and went back to the ground to find our ground staff and team in full flow getting water off the ground. They had the first motor mop I'd seen in operation at a league ground. It was shaped like a lawnmower and could carry an extractor hose or water cannon and did a fantastic job." Hi-spec stuff indeed, although earlier in the season the roller had been overturned by vandals, who painted "legalise cannabis" on the wicket in two-feet-long letters.

While Mikey was studying the *Sporting Life*, the umpires had decided upon a start time and Stephenson had to "go back to the bookies and call Michael". The game was trimmed to 20 eight-ball overs apiece, and Holding's figures – shuffling in gingerly over sodden turf – were an ugly 10-0-98-3, with his betting-shop chaperone slamming 81 of the home team's 157/6, "a mauling that he did not forget, as he showed me when we met again in Tasmania a few months later". Rishton came up 12 short.

* * *

In the midst of the June monsoons came Holding's first head-to-head with Roberts. It was in the Martini Trophy, the second year of a Vermouth-sponsored experiment with the venerable Worsley Cup, which had been a straight knockout until 1980 but was now a four-group round-robin prior to semi-finals, with games of 48 six-ball overs and no restrictions on bowler allocations (yes, this meant the pros would generally bowl 24 of them). Holding had taken 7/32 in the first Martini game as Lowerhouse were knocked over for 102, although Rishton could only crawl to 91/9 in reply, Amarnath's floaty swingers proving nigh-on impossible to get away in a game that finished at 9:22pm. Meanwhile, Roger Bromley had bowled unchanged to take 5/43, including Holding, bowled for a duck, earning the headline 'There's No Holding Roger' in the *Burnley Express*. "I was thrilled to bowl out my hero," says Bromley, "and when he came over in the bar to say 'well bowled' I was shaking with pride."

A week later, Rishton beat Bacup, a game that started in spitting rain and continued with thunder and lightning circling, eventually being suspended and finished over a couple of weekday evenings. Holding's 24 overs yielded 1/73 and a decent amount of annoyance, subsequently channelled into a brutal innings of 52, all but four of which came in sixes. Haslingden had also picked up one Martini win and one loss, Roberts taking 2/37 in victory over Lowerhouse and 0/35 against Bacup, whose top four – stirred, though not shaken – chipped in 33, 27, 30 and 40.

Meanwhile, in the league, the Antiguan had followed his shivering debut in Blackburn with a series of solid contributions, albeit nothing like the devastation he might have been expected to unleash: there were figures of 4/62 and 5/53 in defeats to Burnley and Rawtenstall, their two eventual rivals at the sharp end, before a trio of wins saw him chip in 4/21 (and a bludgeoned 69, including five sixes), 2/50 and 4/56. It was an opportune moment to get the pro's feedback, thought the Haslingden boys.

"We asked him after about half-a-dozen games how the season was going," recalls Ingham, "what he thought of the team, whether there were things we could put right. He said to me: 'There are too many posts in the team', meaning bad fielders. 'He's a post, he's a post, he's alright, you're alright, he's a post, he's a post…' The team were quite amused when they heard about it."

Between the early-June rains, Haslingden were able to avenge the Burnley loss in a game reduced to 22 overs each. Fifteen long years after making his first-team debut alongside a young Clive Lloyd, the 32-year-old Knowles carved his way to a maiden Lancashire League hundred from just 79 balls, the first ton by any Haslingden amateur for 18 years – indication of how tough life could be with A- or B-list pros to face most weeks. If having Holding and Roberts around brought to mind Graham Gooch's famous throwaway line about facing Richard Hadlee's New Zealand – "the World XI at one end and Ilford second XI at the other" – then Lancashire league batters faced this scenario more or less every season. Indeed, against Burnley, Knowles took down one of NZ's Ilford Twos crew – Gary Robertson, a farmer's son from New Plymouth who would share the new ball with RJ Hadlee in his solitary Test appearance – only here Robertson was notionally occupying the Hadlee niche. Yet still he travelled for 5-0-44-0 under the Knowles assault.

Roberts then followed up with 7/44 as Haslingden eased onto the shoulder of leaders Nelson, for whom Kapil Dev was proving a shrewd on-field investment if a somewhat hands-off and aloof presence around the club. Indeed, he had been AWOL and incommunicado until May 16 – officially injured (thus enabling Nelson to engage a sub pro) but actually in Europe on his honeymoon. All of which meant that neither Kapil, Holding nor Roberts had turned out for the Lancashire League XI in the traditional early-season friendly with Lancashire, a contractual obligation mandated by the league itself, a lapse for which only Roberts was fined. Not one to whom smiling came easily, Andy was vexed about this – particularly as, on the day of the fixture, he was in the ante-natal unit of a Leicester hospital with his wife, who was expecting their first child within weeks.

After the blizzards, drizzle, downpours, thunder, lightning, icy winds and mud, the sun finally popped his hat on for the West Indians' Martini *mano a mano* – only the third time they had ever played against each other – and the *Lancashire Evening Telegraph* sent along a snapper to capture a smiling Roberts and Holding shaking hands, the pair photobombed by Knowles's young sons Graham and Barry, resplendent in HCC jumpers. The weather, mercifully, was set fair, yet the pitch remained tricky. And the nervous energy was thrumming, recalls Ingham: "We said to Andy, 'Have a word with your mate. You two can bounce each other and we'll have a few half volleys, if you don't mind!'" (They did mind.)

Set to come in at No.3, Ingham was out there early: "Bryan said, 'It's not as bad as you think it'll be'. The first ball hit Frank Martindale's gloves before I'd even seen it! It wasn't a 'bouncerthon' but he wasn't shy." Ingham, Knowles and Alan Barnes at No.9 each made 18, although Haslingden could only eke out 105 in 46.1 overs of grim doggedness as Mikey bowled unchanged for 5/32, trapping Roberts lbw for 15 – not so much chin music as shin music. Andy returned the favour, cleaning up Holding for two with a sharp nip-backer in a spell of 2/39 off 20.1 overs as Rishton fell for 95. Both teams were eliminated. A crowd of over 2,000, bringing a welcome £745 gate, had enjoyed a long look at these icons as the summer finally started to show its face.

* * *

For Rishton, the cup tie fell between back-to-back mid-season league games against Lowerhouse, in the second of which Holding sent down his quickest spell of the season. The first game came the day before the Martini encounter with Hassy, and followed straight on from three days' Championship cricket (and almost 45 overs) at The Oval, Mikey getting a lift back from 'Flat' Jack Simmons, who insisted as always on stopping at his aunt's chippy in Clayton-le-Moors to refuel – sometimes fish, sometimes a meat pie, sometimes both (a speciality they now call 'The Simmo'), but always with mushy peas, a taste Mikey's palate never acquired.

Unsurprisingly, the bowling crease at Lowerhouse was damp – not such a problem for Amarnath, whose 3/12 from seven overs of shuffling hyper-medoes helped win him that World Cup final Player of the Match – and Holding struggled through 17 overs to pick up 3/60 as Lowerhouse made 134/9, enough to win by five runs.

If the doctored ends were an annoyance, there was also another incident with a non-walking batter to rile him. "In the game at our place," recalls Lowerhouse's No.3 Stan Heaton, who made 25, "Michael hit me on the chin and first slip caught it. Obviously, I didn't walk, because I hadn't hit it. He started to have a pop at me, but then stopped when he could see the blood trickling down my chin." (In the absence of hot-spot, bloodspots provided a passable workaround, although some club batters may well have been tempted to walk anyway.) As well as Heaton played, it was Pankaj Tripathi's 47 that proved decisive. The innings went to his head somewhat, and in the lead-up to the following week's return match there was some bravado-fuelled trash-talk in the paper. Obviously, it backfired spectacularly.

"I know there was quite a lot of fuss in the weeks before Andy and myself arrived," Tripathi might have read in Holding's column in that Saturday's *Lancashire Evening Telegraph*, still floating after his match-winning efforts. "Fears were expressed about intimidatory bowling and I believe that at least one player retired from Lancashire League cricket rather than face the prospect of playing against the likes of me and Andy … Certainly, there has been no intention on my part or Andy's to hurt or frighten anybody. It has never been on our minds. I can promise you that."

A week is a long time in cricket, however.

At the start of the Lancashire summer's first unbroken week of sunshine, Holding had issued instructions for Rishton's groundsman to prepare the quickest wicket possible. The beast had been poked. Mikey may have opted out of the open plains of a full county-cricket grind to check in instead at the safari park of league cricket – food source taken care of and ample grassland for a frolic, if lacking a little edge, a little urgency – but a lion he remained.

The visitors won the toss and, ballsily, decided to bat. It did not go well. Only Amarnath, with 43*, made double-figures – a fact some teammates ascribed to not taking as much of Mikey as a pro might have been expected to – and Lowerhouse were bulldozed for 67. Tripathi was hit in the face by Holding and had his nose broken, temporarily interrupting a short innings of three, compiled over two acts. "He was going to go back out without a helmet," recalls Heaton, "but we persuaded him otherwise and he went back on, although didn't last too long. The wicket was an absolute rock-hard shirt-fronter."

Able to bowl without sawdust for the first time that season – it was June 27! – Holding's figures of 13.3-6-13-9, with seven bowled and two caught behind, provided an eloquently brutal riposte and a reminder, if any were really needed, of the upper gears he could access when not slipping about on muddy wicket ends. "Our cricket manager was quoted as saying he got four with full tosses," adds Heaton, "without mentioning that they were at 90 miles an hour at our tail-enders." As for the *Lancashire Evening Telegraph*, it ran the headline HOLDING AND HILL ROUT 'HOUSE, somewhat overstating Barrie Hill's role in it all.

As you would expect, figures of 9/13 sent moderate shockwaves pulsing through the league's synapses, a little ripple of consternation. Alan Wharton, the ex-Lancashire and England player and Colne's representative on the Lancashire League committee, even wondered whether short-pitched bowling should be banned. It was therefore no surprise for Holding that there was yet more hyper-localised dampness at the following day's re-arranged game at East Lancs – a money-spinner everyone at the club known as 'HQ' was extremely keen to have played, with the possible exception of their batters. "Almost everywhere I went the outfield was wet, the wickets were wet, the run-ups were wet," groused Holding in his autobiography. "We had to put loads of sawdust down because you couldn't keep your footing when running in, so it was far from comfortable for a fast bowler like myself. I developed a niggle in my ankle as a result."

Holding was only able to send down 8-4-9-0 before limping out of the attack with a disc problem that bothered him for the rest of the season (a subsequent x-ray revealed a slight bending of the spinal column, due to his left leg being 1½ inches longer than the right). The irritation bingo card was completed by further non-walking shenanigans, too. Brian Ratcliffe was the guilty party this time and, after getting away with gloving a Holding bumper to leg gully, he went on to make an unbeaten, dine-out-on-this-forever 101 out of 170/6, earning a collection of £44 while East Lancs took £327 on the gate (around £1,225, inflation adjusted).

"Brian immediately started rubbing his head," recalls Martindale, "and the umpire fell for it. Michael turned and asked: 'Why isn't that out?' The umpire said it had hit him on the head. Michael said: 'Umpire, if that had hit him on the head, he would now be dead.' Brian admitted it in the bar later. And that winter, after we had re-signed Michael for the following season – although he didn't come back because of knee surgery – Brian actually joined Rishton himself. He left East Lancs so he wouldn't have to face Michael Holding again!"

Holding's back problem caused him to miss three of the next six matches (for Lancashire, there was a single Sunday League game in a 40-day stretch). The three games he was able to play did bring him combined figures of 15/77, however, starting with 5/36 in defeat at home to Burnley. He had skipped a three-dayer at Chesterfield in the lead-up and Lancashire's physio, Freddie Griffiths, advised more rest on Saturday – advice Holding ignored, deciding he had "a moral obligation to turn out", doubtless to joy unconfined in the Burnley ranks. "He has my blessing but not my consent," said Griffiths, explaining that arrangements had been made to take Holding down to Maidstone for the following day's John Player League game with Kent "in a special vehicle in which he can lie down". Again, one can imagine a few of the Burnley team hoping *they* wouldn't be leaving Blackburn Road in a special vehicle allowing them to lie down.

Bespoke journey undertaken, Holding did play in Kent. But he sat out the away game with Burnley – a blow for the Turf Moor finances, no doubt, if a boon for their top-order batters – with

Sikhander Bakht deputising and helping secure a tie. (A sign of the pulling power of the Lancashire League, the contacts built up over decades of attracting top pros, was shown by Ramsbottom, in need of a sub pro for Ian Callen in mid-July, being able to dial into the Australian touring party, who loaned them Rodney Hogg, battling with Geoff Lawson for the third seamer's slot behind the Lillee-Alderman pairing and about to play the Edgbaston Test ten days later. Hogg took 4/74 and top-scored with 45 in defeat at Enfield, Madan Lal showing him how it was done in those parts with 58 and a nous-laden 6/42.)

Holding missed both games against Todmorden, too, whose pro, Mohsin Khan – a year out from a Test 201* at Lord's – was thus able to plunder a century at home against Mikey's somewhat lower-grade deputy, Sam Parkinson, a left-arm medium-pacer from Adelaide who was turning out for Bucks in the Minor Counties, where he picked up just 23 wickets in ten games.

The other two league games Holding played during this period were both against Nelson. In the first, at Rishton, Kapil made a third of his team's total. Unfortunately, that was only 18 as he fell to the left-arm swingers of Blackburn Rovers centre-half John Waddington, after which Nelson jenga'd from 54/4 to 54 all out in 38 scoreless balls, Holding going for 12 from one of his overs yet finishing with 7/16 from 10.3 in a ten-wicket win, three of them caught at short leg. With a bad back. Indeed, in the middle of his spell he had a message relayed to Lancashire, crying off their JPS game with Essex, and the following week he visited a specialist in Manchester. His efforts earned him a £23 collection, left on the bar.

In the return, Rishton were restricted to 105/9 and, after a long rain break, Nelson stumbled to 45/9 from 19 overs, Kapil top-scoring with 14 before falling again to Waddington, who bagged 5/19, Holding taking 3/25. Once more, Rishton were denied the run-rate win by a single over (although, had they taken the final wicket, the five-point win would have been theirs), symptomatic of a season that was slowly being drained of its lustre. As for Nelson, an aggregate against Rishton of 99/19 – or one Ian Osborne – had dealt a major blow to their own title aspirations.

Next up for Rishton was the first of those mid-August meetings with Haslingden, ahead of which appeared Holding's Saturday

Telegraph column with the headline, 'You've Not Seen the Best of Me' – to which the obvious response was: Yes we have, mate. You took 14/149 five years ago on the flattest pitch of all time at The Oval, when everyone else – including AME Roberts – was basically bowling throwdowns!

"I have not had a very rewarding first season in league cricket," continued Holding, "despite taking 63 wickets at less than ten apiece." Without the incessant rain, the pitch-doctoring and the bad back – and, perhaps, with more of an inclination to put the shits up people, à la Griffith and Gilchrist from a previous era – then he might have gone okay.

* * *

While Holding was dealing with Pankaj Tripathi, Haslingden's tilt for that first title since 1953 had taken a dent with defeat to Bacup in their own late-June double-header, something of a surprise result given their opponents then failed to win any of their remaining 13 games. Bacup had been 27/4 chasing 136 – Roberts with figures of 6-3-5-4 – when a heavy shower trimmed 40 minutes from the innings and turned the game. Upon resumption, Roberts dropped Roger Law on 15, who went on to make 58 as Bacup's 109/8 proved enough for a run-rate win, something with which Messrs Duckworth, Lewis and Stern might have had reason to quibble. The upset's other architect was teenage left-arm spinner Keith Roscoe, snaffling 8/34 not long after being given a two-week ban by the club for arriving only 20 minutes *before* play, a punishment that prompted Law to resign the captaincy.

A win over Ramsbottom 24 hours later, a game played in continuous drizzle, set Haslingden up nicely for the home fixture against table-topping Nelson, for which the motivation wasn't solely overtaking them in the league. "We were very determined to win against them," says Knowles. "We'd signed Kapil Dev the season before, then he'd let us down at the last minute. No reason was offered. We weren't best pleased about it."

Roberts was certainly fresh enough, having played a solitary day's cricket for Leicestershire in June. The Foxes would pay Haslingden £1,250 in compensation for the Antiguan's services that summer

– accounted for under 'donations', which may or may not have been a tax thing – although, as with Holding, his club commitments took precedence. And he took them seriously, despite the often downbeat demeanour. He may not have been the life and soul of the party, but Haslingden badly needed him to come to the party against Nelson.

"I don't think Andy ever *really* bent his back," reflects Ingham. "I'm not saying he just went through the motions; that wouldn't be fair. He was obviously a notch above most of the other pace bowlers in the league. But sometimes, if there was a game we had to win, we'd dip into the club's social fund, a pot we had for social events. If we needed a bit more out of Andy, we'd drop him a few shillings – £50, say – and tell him: 'We need a bit of pace today, Andy. We need to beat these.'"

Nelson were eviscerated for 72, Roberts bagging 7/38 – including Kapil lbw for 11 – with those "posts" backing him up in the field. At one stage, the visitors were 33/8, although 19-year-old debutant Michael Bradley gritted out 19* at No.10 to give them a puncher's chance. Kapil responded, zipping through the first four with 29 on the board, before a breezy 31 from Roberts settled things, Knowles unbeaten on 29, the first of that streak of captainly contributions. Job done.

Before the return game up at Nelson, Haslingden picked up an 83-run win at Accrington and a nervy one-wicket win over Todmorden, whose 20-year-old No.4 Brian Heywood was pretty certain Roberts wasn't holding too much back: "Our captain, Phil Morgan, who played everything off the front foot, twice swatted Roberts bouncers for four. Waiting to go in, I remember thinking, 'Phil, don't do that!' Predictably, Roberts wasn't having it, and went up a yard or two in pace. This was the first time many of us had worn helmets, and our club had also bought hockey-style chest protectors, although I found these too cumbersome to wear."

The apprehensive Heywood entered at 28/2, promptly gloving one of Roberts's trademark rope-a-dope slowish bouncers over the keeper's head for two. "The umpire then riled him further by asking: 'Do you think we might see one or two pitched in his half?' to which Roberts replied: 'You want me to bowl off-spinners, umpire?' Roberts then set off on his walk back – and kept going, all the way to the sight screen, from where he sprinted in like a runaway train.

I remember thinking: 'This is going to be quick.' I saw it briefly as it left his hand – just long enough to know it was short – ducked and was still on my way down when it whistled over the back of my neck. It was the fastest ball I ever faced. My batting partner, Mike Hartley, who played first team cricket for 20 seasons, said it was the fastest ball he ever saw. He went on to make 40, many of them by giving himself room and carving Roberts over gulley. But we eventually lost the match narrowly on run rate."

A week later, Kapil chipped in 32 to Nelson's 168/5, again falling lbw to Roberts, who returned an underwhelming 4/72. The chief contribution was a feisty 77 from self-employed insurance broker Ian Clarkson, who was developing something of a habit of taking down big-name pros, and here – after getting away with a nick through to the keeper off Roberts while still in single figures – successfully took on the short stuff. After tea, Knowles and Ingham steered Hassy to 58/1 but Kapil took them both out then immediately uprooted Roberts's stumps. With four regulars unavailable, the visitors subsided to 101/7 and gave up the chase, Kapil finishing with 6/57.

"If someone comes and 'pros' you – that's what we used to call it: 'How did you get on?' 'We got pro'd' – if someone does that, you're going to lose the game," says Ingham. "Our attitude was: we'll beat the amateurs, let Andy – or whoever it was – take care of the pro." The India vice-captain had won the day and put a dent in Haslingden's title chances, yet it was a score draw between the pros over the two games: 43 runs and 10/94 for Kapil plays Roberts's 41 and 11/110.

Haslingden bounced back with another thumping win over Accrington then headed over the county border to Todmorden, where Mohsin's presence regularly attracted visitors down the Calder Valley from Bradford – although they were mainly there for a glimpse of his wife, Bollywood star Reena Roy. "I was again batting when Mike Hartley came in," recalls Heywood, "and Roberts immediately asked his captain for 'seven gulleys'. He bowled off a short run and concentrated on nipping the ball around. Late in the innings, our opening bowler, John Townend, twice smashed him back over his head onto the adjacent school roof, but Roberts still emerged with figures of four for 49, having bowled through at one end and ensured that Haslingden had a leisurely run chase after tea."

With six games left, Roberts, the most expensive signing in Haslingden's history, had 298 runs at 16.55, the third worst among the pros, and 62 wickets at 12.95, the third best. It was enough for the club to offer terms for the following year – this time, they were led to understand, without any cricket for Leicestershire to sap energy or draw him away from coaching duties. The club had just installed its first artificial nets, too – handy to ensure practice nights went ahead in the snow. Things were looking up. They just needed that elusive league title to cap it all off, Bryan Knowles was perhaps thinking as he laid out his wares on Ormskirk market on a warm August Saturday that would see his men hit the summit for the first time that summer, the day before the first league meeting with Rishton.

* * *

The big local sports news in the lead-up to the first Holding-Roberts league encounter – potentially, Haslingden's biggest earner of the season – concerned the efforts of 29-year-old Bill Moran and 37-year-old Dave Barlow, a pair of cabbies at B-Line in Rawtenstall, who were attempting to break the world record for the longest continuous two-person darts match, which stood at 116 hours. "It was a struggle not to fall asleep for the first couple of days but after 72 hours we couldn't even close our eyes," said Dave, mid-marathon. "Half the time you're like a walking zombie. During Tuesday night I was almost out of my mind. I didn't know which way to turn." A doctor dropped in and deemed them fit to continue, despite the bruised fingers and swollen knees. "We have just kept each other going when one of us has got depressed," added Bill.

Proceeds were to be donated to Rossendale General Hospital, yet the community failed to rally behind them. "We had a lot of support from friends and family, and also the staff at B-Line, but it would have helped if we'd had more support and encouragement from the public," lamented Dave. They eventually abandoned oche after 95 hours, having hit one solitary maximum between them, Dave then throwing Bill under the bus for quitting. A lesson for us all.

By the time Bryan Knowles got home at the end of that long Saturday – four more points bagged, 49 more runs added to the season's pot – 'Beefy' Botham had biffed the Aussies for an 86-ball hundred 30 miles down the road in Manchester, more or less securing the Ashes. Everything in the cricketing garden was rosy, although Mikey Holding loomed on the near horizon.

Opening up the previous evening's *Telegraph* over breakfast that Sunday morning, Bryan perused Michael's column, 'You Haven't Seen the Best of Me', at the end of which the Jamaican turned to the long-awaited double-header with his bestie: "If anyone had asked me to name the side I would like to see win the championship – after Rishton, of course – I would have said Haslingden, because of my friendship with their professional Andy Roberts. But as Rishton still have to play Haslingden home and away, I'm afraid I cannot tip them to win the title. Sorry Andy, but there's no way we intend to let Haslingden beat us twice." Music, no doubt, to the ears of Burnley and Rawtenstall.

As it turned out, of course, Knowles helped himself to those 96 runs, smashing a car windscreen next to the scorebox as he reached his fifty. Frank Martindale denied Haslingden the bonus point, but they were joint top with four to play and Knowles had 846 runs. Meanwhile, the gate had broken three figures for the first time that season, bringing in £272.69 (around £1,020). In the bar, tapping into his £55 collection, Knowles admitted with a shrug that, yes, he had feathered one through to Martindale off Mikey, but what are you going to do? There was some of the best rambling in the country around these parts, but not too many walkers. After a day in which Holding had hurt his wrists attempting to take a boundary catch – not ideal, with Lancashire having that NatWest Trophy semi-final in the week – and ceded bragging rights to his best man, Knowles's admission was just a little too on-the-nose.

Sure enough, Holding was off the long run in the following week's column. Irked by amateur teammates able to brush off a defeat within half-an-hour of stumps, he made it plain that players "don't take it seriously enough", although admitted this could be a professional's perspective. "While on the subject of players' attitudes," he continued, "I was very disappointed by one incident in a recent league game involving Rishton. It followed a claim for a catch behind the wicket. The batsman concerned, who for obvious reasons shall remain nameless, signalled to the umpire that he had not touched the ball yet after the game he admitted that he had done. Umpires make up their own minds and players have to accept their decisions whether they feel they are right or wrong."

Anyone who had seen the photo – one of the most famous in cricket history – of Mikey booting out the middle and off stumps at Dunedin 18 months earlier might have thought that a bit rich. Equally, not many people would have been inclined to point out as much. The subtext was clear, though: I'm coming hard this Sunday, Bryan Knameless.

A long week ticked by, eventually reaching Saturday, Bryan's 33rd birthday. It had started in Ormskirk, with his towels and bedding, and finished at Bentgate with him having scored 62* – taking his tally to 908 – in an eight-wicket victory over Lowerhouse, Roberts following his 3/49, including the big wicket of Amarnath, with 69* and a welcome collection. The other two horses in the race picked up four-point wins, leaving everything as it was with three to play: Haslingden 71, Burnley 71, Rawtenstall 69. Meanwhile, Rishton were demolishing Bacup, whose 40 all out was the lowest total in the league that year, Holding bagging 4/17 as he loosened up for his compadre. And Bryan.

There can be few more formidable barriers between a club cricket team and its first league title for almost 30 years than a simmering Michael Holding. Somehow, though, Haslingden limited him to just two wickets, a fairly sizeable step toward *not getting pro'd*. All that was after tea, however. Beforehand, they had restricted Rishton's amateur batting to 57 runs, including extras, another major step toward victory.

Holding came in at 38/4, sauntering out there bare of head, knowing full-well that nobody was deranged enough to bounce him. Hassy's attempts to get his best man to oblige with an upstairs barrage were not even bothered with, Roberts contenting himself with the performative aggression of a few past the upper torso – the strategically sensible option or a timorous abnegation with a title on the line?

Only one four flew from the mighty heaves of Holding's hefty SS Jumbo, but there were seven sixes sent sailing over those compact boundaries – boundaries short enough to deny him a full run-up, short enough for a supporter not to have to raise his voice to suggest the pro "knock his block off, Michael" as he turned at the top of his run. Dropped on 33 by Knowles and 52 by John Entwistle, Holding clubbed a season's best 75 (out of the 94 scored while he was at the crease), enough to earn him a £56 collection as Rishton fell for 132, Roberts finishing with 5/45. Mike Eddlestone's 13 was the next biggest contribution. Tough chase, under the circumstances.

After a long, dark tea interval of the soul, Knowles and Entwistle shuffled out through the throngs – a gate of £354 from around 1,000 spectators – and into the lion's den. They started well, and there were 35 on the board when Mikey broke through, but Knowles and Ingham dug in and took the score up to 64/1 – so near now that they could taste it, smell it – at which point Barrie Hill, purveyor of the "little floaters" that had denied Knowles his ton the previous Sunday, took four wickets in two overs, including Roberts, trying to smear his way down the short-cut to victory. Was this a choke?

It was now Knowles versus Rishton. Partners disappeared at 81/6, 99/7 and 100/8. Another eight runs were found, at which point, running out of time and faith, Knowles was stumped for 70 off Hill and his LCCC-physio'd shoulder, "trying to hit him out of the ground again!" Haslingden were 117 all out – Hill with a career-best 8/29 (and a collection of £46, around £175 inflation adjusted), Holding with 2/53. The *Lancashire Evening Telegraph* headline? HILL AND HOLDING ROUT HAS'.

Mikey had delivered on his promise to throw a spanner in the works; it just happened to have been with the willow. Knowles had the consolation of having scored 166 runs in two hits against the world's most fearsome pace bowler, earning the Jamaican's respect and £99 in collections (around £370). His run tally was up to 978 with two games left. The rest of the news was not so good.

Burnley had won by three runs off the last ball – Colne having turned 167/5 into 171 all out – and thus were now the outright leaders. Meanwhile, with Franklyn Stephenson's 7/38 demolishing Accrington, Rawtenstall had won an eighth successive game and leapfrogged Haslingden. And they had done it without their skipper, Peter Wood, who was busy making a surprise List 'A' debut at 30 years old after being called up at the 11th hour by Notts skipper Clive Rice, an admirer of Wood's when the South African had been pro at Ramsbottom eight years earlier. The game was at Edgbaston, and Wood was told he was batting No.3.

"Richard Hadlee wasn't in the team but he was in the dressing-room smoking a cigar," Wood recalls. "He said, 'Do you want me to come and bowl some at you?' So I spent lunch with him firing them past me in the nets. Then Gladstone Small turned up and did the same." Wood sat through a 188-run opening stand and was then strangled down the leg side for three off Bob Willis, still floating from his Headingley miracle. He played once more – twice in the interim turning them down to see through Rawtenstall's campaign – run out for 15 while batting with Tim Robinson. "Then I told Clive, 'I'm too old for this' and went back to work."

With two games left, Burnley sat on 76 points, Rawtenstall 74 and Haslingden 72. The permutations for Haslingden's badly wounded chances of that long-awaited title were simplified by the top two playing each other next – simplified, though not helped. The only way Haslingden could head into the final game as (joint) leaders would be a no-result in Burnley while they picked up a five-point win at home to Colne.

* * *

The mayor of Haslingden's chains of office glinted in the late-August sun as he made his way around the hearty crowd that had turned up at Bentgate to see whether Bryan Knowles could become the first Lancashire League amateur for 62 years – and just the third ever – to break the magical four figures. "I didn't think too much about it," Knowles recalls, "but there was quite a bit of build-up in the local press: will he do it or will he not?"

Twenty-two more runs were needed – 35 to go past George Parker's amateur club record of 1,013, set in 1908 – and after 57 balls of graft, a punch through mid on got him there: "It was slightly uppish, and I thought 'oh no, I've holed out', but it just skipped past him for a three." Knowles carried his bat for 68* out of 154 all out, a ninth 50-plus score of the campaign, then Rod Taylor knocked over the first five. Roberts came back on to mop up: five points bagged.

"It's the happiest day of my life," Knowles told reporters, eschewing the usual lip-service to wedding days and children's births. "I thought 1,000 runs in a season was out of anybody's reach in overs cricket. I had such a poor start, only 52 runs in my first five innings, but a committeeman asked me how I felt about dropping down the order to get my confidence back. I said I would give it one more go as opener. In my sixth innings I scored 62 and I've not looked back."

News came in that Rawtenstall had won the top-of-the-table clash by a commanding 74 runs, Stephenson taking 6/31 to rout the home team for 102 after Wood had top-scored with 60, leaving the standings thus, with one to play: Rawtenstall 79, Haslingden 77, Burnley 77. Meanwhile, Holding turned out for Rishton *on the rest day* of the Roses game at Headingley – which brought him match figures of 10/115 and a spell of 27 overs on the spin in the second innings – to bag 4/54 in defeat to lowly Accrington. He signed off with 4/62 and another seven sixes in an end-of-term 52 against Bacup, the peppering of Rishton's short straight boundaries off 19-year-old Keith Roscoe earning him a £27.60 collection, "which will help me pay the speeding ticket I picked up during the week," he quipped.

"I remember it well," says Roscoe. "He hit the first four balls of the over for 24 – four consecutive sixes – and I had him stumped on the fifth. Now that's what you'd call buying a wicket! One of our lads got injured crashing into the sightscreen trying to catch the fourth of them. It had everything that over: runs, wicket and an injury. It's a good job I got him when I did, though, what with 'em being eight-ball overs back then…" It was indeed a wily piece of bowling from 'Kes', who later ran a racing-pigeon accessories firm, played rhythm guitar in new-wave and punk band Riflemen of War, and would still be going strong in 2024, aged 62 – some 935 Lancashire League appearances, 58,993 deliveries and a league-record 1,886 wickets in the bank.

If the defeat at Rishton 13 days earlier had knocked some wind from their sails, Haslingden had to take care of their own business at Lowerhouse on the final afternoon and hope that East Lancs, the reigning champions and Martini Trophy winners, could do them a favour against Rawtenstall. Once more they dipped into the social fund, yet Roberts could not rise to the occasion, taking a disappointing 2/58 as Phil Astin's 70 steered Lowerhouse to 187/8. The Antiguan's final balance-sheet would show eight four-fors and only four five-fors, albeit three of them against teams in the top four.

In reply, Haslingden fell to 9/2, Knowles gone, before 'Fruits' began to hit out, racing to 81 with nine fours and four enormous sixes. At 148/4, the game looked settled, but Graham Bushell snuck one through Roberts and Mohinder Amarnath strangled the life out of the lower order, finishing with 6/43 as Haslingden came up 15 short with 29 balls remaining.

In the end it mattered not as Rawtenstall, the best supported club in the league, triumphed on home turf in front of 2,500 devotees. John Swanney made 118* – the only Lancashire League hundred of his life, netting him a collection of £106 – to push the Rawtenstall total to a formidable 235/8, more or less sealing it, before Stephenson knocked over the first six to take him past the 100-wicket mark. Burnley lost, meaning Haslingden won the Holland Cup, given to the runners-up.

The champions had won ten on the spin, Stephenson taking 54 wickets at 7.24 in that run – all faithfully recorded by the club's future TMS scorer Malcolm Ashton – to give him a final tally of 105 at 9.26, top on both counts. Holding was second with 86 at 10.74 – a decent effort considering there were four games in which he didn't bowl, that his first game without sawdust was June 27, that he twanged his back on June 28, and that he largely observed a self-imposed ban on chin music – while Roberts was third (82 at 13.10), Kapil Dev fourth (71 at 14.57) and Amarnath fifth (69 at 15.24), a list that makes Knowles's achievement all the more staggering.

Roberts and Holding stuck around for the end of the county campaigns – the Antiguan recording match figures of 10/120 against Glamorgan three days after Lowerhouse had nullified him – culminating in a ten-over hit and giggle against each other at Stamford Bridge in the final of the Lambert & Butler seven-a-side competition. Challenging as it had been for the amateurs to face them, their star quality had been a boon for the Lancashire League as a whole. Only Holding – and, later, Vivian Richards – had been able to reverse the slow decline in crowd numbers since the 1950s, with gate receipts up from £10,516 in 1980 to £15,500, with another £6,552 in the Martini. Holding's presence had pulled in £1,800 at Rishton's away games, while home matches raised £2,400 – £1,600 above their recent average – along with another £1,200 in two cup games. Throw in what Lancashire paid Rishton and it had proven a sound investment.

Despite the notes of on-field disappointment, both clubs agreed for their spearheads to return. That knee niggle ultimately prevented

Holding from taking up his contract, although he was back at Blackburn Road in 1988 for a one-off game as sub pro, warmly greeted, he later remembered, by "Betty, our most loyal supporter, whose criticism or support could be heard from the other side of the ground". Haslingden, meanwhile, got wind that Roberts had again signed a midweek deal to play for Leicestershire, so terminated the agreement and requested he be given a *sine die* ban for breach of contract. The league declined, yet Roberts headed instead to Littleborough in the Central Lancs.

The 1982 season saw Rawtenstall (and Stephenson) retain the title, while the year after that, with Hartley Alleyne firing the rockets, Haslingden's 30-year wait was over, the first of seven championships in 11 seasons. At the heart of it was Bryan Knowles, in his late-blooming prime: leading amateur run-scorer again in 1982, with 935; second in 1983; top again in 1984, once more clearing 900. His main competitor during this period and subsequently his golfing partner was the late Peter Wood, the Lancashire League's top amateur batter six times to Knowles's four. "Did he rib me? No, I always ribbed him because his ground was a lot smaller than ours," says Knowles. "He only used to play on a pool table."

When Knowles was made captain of the League Cricket Conference team – driving to Hilton Park services on the M6 for selection meetings, cherry-picking the likes of Ezra Moseley, Winston Benjamin, Patrick Patterson and Tony Merrick from club cricket to beef up the LCC attack for games against the touring West Indians, Australians and Indians – he pulled rank and slid in one place above the Rawtenstall man. Nevertheless, ten years after Knowles's golden summer, ten years after Clive Rice had plucked him from obscurity to play for Notts, Wood would compile what remains the Lancashire League's amateur record of 1,227 runs, a number posthumously immortalised in his honour at the renamed club bar after he had departed the crease.

While Michael Holding had studiously avoided pinpointing individuals in his *Lancashire Evening Telegraph* columns, there was one exception: "One name I am prepared to mention is Peter Wood, the Rawtenstall captain. Peter has loads of ability and uses his experience excellently. With his composed, determined batting, he is the player who has most impressed me in the Lancashire League;

not an easy batsman to dismiss and a player of quality." Quite the shot of confidence.

Going toe-to-toe with two West Indies greats in 1981 brought lifelong memories, grand or grisly, for a number of Lancashire League players. Accrington's Graham Beech took 87 and 67 off Roberts and 45 off Holding en route to 938 runs – more than any of the pros managed. There was Ian Osborne with his four sixes, Mike Everett with his four off the meat, Pankaj Tripathi with his broken nose, Brian Ratcliffe with his ton (most of it after Mikey had limped off, but let's not get bogged down in details). Then there was Knowles with his 1,050 runs – the first amateur to top the run charts for 15 years – his 70 out of 117 and his 96 against Rishton, an innings that *The Times* of London, which gave him a half-page feature, described as "zenithal". It wasn't only Ian Botham that carved his name in the cricketing folklore that summer.

Knowles picked up 11 awards at Haslingden's end-of-season do, including a clock presented by the club and an engraved silver platter from the Lancashire League. He received a cheque for £45 from the league's chief sponsors, brewers Matthew Brown, and was *Sports Pink* Player of the Year. But the most cherished prize, the one to which his mind drifted on slow days at the market, was being the batter who had popped Michael Holding back over his head for a one-bounce four. "Not that he bowled you too many to drive," quips Knowles, proud of his achievements yet realistic about them, too.

"I was never worried about facing fast bowling," he adds. "Working all week, you'd look at who you were playing at the weekend and look forward to the challenge. The pitches evened the contest up a little bit. If I'd have been batting against Michael Holding in the West Indies, he'd have most likely knocked my head off."

Bibliography

Birley, Derek. *A Social History of English Cricket*
Brookes, Nicholas. *An Island's XI: The Story of Sri Lankan Cricket*
Cavanagh, Roy. *Cotton-Town Cricket*
Chapman, Jack. *Cream Teas and Nutty Slack: A History of Club Cricket in Durham*
Davis, Alex P. *First in the Field: The History of the Birmingham & District Cricket League*.
Edmundson, David. *See the Conquering Hero: The Story of the Lancashire League, 1892-1992*
Holding, Michael. *No Holding Back*
Kay, John. *Cricket in the Leagues*
Lillee, Dennis. *Menace: The Autobiography*
Lillee, Dennis. *Back to the Mark*
Pearson, Harry. *Slipless in Settle: A Slow Walk around Northern Club Cricket*
Ryan, Christian. *Golden Boy: Kim Hughes and the Bad Old Days of Australian Cricket*
Samiuddin, Osman. *The Unquiet Ones: A History of Pakistan Cricket*
Shelley, Don. *History of the Middlesex County League*
Stephenson, Franklyn. *My Song Shall be Cricket*
Wild, Noel. *The Greatest Show on Turf (commemoration of centenary year of the Lancashire League)*